The False
Promise of
Codetermination

The False Promise of Codetermination

The Changing Nature of European Workers' Participation

Alfred L. Thimm
Union College

LexingtonBooks
D.C. Heath and Company
Lexington, Massachusetts
Toronto

Library of Congress Cataloging in Publication Data

Thimm, Alfred L
   The false promise of codetermination.

   Includes index.
   1. Employees' representation in management—Europe—Case studies.
2. Employees' representation in management—Germany, West. 3. Works
councils—Germany, West.
I. Title.
HD5660.E9T45   331'.01'12   80-8422
ISBN 0-669-04108-4

Published simultaneously in Canada

Printed in the United States of America

International Standard Book Number: 0-669-04108-4

Library of Congress Catalog Card Number: 80-8422

Contents

List of Figures

List of Tables

Preface and Acknowledgments

The concept of employee participation in enterprise decision making has had an intuitive appeal to both the egalitarian aspirations of Anglo-American liberalism and the conserving principles of the Christian-Democratic movement. This study explores the deep historical roots of the Central-European "codetermination" phenomenon, its impact on the labor-management relations of its neighbors, and the ever-changing nature of the legal-political framework that determines its effectiveness. Both the small amount of U.S. as well as the immense volume of European codetermination literature has emphasized the theoretical, normative aspects of the ideological and legal foundations of employee and union participation in the management process of form and industry. Through case studies and empirical observations, I have shown how "codetermination" has worked in the praxis, how the praxis has been changing constantly, and how often widely supported legislation has had and will have consequences quite different from those intended.

Since the legal and political framework of codetermination has acquired an aura that makes it difficult to publicly criticize, all managers, civil servants, and employees interviewed were assured anonymity, though a good many were willing to be quoted. Differences between publicly and privately stated views, however, have been particularly significant in this context.

It is with great pleasure that I acknowledge the help, encouragement, and advice of Professor Eberhard Witte and his associates at the University of Munich's Institute of Organization. Both during my stay at the University of Munich during 1974-1975 and during the subsequent years, I have benefited greatly from the Institute's empirical codetermination research and Professor Witte's many helpful suggestions. I must also acknowledge the help of Professor Grün (Wirtschaftsuniversität, Vienna) who opened many doors for me in Vienna, as well as the assistance of my friend and colleague, Professor Board, in preparing the Scandinavian chapter. Professor H. Northrup from the University of Pennsylvania read and criticized several drafts; for his many suggestions, most of which I took to heart, I have been immensely grateful. None of the above are, of course, responsible for the views expressed in this book.

The section in chapter 7 on codetermination in Luxembourg has been taken from Janice R. Bellace's *Codetermination in Germany, The Netherlands, and Luxembourg*, prepared for the Multinational Industrial Relations Program of the Industrial Research Unit, The Wharton School, University of Pennsylvania, 1976. Copyright © 1976 Trustees of the University of Pennsylvania. This material is reprinted with the kind permission of the copyright owner and the author.

The public-affairs offices of Volkswagen, BASF, and Siemens have been extremely helpful in supplying me with information for the three case studies. Mr. Werner Osel of Siemens' Munich information office and Mr. Fred Jacobson, public-affairs director of BASF-Wyandotte Corporation, have my special gratitude for their assistance and cooperation.

Introduction

During the 1970s, the disillusionment in the institutions of American representative democracy rekindled an interest in worker participation in the economic decisions of the enterprise as a vital expression of direct democracy. Because West Germany had the most elaborate system of mandatory employee codetermination, numerous articles in key journals and newspapers presented to American readers an enthusiastic description of the new and expanding industrial democracy in the Federal Republic.[1]

The admiration of academicians and journalists for the political aspects of German codetermination was equaled by the interest of American management in the stable nature of German labor relations, which seemed to explain the monetary stability and high growth rate of the German economy. This was the message that even business publications seemed to convey.[2] It was no wonder then that German codetermination began to be viewed as the wave of the future, which every country would have to adopt if it was not to be left behind.

This book will show that the subject is quite complex. German codetermination law alone is not a stable, well-defined concept. Rather it expresses an ever-shifting compromise between two entirely different and mutually exclusive visions of worker participation, which consistently reflects changing political and economic conditions. German codetermination has changed greatly from 1952 to 1972 to 1980 and may be subject to further changes. Moreover, other European countries have not been able or willing to adopt German codetermination legislation since they lacked the necessary historical and political traditions of Germany, although there have been ideological movements to support worker participation throughout Europe.

This book will demonstrate that an analysis of European codetermination phenomena must consider the following points:

1. Employee codetermination practices and legislation are deeply rooted in a country's history and institutions and cannot be easily exported from one country to the next.
2. Codetermination laws change with political and economic conditions. A socialist government during a period of stagnation, for instance, will provide an entirely different environment for employee-union participation in economic decision making than will a liberal (nonstatist) administration during an economic-expansion phase.
3. There is a significant difference between employee codetermination and union codetermination, though frequently this issue is not recognized. Moreover, neither form of codetermination may have any relationship to industrial democracy, an elusive and much-abused term.

4. Recent significant economic and political changes in Europe have changed the union-management equilibrium and will tend to give existing codetermination practices an entirely new complexion.
5. Any major change in a complex system will have unexpected consequences. Existing codetermination practices have already changed management behavior in various European countries, and further changes will occur over time. An examination of employee participation in the decision-making process of the firm must call attention to possible long-run results that barely can be perceived today.

Notes

1. Typical of this literature has been Paul Kemezis, "Keeping Labor Peace in Germany," *New York Times*, 11 April 1976. Chapters 1 and 2 of this book contain further examples.

2. See, for instance, Robert Ball, "The Hard Hats in Europe's Boardroom," *Fortune* (June 1976).

The False
Promise of
Codetermination

1

The Origins of Codetermination, 1848-1950

Employee codetermination in the management of German enterprise has been Europe's major social innovation of the postwar period. Overshadowed for many years by the economic miracle of postwar recovery, German codetermination has prompted attempts to imitate it throughout Europe, just when the controversy generated by the 1976 codetermination reform legislation may have ended the era of harmonious labor-management cooperation in the Federal Republic. Employee codetermination in Germany, however, has not been a historical accident, imposed by British occupation authorities, as widely believed. Rather it has been the result of historical forces that at the very least go back to 1848. Codetermination has its roots in both Christian-conservative and socialist-radical thought and therefore has evolved into two entirely distinct and mutually exclusive concepts of worker participation in enterprise management.

The crushing military defeat of 1945 and the subsequent repudiation of left- and right-wing extremism introduced into German society a willingness to compromise. This new pragmatism permitted the simultaneous development of two distinct codetermination laws. One applied to the coal-iron-steel industry only and expressed the radical syndicalistic concepts of worker-union participation in enterprise management, and the other established joint employee-management decision procedures in the rest of the economy and emphasized the common interests that unite the members of a firm. Together these two laws, passed in 1950 and 1951, respectively, constituted Germany's postwar codetermination legislation, which has strong popular support and was acceptable for the next twenty years to conservatives, liberals, intellectuals, employers, and unions. Until 1976, at least, a workable model of codetermination had been responsible for creating an unprecedented era of social cooperation that laid the foundation for Germany's economic growth. A knowledge of the deep roots and gradual growth of employee codetermination in Germany is necessary for an understanding of the far-reaching political implications of this phenomenon.

Early Beginnings, 1848-1933

The roots of worker participation and codetermination go back to the first half of the nineteenth century when the anxieties caused by the onset of

1

industrialization and the visible growth of urban squalor triggered a wave of romanticism that engulfed intellectuals from Vienna to Paris. Opposed to the atomistic rationalism of classical liberalism, romanticism emphasized the organic, noncompetitive nature of the preindustrial society; it preferred the farm to the factory, the artisan to the manufacturer, social cooperation to competition, state regulation to laissez-faire. This romantic counter-revolution provided the common basis for the anticapitalistic, antiliberal movements of the Right and the Left. Therefore it was not accidental that both socialists and conservatives looked to some form of worker participation in the decision-making process of the firm as a means of reintegrating the urban proletariat into society.

Marx believed that worker participation in the production process was incompatible with capitalism; it was left, therefore, to the utopian and reformist socialists to develop cooperative models that could exist within a capitalistic society.[1] Hostile to the concept of competition and a market system directed by the individual's profit motive and selfish interests, these romantic models were designed to eliminate class conflicts rather than emphasize them.

Catholic and Conservative Philosophy

Cooperative production was also advocated by the Catholic reform movements of the late nineteenth and early twentieth centuries. Guided by Pope Leo's encyclical, *De Rerum Novarum* (1890), the Christian-Social movement opposed rationalistic, cosmopolitan (classical) liberalism and class warfare; it valued cooperation over competition, peasants and artisans over manufacturers, the small organization over the big. In a language similar to the rhetoric of the American populists, it condemned international (Jewish) bankers and big business, and it looked toward government regulation to protect artisans and small business from the economies of large-scale production.

Suspicious of liberal democracy, the Christian-Social movement in Austria and southern Germany relied upon the still-existing corporate remnants of the precapitalistic society—the chambers of artisans, peasants, labor, professionals, and others—to achieve the collective participation of employees in the economy in lieu of class warfare. Under the influence of Pope Pius XI's encyclical, *Quadragesimo Anno* (1931), the Christian-Social parties became increasingly hostile to the entire superstructure of liberal capitalism and parliamentary democracy during the interwar period.[2]

The catastrophes of the Hitler government and World War II ended the Christian-Social movement's flirtation with authoritarian forms of government. Although culturally conservative, the Christian-Social movement has held an essentially populist position on economic-political issues.[3] Distrustful of central economic planning and government bureaucracy, it does look today toward market solution of economic problems but does not hesitate to soften impersonal market decisions through agreements among the corporate economic partners (labor and capital, represented by their chambers) and through worker participation in the decision-making process of the firm; if necessary, government regulation of economic processes is accepted. This system is referred to today as social market economy, an adequate description of the actual conditions prevailing in West Germany and Austria.

In a social market economy, the firm is no longer guided by profit-maximization opportunities. Instead it becomes an institution in which employers and employees cooperate in satisfying the demands of the market within given social constraints. The cooperation between owners and employees at the microlevel of the firm reflects the cooperation between the collective institutions of capital and labor at the macrolevel, a cooperation that is dominated by the precapitalistic notion of fair profit and fair wages. (Since 1976, for instance, the German government has been able to convince both the German public and the German unions that wage increases in excess of the inflation rate would not be fair.)

In the context of a social market economy, employee codetermination becomes an additional, significant institution of an economy that strives to integrate all strata of society. The social market economy and employee codetermination therefore have the support of conservatives and Catholics.[5] The labor unions and the overwhelming anti-Marxist majority of German and Austrian Social-Democrats today are almost equally committed to the social market concept as the proper context for employee codetermination. The socialist support of worker participation in the firm, however, has been based upon a view of society that differs from the Conservative-Christian philosophy.[6]

Socialist Philosophy

Early socialist thought—utopian, reformist, and Marxist—emphasized the alienation of workers from the work process and viewed the competitive market as chaotic and wasteful. As a consequence, generally unworkable models of utopian, socialist societies appeared, alongside real efforts by trade unions and labor parties to develop consumer and producer cooperatives. In Germany and Austria the cooperative movement became an integral part of a social-democratic life-style in which party members, from infancy to old age, could spend their lives in a completely segregated environment.

Although producers' and consumers' societies originally had adopted cooperative ways of living, they were also influenced by the conflicting Marxist and non-Marxist reformist trends in the pre-World War I Social Democratic parties.[7] While Marxists considered the cooperative movement, the trade-union movement, and the existing factory councils as acute or potential tools of class warfare, the reformistic-nationalistic elements in the Social Democratic parties viewed these institutions as devices that would help reintegrate the proletariat into society.

Attempts to limit the economic power of employers and to remedy the alienating impact of industrialization also received strong support from the dominant intellectual movements of the day. Most important for preparing an interventionist climate was the historical school, a group of political economists and law professors—appropriately called *Kathedersozialisten* (socialists of the professorial chair)—who dominated German, and especially Prussian, universities during the last third of the nineteenth century and set the stage for Bismarck's social legislation.[8] The *Kathedersozialisten* advocated government intervention to equalize the bargaining position between employers and employees and encouraged joint factory committees.[9]

Early Codetermination Laws

Catholic and Protestant trade unions, as well as the Conservative and Catholic (*Zentrum*) parties in Germany, supported all efforts to "reintegrate" the working class into society.[10] Bismarck especially (and Emperor Franz Joseph in Austria) looked toward a state-supporting (*staatstragende*) alliance of workers and peasants, with the precapitalistic establishment as a remedy for the economic and social strains that threatened the nation.[11]

The notion that the common interest of workers and employers requires joint arbitration committees has its roots in the guild systems of the Germanic countries and was transmitted to the emerging nineteenth-century labor movement by Catholic and Protestant trade unions.[12] This essentially conservative sentiment was strong enough to emerge even in the national-liberal laissez-faire atmosphere of the Frankfurter Parliament of 1848-1849, which advocated the establishment of joint (owner-employees) factory arbitration committees.[13] The hostile response of the Prussian court to the Frankfurter Parliament ended any further serious discussion of the joint factory committees for several decades, though during the second half of the nineteenth century, liberal and paternalistic employers in the Rhineland voluntarily formed such committees that did make contributions to safety and productivity.[14]

The success of the voluntary joint committees led to increased worker participation in the administration of safety legislation in the 1880s. The worker-protection legislation of 1891 required employers to consult their work force before drafting shop rules (*Fabrikordnung*), and it encouraged the voluntary establishment of committees to process grievances and administer both internal work rules and national factory legislation.

For the first time, mandatory works councils were established by Bavarian and Prussian mining laws (*Bergwerkgesetze*, 1900 and 1905, respectively); though still primarily advisory, the Bavarian and Prussian works councils administered safety rules, cooperated with management on raising productivity, and provided the model for further codetermination legislation.

These integrationist efforts culminated during World War I in the munitions-industry legislation (*Hilfsdienstgesetze*) of 1916 and 1917 that mandated the establishment of joint factory councils in the defense industry as an expression of social cooperation. These councils in every respect were the predecessors of the contemporary German and Austrian works councils.

Codetermination in the Weimar Republic

Worker participation as a tool to overcome alienation and class conflict reached its initial peak with the World War I munitions-industry legislation. The revolution of 1919 not only overthrew the imperial constitution in Germany (and Austria), but for a brief two- to three-year period sharply increased the role of Marxists and radical socialists within the Social Democratic party, the labor unions, and Parliament. Although the avowedly revolutionary Marxists remained a minority in the socialist movement, their rhetoric did color the Weimar Constitution and much of the social legislation of the immediate postwar period of 1918-1920. Thus article 165 of the Weimar Constitution expressed the view that the socialization (*Sozialisierung*) of society was desirable; hence the ownership of the means of production of appropriate industries should be transferred to the community (*Gemeineigentum*).

The notion of communal ownership was not defined further, but it seemed to exclude formal nationalization (*Staatskapitalismus*). Instead the transformation of property was to be accompanied by the development of a set of interlocking councils (*Rätesystem*).[15] An additional layer of regional and national worker and economic councils was to have been developed, which ultimately would have absorbed most of the tasks performed by the state and federal parliaments.

Among these economic councils, the *Reichswirtschaftsausschuss* (state economic committee)—a national forum for top-level industrial and labor leaders to make joint macroeconomic decisions—has played a particular role in German labor-union mythology. From 1919 until today labor leaders have demanded that the joint macroeconomic labor-management decision forum, promised in the Weimar Constitution, be instituted. The business leaders in 1919 (as well as in 1946 and 1979), however, have been reluctant either to commit themselves to a quasi-corporate (*Stände-Staat*) codecision-making forum or to reject the labor overtures outright.

A union-entrepreneur central cooperative body (*Zentralarbeitsge-meinschaft*) was formed in 1918 as a compromise designed to achieve "the common selection of all economic and social problems affecting industry and trade, as well as [joint consideration] of all legislative and administrative matters pertaining to those problems." This central cooperative body dissolved in the 1920s, to reappear in 1972 under the name *Konzentrierte Aktion* as a tripartite labor-management-government body. In both cases these top-level consultative forums were symbols of the prevailing spirit of social cooperation rather than decision makers. During periods of labor-management conflicts, in 1923 and 1977, these joint councils fell apart.[17]

The works councils of Weimar Germany inherited two conflicting traditions: the integrationist joint-factory committees of imperial Germany and the quasi-revolutionary works councils that sprang up in the revolutionary November of 1918. Initially the image of the Russian worker-soldier soviets dominated and shaped the aspirations and language of the *Arbeiter-Soldaten Räte* throughout Germany; within a year, however, the integrationistic-reformistic attitude had reasserted itself in the factories.

The works-council legislation (*Betriebsrätegesetz*) of 1920 restated article 165 of the Weimar Constitution and was meant to be the first step toward the transformation of society. In 1922, a works-constitution law reserved a minimum of one board-of-directors seat—normally two—for a works-council member. This was, however, the last attempt to broaden labor's role in society, because even by 1920, the radical rhetoric of the Social Democratic parliamentarians already had been out of step with the political realities.[18]

In the face of attempted coups by the extreme Left and Right (especially the Spartacus and Kapp uprisings), the Social Democratic government under the leadership of Friedrich Ebert (president, 1919-1925) and Gustav Noske (defense minister, 1919-1920) cut all ties to the revolutionary radical groups, forcefully reestablished law and order, and moved toward cooperation with the bourgeois center parties, especially the Catholic *Zentrum*. Under these changed conditions the works councils lost their revolutionary pretensions, but they contributed to the democratization of German industry and the reintegration of the worker into society. The Works Council Law of 1920 served effectively for thirteen years to humanize factory life and to train workers to join with management in shaping personnel policy on the shop floor.

The spirit of shop-floor labor-management cooperation provided the basis for converting collective-bargaining agreements into binding legal instruments; furthermore it enabled the transformation of the industrial and trade courts into labor courts in which a judge presided over a council of employer and worker delegates (assessors). These tripartite courts settled industrial disputes and excelled in the pragmatic interpretations of collective bargaining agreements. The willingness to arbitrate social conflicts epitomized the principle of social obligations and cooperation that has prevailed under the Weimar Republic, National Socialism, and the current Federal Republic.[19] The success of the Weimer Republic's works councils in establishing effective shop-floor-level labor-management cooperation was a major factor in the development of the post-World War II codetermination legislation in Germany.

Codetermination, 1933-1945

The National Socialist government dissolved the works councils and trade unions in January 1934 and replaced them with the *Deutsche Arbeits Front* (DAF) in a vertical, unitary organization that included all employees, including top management (*Vorstand*) and even the owner, whenever the owner performed managerial tasks. Under the leadership concept (*Führerprinzip*), the chief executive-owner of each enterprise was also the titular leader of the DAF unit. The works councils were, nominally, replaced by a "committee of trusted men" (*Vertrauensleute*), which was encourged to advise management on both production and personnel questions. The DAF, in emphasizing the organic unity of both enterprise and society, merely adapted its political ideology to the traditional German principle of social cooperation; class warfare and cutthroat competition were either Marxist or plutocratic characteristics, which had no place in the new national-socialist society. The DAF took over the social functions of the individual unions and expanded greatly the leisure-time activities; the fundamental conditions in individual enterprises did not really change, especially not during the peacetime years of 1933-1939.[20] Operationally the shop committees of "trusted men" were closer to the works councils of the Weimar Republic than to the more paternalistic joint production and joint factory committees of Hohenzollern Germany.

The increase in income and employment during those years ceated a climate in which the ideological emphasis on the community of interest of employees and employers, enterprise and society, gained further acceptance, especially since working conditions and labor-management relations

on the shop floor remained substantially the same. The elected representatives of the pre-1933 works councils generally retained the confidence of
both the work force and the professional management. An infomal type of
codetermination seems to have continued throughout the period 1933-1945.

Postwar Developments

At the end of the war in 1945, works councils and trade unions reappeared
fully and instantaneously, in many instances even prior to the arrival of occupation forces.[21] Cooperation between employers and trade unions formed
the basis for the economic reconstruction of Germany. The constitutions of
the newly formed self-governing provinces (*Länder*) in the American,
British, and French occupation zones reflected the virtually unanimous sentiment among all political parties "to reorder society" and to achieve "industrial democracy"; this *Wirtschaftsdemokratie* was defined as the right
of labor to share equally with capital in the management of the enterprise
and the economy.[22]

Allied Labor Policy

The works-council codetermination laws proposed by the provincial
legislators, however, did not gain the necessary Allied High Command approval because they conflicted with overall Allied labor policy as stated in
the quadripartite Allied Control Legislation 22 (10 April 1946). ACC law 22
did approve formally the establishment of works councils that were to
represent the occupational, economic, and social interests of workers and
salaried employees. Article V redefined the works councils' role in accordance with the 1920 Weimar law, but unlike the Weimar legislation did not
specifically require employee participation in management through
representation on the supervisory boards.

　　Under American influence, the Allied Control Council left the precise
role of the individual works councils to be determined through free collective bargaining. As a consequence, the works councils' participatory role
was, briefly, determined by a few local union-management agreements in
the steel industry, which, though patterned after the 1920 legislation, did expand greatly the works councils' powers of codetermination. With the exception of the iron and steel industry, neither labor nor management nor the
political parties felt at ease with permitting the collective bargaining process
to change the structure of society. Subsequent to Allied law 22, the German
Länder therefore passed works-council laws that attempted to reconcile the
codetermination philosophy of the Länder constitutions with the apparent
limitation on employee participation imposed by law 22.

The resulting legislation was similar in language to the Allied control legislation but extended the participatory role of the works council through an imaginative reinterpretation of article V of control law 22. In effect, the Länder works-council laws overcame in the French and British zones the limitation imposed on employee codetermination by the Allied Control Council.[23] The traditional participatory (*Mitwirkungsrecht*) role of the works council in matters affecting working conditions was extended to include the formulation and execution of hiring, promotion, transfer, and dismissal policies. The works councils received, moreover, entirely new codetermination rights (*Mitbestimmungsrechte*) on all economic issues that were of fundamental interest to employees. In a language that closely anticipated the works-council legislation (*Betriebsverfassungsgesetz*) of 1952, the councils had to be kept informed by management on all matters relating to the economic performance of the firm; the councils had to approve all decisions pertaining to the expansion, merger, or contraction of the firm, the development of new methods or products, and the disposition of profits.

In case management and the works council failed to agree, the laws provided for an intricate arbitration system, which included the labor court. The very last word, in case arbitration failed, was to have remained with the stockholder meeting (*Generalversammlung*).

The codetermination provision of the works-council legislations passed by the Länder was suspended in September 1948 in the American zone by the high commissioner, General Lucius Clay, who believed that the full issue of employee codetermination in industry should be decided ultimately by the West German state and not by the individual provinces. Clay and his advisers seemed to have been particularly disturbed by the works-council law passed by the Land Hesse, which gave the council an especially effective veto power on all economic issues. Management could not make a major economic decision affecting employment without the union's consent. In the absence of consent, the status quo prevailed.

In the spring of 1949 the German Federal Republic was established. Its constitution (*Grundgesetz*) provided that federal labor legislation would supersede any state law (article 31). Consequently John McCloy, the new high commissioner, lifted the suspension in April 1950, and the new republic was immediately faced with the potentially divisive task of formulating federal codetermination legislation that would reconcile the conflicting ideologies, experiences, and interests.

The major difficulty in formulating an acceptable federal codetermination law was not presented by the comparatively slight difference between, say, the Bavarian and Hessian legislation but by the significant difference between the role of the unions in the codetermination process that existed in the iron-coal-steel (*Montan*) industry and the rest of the economy.

Existing works council legislation and practice outside the Montan industry were compatible with the Conservative-Christian view of worker participation, centered around the employees of a firm (*Belegschaft*) and did not explicitly reserve a role for the unions, while the labor unions emerged as the main instruments of employee codetermination in the British-sector Montan industry, in line with the syndicalist view of codetermination.

Codetermination in the Montan
Industry during the Occupation

Although post-World War II labor-management relations had been firmly based both on old Weimar institutions (works councils and labor courts) and the new resolve not to repeat the errors of the Weimar Republic, the policies of the occupation powers did influence the precise forms of employee codetermination. During the immediate postwar occupation era, the British forces occupying the Ruhr area—the industrial heartland of Germany—began, in cooperation with the work force, to reconstruct and ultimately operate the key German coal, iron, and steel plants.[24] Partially prompted by the socialist ideology of the British Labour government, partially by a historical theory that blamed the Ruhr barons for the rise of National Socialism, in December 1946 the British occupation authorities attempted to break up the Montan concerns into many small, uneconomic units. The owners of the major firms appealed to the Montan unions (I.G. Bergbau and I.G. Metall) for help in preventing what they referred to as the cannabilization of the integrated coal-iron-steel industry, and in early 1947 offered the unions in return full codetermination through a 50 percent share of the supervisory board seats, after the industry had been returned to its owners.[25]

The unions accepted immediately the codetermination offer, and the Allies approved. Subsequently legislation 27 of the Allied High Commission allocated 50 percent of the supervisory board seats of the decartelized steel-coal enterprises to employees and unions in the Montan industry. Although the owners of the Montan industry opposed the decartelization aspect of law 27, they fully approved its codetermination provisions, including the mandatory promotion of a union-approved personnel director (*Arbeitsdirektor*) to the top management executive committee. The Allied law, however, merely expressed its approval of the already prevailing conditions in the Montan industry by giving the existing union-management agreements the force of law.

The role of the British occupation forces in establishing employee-codetermination practices in the Ruhr industry has been overemphasized by American observers. Despite the fragmented nature of their own trade unions, the British certainly played an active part in promoting the establishment of a democratic nonpartisan industrial trade-union federation (*Einheitsgewerkschaft*) in lieu of the many political unions of the Weimar Republic. The British support of employee participation in enterprise management was based, however, on the already existing works council and labor court institutions that had survived the Nazi era because they had been representative both of the social production process of German industry, and the spirit of the immediate postwar period.[16] Chancellor Helmut Schmidt has observed, "It is wrong to say that codetermination was forced upon us Germans from the outside. The realization of codetermination's necessity in general, and in the Ruhr specifically, was universally accepted [in Germany] after the war."[27]

While management in the British- and American-occupied zones was primarily motivated by the short-run problems of rebuilding devastated production units, the union's position was determined by its long-run view of labor-capital codetermination: equal codetermination of labor through the unions in the shop, on the supervisory board, and in the economy.[28] Codetermination in the Montan industry came close to satisfying the most ambitious goals of the union leadership.

Codetermination in the Transition Period, 1948-1950

By 1948 employee participation in the management of the enterprise had become an established and accepted fact of life in postwar Germany, as well as a ray of hope for a better, more cohesive society. However, two different systems of employee codetermination had developed simultaneously in West Germany: one in the Montan industry, and the other in the rest of the economy. The existence of two conflicting codetermination models shifted the debate over the scope and desirability of codetermination to selecting the codetermination model best fitted for a democratic, nonbureaucratic Germany.

In the steel industry, a union-management codetermination prevailed in which employers and employees specifically recognized the leadership of I.G. Metall (the steel union) and I.G. Bergbau (the mine union) as the representatives of labor and the trade unions as the corporate and equal partner of capital in the management of enterprise and industry.[29] This equal partnership was characterized by the equal representation on the supervisory board (*Aufsichtsrat*) of unions and stockholders.

In the rest of the economy, codetermination on the shop floor and on the supervisory board was carried out by the chosen representatives of a firm's employees, who themselves had to be employed by the enterprise. Local union officials could be chosen by the employees, and of course were frequently elected, if they evoked sufficient confidence, but the unions had no official position in the codetermination process. An American observer, Paul Fisher, searching for the ideological position of codetermination, asked in 1951:

> Is it [codetermination] in fact the first step toward communism? Is it . . . "an attempt on a grand scale to socialize power without socializing owner-ship," a procedure to "seize authority from the employer without confer-ring it on the state"? Is it a step in the development of a corporate state, or of an economy based on the teachings of the Catholic church? "Does it represent the victory of the Catholic wing over the socialist forces in the German labor movement? Is it a revival of syndicalist tendencies?"[30]

Fisher, however, had failed to discern the existence of two entirely dif-ferent codetermination models based upon different ideologies, and therefore he chose to answer his own questions with the ambivalent statement that "codetermination springs from all these sources." Since that time we have gained much additional knowledge of the sociopolitical forces that have shaped the codetermination process in the Federal Republic. Between 1972 and 1979 a vigorous and acrimonious debate over the extension and reform of employee codetermination occurred in West Germany. This debate bore a striking resemblance to the divisive controversy over the scope and nature of Federal codetermination legislation that had threatened the social peace of the new republic from 1948, the year preceding the birth of the Federal Republic, to the passage of the Montan codetermination law of May 1951.[31]

Conflicting Concepts of Codetermination

The advantage of thirty years of actual and varied codetermination ex-periences, as well as further ideological debates, enables us to distinguish more accurately between the two different ideological models than was possible in 1951.[32]

The Christian Model

The Christian-conservative view of employee codetermination emphasized the cooperative role of the individual in the production of goods and ser-vices for the benefit of people rather than for profit. Although the use of profit as a guide to the allocation of resources was not questioned—and in the 1960s was strongly supported as the only alternative to bureaucratic planning—moral and social considerations were to transcend mere eco-nomic objectives. Employee codetermination in personal, social, and economic matters was to be merely one aspect of a cooperative production process in which employee and employer, along with self-employed professionals, artisans, and peasants, would join in creating a new society that would place people at the center of economic activity. Although there was a far-reaching agreement among Protestants and Catholics in postwar Germany on the nature of both employee codetermination and a "Christian market-economy," later called *soziale Marktwirtschaft* ("social market economy"), it was left primarily to Catholic intellectuals to define and defend the Christian codetermination model that was fully compatible with the tenets of *Quadragesimo Anno*, "on the Reconstruction of the Social Order." A true, creative, and Christian employer-employee cooperation on both local and national levels required the exclusion of all outsiders—especially national labor union or government functionaries—from this relationship.

The Christian-conservative codetermination model was finally codified in the Christian Democratic Union-Christian Social Union (CDU-CSU) bill that was submitted to Parliament in May 1950.[33] In its programmatic part, the bill emphasized the employees' codecision-making functions in all issues pertaining to the work place through the works council. The works council, elected by the individual employee and consisting of employees of the enterprise, helps transform the hired help into coworkers (*Mitarbeiter*) who can no longer be hired and fired at the whim of the employer because they have a vested right in their job and must be informed and consulted on all personal, social, and economic issues pertaining to their job.[34]

The Christian-conservative model has been concerned primarily with establishing economic democracy at the work place and transforming individual employees into coworkers; it also looked for a format to enable the employees of a firm to participate collectively in the overall management of the enterprise. The CDU-CSU bill (and the subsequent works-council legislation of 1952) allocated one-third of the board of directors' seats to works-council members who are elected by all employees.[35]

The supervisory board, the Central European version of the Anglo-American board of directors, is not a component of a two-tier management system, as repeatedly and wrongly maintained in American journals, but has played essentially the same advisory role, especially during the postwar decade, as its American counterpart.[36] The major distinction between the Anglo-American board and the German supervisory council is the mandatory exclusion of top managers from the German model. The supervisory board appoints the top-management committee, approves major investment decisions, and accepts management's annual performance report (*Jahresabschluss*) for submittal to the general stockholders' meeting (see table 1-1 for a glossary of German management terms). The CDU-CSU bill allocated one-third of the board seats to employee representatives to enable the employees to participate in setting long-run objectives and, further-

Table 1-1
Glossary of German Management Terms

German Term	American Equivalent	Term Used in Book
Aktien	Shares	Shares
Aufsichtsrat	Board of directors	Supervisory board
Aufsichtsratmitglied	Member of the board; director	Board member or director
Aufsichtsratsvorsitzender	Chairman of the board	Board Chairman
Betriebsrat	No American equivalent	Works council
Betriebsverfassungsgesetz	No American equivalent	Works-council legislation or works legislation
Mitbestimmung	No American equivalent	(Employee) Codetermination
Montan Industrie	Coal-iron-steel industry	Montan industry
Paritätische Mitbestimmung	No American equivalent	Equal codetermination
Unternehmensverfassung	No American equivalent	Enterprise legislation
Vorstand	Top management executive Committee	Management board or management executive committee
Vorstandsmitglied	Senior vice-president	Management board member
Vorstandsvorsitzender	Company president	President; chief executive officer (CEO)

more, to acquaint employees with the general business, economic, and social issues that confront the firm.

The most important aspect of the CDU-CSU bill was the lack of any specific reference to the labor unions in it. The employees could, and did, elect union members and local union officials who were employed by the firm to the works council and to the supervisory board, but no specific role was reserved for the union. Although ordinarily a majority of works-council members have belonged to the union (about 80 percent between 1948 and 1950), the works council could and did function independently of the local union, and possibly in competition with it.[37] The CDU-CSU most certainly recognized the role that democratic labor unions had to play in postwar Germany but wished to direct union activity into negotiating industry-wide wage and collective-bargaining agreements. The local union and local union leadership were expected to play a significant role in the election of the works council and to continue to provide leadership in the internal decision-making process.[38] Hierarchical, bureaucratic institutions and their functionaries were to be excluded from the codetermination process, however. Employee codetermination in the firm was to be undertaken by and for the individual employee.

Social-Democratic Trade-Union Model

The trade-union model of employee codetermination, on the other hand, viewed the German Union Federation (DGB) as the appropriate collective instrument for transforming the employer-worker wage relationship into an equal partnership of capital and labor for the management of the enterprise and the economy. The labor union as the corporate representative of labor corresponded to both radical syndicalistic and medieval guild views of society; however, the union codetermination model was also merely a first step toward a reordering of society in which the labor-union leadership would play a major but ill-defined role in directing the economy and supplementing or replacing significant aspects of the market-economy. This essential goal of the union leadership has remained amazingly constant since 1919.

After lengthy internal discussions, the DGB in 1950 submitted to Parliament a proposed codetermination bill under the appropriate title, "Reorganization of the Germany Economy."[39] This counterproposal to the CDU-CSU bill offered a clear description of the trade-union view of codetermination, which demonstrated that the ideological outlook of the union leadership had hardly changed since 1919.[40] Moreover the DGB's codetermination goals of 1950 still motivate its leadership in 1980, and therefore deserve closer examination. The proposed DGB bill can be divided into three sections; union-employee codetermination at the work-place level; equal union-employee participation in the management of the enterprise; and equal union leadership representation on a national macroeconomic planning board.

Codetermination on the work-place level in the DGB model was quite similar to both existing conditions in the 1946-1950 period and to the works-council provisions in the CDU-CSU bill, with one important exception: the union was to exercise a veto right over works-council nominations. Only employees acceptable to the local and national union leadership could stand for election.

On the enterprise level, the DGB proposal allocated 50 percent of the supervisory board seats in large companies (with at least three hundred employees) to employee representatives, one-half of them to be chosen from DGB functionaries ("outside" representatives), the other half to be elected from a union-submitted nomination list of employees.[41] Furthermore the manager of personnel (*Arbeitsdirektor*) could be appointed only with the approval of the majority of the employees' representatives on the board, with the imprimatur of the national union leadership.[42]

The union model of codetermination demanded the equal participation of labor (trade unions) in the management of the firm. The DGB proposal hence provided for equal representation on the supervisory board, and for one seat on the management board, since even in the 1949-1950 period there was little chance that the public and Parliament would have accepted a larger union representation on the management board.[43] The DGB proposal also provided for the establishment of a joint management-employee economic committee (*Wirtschaftsauschuss*) to receive and discuss all pertinent production, investment, sales, and employment information.

The committee was to be staffed equally by management and employee delegates, the latter to be nominated by the works council in cooperation with the unions. The economic committee was meant to have both advisory and decision-making functions, which would have usurped the strategic role of the Vorstand. In case of unresolved disagreement between its management and employee members on issues of fundamental interest to labor, the enterprise management would have had to refrain from implementing its decisions in the disputed area (for example, it could not stop the production of an unprofitable product).[44]

The economic council was the only feature of the DGB's enterprise codetermination draft that ultimately was incorporated by Parliament into its 1952 works-council legislation, although in an emasculated version in which all decision-making authority had been removed.

On the macroeconomic level, the DGB proposal provided for the creation of a federal economic council (*Bundeswirtschaftsrat*) that would advise Parliament on macroeconomic policy and regional corporative economic, artisan, and agriculture chambers, as well as provincial economic councils. One-half of the seats on all these councils were to be reserved for labor (actually union functionaries). On the federal economic council, the other half of the seats were to be allocated to representatives of corporate managers; on the chambers and the economic councils, corporate employers were to share their half with the representatives of small business, artisans, and farmers. The regional chambers were scheduled to assume autonomous regulatory powers, quite similar to the NRA's industry-wide councils in the first Roosevelt administration, while the provincial economic councils were to advise the state legislatures on economic policy.[45]

Political Implications of the Two Models

The provisions of the DGB proposal that dealt with codetermination at the work place and on the supervisory board reflected, for the most part, conditions that had already been achieved in the Montan industry. When the DGB defined its concept of equal labor participation in the macroeconomic guidance of the economy, however, it returned fully to article 35 of the Weimar Constitution and its promise to encourage a hierarchical system of local, regional, and national councils as a means of "overcoming capitalism." Although the Marxian rhetoric of the 1919-1920 period was absent from the 1950 DGB proposal, still the proposed federal economic council was a copy of the *Reichswirtschaftsrat* of 1919, and the provincial chambers and councils were somewhat less ambitious devices for creating extraparliamentary, corporate bodies designed to curb the independence of provincial and municipal legislatures.

The tenacity with which the German union leadership has continued to demand the establishment of a quasi-corporate, union-management economic council as promised in 1919 throws a special light on the long-run goals of codetermination in the labor-union model. Already in 1950 and certainly in the 1970s, the proposed regional councils had long lost the revolutionary Leninist implications of 1919. What had not been lost, however, was the determination of the union leadership to share at least equally in the management of the entire economy in a manner that would impose a certain measure of investment planning on the market economy.[46]

The periodic discussion of the German codetermination experience in North America and Great Britain has not only neglected to distinguish between the two existing and mutually exclusive models of codetermination; it has also overlooked that employee codetermination in the management of the firm was to have been merely one step toward a reordering of society in the ideological context of both codetermination proponents: the labor union-Social Democratic party coalition, and the Christian-conservative advocates of a cooperative market society.[47]

In the Montan industry, the labor unions had won acceptance as the appropriate agents of an employee codetermination format that emphasized collective participation in the management of the firm at the top level, while in the rest of the economy codetermination was based upon individual employees, who were concerned primarily with being able to control their immediate work environment. From the first day of the new republic, the struggle over the final shape of codetermination began between the proponents of the two conflicting models. The outcome of this struggle will ultimately determine the nature of German society. (See table 1-2 for a summary of codetermination legislation.)

Table 1-2
German Codetermination Legislation

Date	Title	Description
1891	Work protection legislation (*Arbeitsschutzgesetz*, part of *Gewerbeordnung* of 1891)	Provided for the creation of worker committees with participation rights in the development of shop procedures and welfare provisions (*Mitwirkungsrecht*)
1900	Revision of Bavarian Mining Law (*Novelle zum Bayrischen Bergwerkgesetz*)	
1905 and 1909	Revisions of Prussian mining legislation (*Novellen zum Pr. Bergwerkgesetz*)	Extended committee participation in safety regulation to de facto codetermination
1916, 1917	Defense industry legislation (*Vaterländischer Hilfsdienst*)	Further extension of participatory rights of worker committees; joint production committees
1919	Article 165, Weimar Constitution	Provides for the development of a system of works and regional worker councils, national economy council
1920	Works-Council Law (*Betriebsrätegesetz*)	Works council is given codetermination rights for work procedures and redundancy policies in factories with at least twenty employees
1922	Extension of Corporation Law (*Novelle zum Aktien-Gesellschaftsrecht*)	At least one seat on supervisory board reserved for works-council member
1951	Montan Codetermination Law (*Montan Mitbestimmungsgesetz*)	Gives employees 50 percent of supervisory board seats. Three-fifths national union functionaries, only two-fifths actual employees. Valid only in coal-iron-steel industry

1952	Works Council Law of 1952 (1952 *Betriebsverfassungsgesetz*)	Established works council; codetermination rights in establishing work, promotion, and layoff rules. Also gave employees one-third of supervisory board seats. No outside representatives permitted; no specific role for union
1972	Works Council Law of 1972 (1972 *Betriebsverfassungsgesetz*)	Extends codetermination rights of works council. Defines relationship between local unions and works councils; strengthens position of unions on works councils
1976	("Reform") Codetermination Law of 1976 (*Mitbestimmungsgesetz*, 1976)	Reforms the enterprise legislation of the 1952 law. Employees receive half of supervisory board seats, but the chairman, chosen by stockholders, has two votes in case of tie. Role of union strengthened. Depending on size of supervisory board, one-third, one-fourth, or three-tenths of employee seats reserved for outside national union functionaries. Applies only to firms with over two thousand employees. For firms with fewer than two thousand employees, the 1952 legislation remains intact.

Notes

1. See J. Finkelstein and A.L. Thimm, *Economists and Society*, (New York: Harper & Row, 1973), pp. 120-128, for a discussion of the utopian socialists as the predecessors of the New Left. The most influential utopians were Louis Blanc, Etien Cerbet, Charles Fourier, Robert Owen, and André Saint-Simon.

2. Actually both *De Reum Novarum* and *Quadrangesimo Anno* were bulls, official ex cathedra pronouncements of the pope to the faithful, rather than encyclicals (letters to the bishops). In American usage the term *bull* has been replaced by *encyclical* even when not appropriate.

3. At the same time that the stoutly Catholic Christian-Social movement (and parties) of the southern Germanies developed, Protestant Christian-Social parties emerged in northern Europe and Switzerland. The most significant of these parties outside Germany has been the Calvinistic Dutch Christian-Social movement, whose strong attachment to the corporate (*Stände*) society gave it an ideological complexion closely resembling its Austrian and Bavarian counterparts. In today's European parliaments, the Protestant and Catholic Christian-Social parties form a common parliamentary Christian Democratic party. See R. Hagoort, *De christelijk-social beweging* (T. Wever, Frankeker, 1965) and Michael Fogarty, *The Rise of Christian Democracy, 1820-1953* (Notre Dame, Ind.: Notre Dame University Press, 1957).

4. The permanent impact of the papal encyclicals on German Catholicism is best demonstrated by quoting Cardinal Frings, archbishop of Cologne: "Contrary to the false tenets of liberal capitalism, which reserves for Capital and providers of Capital the undisputable primacy in the economy, the only correct view is gaining wider and wider acceptance, not least as a result of the clear pronouncement of the popes, that capital and labor are the two *equal* promotive and formative forces in the economy." Joseph Kardinal Frings, *Verantwortung und Mitverantwortung in der Wirtschaft* (Cologne: n.p., 1949), pp. 104-105 (my translation, my italics.)

5. The terms *liberal* and *conservative* have had a different meaning in Europe and North America. At least until the 1960s the European liberal parties represented the interests of the bourgeoisie and were anticlerical, anti-big government; they strongly endorsed the free market and had more in common with American Republicans than with New Deal liberals. During the interwar and immediate post-World War II periods, the liberal parties in Europe often joined with the conservatives to form anti-Marxist coalition governments. During the 1960s the liberal parties of the United Kingdom, Germany, Scandinavia, and France lost part of their following to the conservatives but attracted segments of the professional classes instead. As a consequence, the liberal parties in Europe, especially in the United

Kingdom and in Germany, have moved significantly to the left and are now found not infrequently as coalition partners of non-Marxist socialist governments. The difference between North American and European liberals has decreased substantially, though the latter have retained their preference for market forces over government regulation.

6. After World War II, the Christian Democratic party was formed in Germany as a nondenominational center party that united various Catholic and Protestant groups. In the Rhineland, the CDU was clearly the successor to the prewar Catholic Zentrum party, which had been the effective representative of the Catholic bourgeoisie. In Bavaria this new centrist coalition retained its predominantly Catholic image and formed the Christian Social Union, a sister party of the CDU; together these two parties form the CDU-CSU, which acts as one party in Parliament. Since the death of Konrad Adenauer in 1967, the differences between the CDU and the CSU have become more noticeable. The CSU has a stronger peasant-petty bourgeoisie base and emphasizes simultaneously both its Bavarian identity and its German nationalism, while the CDU, culturally more liberal, appeals to a broader sociological coalition, ranging from corporate managers to skilled workers and professionals.

7. Much of this material applies also to Switzerland, the Scandinavian countries, and Holland, especially prior to World War II.

8. The most important representatives of the (younger) historical school were G. v. Schmoller (1838-1917) and L. Brentano (1844-1931). Max Weber (1869-1920) and Werner Sombart (1863-1941) can be considered as the culmination of this movement.

9. R. v. Mohl, law professor at Tübingen, in 1825 was one of the first explicit advocates of joint factory committees for improving working conditions. W. Hansen, *Mitbestimmung der Arbeitnehmer* (Düsseldorf: DGB, 1968), p. 10.

10. The social climate in Prussia at the turn of the century was greatly influenced by the Protestant minister Adolf Stoecker, who founded first the (Protestant) Christian-Social movement within the Conservative party and, later, the Protestant workers' movement, which became a strong supporter of Bismarck's social legislation.

11. In Austria, Emperor Franz Josef had hoped that the Social Democratic party would become a unifying factor that would overcome the centrifugal forces of nationalism. The Social Democrats of the Austro-Hungarian monarchy, however, developed a loose federation of national parties, divided along linguistic and nationalistic lines (such as German, Czech, and Hungarian parties). The absence of an effective central party machinery did not prevent frequent cooperation between Social Democrats and the court on specific social issues. It also strengthened the reformistic, non-Marxist views in the monarchy's Social Democratic parties, at least until 1918. In Germany, Bismarck's social legislation of the 1880s and early

1890s—especially the workers' protection laws (*Gewerbeordnung*) of 1891 but also subsequent old-age and health-insurance legislation—may not have weakened the Social Democrats significantly, but the social legislation succeeded in strengthening the reformistic wing within the SDP Germany, muting its class-warfare rhetoric and reestablishing social cooperation as a characteristic of modern Germany.

12. In the Scandinavian countries the early trade unions clearly represented a continuation of the guilds. See (W. Galenson, "Scandinavia," in *Contemporary Labor Movements*, ed. W. Galenson (New York: Prentice-Hall, 1952). In Switzerland, the guilds coexisted with trade unions for centuries and have maintained social functions until today, as any visitor to the *Zunfthaüser* on Zurich's Limmat Kai can witness. In Holland, the transition from guilds to trade unionism is less apparent, although the Protestant workingmen's association (*Patrimonium*) tried to maintain the Christian values of the medieval guilds. See Hagoort, *De christelijk-social beweging*.

13. The most ambitious proposal, submitted to the assembly by delegates Carl Degenkolb, Moritz Veit, Friedrich Becker, and Wilhelm Lette, provided for a tripartite mandatory factory committee consisting of delegates from each "independent worker-association," master craftsmen (*Werkmeister*) (both elected by the work force), and the owner or his representative. See Hugo Müller-Vogg, "Von Fabriksausschuss zur Mitbestimmung" [From factory committees to codetermination], in *Frankfurter Allgemeine Zeitung*, 10 March 1979, p. 15.

14. From 1815 to 1866, Frankfurt was the seat of the German confederacy (*Deutscher Bund*), a nominal federation of German states that included Austria and Prussia. The liberal-nationalist revolutions of 1848 produced the Frankfurter Parliament, which actually attempted to serve as a constitutional assembly. It offered to crown William I, king of Prussia, as emperor of Germany. William brusquely refused to deal with the bourgeois assembly, and the Frankfurter Parliament dissolved in 1849. Its impact on German liberalism exceeded its short and ineffective existence, however. In the area of labor relations, the efforts of the Parliament coincided with the emergence of the liberal ultramontane movements of French Christian Socialists across the Rhine. Joint works councils were strongly advocated by Fr. Lamennais and his periodical *L'Avenir*.

15. The term *Räte* ("councils") takes on a specific meaning in the context of the postrevolutionary period (1918-1921). The Russian revolution created worker, peasant, and soldier soviets (*Räte* in German, "councils" in English translation); the Soviet Union during this period was known as the Räte Republik in Germany, and the term *Räte* in German political language carried with it a radical connotation that lasted until the end of World War II.

16. See *Vom Sozialistengesetz zur Mitbestimmung*, ed. H.O. Vetter (Cologne: DGB, 1975), p. 230 (my translation).

17. The labor leaders withdrew from the Konzentrierte Aktion in July 1977 because the employer association decided to contest before the courts the codetermination reform legislation of 1976. They declared their willingness to return in November 1977, though the Konzentrierte Aktion did not meet again until September 1979, and then only in an informal manner.

18. See Fritz Fabricius, "Naturrecht und Mitbestimmung," *Mitbestimmungsgesetz* (Darmstadt: Hermann Luchterhand Verlag, 1976), pp. 83-84.

19. "The principle of social cooperation . . . is an ideology rooted in the common interest of employer and employee in the welfare of the enterprise and confirmed by fascism and the 'economic miracle.'" Thilo Ramm, "Codetermination and the German Works Constitution Act of 1972," *Industrial Law Journal* (March 1974):25.

20. Not much has been written about the DAF; in 1968 while I was a visiting professor at the Technical University at Graz, I studied the role of the trade unions in resisting Communist domination in the Russian-occupied part of Austria between 1945 and 1955. In the course of this work, I gained insight into the prevailing shop-floor relations during the period 1938-1945.

21. Officially labor unions were first permitted to reestablish themselves in the British sector in September 1945, and shortly thereafter in the American occupation zone. Informally contracts between labor union officials and occupation authorities existed from the day Allied troops entered Germany. The *Einheitsgewerkschaft* (United Unions) in the British zone was the predecessor of the German Union Federation (DGB).

22. For example, the Bavarian Constitution contained the following typical passage: "In all economic enterprises, employees have the right to participate in all matters which concern them. In all important endeavors they have direct influence on the policy and management of the firm. Works councils are to be formed for this purpose in accordance with the provisions of a special law [to be passed by the Bavarian legislature]." Bavarian Constitution, October 1946, art. 175.

23. Allied Control legislation 22 applied also to Russian-occupied Germany, and up to June 1947, works councils in the Soviet zone operated very much along the lines of the 1920 Weimar legislation. On 6 June 1947, the Russians dissolved the works councils in the nationalized sector "to free [management] from the interference of irresponsible works councils." See Otto Stammer, "Mitbestimmung in der Zone," *Gewerkschaftliche Monatshefte* (June 1950):250-254.

24. The coal-iron-steel sector of the economy is called the Montan industry in German; its unions are often referred to as *Montan Gewerkschaften*, although originally this term referred only to mine workers.

After January 1947, the Montan industry in the British zone was administered by the North German Iron and Steel Control Board. The board in turn set up an employer-union Steel Trustee Association to manage the confiscated property of the old steel barons. The unions held four of eleven seats on this board; those of the other seven were nominated by the previous owners; and all were appointed by the British and, later, the Allies.

25. "In order to carry out a decartelization which will not endanger the economic viability of the firms, the appropriate [British] measures must be influenced by those who are familiar with the administrative and works condition, that is, management and works councils in cooperation with the union." Dr. E. Reusch and Dr. E. Hilbert, Montan industry executives (Vorstand, Gutehoffnungshütte), in a January 1947 letter to the Montaneinheitsgewerkschaft (the united union of steelworkers and coal and iron miners) in Cologne, quoted by Helmut Schmidt in "Die Mitbestimmung der Arbeiter," Special Reprint from *Konrad Adenauer und seine Zeit*, ed. D. Blumenwitz et al. (Augsburg: Deutsche Verlags Anstalt, 1976), p. 6 (my translation). Dr. Karl Jarres v. Klöckner, president, Klöckner-Works, went even further in a similar letter to the Montan union leaders in Cologne and offered immediately, in early 1947, supervisory board seats to representatives of employees and union. The Klöckner-Werke was the first firm to reorganize its board of directors in accordance with the concept of the equality of capital and labor; 50 percent of all supervisory seats were allocated to employee-union representatives in the summer of 1947.

26. For example, Adenauer's Christian Democratic Union (CDU), meeting in the town of Ahlen in 1947 to determine its first "party platform" (Ahlener program) demanded the equal codetermination of employees in their firm as a step toward achieving economic democracy (*Wirtschaftsdemokratie*). Similar motions were passed by the Catholic Conference in Bochum (1949) and the Council of the Lutheran (Evangelische) Church in Essen (1950).

27. Schmidt, "die Mitbestimmung der Arbeiter," p. 6.

28. The union viewpoint was clearly stated by Hans Böckler, a trade-union leader of the Weimar period who had emerged as the most influential labor spokesman in the British occupation zone during the 1945-1948 period. In the first trade-union conference (in the British occupation zone) in Hannover, March 1946, Böckler remarked: "We [the union leaders] had told each other immediately at the beginning of the complete defeat [of Nationalist-Socialist Germany]: it must not happen a second time, what happened to the German workers in 1920-21, that after honest endeavor [to create a democratic society] in the end they are again deceived. We [the workers] must, therefore, be represented *equally* in the entire economy, not only in individual economic institutions, *but in the entire economy*. Hence the concept is: representation on the top management committees and on

the supervisory boards of the corporations." Minutes (*Protokoll*) of the First Trade-Union Conference in the British Zone, Hannover, 12-14 March 1946, p. 19 (my translation, my italics). Note the reference to equal representation in the entire economy, once more a reference to the Labor-Management Economic Council promised in the Weimar Constitution.

29. The initials I.G. stand for *Industry Gewerkschaft* or "industrial union."

30. Paul Fisher, "Labor Codetermination in Germany," *Social Research* (December 1951):466.

31. The full title of this law—commonly referred to in German as the *Montan-Mitbetimmungsgesetz*—reads in translation, "Law concerning employee codetermination in the supervisory and management boards of the mining, iron and steel industry," 21 May 1951.

32. In actual practice, codetermination varies from firm to firm to a much greater extent than has been believed by academic observers. At the University of Munich, Professor E. Witte's Institute for Organization has been carrying on a major empirical study of the actual decision-making process in every German-owned firm subject to the Reform Codetermination Law of 1976. Without in any way anticipating the formal publication of this study, it should be stated that codetermination in practice has had many more variations and has been much more dependent on the people involved than any ideologues could have anticipated. For a specific case study, see Alfred L. Thimm, "Decision-Making at Volkswagen, 1972-1975," *Columbia Journal of World Business* (Spring 1976):94-103.

33. In its rhetoric the bill drew heavily on the codetermination programs developed at the *Bochumer Katholikentag* (Catholic Assembly) of 1949 and the *Evangelischer Kirchentag* (Lutheran Assembly) at Essen in 1940, which had demanded that the wage relationship between employer and employee be overcome through codetermination, both on the level of the firm and in society as a whole. The Catholic Assembly had demanded the "codetermination right for all 'co-workers' [*Mitarbeitende*] on all social personal and economic issues." See Deutscher Katholikentag Bochum, 1949, p. 114. The use of the term *coworker* instead of *employee* was a subtle change, denoting the shift from the concept of hired labor as a factor of production to the joint cooperation of owners and coworkers, both equal, with common interest in the success of the enterprise. *Rat der Evangelischen Kirch Deutschlands*, Essen (1950). The statement of the Protestant Assembly did not go into detail; it was especially vague concerning the way codetermination on a higher level (*überbetribliche Mitbestimmung*, or "codetermination beyond the enterprise") was to be organized.

34. Actually employees in Germany (and most of Europe) have enjoyed considerable protection against both individual and mass layoffs since 1919. Firing a worker with some seniority (say ten years) has been quite costly

since World War I. The works-council legislation requires the employer not only to consult and inform the works council of planned layoffs but also obtain its approval. The works council rather than social legislation becomes the primary protector of employee interests. The CDU-CSU bill, emphasizing individuals rather than the union, drew heavily upon the works-council provisions of the 1946-1948 codetermination legislation of the various provinces (especially the Bavarian legislation); eventually the works-council legislation of 1952 conformed quite closely to the bill that the CDU-CSU submitted to Parliament in 1950.

35. All members of the firm except the half-dozen top managers who comprise the management board were considered employees; this definition has prevailed in the law.

36. Interestingly the Montan codetermination legislation of 1951 and the subsequent codetermination reform legislation of 1976 have strengthened the managerial role of the supervisory board: "Through the [Montan] codetermination legislation, the supervisory board receives a superior position in the structure of a corporation; the supervisory board is no longer a mere stockholder committee but a decision-making forum, in which various interests are respresented, and which has definite, legally conferred jurisdiction." Norbert Reich, "Die Stellung des Aufsichtsrat in mitbestimmten Unternehmen," *Mitbestimmungsgesetz* (Darmstadt: H. Luchterhand Darmstadt, 1976), p. 165 (my translation).

37. Clark Kerr, in "The Trade Union Movement and the Redistribution of Power in Postwar Germany," *Quarterly Journal of Economics Q.J.E.* (November 1954):537-539, 557, repeatedly refers to the potential competition between works council and union. Kerr expressed the view of American labor-union functionaries who were surprised that German unions advocated codetermination and the extension of works-council jurisdiction. Kerr and the American observers greatly exaggerated potential or actual works-council-union conflict, at least partially because their views of German reality had been badly distorted by American war propaganda, which had turned the "worker-union leader" into an antifascist hero and the employer-stockholder into a proto-Nazi; reality was much more complex. For a more sophisticated description of works council-union relationships, see A. Mausolff, *Gewerkchaft und Betriebsrat im Urteil der Arbeitnehmer* (Darmstadt: E. Rother Verlag, 1952).

38. Catholic and Protestant labor leaders and theologians played a major role in developing the postwar codetermination model; hence there was no antiunion bias in its formulation, and certainly the local union was in no way precluded from playing a role if it enjoyed the confidence of the employees.

39. *Gesetzesvorschlag zur Neuordnung der deutschen Wirschaft* (Düsseldorf, DGB, 22 May 1950).

40. Moreover, the position taken by the DGB during the 1970s is still fully compatible with its public statements of 1919 and 1950. DGB President H.O. Vetter expressed greater confidence in the social market economy in 1950 than in 1976 or 1980.

41. In small firms (defined as having between twenty and three hundred employees), the Weimar legislation was to be revived, and two works-council members were to join the supervisory board.

42. *Arbeitsdirektor* does not mean "worker director" (Arbeiter-direktor) as often mistranslated in the United States. The literal translation might be "work manager" or, more freely, "director of industrial relations." Since white-collar, professonal, and managerial employees also fall under the jurisdiction of the Arbeitsdirektor, the translation "personnel vice-president" is the best.

43. The *Vorstand* (management board or management executive committee) has between three and twelve members, although five is the most frequent number, comprised of a chairman, plus technical, financial, commercial, and personnel managers (*Resortschefs*). During the 1946-1949 period, three member boards were common in the Montan industry in order to give greater voice to the union-selected Arbeitsdirektor, and hence to the union leadership. The chairman of the management board (*Vorstandsvorsitzender*) is the chief executive officer of the firm, previously called *Generaldirektor*, a term still in use in Austria and Switzerland.

44. The economics' committee veto power over management decision also reappeared in the 1976 Swedish Act of Employee Participation.

45. Separate federal and regional economy chambers (*Wirtschafts Kammer*) and artisan and agricultural chambers exist in the Federal Republic and have existed before in Weimar and Imperial Germany. The DGB proposal would have unified these three separate chambers with the chamber of labor (*Arbeiterkammer*), given 50 percent of the seats to labor (unions), and enhanced enormously the political and regulatory powers of these indestructible corporate remnants of the Holy Roman Empire.

46. In Sweden, after sharing power equally with the employer associations, the union leadership had suddenly demanded to participate in the profits of the enterprises in a manner that would give them virtual ownership of the industry within twenty years.

47. In emphasizing the predominantly Catholic viewpoint in the development of the Christian cooperative codetermination model, the intellectual contribution of a group of influential neoliberals, associated generally with Adenauer's economics minister, Ludwig Erhardt, has been neglected. The major intellectual influence in this group emanated, however, from Wilhelm Roepke's romantic-neoliberal views: see his *Economics of a Free Society* (Chicago: Henry Regnery, 1963), esp. chap. 5.

2 The Golden Age of Codetermination, 1950-1972

The highly ideological nature of the political controversies in the Weimar Republic had made compromise difficult, reasoned parliamentary debate virtually impossible. The new West German Republic viewed the supposedly nonideological, well-mannered, pragmatic nature of Anglo-American politics as the necessary prerequisite to the successful development of a parliamentary democracy. It was resolved, therefore, to hold debates on an operational, nonideological level henceforth and to strive for consensus rather than total victory. The attempt to draft a new uniform codetermination law tested the good intentions of the new democracy. The concept of employee codetermination as a means of strengthening the fabric of society and preventing the alienation of the workers had the full support of all political parties, the churches, the newspapers, the intellectuals, and perhaps even the workers'. Nevertheless the nature and degree of codetermination was a highly controversial issue that had far-reaching implications for the future of Germany.

Codetermination Compromise

The fact that two different modes of codetermination already existed in 1949 contributed initially to the divisive and acrimonious struggle over the proposed new uniform codetermination law, but ultimately it also presented the compromise solution. The Adenauer government, supported by a strong conservative-liberal (CDU-CSU and FDP) majority in Parliament, at first had attempted to adopt the CDU-CSU codetermination bill, which was quite compatible with the prevailing conditions outside the iron-steel-coal (Montan) industry. The extension of the works council-centered codetermination legislation to the Montan industry would have required the Montan unions to relinquish their role on the supervisory board and to accept a weaker position within the mines and factories.

Quite naturally, the two affected unions, I.G. Metall and I.G. Bergbau (mine workers), furiously opposed any proposal that threatened their established position in the Montan industry.[2] They were fully supported by the DGB leadership, which said it would call a general strike if the parliamentary majority imposed its codetermination model upon the Montan industry. A general strike in support of a political goal would have been illegal and would have been opposed by a large majority of the population.[3] It also would have poisoned the relationship between the unions and society, between the DGB leadership and the Adenauer government. The postwar attempt to depoliticize the trade unions and to convert them from instruments of class warfare to American-type representatives of their members' economic interests would have failed irreversibly.

Legalizing the Union View of Codetermination in the Montan Industry

Adenauer took the leadership in working out a compromise that preserved the union gains in the Montan industry.[4] It also permitted the government majority to establish subsequently their own version of employee codetermination for all other sectors of the West German economy.[5]

In line with this 25-27 January 1951 compromise agreement between unions and government, the German parliament passed on 19 April 1951 the Montan *Mitbestimmungsgesetz*, which gave legal recognition to the equal representation of union and employee representatives in the coal-iron-steel industry and generally confirmed the existing management-union relations on the supervisory and management board.[6] Specifically the Montan unions maintained their 50 percent share of the supervisory seats; the prerogative to choose the personnel vice-president and hence have some representation on the management executive committee; and, perhaps most importantly, the recognition of the Montan trade unions as the instrument of worker codetermination.

Implicit in the DGB-Adenauer compromise was the union leadership's promise to permit Parliament to determine the codetermination legislation for the rest of West German industry without resorting to extraparliamentary measures if the final law did not meet the demands of organized labor. The German unions, of course, did not give up their right to lobby in the strongest form possible for the codetermination bill the DGB had submitted to Parliament in 1950.

Adoption of the Catholic-Conservative View for All Other Industries

In spite of heavy SDP-union opposition, the Parliament adopted in 1952 a pragmatic version of the original CDU-CSU codetermination bill; the *Betriebsverfassungsgesetz* (literally, "works constitution act") of 1952 was a clear expression of the Catholic-conservative view of codetermination, only slightly modified by political and practical considerations.[7] The law consisted of two distinct parts: the works legislation, which defined the codetermination rights of the individual workers whose social, personal, and economic interests in the firm were to be represented by a works council, and the enterprise legislation (*Unternehmungverfassung*), which provided for the collective codetermination of a firm's personnel by allocating one-third of the supervisory seats to employee representatives.[8] The works legislation applied to all German companies with at least five employees, while the enterprise legislation applied only to corporations and limited-liability companies outside the Montan industry with more than five hundred employees.

Significance of the Compromise

The 1951-1952 compromise legislation is of considerable interest today for three reasons. First, the two distinct codetermination models are clearly expressed by the two different laws; thus they provide a unique opportunity to compare their effectiveness over the next twenty years. Second, the legislation represented the high-water mark of the conservative codetermination model, which emphasized the organic unity of enterprise owners and employees and rejected the claim of the national unions to speak for labor. Each subsequent codetermination amendment in 1972 and 1976 strengthened the role of the national trade unions in enterprise codetermination and weakened the role of individual employees. And third, the DGB leadership had never accepted the 1951-1952 compromise as a final solution but has striven until today to extend the Montan codetermination to the entire country. Moreover, the equal participation of labor and capital in the management of the enterprise has become a trade-union demand throughout Europe. Although American unions have shown little, if any, interest in any form of management participation, some American intellectuals have been eagerly pressing the half-understood German model on reluctant labor leaders.[9]

Corporate Environment of Codetermination

The German corporation has stockholders, a supervisory board, a management executive committee, and employees. The employees are separated into three groups: managers (*Leitender Angestellte*), salaried employees (*Angestellte*), and workers (*Arbeiter*). In the actual performance of their duties, the supervisory board and the management executive committee have greatly resembled their Anglo-American equivalents, although their legal status has been different; moreover, the allocation of 50 percent of the supervisory board seats to union-employee representatives in the Montan industry has changed the operational nature of the supervisory board in the coal-steel sector.[10]

During the early phases of the developing corporation law in the nineteenth century, German, especially Prussian, firms actually did have a two-tier board system, quite similar in intention and operation to the strategic and operational management committees of the pre-World War I Du Pont company.[11] The stockholders chose a *Verwaltungsrat* ("administration committee"), made up of major shareholders, to set long-run policy and to represent the company to outsiders. The Verwaltungsrat appointed the operational managers. In subsequent legislation (1861-1864), the Verwaltungsrat was replaced by two committees: a professional management committee, which combined the legal and strategic functions of the Verwaltungsrat with the duties of the operational managers, and the supervisory board, elected by stockholders, whose legal responsibility was the supervision of the Vorstand.

Current German corporation law still merely requires the Aufsichtsrat to supervise in a fiduciary manner the management of the firm.[12] In practice, however, the supervisory board's behavior has been virtually identical with that of the Anglo-American board, except for the fact that no member of the Vorstand can simultaneously be a member of the firm's supervisory board. In the United States, the board appoints the president and may offer advice on the selection of a few key executives. The German supervisory board appoints the entire Vorstand (ordinarily three to nine *Direktors*), which assigns different duties to each member but is responsible, collectively and individually, for the sound management of the enterprise. In practice, and especially since the advent of codetermination, the supervisory board approves major strategic and investment decisions. In many cases, however, a strong *Vorstandsvorsitzender* (chairman of the management committee) will virtually tell the board whom to appoint to the Vorstand and whom to fire; similarly many German boards, just like American boards, may rubber-stamp all major decisions brought before them.

Legally the position of the German top executives is stronger than that of their Anglo-American counterparts because the Vorstand is the company before the law. Whenever codetermination legislation refers to the employer, it really means the Vorstand. The members of the management committee are required to serve the company as professionals, and the supervisory board cannot legally interfere. The board can discharge Vorstand members—who usually hold three- to five-year contracts—but it must abstain from offering directives, although it may veto management's investment proposals. In such a case, the Vorstand may appeal directly to a specially called stockholder assembly and can be upheld if supported by three-quarters of the shares voted. In practice, however, supervisory board vetoes are extremely scarce. Moreover, because of the Vorstand's explicit position as professionals, the stockholder assemblies ordinarily elect supervisory board members at the recommendation of the chief executive, and supervisory boards rarely quarrel with their management.

The top management of large corporations views the supervisory board as a source of advice and support, not as the shareholders' watchdog, and recommends to the shareholders leading managers and bankers for election to the board. In his investigation of the changing nature of the codetermined supervisory board, E. Gutenberg found that the contemporary Vorstand discusses major decisions with key board members before acting, thus changing the nature of the board from a controlling to an advisory function.[13]

From the point of view of the trade unions, however, the supervisory board was chosen as the agent of participation in management decisions because it could appoint and dismiss the top management; the trade unions, therefore, perceived the potential role of the supervisory board and disregarded the actual function performed in the interwar period. It will be important to analyze how much the nature of German management has changed, or may still change in the future, as a consequence of the codetermination legislation.

Montan Codetermination Law of 1951

The 1951 law (*Mitbestimmungsgesetz*) dealt exclusively with the selection of union-employee representatives for the supervisory and management boards in the Montan industry, without prescribing specific responsibilities or conduct for the new board members.

The Mitbestimmungsgesetz applies to all corporations and limited-liability companies in the coal-iron-steel industry with more than a thousand employees. Each of these firms has to form a supervisory board, which ordinarily has eleven members.[14] All members of the board have equal rights and obligations and cannot be bound by any directives.

The supervisory board ordinarily consists of five stockholder representatives, five employee representatives, and a neutral member who is elected by the other ten members. The employee and stockholder delegations each include a "further member" (*weiteres Mitglied*), who can be neither an employee, nor a stockholder, nor a functionary of union or employer organizations. It had been the intention of the law that the two further members, as well as the neutral member, would represent the interests of the public. This has not been the case.[15]

The five employee-union representatives on the supervisory board are selected through a complex process. Three representatives, including the further members, are chosen by the national unions represented in the Montan enterprise, after previous consultations with the local works council and union officials.[16] The two remaining representatives must be employees of the firm; one must be a worker, the other a salaried employee (*Angestellter*).[17] The workers and employees form two different electoral colleges, one of the few significant changes in the 1951 law from the previous prevailing codetermination conditions in the Montan industry. Each college elects its representative by secret ballot from nominations submitted by the works councils; the works councils in turn compile their nominating lists after consultations with local and national union officials. After the election, the works council must inform the appropriate national unions of the victorious candidates' names. Although each employee is eligible for election, the national union may veto the winner if there are reasonable grounds that, in the union's view, the nominee might endanger the enterprise or the national economy.[18] Should the works council reject the union's objection, and should the union maintain its veto, the federal minister of labor must make the final decision.

In order to make the 1951 law compatible with the existing corporation law, the Mitbestimmungsgesetz still provides that the general stockholder meeting (*Hauptversammlung*) continue to elect all supervisory board members, stockholder as well as union-employee representatives. In the election of the union-employee representatives, the stockholder meeting is bound by the 1951 law to accept the five union-employee selections. It is not quite clear legally what would happen if the general stockholder meeting refused to be bound, but this situation has never occurred.

The management executive committee must include the Arbeitsdirektor who, however, can be appointed only with the approval of the majority of the employee representatives (thus, the national union).[19] The duties of the Arbeitsdirektor are not specified by the law—quite unusual for German legislation—but are left to be determined by the supervisory board of each firm. As a member of the management committee, the Arbeitsdirektor is legally responsible for the entire enterprise, although politically that person is indebted to the union leadership for appointment and dependent upon their goodwill for job tenure.

The neutral member of the board is also formally appointed by the stockholder assembly upon nomination by the other ten supervisory board members. The nomination is by majority vote, but at least three members each of the employer and employee representatives must support the nomination. If the supervisory board cannot agree on the neutral member or if the stockholders reject the nominated candidate, a complicated mediation process ensues. If all mediation fails, the stockholders ultimately can select a neutral member of their choice. There has been no known instance in which the board failed to agree on a neutral member.

The 1951 law does not specify how the chairman and vice-chairman of the supervisory board ought to be elected, an omission that could have caused considerable difficulties in developing an operational board. Unions and employers agreed, however, to follow the procedure established during the occupation period and select the supervisory board chairman from the stockholder representatives and the vice-chairman from the employee representatives. In most cases, Montan boards appointed an executive committee (*Presidium*), which consisted of the chairman, the vice-chairman, and the neutral member.

The 1951 Mitbestimmungs law maintained existing codetermination relations in the Montan industry, where management and union had already learned to cooperate during the preceding years. The 1951 legislation itself provided merely the assurance that, in spite of some minor revisions, the existing institutional relationships were to remain intact. Officially employer and union spokesmen professed satisfaction with the Montan codetermination law. The employers stressed in their public statements, however, that conditions in the Montan industry were very special and quite different from those in other sectors of the economy; hence no general conclusions ought to be drawn. The union leaders, on the other hand, cited the smoothly working codetermination process in the Montan industry as supporting evidence for their demand to extend equal codetermination to the entire economy.[20]

The importance of the Montan codetermination model for the further growth of union power in Germany and throughout Europe requires a close look at its operational effectiveness, but this is done best by viewing it in comparison and in conjunction with the 1952 legislation; hence I shall first discuss the latter.

Works Legislation Act of 1952

The 1952 law (*Betriebsverfassungsgesetz*, hereafter referred to as Betr. V.G., 1952) viewed the works councils, elected by the personnel of each plant, as the instrument of employee participation in the economic and social decisions affecting the individual's work place. It is an agent of social cooperation; hence the works council cannot call strikes nor undertake any other job action. In cases of disagreement with management in codetermination areas, arbitration and, finally, appeals to the labor courts are the only permissible steps to settle conflicts.

In order to strengthen the position of the works council and improve the communication between management and employees, the 1952 law also provided for works-council representation on the supervisory board. The 1952 law, therefore, consists of two components. The enterprise legislation provides for employee representation on the supervisory board of all corporations and limited-liability companies with more than five hundred employees outside the Montan industry. And the works-council legislation regulates employee participation in the social, personal, and economic decisions of the enterprise through the works council, which must be formed in all firms that have at least five employees (ten in the agricultural sector). The works-council legislation applies also to the Montan industry, where it supplements the codetermination act, and thereby establishes uniform election standards for the works councils throughout West Germany.

Enterprise Legislation

The enterprise aspect of the 1952 law, which is still in effect for German corporations with fewer than two thousand employees, contained four key provisions.[21]

1. Employee representatives must hold one-third of the supervisory board seats in all corporations and limited-liability companies with more than five hundred employees (firms that are not included in the Montan codetermination law of 1951) subject to sections 76 and 77 of the Betr.V.G., 1952. The law excludes family-owned corporations with fewer than five hundred employees. But cooperatives employing more than five hundred persons are included and must form appropriate supervisory boards. Supervisory boards must have at least three members; any number divisible by three but not exceeding fifteen is acceptable.

2. The employee representatives are directly elected by secret ballot. The employee representative (also sometimes referred to as "employee director" in American literature) must be employed by the enterprise if only one supervisory board member is to be elected. If two or more employee directors are to be chosen, at least two representatives from the enterprise—one a worker, the other a salaried employee—must be selected. The law thus permits, implicitly, the election of an outsider, presumably a union functionary, if the supervisory board contains nine or more members. As a consequence, many corporations reduced their supervisory boards to six members.

3. Works-council members as well as individual employees can submit nominations for the board election. The individual nominations, however, must be signed by either 10 percent of the electorate or one hundred employees.

4. The recall of an elected supervisory board member is possible if either the works council or one-fifth of the eligible employees demand a recall vote. The recall is successful if it is supported by at least three-fourths of the ballots cast. In practice, such a recall has occurred only rarely.

These four points are the significant enterprise provisions in the 1952 legislation. The actual duties of the supervisory board are not specified. German company law, however, requires that the management executive committee inform the supervisory board extensively about enterprise operation. Moreover, the board is not required to play merely a passive role but may demand specific reports from the management. Nothing in the 1951 law precluded or encouraged the employee directors to exhaust all possibilities of their position to influence the decision process.

Works Legislation Wc 1952

The works legislation of the 1952 law is much more important than the enterprise component.

1. All enterprises with at least five employees must form works councils.[22] Specifically excluded are all public institutions (federal, provincial, or municipal), as well as religious and political organizations.[23]

2. The tasks of unions and employer associations are not affected by the Betr.V.G. of 1952.

3. The works councils vary in size. Firms with fewer than twenty-one employees will have only a works council of one, while the largest with more than nine thousand employees may have up to thirty-five works-council members. If the works council has at least three members, both workers and salaried employees must be represented; a rather complicated key assures either group a minimum representation somewhat in excess of its true proportions.[24]

4. Workers and salaried employees will vote separately, by secret ballot, to elect their respective works council member. In case of a one-person works council, salaried employees and workers will vote jointly.[25]

5. Works-council members are chosen by a proportional election system for a two-year term to guarantee the representation of different interests among the employees. All employees (and by implication the local union) can submit nomination lists, provided they are supported by the signatures of at least 10 percent of the total personnel. A union representative may attend the works-council meeting in an advisory capacity if at least one-fourth of the council members request it.

6. The works council has to report once a year to the works assembly (*Betriebsversammlung*), which comprises all employees of the firm. The employer must be invited to the works assembly and is entitled to present his views; similarly, representatives of the national unions may attend the works assembly. Additional works assemblies may be called if the employer or at least 25 percent of the employees demand it and present an appropriate agenda.

7. Employer and works councils are expected to cooperate in a spirit of mutual trust and in the best interests of the enterprise, employees, and public. Their mutual cooperation operates within the framework of the industry-wide collective-bargaining agreement and with the support of the national union and employer organization. Both employer and works-council members are expected to abstain from all activities that might endanger the internal peace and the mission of the enterprise. They are to refrain especially from political activities within the enterprise.

8. The works council has three general tasks: to propose measures to the employer that further the interests of the enterprise and the employees; to monitor the existing collective-bargaining agreements, internal-enterprise agreements, and social legislation; and to take complaints from the employees and, should the council decide they are justified, negotiate settlements with the employer.

Depending on the subject matter, the works council's functions include codetermination (*Mitbestimmen*), cooperation (*Mitwirken*), and consultation (*Beraten*); concomitant with its active function is its right to obtain information on virtually all aspects of the enterprise.

Definitions of Terms

Codetermination requires that the works council arrive at a decision jointly with management. In case of disagreement (absence of codetermination), binding arbitration is required unless both sides decide to drop the matter.

Cooperation and consultation require extensive discussions between management and works councils prior to implementing management decisions. In the 1952 law the terms *cooperation*, *consultation*, and *information* are defined only implicitly through the context.

Codetermination rights apply to all social issues, such as starting and quitting times, vacation scheduling, vocational training, administration of fringe benefits, internal discipline and work morale, administration of piece wages, wage and salary administration, and safety.

Actual wages are set by collective bargaining; the council codetermines the administration of the contract. In fact, of course, this division of responsibilities is often difficult to defend and to maintain.

The works council also has quasi-codetermination rights in the case of structural changes (*Betriebsänderungen*), including closing of departments, plants, or the entire enterprise; geographical transfer of the plant or departments; mergers; significant changes in plant or product; and introduction of new methods that are not obviously determined by technological advances. In case works council and management cannot agree and in case the complex arbitration procedure is not successful, management ultimately prevails.[26]

Codetermination and cooperation rights pertain to all personnel matters, provided the firm has more than twenty employees. Personnel matters are defined as hiring, reorganization, and transfer and firing of individuals, (not layoffs). Whenever an opening occurs, the employer has to inform the works council about both the job description and the candidate(s). If the works council has reservations about the candidate or the nature of the job, it must advise the employer accordingly. If employer and council fail to agree, management can proceed provisionally. The works council, in turn, can request the labor court to determine the merits of the case. The council can also demand the dismissal of an employee who has repeatedly violated the social and/or legal norms of the enterprise. If management does not dismiss such an employee, the case goes before the labor court for settlement.

Of special interest are the works council's rights in the case of mass layoffs (defined as layoffs of at least 10 percent). The employer must inform the council whenever the possibility of mass layoffs (or mass hiring) arises so that both can consider jointly how the social consequences of a layoff could be minimized. Since cooperation, but not codetermination, is involved, works-council agreement is not legally necessary, although only rarely will management order mass layoffs without first having gained works-council approval.

Consultation with the works council and management's obligation to inform extend primarily to economic matters. In order to promote trust and cooperation among works council and employer, an economics committee is to be established in all firms with more than one hundred employees. The economics committee consists of four to eight qualified members, at least one of whom is a works-council member; half of the members are chosen by the employer, half by the works council. The economics committee is to meet once a month to discuss economic issues of interest to the enterprise; the annual financial report is to be explained by the management to a joint economics committee-works council meeting. The primary purpose of the economics committee is the dissemination of economic intelligence throughout the enterprise and to further the mutual understanding of the economic issues facing employers and employees.

It is important to emphasize once more that the Betr.V.G., 1952, is based upon the social cooperation of employer and employee. The works council, elected by the employees, responsible to the employees collectively, and organized in a manner to provide maximum contact with each individual employee, is the instrument of employee participation in the decision processes that affect the organization of the employee's work place, career, job security, and pride in the firm. The allotment of supervisory seats to employee representatives is primarily a step to create an additional forum for communication, information, and participation.

Performance Comparison of the Codetermination Laws

The significant differences in spirit, purpose, and procedure between the Montan codetermination legislation of 1951 and the works-council legislation of 1952 require a careful comparison of their respective impact on the decision-making processes and on employee morale.[27] Moreover, the union's insistent demand that the Montan codetermination be extended to the entire economy—a demand that was almost, but not completely, satisfied in 1976 in Germany, and may be the issue throughout Europe in the 1980s—makes it even more important to assess the operational effectiveness and the sociopolitical implications of the codetermination and works council legislation.

In assessing the microeconomic and macroeconomic impact of the two codetermination models, I will draw on the so-called Biedenkopf report (1970), the 1974 hearings before the parliamentary labor committee, the 1976 reports of the parliamentary labor committee, the empirical investigation of decision processes under codetermination carried out by the Institut für Organisation at the University of Munich (1974-1979) under Professor Eberhard Witte, my own research, interviews, and case studies over the same period, and other published material.[28]

Biedenkopf Report

The Biedenkopf report deserves special comment, partly because of the national and international attention it has received and partly because of the research methodology, which raises a few questions.

In January 1967, Chancellor Kurt Kiesinger appointed a bipartisan committee of nine university professors under the chairmanship of Kurt Biedenkopf, then the University of Bochum's rector, today a member of Parliament and a leader in the CDU. The committee, advised by a bipartisan group of six experts drawn from union and employer organizations, questioned personally fifty-four senior managers, works-council chairmen, and union leaders about their experience with the two codetermination models. In addition, and partially based on the experience gained in the confidential interviews, the committee evaluated 1,091 individual questionnaires, about 81 percent of the total number mailed.

The report of the committee represents a classic achievement in the intelligent evaluation of nonrandom surveys; both the skill of its chairman obtaining a unanimous evaluation on most issues and the stylistic clarity of the exposition must be admired.[29] Still the committee's research methodology raises a few doubts. In view of the broad official consensus that codetermination is beneficial, it is hardly likely that any manager or union official who opposed codetermination for practical or ideological reasons would have admitted this to the committee, even if assured anonymity. How many American managers or union leaders would tell a committee of university professors that they oppose affirmative action?

More importantly, the Biedenkopf committee accepted the prevailing German definition of the codetermination of labor and capital. Again and again the Vorstand is considered to be either representing the owners or to be virtually identical with the owners. In spite of the abundant American, and more recently, German literature on the separation of management and control, German politicians, union leaders, and even managers still continue to speak as if professional management did not exist, as if maximizing the return on capital investment were still the paramount decision rule for German entrepreneurs. As a result, the Biedenkopf committee did not always ask the proper questions, nor did it always receive the appropriate answers. The same criticism applies to the parliamentary committees' discussions and testimonies. We shall therefore examine the impact of various forms of codetermination on management behavior, on the separation of ownership and control, and on the nature of enterprise decision processes.

Works Councils: Employee Participation in Practice, 1951-1972

The works-council component of the Betr.V.G., 1952, is by far the least controversial and most widely approved codetermination institution. It was also the only one that applied to all firms throughout the entire economy.

The 1952 legislation confirmed the positions of the works councils, eliminated the minor disparities in their legal status that had prevailed in different Länder, and extended the codetermination role of the councils in the economic sphere. Since management and works-council members had been dealing with each other quite effectively since 1919, the 1952 legislation prompted few noticeable immediate changes in the day-to-day operations.

For the most part over the next twenty years, the works councils became increasingly integrated into the management of the enterprise, although the role of the councils differs greatly from industry to industry and even within multiplant firms. As a rule, the works councils proceeded from harmonious cooperation with management in the 1950s to the absorption of operational management functions in the 1960s and early 1970s. In the firm of Siemens, for example, personnel policies and social programs are administered by the works councils within company-wide guidelines developed jointly by the *Konzern Betriebsrat* (corporate works council) and top management.[30] Siemens adheres to the exception principle in its personnel policy and has left it to the various works councils to deal with the exceptions to standard operating procedures.

Council Participation

Works councils are formed on a plant level, and in cases of multiplant firms, with divisional and corporate level works councils above them.[31] The influence of each works-council chairman varies with his leadership ability, but able and aggressive personalities can carve out a managerial role that goes way beyond the intent of the legislation. Especially on the divisional and corporate-level works councils powerful chairmen—called *Betriebspäpste* ("works popes")—became for most employees indistinguishable from management. These leaders, however, can maintain their positions only if they are periodically reelected, and hence satisfy the needs and expectations of their electorates. They can maintain their harmonious relationship with the Vorstand only if they continue to demonstrate their managerial skills and entrepreneurial instincts.

Works-council members are not paid for their services but continue to receive the wages of the position they held prior to election (for most, of course, the works council is not a full-time assignment, and they continue with their regular job on a part-time basis). Works-council chairmen, especially on the higher-level councils, are provided such management perquisites as offices, secretaries, expense accounts, and occasionally even company cars.

Throughout German industry, works-council chairmen and vice-chairmen are reelected regularly, thus transforming their function into a quasi-professional bureaucratic position that may provide ample rewards to the individuals concerned but discourages direct, shop-floor participation by the employee. This trend was greatly accelerated by the 1972 legislation.

Since the material rewards for key works-council chairmen are rather limited, the enterprise acquires a group of managers who serve because they enjoy the practice of management and who maintain their positions only as long as they can continue to reconcile the interests of the firm and the employees. The most successful Betriebspäpste would say that the interest of the personnel and the enterprise are identical, and this view is transmitted to the entire organization. This means that workers on the lowest level will have a sense of participation if they can identify themselves with the enterprise and with their work groups. Employees with more individualistic personalities may find, on the other hand, the works council in a Siemens-type enterprise to be a stern disciplinarian.

For the most part, skilled older workers and higher-level professionals are elected to the works councils, while younger, unskilled employees seem to exclude themselves almost voluntarily from both the passive and the active election process. The contact between the works council and the underrepresented groups in the organization varies widely. Small firms and, on occasion, especially motivated works councils at larger firms manage to in-

Table 2-1
Survey on Employee Attitudes
(Answers in percentage; N = 8008)

Statement	Agree	Agree Partially	Disagree	Don't Know
If I make enough money, I don't care about codetermination.	27	28	43	2
In the "works," as in life, who talks too much gets into trouble.	42	38	16	4
Who wants to participate in decision making, must first achieve something.	91	4	3	2
Managerial decisions should be left to those who understand something about it, and that is management.	42	38	16	4
Each one shall solve his own problems first, and shouldn't bother other people with it.	28	27	40	5
It is nonsense that worker and employees should interfere with management decisions; only the owner bears the risk and, therefore, should alone decide.	21	39	34	6
Participation in determining one's work increases the fun of working.	73	18	4	5
Anyone, today, who does a good job, does not need "Codetermination."	41	37	18	4

Source: Adapted from *Mitbestimmung in Österreich*, Chamber for Worker and Employees (Vienna, 1975), p. 19, [author's translation].

clude the low-skilled, younger employees in their activities and thus actually realize the industrial democracy that the entire process is meant to accomplish. For the most part, however, large segments of the work force do not participate directly in works-council activities and exhibit only moderate interest and approval of works-council codetermination. In 1975 the Austrian Chamber of Labor, a corporate institution with close ties to the trade unions, sponsored a large opinion survey to determine employee attitudes toward codetermination. The results, summarized in table 2-1, support earlier studies in the Federal Republic.[32]

Role of Councils

The smooth absorption into the German industry of millions of guest workers from Italy, Yugoslavia, and Turkey, on the other hand, undoubtedly has been a result of worker participation in the social sector in which the line between works council and personnel departments is difficult to determine. For example, an Italian works-council member who has been employed at Volkswagen for fifteen years will play a major role in socializing new young immigrants from Sicily both in the plant and in the company housing projects. Directives from an Italian works-council member concerning work discipline and living habits are more effective than commands from a German manager and cause much less resentment.

The high level of social cooperation between employees and management that has prevailed in the model codetermination firms is not typical for works-council codetermination throughout Germany. In many enterprises, especially limited-liability companies (in German, GMBH) with fewer than five hundred employees, the works councils play a negligible role, and strong management reduces codetermination to a one-way flow of information. Moreover, there are other sectors in which social cooperation is quite absent although the works councils are strong and active. Sections of the printing and automobile industry (General Motors' Adam Opel works is an example), for instance, have been dominated by comparatively radical unions, (by German criteria) which have prevented the full development of social cooperation between management and employees.

In the chemical industry the unions at the BASF installation in Ludwigshafen have been infiltrated by radical left-wing socialists and occasionally even Communists, who succeeded in creating an adversary relationship toward management.[33] A majority of the salaried employees and a strong minority among the workers have disapproved of this policy and elected moderates to the works council. The highly politicized council became, especially on the higher levels, a forum for ideological controversies between left-wing and moderate council members. Whenever the left wing dominated, the works councils became the instruments of empl management confrontations.[34]

In general, however, the works councils in the chemical industry ha cooperated with the industrial-relations department in administering tl personnel and social policies of the enterprise. Controversies arose mainly over layoff procedures during recession periods and, occasionally, over promotion and training decisions. These controversies often ended through compromise. The number of temporary layoffs was reduced if, for instance, the works council approved and supported an early retirement drive; mandatory overtime during peak periods was approved by the works council if, consequently, vacations were further liberalized.[35] The difference between confrontation codetermination and social cooperation codetermination is expressed primarily in the decision horizon of the works councils; confrontation prompts short-run decisions, social cooperation emphasizes the long run.

Council-Union Relationship

The works council-union relationship was generally stable and quite well defined during the twenty-year period from 1952 to 1972. Although 75 to 80 percent of works-council members had been affiliated with the unions, the councils operated independently from the national union. The influence of the local unions depended primarily on personal factors, although real and open conflicts occurred rarely. The local unions were generally satisfied if the works-council members were reasonably compatible with the union leadership, and they refrained ordinarily from exerting direct pressures, in accordance with the 1952 legislation.

Legally the main task of the national union was to negotiate industrywide collective-bargaining agreements, which determined wages and fringe benefits. Local unions could modify the national agreements through plant or enterprise negotiations, but they played a relatively subordinate role. Although the works councils were designed to be an instrument of social cooperation, German labor law recognized and protected the adversary role of management and unions by forbidding all interference with the bargaining process. This concept, called *Tarifautonomie* (roughly translated as "autonomous wage bargaining") becomes a crucial issue in the subsequent controversy about equal codetermination.

The unions generally did not welcome the emergence of strong, independent Betriebspäpste, who certainly reduced the unions' influence in the plants. American observers had viewed the works councils as potential competitors to the unions, and in several instances the unions became acutely aware of this danger. Their response was twofold. On the political level their insistent demand for new equal-codetermination legislation also included a strengthening of the union position within the firm, while simultaneously the unions began to appoint union shop stewards within certain plants so that they would be in a stronger position to deal with the works councils. Union shop stewards appeared most often in the automotive and chemical industries, where they used ideological and political arguments to influence both the workers and the works councils, but in turn had to meet opposition from the Left and the Right. In the Montan industry, the influence of the unions on both the election of works-council members and their subsequent behavior was greater than in the rest of the economy, but the I.G. Metall still found it necessary to establish union *Vertauensmänner* even in the steel industry, where they played a particularly effective role in the 1978-1979 steel strike.

In summary, the works councils had been an effective device for employee participation in the organization of their work place during the period 1952-1972; they improved the security of individuals and protected them from arbitrary hierarchical decisions. Although the actual effectiveness and efficiency of the works councils varied widely from enterprise to enterprise, German executives seemed to have adjusted themselves well to the loss of management prerogatives. In certain cases, as for instance Siemens, management had been able to incorporate works-council participation in its entire personnel administration structure. In the most successful cases, the effects of the 1952 legislation seemed to correspond to Peter Drucker's prescription to turn every employee into a manager.[36] The works councils have certainly been a factor in furthering decentralization and delegation of authority in German management.

Enterprise Legislations: Codetermination Through the Supervisory Board, 1950-1976

Union and employee codetermination through their representatives on the supervisory board has been the truly controversial aspect of work-force participation in managerial decision making. The Montan codetermination model is of special interest since the unions have consistently demanded its extension to the entire economy, and almost succeeded in 1976. Moreover, other European unions and their intellectual supporters have demanded the equal participation of labor in the supervisory boards as a necessary step to obtain industrial democracy. We shall attempt to assess the Montan codetermination on its own merit, compare it with the one-third employee representation on the supervisory boards of firms subject to the Betr.V.G., 1952, and last consider the issue of industrial democracy.

Montan Codetermination in Practice

In order to assess properly the Montan codetermination, the unique economic and political nature of the German coal-iron-steel industry must be understood. The Allies, and especially the British, succeeded after World War II in breaking up the vertically integrated steel industry into its production components, and the American-inspired antitrust agency (Kartell Amt) was to guarantee the proper competitive behavior of the decartelized industry.[37] Once the reconstruction of the coal-iron-steel industry had been completed by 1951, excess capacity in coal mining and modernization in steel production prompted both reconcentration and government intervention.

The creation of the Coal and Steel Community in 1953, the nucleus of the European Common Market, introduced a strong noncompetitive influence into the Montan industry through marketing orders, as well as pricing and production directives. The survival of a strong coal and steel industry demanded the closing of inefficient mines and mills, as well as heavy capital investment in high-technology, lavor-saving equipment. On the supervisory boards, the union leaders cooperated with management to obtain employee and stockholder assent to channeling investment into the most efficient locations, to reintegrate vertically Montan enterprises, and simultaneously to reduce coal and iron mining capacity sharply. Between 1951 and 1969 the number of steel and iron manufacturing firms decreased from thirty-four to nineteen, the number of coal and iron mines from seventy-one to thirty-two.[38]

The structural changes in the Montan industry throughout the entire community and particularly in Germany were carried through with strong government intervention, which resulted ultimately in full or partial government ownership of such key enterprises as Ruhrkohle AG and Saltzgitter AG (steel).[39] The high concentration, government ownership, subsidies, and intervention, as well as the overall control and guidelines by the community commissioners, have given the Montan economy the appearance of a regulated utility rather than a free-enterprise industry. From the point of view of American observers, there is little difference between the behavior of European prewar capitalistic cartels and postwar bureaucratic supranational agencies.

The structural changes in the Montan industry during the 1950s and 1960s could not have been carried out without the full support of the national union leadership and their representatives on the supervisory boards, who placed long-run regional and national interests above the short-run concerns of employees and stockholders. According to Biedenkopf, the close cooperation of management and union representatives on the supervisory boards, often over the objections of employee and stockholder representatives, may have provided a particular flavor to the Montan codetermination that cannot be replicated in other industries and at other times.[40]

The picture presented by the Biedenkopf report of farsighted managers and union leaders, standing shoulder to shoulder against shortsighted employees and stockholders, on and off the supervisory board, is somewhat overdrawn. First, it does not allow for the significant role the government and the Common Market (Montan community) have played; second, the considerable differences in the practice of codetermination and the influence of unions among different firms in the Montan industry are frequently ignored; third, and importantly, the so-called stockholder representatives on the supervisory boards were often closer to top management than to the stockholders. The entire concept that the supervisory board is the appropriate location for capital and labor to join in guiding the enterprise rests on an archaic nineteenth-century view of the firm; it fails to recognize that both management and unions have become vital institutions with their own ideology and objectives, which may have little in common with the interests of individual stockholders or employees.[41] The unique institutional framework of the Montan industry, including minimum prices, production quotas, and strict domestic antidumping provisions, provided some short-run insulation against market forces, thus granting Vorstand and unions more room for compromise and cooperation.[42]

Behavior of Supervisory Boards under Differing Legislations

The representation of employees on the supervisory boards in accordance with the provisions of the Betr.V.G., 1952, was not very controversial during the 1951-1972 period, although opinions somewhat differed about the justification, effectiveness, and importance of this form of codetermination. Since 1972 there have been volatile union-management controversies at Mannersmann (1977) and Saltzgitter (1978), which illuminated the worsening labor relations in the steel industry that culminated in the 1978-1979 steel strike. I shall therefore compare to what extent the different forms of board codetermination affected either the speed and efficiency of the decision process or actual employee participation during this period.

The supervisory board, inside and outside the Montan industry, has been considered by the proponents of equal codetermination as the appropriate body to afford employees the opportunity to participate in the managerial decision processes (*Willensbildung*). Legally the supervisory board was restricted to the fiduciary supervision of the management committee, although its authority to appoint the Vorstand did give it potential veto right and, hence, important reserve powers. For the most part, however, the supervisory board had played a rather unimportant role prior to codetermination; on occasion, however, a supervisory board that had been selected at the recommendation of the Vorstand for its managerial aptitude chose a chairman, vice-chairman, and committee chairmen who coalesced with the Vorstand in a Praesidium (executive committee) that operated exactly like an Anglo-American board. It seems very likely that both the precedent of presidia that developed long-run policies and the ability of the supervisory board to appoint the Vorstand prompted the union leadership and their intellectual allies to choose this forum as an instrument of codetermination of capital and labor. The very fact that those firms that produced a presidium were the best examples of the separation of ownership and control that Germany had to offer never seemed important to those who debated the equality of capital and labor.

There seems little doubt, however, that the supervisory board has expanded its role through the codetermination laws and has become an advisory forum to top management, very much like the Anglo-American board.[43] This process has taken place under the influence of the Montan codetermination law of 1951 and also the Betr.V.G., 1952. Although Biedenkopf still believed that this process was more noticeable in the Montan industry, the latest empirical research does indicate that the differences within each sector (Montan, non-Montan industry) are not greater than the differences between the two sectors. It is true that the changing nature of the supervisory board first became noticeable in the Montan industry where Vorstand and union functionaries on the supervisory board cooperated in many instances to develop merger and investment programs as well as schedules to close excess iron and coal mines. Only after Vorstand and unions were in agreement did management submit these policies to the supervisory board for pro forma approval.

During the period of rapid economic growth in Germany (1950-1965), the union influence on the supervisory board in the Montan industry served in many, but not all, firms to emphasize further the separation of ownership and control. Although union-management cooperation may have achieved efficient structural changes in the industry, it is rather difficult to describe this issue as codetermination between capital and labor. Although the employee representatives were often reluctant to approve closing and merger proposals, they did, in the end, vote unfailingly with the union functionaries en bloc. The so-called stockholder representatives—"so-called" because they were often closer to management than to the ephemeral stockholder—could not easily vote against their Vorstand and almost invariably approved management proposals that had already received union support.

A similar process also occurred outside the Montan industry, especially in companies that had experienced rapid growth. The strong support of the employee representatives at Daimler-Benz and BMW for management's aggressive investment programs certainly strengthened the position of the Vorstand against the supervisory board and the stockholders. By 1970 most supervisory boards throughout West Germany had extended their influence beyond the limits of their charter (*Satzung*) to become a management decision forum by demanding that an increasing number of strategic investment and marketing decisions require their approval.[44] In many instances, especially in those firms that developed a joint supervisory board-management executive committee, these approvals were merely a formality; in others, lengthy internal battles took place before the supervisory board arrived at a decision.[45]

The union-employee representatives in the Montan industry invariably voted as a bloc at each meeting along the lines previously determined in separate caucus sessions (called *Fraktions-sitzung* and analogous to the party caucuses in Parliament). Serious differences of opinion occurred in these caucuses between union functionaries and employee representatives, but the union officials invariably succeeded in having their views prevail. They succeeded partially because they held a three-to-two majority (or six to four in enlarged supervisory councils of conglomerates); partially, especially in the 1950s, because the union functionaries had superior academic training and experience; partially because the unions had achieved such a dominant position in the Montan industry that the individual employee representatives sooner or later had to fall in line.[46]

Among firms outside the Montan industry, external union functionaries only rarely were elected to the supervisory board, where they had little influence on the attitude of the employee representatives. Employee representatives on the supervisory board in and outside the Montan industry in almost all cases were also works-council members, with very similar experiences. Moreover, top managers from all sectors have repeatedly praised the loyalty and entrepreneurial attitude of the internal employee board members.[47] The difference in the influence of union functionaries on the caucuses of employee supervisory board members is, therefore, best explained by the different position of the union in the Montan industry.

Board Codetermination and Industrial Democracy

In subsequent years, employees outside the Montan industry virtually ceased to elect anyone to the supervisory council who did not work for the enterprise. Those who favored the mandatory inclusion of national union functionaries among employee representatives cited the frequent statements by Montan managers that union officials on the board, unlike employee representatives, were able to consider industry-wide and national aspects of the issues under consideration; moreover, Montan managers and union functionaries publicly agreed that the employee representatives had been motivated entirely by enterprise egoism (*Betriebsegoismus*). Those opposed to the presence of external union officials on supervisory boards believed that the advantage of codetermination was to confront the employee representatives with the reality of enterprise policy in the context of a market economy.[48]

The elitist statement that "for their own good" the employees be compelled to accept union officials among their board representatives may be quite true, but it hardly deserves the term employee codetermination nor can it be argued that mandatory allocation of board seats to union functionaries contributes to industrial democracy. The fact that professional managers and stockholders do not always have common interests has been thoroughly examined in the literature, and perhaps even overemphasized.[49] The perhaps even greater divergence in the objectives of employees and national union functionaries is ignored quite often. The employees and their elected representatives are motivated primarily by narrow economic interests, while labor unions, especially in Europe, are political organizations with ideological values and pragmatic, national objectives. In Germany the differences in employee and union objectives were less noticeable in the first two postwar decades, when the economic goal of rebuilding the country overcame all sectional and group interests.

Union officials have dominated the employee representatives on the Montan supervisory boards and have greatly influenced the behavior of works councils in the Montan industry. To the extent that the works councils determine training and advancements on the lower levels of the organization, and the union-selected Arbeitsdirektor is responsible for promotion on the higher levels in the organization, the unions are in a strong position to reward their friends. From a managerial viewpoint, this informal trade-union variant of the old boys' network separates management responsibility from union authority; politically this is the antithesis of industrial democracy.

Individual employees, though often loyal members of militant unions, have recognized that their interests do not necessarily coincide with those of the national union leadership and have refused to elect voluntarily outside union functionaries to the supervisory board. The Biedenkopf committee recognized this fact:

> According to the unanimous testimony [of managers, employers and union officials], the reason for the small number of outsiders [persons not employed by the firm] as employee representatives in the enterprises subject to the "works constitution law" [Betr.V.G., 1952] is due to the preference of the work force for employee representatives who are employed in the enterprise. . . . On the basis of the testimony, the commission gained the impression that the presence of "outside" employee-representatives [national union officials], if desired, *can only* be assured through mandatory *legislation.*[50]

The unions have tried consistently to make a strong case for legislation requiring the selection of union officials to supervisory boards. The testimony by union officials concerning the lack of entrepreneurial understanding among employee representatives, their inability to understand and judge entrepreneurial problems in their totality, especially if contrasted with the superior technical qualifications and broader economic understanding of union officials, would have been vigorously attacked by all proponents of codetermination if they had been made by managers rather than by union spokesmen.[51]

Both the Biedenkopf committee and, several years later, union and SDP officials in subsequent testimony before the parliamentary committee (1972-1974) emphasized that, for the most part, Montan managers had acknowledged the superior qualifications of the national union functionaries. Neither the management outside the Montan industry nor I, however, has been convinced that the presence of union functionaries improved the decision processes in the supervisory board. Management outside the Montan industry invariably has supported the efforts of its personnel to keep outsiders off the board; in those cases where especially strong national unions (such as I.G. Metall and I.G. Chemie) were likely to place a national union functionary among the employee representatives, management reduced the supervisory board to six members, thus making it impossible to add an outsider to the employee representatives.[52] Even the Biedenkopf report concedes, furthermore, that the most effective codetermination process developed in highly decentralized firms which elected a relatively large number of middle- and upper-level managers to the works councils and to the supervisory board. Under these circumstances, codetermination evolved into a truly participatory management in which the works councils and the supervisory board emerged as extrahierarchical information and decision forums.

There can be little doubt that in the immediate postwar period and during the 1950s, the leaders of the coal and metal unions were quite superior in training and sophistication to many employee representatives; moreover, the overall union policy on the restructuring of the Montan industry coincided with management's goals and with the views of the coal and steel community. It was this period of close union-management cooperation that justified the testimony of the Montan executives, which praised the national viewpoint of the union representatives on the Montan supervisory boards. By the 1960s, however, employee representatives, especially outside the Montan industry, were no longer inferior to the union officials in political and economic sophistication and quite superior in their understanding of the enterprise problems.

The picture of the calloused toiler in the boardroom was only rarely accurate, even in the immediate postwar period, and had become a myth by the 1960s.[53] The salaried employees, of course, almost invariably elected representatives with extensive managerial experience and ability to the board, while the workers elected almost exclusively skilled craftsmen with ample works-council experience. As the testimony before the Biedenkopf committee showed, both workers and salaried employees, inside and outside the Montan industry, almost without fail have elected only works-council members to the supervisory board. At BASF, for instance, the chairman of its Ludwigshafen works council for twelve years had also been chairman of the BASF corporate works council and a member of the supervisory board for eight years before he was defeated in the 1978 supervisory board election. By 1970 most employee representatives with previous works-council service had become skilled and competent managers with several years of upper-level management experience in the industrial relations-personnel area and hardly fitted the rather patronizing picture of the inexperienced, short-sighted employee representative that the Montan managers and union spokesmen described before the Biedenkopf committee and before the parliamentary committees.

The approval of the union functionaries' role on the supervisory board expressed by most—though not all—Montan executives before the various committees was taken completely on its face value by Biedenkopf and his colleagues. A striking exception to the prevailing viewpoint of Montan executives were the blunt statements by the Mannesmann Vorstand, especially its colorful CEO, Egon Overbeck, who did not concede the slightest benefit to the Montanmitbestimmung, least of all the presence of union functionaries on the Mannesmann supervisory board. A former Vorstand member of a Montan enterprise, and later the NSU (VW subsidiary) Vorstand and currently CEO of an American-owned German subsidiary, assured me that many, if not most, Montan executives agree with Overbeck but will not say so publicly or before a committee, even if assured anonymity. Overbeck has remained the only senior steel executive who has publicly criticized the Montan codetermination law.

Board Codetermination and Management Behavior

There can be little doubt that the responsibility and good sense displayed by the German coal and steel union leadership during the 1950s made a major contribution to Germany's economic recovery and, in the long run, to the economic well-being of union members. There were, however, at least two additional reasons for the Montan management's qualified support for the Montan codetermination that have not received appropriate consideration in the Biedenkopf committee or in subsequent discussions. First, the leaders of the mining and steel unions have been firmly entrenched for decades in the supervisory boards of the Montan industry, and there was no possibility that this might change. Especially in the 1950s and 1960s, these labor leaders were responsible, intelligent, and well mannered, qualities that led to a reasonable, smooth-working relationship between labor leaders and top managers. There was no sense in endangering this relationship by a testimony that would needlessly jeopardize a working partnership. In the case of Overbeck's testimony, no existing relationship was threatened, since the union-management relations at Mannesmann had never been cordial; moreover, Overbeck's views were well known throughout the industry.

Another reason for the qualified public support extended by the Montan management to the union officials on their supervisory boards was the help that the mining and steel unions had given to the rationalization—productivity improvements through replacing manpower by machinery—and recartelization—the reestablishing of cartels—that had been taking place in the coal and steel community. Within this community the German companies developed especially close ties with Dutch, Belgian, and Luxembourg firms that led to a close coordination of investment, marketing, and pricing decisions. This stabilization policy (a euphemism for eliminating competition) has had the full support of the German Montan unions, who have been very helpful in stifling anti-German and anticartel sentiments in the socialist parties of the Benelux countries.

The Montan management's repeated emphasis on the union officials' sophisticated viewpoint with respect to the regional and national needs of the industry should have alerted the Biedenkopf committee to the help that unions can provide in replacing the market with a quasi-neomercantilistic, corporate cooperation between big business and big labor. Such cooperation is especially likely in the Montan industry, where neither management nor unions have been known for their attachment to the free market. The overriding impression one obtains from the equal codetermination in the coal-steel industry during the 1950s and 1960s is the conversion of joint decision making of capital and labor into close cooperation between union leadership and the top management of several key companies, especially the government-owned ones, with the actual influence of private stockholders and employees reduced to a minimum.

The consolidation in the Montan industry had the support of the German government. Its subtle but effective influence during this consolidation period has been a neglected factor in the account of union-management cooperation during this period. The Biedenkopf report, for instance, emphasizes the joint management-union efforts in obtaining employee and stockholder approval of mergers and plant closings but omits any reference to government policy. Codetermination in the Montan industry has been a further step in the managerial revolution that leads to the complete separation of ownership and control; it may also have been a first step away from a market economy toward a new corporate state.

The prevailing cooperation between Montan management and union officials on the boards resulted frequently in working arrangements that generally avoided divisive votes (*Kampfabstimmung*) on the supervisory board. Since the employee-union representatives invariably caucused before a board meeting and voted together during the meeting, advance approval of any management proposal had to be obtained from the key union officials if it was to be adopted by the board. Top managers (Vorstand members) would meet first with the leading union official. If agreement was reached in principle, preparatory meetings were held between the employee-union board representatives and members of the management executive committee. Only if full agreement could be reached at these preliminary meetings did management submit the issue to the entire supervisory board, which generally would approve the proposal with very little debate.

In case no agreement could be reached in the preliminary sessions, management would refrain from bringing the issue before the board. The custom of preparatory meetings, separate caucuses, and exploratory negotiations between management and union greatly reduced the importance of the board in many Montan enterprises as a discussion or consulting forum. To the extent that successful prior negotiation between management and union officials strengthened the Vorstand's position in its relations with the so-called stockholder board representatives, one could even say that the supervisory function of the board was impaired in many cases.

Preliminary meetings between management and employee representatives also occurred outside the Montan industry and were well received by all employee representatives. In those instances, the major purpose of these meetings seemed to have been to inform and to solicit employee opinions at an early stage. Since the employee members of the board could not reject a management proposal, these preparatory meetings did not serve as a filter to eliminate controversial topics from board meetings. In the Montan industry, on the other hand, it has been precisely this filtering quality that seems to have been the chief drawback of the exploratory meetings. Not only were strategic management decisions delayed until the approval of the union officials could be obtained, but key issues in the coal and later the steel industry were never debated but rather kept quiet under this policy.

Even the Biedenkopf report conceded that the very nature of codetermination and the concomitant caucuses caused considerable delay in the decision process.[54] The only question is how serious the consequences were. Certain delays may help to stabilize the system, but others may cause immediate oscillations that may even destroy the system in the long run. According to industry spokesman Dr. Gottfried Walther and to Mannesmann's Overbeck, the Montan Mitbestimmung made it more difficult to adapt industry to changing conditions. Union spokesmen, on the other hand, stress that the delays in the decision processes were important in enabling management to obtain the cooperation of union and employees through supervisory board codetermination.[55] Still, the process of obtaining the support of the employee representatives was often quite costly since approval of management proposals had to be obtained through concessions in other areas.[56]

The Biedenkopf report understandably equivocates on the entire issue of delays and bargaining in the decision processes, but it omits a crucial aspect. The structural changes in the Montan industry occurred during an unprecedented period of economic growth and social cooperation on the macrolevel. How much the board atmosphere can be changed when one or the other of these preconditions is absent is indicated by the fact that "more divisive votes occurred in 1970 than in the previous eighteen years."[57] Yet if the costs of Montan codetermination were either controversial or difficult to assess, the benefits were obvious: union support for a painful policy of industrial reorganization. If we compare the performance of the German coal and steel industry with that of the British during this time, the benefits seem overwhelming.

Board Codetermination and Enterprise Objectives

This discussion of supervisory board codetermination has observed only management conduct to gain necessary approval of major merger or investment decisions. For the long run the question of to what extent codetermination affects enterprise objectives is more important. In the enterprises outside the Montan industry, there has been no indication that codetermination affected strategic behavior, at least certainly not before 1976. In the best management firms—IBM Germany, BMW, Daimler-Benz, Siemens—the presence of responsible employee representatives on the supervisory board improved the two-way flow of communication, enabled middle-level executives who represented the salaried employees to participate in strategic board decisions, and generally melded works councils and personnel administration into a smoothly functioning manpower management component.

A high degree of effective internal communications can and does occur in other systems of management, of course. The point is that the best examples of German corporate management were able to integrate successfully the mandatory codetermination legislation into their existing framework. Their success is a testimonial to the managerial skill of the enterprises rather than to the codetermination system. Developments since 1976 also raise the question whether such a successful integration can continue to exist in a less prosperous and cooperative era.

It is quite possible, however, that the integration of employee participation in the management process added additional weight to the full employment objective in the hierarchy of enterprise goals. If we except the American IBM Corporation, there is certainly more reluctance among German than among American management to correct market fluctuations through layoffs. It is rather doubtful, however, that the allocation of board seats to employees had a significant effect on the leadership of those enterprises in which the social cooperation of management and employees had developed fully.

There were examples of other firms, however, in which the stockholder representatives exploited their two-thirds majority to dominate the board meetings. In a few extreme cases, supervisory board executive committees even excluded employee representatives and decided important topics alone, thus effectively preventing employee participation in supervisory board deliberation. These instances were frequently cited by union officials before the Biedenkopf and the parliamentary subcommittee hearings. Although these events undoubtedly occurred during the 1950s, most evidence indicates that formal discrimination against employee board members had disappeared by the late 1960s, although vigorous entrepreneurs in medium-sized, family-owned firms (especially limited-liability companies, called GMBHs in German) have continued to dominate the enterprise, including the supervisory boards, through their overwhelming presonality.[58] The empirical research of the University of Munich-Witte group has reaffirmed that the close personal contact between owner-managers has discouraged employee interest in supervisory board participation, especially since the supervisory board in GMBHs has no practical management purpose.

The existing apathy among employees toward participation on the supervisory board level, as well as the unimportant role the board has played in many enterprises, have been the real explanation for the absence of effective employee participation in many enterprises outside the Montan industry. The trade unions have demanded that outside union officials be added to the boards of all German companies, including GMBHs, even though the employees have invariably shown their opposition to the role of outsiders in the codetermination process. The addition of unwanted union officials undoubtedly would enhance the managerial importance of the supervisory board, but it is rather doubtful whether a quasi-mandatory participation could still be called employee codetermination.

During the 1950s and 1960s the German unions were quite moderate in their wage demands in order to enable management to maintain a high investment level. During this economic-growth period, management, unions, employees, and stockholders exhibited an unusual consensus concerning the disposal of enterprise profits. Therefore it was not surprising that during this period of stable prices and profits union and employee representatives on the Montan supervisory boards made no attempt to interfere with management's dividend policies. We know today that this era of good feeling was due as much to the prosperity of these two decades as to the cooperative attitude of the union leadership on and off the supervisory boards.

The Biedenkopf report recognized the impact of the business cycles on the nature of employee codetermination and hence on management objectives.[59] With the advantage of ten years' hindsight, we can say that supervisory board codetermination in the Montan industry amplified the impact of the business cycle on management behavior and objectives. In the expansionary phase of the business cycle, management's expansionary investment programs were vigorously supported by the union-employee representatives against the stockholders; during the contraction phase, the same board members resisted or delayed the necessary capacity reduction, automation, or mergers.[60]

Mergers have been resisted by the union-employee delegation only if they resulted in employment reduction. On the other hand, mergers that strengthen the market and profit position of the firm by decreasing competition ordinarily have been enthusiastically supported by union and employee representatives. The notion of the British occupying powers and early American observers that union participation would prevent the recartelization of the steel industry was completely wrong.[61]

Impact of Arbeitsdirektor

The presence of the Arbeitsdirektor on the Vorstand in the Montan industry, and the concomitant strengthening of the role of the personnel vice-president throughout the economy, provide at least one clear-cut indication of the impact of codetermination on management objectives. The 1951 and 1952 legislation advanced social and personnel matters into the purviews of top management. If one accepts the view that management primarily "satisfices" rather than maximizes, the social and personnel concerns become important constraints, which any feasible long-run stragegy has to satisfy even before its other merits could be explored.

The actual role of the Arbeitsdirektor, the Vorstand member approved by the union leadership and serving at the pleasure of the union-employee directors, is more difficult to assess. Although Arbeitsdirektors invariably assert that they carry out their responsibilities without any undue union influence, the Biedenkopf committee had been sufficiently impressed by the ambiguity of the Arbeitsdirektor's position that it recommended the abolition of the Montan Arbeitsdirektor in its final report.

Of much greater interest is the question concerning what impact the Montan codetermination has had, or will have, on middle-management

behavior. Without union approval (through its supervisory board representatives) no senior executive can hope to become a Vorstand member;
without the support of the Arbeitsdirektor, promotion within the company
will be difficult; without works-council approval, an employee may never obtain the training to climb the first rung of the managerial ladder. The
Biedenkopf report is rather evasive on this point, but it does convey its impression that the unions have not misused their power.[62] The proper function of an institution cannot depend on the good behavior of a few key
members in the long run, however. Moreover, the very fact that union
power might be used to reward friends and punish enemies may prompt
behavior changes that might become discernible only years later. By 1970,
there was not very much evidence that the Montan Mitbestimmung and the
Arbeitsdirektor had any noticeable impact on upper- and middle-
management behavior.

Summary of Assessments

The works councils have provided participation in personnel and social
decisions for key employees directly, and for the majority of employees indirectly. The councils have strengthened the importance of social and personnel considerations without any noticeable weakening in the managerial
decision processes and with great gains in the social cooperation between
management and employees. The election of works-council members to the
supervisory boards outside the Montan industry generally seemed to have
increased the flow of communication and may have brought new viewpoints
into the managerial decision processes. Its overall significance was probably
limited, however.

   The equal participation in the Montan industry has made the unions
rather than the employees the true codetermination partners and has
delayed the decision processes, but it has enabled the coal-steel sector to
undergo serious structural adjustments without labor unrest. The rather
peculiar economic aspects of the coal and steel industry and the special
management-union relationships that have been shaped by the occupation
period make a precise assessment of Montan codetermination's impact on
enterprise behavior difficult. Even by 1970, however, there were clear indications, only unwillingly perceived by the Biedenkopf committee, that
the power given to the unions in the Montan legislation could bring about
a neomercantilistic corporate state in which union and management
bureaucracies would paternally codetermine the fate of employees and
consumers. Such a corporate state would become increasingly incompatible with a free market or with grass-roots participation in managerial decisions.

In the Montan industry, cooperation between union and management helped in closing uneconomic mines and factories during the 1950s and 1960s, but this was a period of vigorous economic growth throughout the German economy. In a period of economic stagnation, the problem of industrial excess capacity is much more likely to divide management and national union leaders. While top management must take all necessary steps to ensure the long-run survival of the firm, union leaders are concerned primarily with maintaining employment. Union leaders, unlike German executives, do not enjoy the luxury of long-run contracts and are under great political pressure to take the short-run viewpoint. Under such conditions the harmony between top management and national union leaders quickly disappears. The steel strike of 1978-1979 is convincing evidence that the much-praised union-management cooperation in the coal-steel industry was a phenomenon of the 1950s and 1960s rather than a result of the Montan codetermination law.

Notes

1. In 1950, an opinion poll taken by the independent Forschungstelle für Volkspsychologie showed that 59 percent of lower-income recipients approved a rather vaguely defined concept of work-place codetermination. In January 1951 the prestigious Institut für Demoskopie reported that 69 percent of factory workers favored some form of personal codetermination; only 48 percent of factory workers and only 37 percent of all employees (including workers) favored the more-extensive works-council type of codetermination, as it existed outside the Montan industry. Only 18 percent of employees (37 percent of all factory workers) favored an undefined "voice in business decisions"; the term "voice in business decisions" referred, however, to the union demand to obtain one-half of all supervisory seats. Although subsequent polls have shown an increased approval of work-place codetermination, the proportion of workers showing an interest in influencing top management decisions has remained small until 1980.

2. Industrie Gewerkschaft Metall, the industrial union of metal workers, Germany's strongest union, organizes all workers employed in the production and manufacture of steel and steel products. Its two power centers are the steel industry and the automobile industry. In the automobile industry, the union had gained a commanding position within the Volkswagen Corporation, which strengthened further its political and economic position in West Germany. See A. Thimm, "Decision Making at Volkswagen, 1972-1975," *Columbia Journal of World Business* (Spring 1976):94-103.

3. The German strike legislation has been developed primarily by federal labor court decisions, which have emphasized social partnership

among the classes and mutual cooperation between management and labor. Political strikes as well as wildcat strikes are not sanctioned by German collective labor law and thus are illegal. Participants in illegal strikes are not protected; they can be dismissed or even sued; see Thilo Ramm, "Codetermination and the German Works Constitution Act of 1972," *Industrial Law Journal* (March 1974):21, and Thilo Ramm, "Codetermination and Constitution" (lecture at the Conference of the Industrial Law Society, Oxford, England, 7-10 September 1973.)

4. Although this compromise undoubtedly was necessary to avoid a divisive and potentially disastrous struggle with the DGB leadership, it de monstrated an important political fact of postwar Europe: once the trade unions have won a particular position, their gain is irreversible. Not even a Konrad Adenauer, supported by a strong majority inside and outside Parliament, could dislodge the Montan union leadership from the politically and economically powerful position they had gained in the steel industry. What Adenauer could not achieve in Germany in 1950, Heath could not achieve in England in 1972, nor Fälldin in Sweden in 1978.

I have referred to this "irreversibility phenomenon" as the iron law of industrial relations: what the unions have gained is theirs; all else is negotiable.

5. "[It was] the historical achievement of Konrad Adenauer to support the realization of codetermination in the Montan industry (in line with already existing conditions)." Chancellor Helmut Schmidt, in *Die Mitbestimmung der Arbeiter*, special reprint from *Konrad Adenauer und seine Zeit*, ed. D. Blumenwitz et al. (Augsburg: Deutsche Verlagsanstalt, 1976), p. 8.

6. Actually the coal industry was for the first time formally included in the Montan industry by the 1951 legislation. Though the coal mines had not been under the jurisdiction of the Allied Steel Trustee Association, the "captive coal mines" of the steel industry had adopted equal codetermination whenever it was introduced into the parent organization. In most other cases the Bergbau union had gained equal representation on the supervisory board through collective bargaining. The 1951 legislation applied to 105 enterprises: 34 iron and steel manufacturers, 65 coal mining industries, and 6 iron mining concerns.

7. The term *Betriebsverfassung* is literally translated as "works constitution." The word *constitution*, however, has a much more narrowly defined meaning in English than does *Verfassung* in German; hence in this book the law is generally referred to by its German abbreviation, Betr.V.G., 1952.

8. In the Montan industry, the works-council provisions of the 1952 Betriebsverfassungsgesetz was considered supplementary (*ergänzend*) to the 1951 Montan Mitbestimmungsgesetz. It changed only slightly the operation

of the already-existing works councils in the Montan industry, which had been reestablished in the Weimar tradition after 1945 through local collective-bargaining agreements.

9. Typical for the enthusiastic, though superficial and misleading American comments on codetermination is Paul Kemezis, "Keeping Labor Peace in Germany," *New York Times*, April 11, 1976. Kemezis chose not only the untypical VW experience to paint a glowing picture of union-management relations but then picked on the much-delayed decision of the VW board to build an American assembly plant as a prime example of union-management cooperation. It had been, however, precisely the conflict between the VW management and the union leadership (Loderer, I.G. Metall) on the VW supervisory board that had been responsible for the inability of the VW management to cope with the economic and technical difficulties that had developed between 1972 and 1975. The battles between top management and Loderer have caused scars that will never disappear.

10. For a detailed discussion of the changing nature of the supervisory board, see Erich Gutenberg, "Funktionswandlung des Aufsichtsrat," *Zeitschrift für Betriebswirtschaft* (December 1970):1-10. The most detailed comparison of the different European supervisory boards with the Anglo-American board is found in Pan. Stratoudakis, *Organisation der Unternehmungsführung* (Wiesbaden, F. Steiner Verlag 1961).

11. A. Chandler, *Strategy and Structure*, (New York: Doubleday, 1966), pp. 63-93.

12. Section 111 of German Corporation Law (AKT.G) of 1937, revised in 1965, is the current law.

"German company law prevents the 'supervisory' board of a German company from exercising control over the functioning of the management board, contrary to what one might expect from the terminology." Janice R. Bellace, *Codetermination in Germany, the Netherlands, and Luxembourg*, (Philadelphia: Industrial Research Unit, Wharton School, 1976), p. 3.

13. Gutenberg, "Funktionswandlung des Aufsichtsrat."

14. Prior to the 1951 law, limited-liability companies had not been required to have supervisory boards. In this context, the 1951 and 1952 laws modified the German company legislation (*Gesellschaftsrecht*).

15. Cf. *Mitbestimmung in Unternehmen* [Codetermination in the enterprise], ed., Mitbestimmungskommission, (codetermination committee) Bonn, Deutscher Bundestag (Parliament) January 1970; reprinted by W. Kohlhammer GMBH, Stuttgart, 1970 pp. 69ff. All references are to the Kohlhammer edition. The report of this prestigious commission, called the Biedenkopf committee after its chairman, merely reaffirmed the virtually unanimous testimony concerning the relative ineffectiveness of the neutral members. In the commission's reform recommendation (part V), no provisions are made for neutral supervisory board members.

16. In practice either I.G. Metall or I.G. Bergbau. Until 1976, only one union ordinarily represented the workers in a plant or mine, though more than one union may have been represented in the various plants of a corporation. The German industrial unions are very similar in organization to American CIO unions.

17. The 1951 codetermination law did not distinguish between salaried employees and managers (*Leitende Angestellte*); hence managers occasionally were selected by the employees in the Montan industry to represent their interests on the supervisory board. In all non-Montan enterprises, key managers repeatedly were sent into the supervisory board by the employees.

18. The Weimar codetermination law of March 1922 required that the two employee representatives on the supervisory board be chosen from the works-council members. Similarly only works-council members were chosen as employee representatives on the Montan industry boards in the 1946-1950 period. Opponents of the 1951 law have pointed out that the employee representation on the supervisory board had not improved in comparison with the Weimar legislation; merely there additional union representatives, another outside force, had been added.

19. The term *director* has different meaning in American and German usage. In German a *Direktor* is a member of the management executive committee and comparable to a senior vice-president; the title *Generaldirektor*, still used in Austria and Switzerland, referred to the chairman of the management executive committee, though today the term *Vorstandsvorsitzender* ("chairman of the Vorstand") is used.

20. *Equal codetermination (paritätische Mitbestimmung)* is the term used to describe the codetermination model in which union-employee representatives hold 50 percent of the supervisory seats.

21. Betriebsverfassungsgesetz, 11 October 1952, Sec. 76, 77, 84, *Bundesgesetzblatt* (Bonn 1952).

22. Betriebsverfassungsgesetz, Sec. 49. The enterprise legislation component of the 1952 law applies to firms with more than five hundred employees, while the works legislation component applies to firms with more than five employees.

23. All public institutions were included in the Personalvertretungsgesetz of 1955 (personnel representation law), which established a quasi-shop steward system for civil-service employees. The shop stewards guard the interests of the employees but cannot influence the decision process. In the government-owned railroads the employees elect one-fourth of the supervisory board and, through the Arbeitsdirektor, one-fourth of the management executive committee.

24. Clark Kerr has commented on the separate electoral bodies: "The working class had its tendencies toward stratification further encouraged and its right of center elements, the salaried workers, strengthened in their

influence; power was not additionally (i.e., in comparison with Weimar) shared in any meaningful way with the workers." "The Trade Union Movement and the Redistribution of Power in Postwar Germany," *Quarterly Journal of Economics* (November 1951):557. Kerr grossly underestimated both the provisions of the Betr.V.G., 1952, that greatly extended the authority and jurisdiction of the works council in comparison with the Weimar law and the ability of the councils to use every provision of the law. His inclusion of Germany's salaried employees in the working class is remarkable. Not even a Marxist, or perhaps especially not a Marxist, would be so rash as to refer to the German Angestellten as members of the working class, even if this term did not include vice-presidents, research scientists, engineers, and economists, among others. Kerr was correct, however, when he recognized that the separate electoral bodies weakened the power of the unions.

25. The unions had strongly opposed the formation of two separate electoral bodies and through collective bargaining had succeeded in avoiding separate constituencies in the Montan industry. Since the Betr.V.G., 1952, also applied to the coal-iron-steel industry, however, this is one instance where the 1952 legislation weakened previous union gains. In order to make this defect more palatable, the 1952 law also provided that workers and salaried employees could vote jointly if both groups decided in separate and secret elections to form a common electoral body. There was little likelihood in 1952 that such a vote would take place; there is even less today.

26. In subsequent legislation the laid-off workers were given the right to sue before the labor courts to obtain redundancy payments (Sec. 74, Betr.V.G., 1972).

27. Although the Betr.V.G., 1952, is also applicable to the Montan industry, the much stronger position of the unions in the Montan industry through the Montan codetermination law changed the spirit of the works council-management relations significantly. The 1951 law dominated the 1952 law.

28. Auschuss für Arbeit und Sozialordnung (Committee for Work and Social Organization).

Parliamentary Labor Committee Reports of 23 February 1976, and 10 March 1976 (7/4787, 7/4845, Deutscher Bundestag, 7. Wahlperiode).

I participated in the initial research of the Institut für Organisation in 1974-1975 and since have stayed in close touch with the ongoing work through numerous exchanges of visits.

29. *Mitbestimmung im Unternehmen* [Codetermination in the enterprise], Bericht der Sachverständigen Kommission, [Report of expert commission] January 1970, W. Kohlhammer, GMBH, Stuttgart, 1970 (referred to hereafter as Biedenkopf report).

30. Siemens may be a somewhat atypical example because the firm has a long history of a wise, paternalistic personnel policy and an excellent esprit de corps. Typically the management refers to the company as the house of Siemens, a term that loses its feudal connotation in English but implies that mere profits are not really the main purpose of the enterprise. Note F. Fürstenberg's excellent monograph about codetermination at Siemens during the late 1960s, *Die Anwendung des BVG im Hause Siemens* (Munich: Siemens A.G., 1970).

31. In American terms this would mean that, for instance, the General Electric plant in Schenectady, New York, would have a works council for each department (steam turbine, gas turbine, generators, and so forth). In addition, there would be a works council for the entire turbine business, including all locations in which turbines are manufactured or sold, and finally, a corporate works council. The Siemens organization is somewhat flatter then GE's, with larger spans of control, and hence fewer layers of works councils than would be the case for GE.

32. There have been a number of empirical but statistically unsophisticated surveys between 1950 and 1976 that show only moderate employee interest in works-council participation and total disinterest in supervisory board codetermination. Until the University of Munich group completes its large-scale research, the most quoted survey continues to be Otto Blume, Helmut Duvernell, and Erich Pothoff, *Zwischenbilanz der Mitbestimmung* (Tübingen: J.C.B. Mohr and P. Siebeck, 1962), esp. p. 321. A more recent study by H. Kothoff, *Sociale Wirksamkeit des Betriebsverfassungsgesetz* (University of Freiburg, 1976), has been available only in mimeographed form, and has received little attention.

33. The Communist works-council member, Otto Zimpelman, came very close to being elected to the supervisory board in 1978. He failed only at the last minute because the national union, I.G. Chemie, worked vigorously to oppose him. In late 1977 a Communist works-council member, Franz Braun, was elected to the supervisory board of Grundig A.G., Germany's biggest television manufacturer, with the support of the I.G. Metall. The I.G. Metall very recently has displayed an unprecedented cooperative attitude toward Communists. In the 1978 works-council elections at GM's Opel, "at least 10 members of the German Communist party were nominated" by the union. *Frankfurter Allgemeine Zeitung*, 5 May 1978, p. 12.

34. The ideological frontiers have hardened since 1976. As a consequence the I.G. Chemie is confronted internally with a coalition of competing unions that do not belong to the DGB. In the December 1977 election, the opposing unions (German Employees Union—DAG, and Christian Chemical and Energy Union) gained nearly 50 percent of the salaried employee votes and 25 percent of the worker votes. Since only 58

percent of the electorate voted, the I.G. Chemie represents not more than 35 percent of the personnel. See, Horst-Udo Niedenhoff "Die Betriebsrat-wahlen 1978", *Gewerkschafts Report*, December 1978, pp. 17-22.

35. Almost all German firms grant at least four weeks' vacation, many five, and the steel industry six. In addition workers may take sick leave, generally not abused in Germany, and personal time off. Fringe benefits generally amount to 80 percent of wage costs.

36. Peter Drucker, *The Practice of Management* (New York: Harper & Row, 1954), p. 51.

37. The similar attempt to split the vertically integrated I.G. Farben into horizontal enterprises forced each successor company to expand both forward and backward in the production process. As a result, each one of the four I.G. Farben successors is today relatively and absolutely larger than the original corporation, and two of them, BASF and Hoechst, have begun to penetrate the American market successfully.

38. Over the same period the number of coal miners decreased from 578,000 to fewer than 300,000; the number of steel workers increased from 220,000 to 322,000; including iron miners, the entire Montan employment decreased by almost 200,000. *Statistische Jahrbücher*, BRD, 1950, 1954, 1958, 1969.

39. The French Montan industry, by comparison, was less successful in shedding excess capacity. When Prime Minister Raymond Barre finally decided to force the rationalization of the French steel industry during 1978-1979, the consequent massive layoffs threatened the survival of his government. See *Economist*, 8 April 1978, pp. 88, 90; 23 September 1978, pp. 95-96; 10 February 1979, p. 98; 10 March 1979, pp. 78-79; and *Fortune*, 9 April 1979, pp. 66-74.

40. See Biedenkopf report, pp. 21-24.

41. I examined in *Business Ideologies in the Reform-Progressive Era, 1880-1914* (University: University of Alabama Press, 1976) the discrepancy between the perceived and actual role of American businessmen at the turn of the century. In the United States the non-Marxist Left, from Veblen to Berle and Means to Galbraith, has consistently attacked the false self-image that American managers have presented to the public. In Germany there seems to be a tacit agreement among the spokesmen for the union and employer associations, the SDP and the CDU, to persevere in applying nineteenth-century terminology to twentieth-century managerial capitalism in order that the Ricardian-Marxian terms of "capital and labor" still retain the validity they might have had 150 years ago.

42. In the long run, the Montan industry, and especially its privately owned sector, has continued to adjust to changing market conditions, although under great difficulties. The well-managed Klökner-Werke, for instance, has reduced its steel capacity since 1971 by 8 million tons,

simultaneously with heavy investment in labor-saving equipment. Since 1971 employment in the firms has been reduced by 8,000, at a saving of DM 300 million (about $150 million at May 1978 rates). On the other hand, wage increases over the same period amounted also to exactly DM 300 million, thus preventing decreases in the direct production costs. By the end of 1978, an additional 1,600 employees was laid off with the approval of the works council; the cost savings equaled the wage increases agreed upon in the spring 1978 negotiations. *FAZ*, 11 May 1978. Still, even after tightening of Common Market minimum pricing provisions, Klöckner has operated at around 60 percent of capacity since approximately 1972, therefore requiring further reduction in manpower capacity but also continuing its investment in automated equipment.

43. See Biedenkopf report, pp. 55-72; Heine, *op. cit.*, passim.

44. See Biedenkopf report, pp. 55-56.

45. At VW, the chief executive officer, Rudolf Leiding, proposed an American assembly plant in 1971; the final approval was obtained in 1977. See Thimm, "Decision Making at Volkswagen."

46. Biedenkopf report, p. 58; *Hearings*, Ausschuss für Arbeit und Sozialordnung. Deutscher Bundestag, 7th legislative period, subsequently referred to as "Hearings," 1972-1974.

47. Biedenkopf report, p. 58 (my translation).

48. Biedenkopf report, pp. 58, 59. Testimony of union leaders before parliamentary committee.

49. The classic source is A.A. Berle and Gardiner Means, *The Modern Corporation and Private Property* (New York: MacMillan, 1933).

50. Biedenkopf report, part IV, sec. 16, p. 60.

51. All quotations are free translations of union statements, which appeared in Biedenkopf report, p. 37. Similar statements were made by union officials before the parliamentary commission in 1972-1974.

52. Under the Betr. V.G., 1952, the employees receive one-third of the supervisory seats, but workers and salaried employees each must have at least one representative on the supervisory board.

53. This myth is perpetuated in the United States by articles with catchy but inaccurate titles, such as Robert Ball's "The Hard Hats in Europe's Boardrooms," *Fortune* (June 1976). Loderer, president of the I.G. Metall and the highly praised representative of the "toiling masses" in the *Fortune* article, is much more likely to wear a custom-tailored suit than a hard hat. During his stay in Switzerland, Lenin is supposed to have observed that "the calloused hand of the worker turns into the manicured hand of the union leader." In the contemporary German context, this process takes place only rarely, since a large share of union officials are recruited directly from the universities. For instance, on the advisory council to the Biedenkopf committee, all three union representatives had academic

degrees, two held doctorates, and none had shop-level experience. This entire development is discussed in Heinz Hartmann's "Works Councils and the Iron Law of Oligarchy," *British Journal of Industrial Relations* (March, 1979).

54. "The participation of employee representatives in the supervisory boards of the Montan enterprises caused delays in the decision processes, according to the overwhelming testimony [before the commission]." Biedenkopf report, p. 71 (my translation).

55. For example, see the testimony of E. Bergh, official of I.G. Chemie, before the parliamentary committee in 1974. Hearings of Bundestag Committee for Labor and Social Affairs, D.Bundestag, Drucksache, 31 July 1972, p. 50.

56. The Biedenkopf report states that this "quid pro quo" bargaining concerned "above all" issues pertaining to merger and closing decisions, such as appropriate redundancy payments. I strongly question the "above-all" phrase. Personal inverviews, as well as a close reading of the hearings, and the newspapers, supply abundant evidence that in many cases the bargaining demands concerned merely the privileges and power of the union-employee fraction on the supervisory board. For example, approval of management proposals was coupled to demands to enlarge the jurisdiction of the Arbeitsdirektor by assigning him sole veto power over all promotions, or to give an employee who was also a local union official the editorship of the company newsletter, or to allocate to another local official the authority to assign offices and telephone extensions. In each case each demand was designed to increase the authority of the union over the career expectations of middle-level management.

57. Paraphrased statement of H.G. Sohl, president of the German Federation of Industries (Bund Deutscher Industry), previously Vorstand and supervisory board chairman of August Thyssen Hütte. Testimony before parliamentary subcommittee, p. 58.

58. The German limited-liability companies are comparable to incorporated firms in the United States whose stock is held solely by the owner(s); these owner-managed firms and their employees have often shown little interest in codetermination on the supervisory board level.

59. Biedenkopf report, p. 76.

60. As a consequence of the high merger rate and the absorption of Montan enterprises into non-Montan conglomerates, an amended codetermination law was passed in 1956 (*Mitbestimmungs Ergänzugsgesetz*, 1956) that applied the Montan law to holding companies, provided the Montan enterprises contribute more than 50 percent of total sales. In holding companies, the supervisory board consists of fifteen members. Four members are employees who are indirectly chosen by their peers; three members are selected by the unions. This law again is a compromise. The unions

prevented a substantial decline in the number of enterprises subject to the 1951 Montan legislation but had to pay for it by accepting a smaller ration of union officials on the union-employee delegation.

61. Note especially Kerr, "Trade Union Movement."

62. Biedenkopf report, pp. 84-87. Even the Biedenkopf report, however, admitted that during the late 1960s, union representatives, especially Loderer, made a greater effort to select supporters for the Vorstand positions. Others testified that positions could be filled with qualified people only if completely unrelated concessions were made to the union-employee representatives. Biedenkopf avoids the entire question of rewarding friends by stating that both union-employee as well as stockholder representatives are interested in technically qualified managers. This, of course, is not the issue; what we shall explore later is whether technical excellence is merely a necessary or also a sufficient condition for promotion. Similarly, Biedenkopf finds that blacklisting of hard-nosed managers has not occurred. The question is, Can it occur in 1980 or 1982 under current legislation?

3

The German Steel Strike of 1978-1979: Implications and Consequences

On 28 November 1978 the I.G. Metall, Germany's most militant union, struck the steel companies in the Ruhr area. This first major work stoppage in the steel industry during the last fifty years illustrated the sharply deteriorating relations between unions and employers that had afflicted Germany for the previous three years.[1] Not by coincidence, the strike began on the same day that the German Constitution Court (*Verfassungsgericht*) began its examination of the constitutionality of the 1976 codetermination law.

There was a relationship between the steel strike and the employers' challenge to the 1976 codetermination reform legislation, primarily because the 1976 law has aggravated union-management relations rather than improved cooperation as some of its enthusiastic supporters on both sides of the Atlantic predicted.[2] Still, the actual issues that led to the deteriorating union-management conditions in general, and the steel management-I.G. Metall confrontation in particular, are much more complex. The German steel strike provides an excellent opportunity to observe the various destabilizing economic, institutional, and political forces that were exposed by this conflict and led to the reexamination of a number of key assumptions held by management, unions, and the public.

Events Surrounding the Steel Strike

Negotiations for the renewal of the collective-bargaining agreement between the I.G. Metall and the steel-owners association in the Ruhr (actually the regions Rheinland-Westfalen, Osnabrück, and Bremen) began three months before the contract expired.[3] Although the German economy, and especially the steel industry, had recovered substantially from the recession—steel had had four very bad years between 1974 and 1977—the growth rate in the economy had hovered around 3 percent, apparently insufficient to absorb fully the baby-boom generation, which was just reaching working age. A low inflation rate had failed to encourage business to increase investment sufficiently to reduce the 4 percent unemployment rate (equal to about

This is an abbreviated and updated version of an article under the same name that appeared in the *Columbia Journal of World Business*, Summer 1979; it is reprinted with the kind permission of the *Journal*'s editors.

6 percent by the American definition of unemployment. School dropouts or housewives entering the labor market are not counted as unemployed in Germany). High labor costs, the metamorphosis of labor into a fixed factor of production as a consequence of the social legislation of the last sixty years, and the ever-appreciating value of the German mark prompted industry to channel its investment into rationalizing existing plants. As the steel industry, especially, closed obsolete plants, it was also purchasing highly automated equipment, thus increasing its productivity by better than 5 percent a year (average German productivity growth has been 4 percent for the period 1976-1979).

From the very inception of the wage negotiations, the I.G. Metall demanded the gradual introduction of the thirty-five-hour week with a forty-hour week wage in the steel industry and a 5.5 percent wage increase. The steel industry, still operating below 80 percent capacity and just recovering from four bad years, offered a 2.5 percent wage increase and two additional days of vacation. The steel employers—the management boards—were under great pressure from the German employer associations who realized that a thirty-five-hour week in the steel industry would lead quickly to a uniform thirty-five-hour week throughout Germany.

In recent years several union and SDP functionaries had been looking toward the thirty-five-hour week as a solution to creeping unemployment in Germany.[4] Also F. Steinkühler, the I.G. Metall leader in Stuttgart, had briefly raised the thirty-five-hour issue during the Daimler-Benz strike the previous year.[5] The I.G. Metall chairman, Eugen Loderer, like most senior German Trade Union Federation (DGB) leaders and Social Democratic party ministers, however, had rejected the thirty-five-hour week only a year ago in a major speech at an I.G. Metall conference. The sudden turn in union strategy has never been explained publicly.

The negotiations between I.G. Metall and the steel and iron employers' association took place on two different levels. One team negotiated wages (*Tarifabkommen*) and the other the union demand for a work-week reduction, which, ultimately, was to lead to the thirty-five-hour week. There were no other issues.

By the middle of November, the actual differences had been narrowed, although each side still projected the opponent as unyielding. The I.G. Metall now demanded a 5 percent weekly wage increase while the employers offered 3 percent. On the work-week sector, the employers offered six weeks vacation (an average increase of four free days; nine more vacation days for new employees, and three more for old employees), while the union demanded a one-hour work week reduction with full forty-hour pay as a first step toward the thirty-five-hour week.[6] The actual difference in the yearly hours worked under the two proposals was quite small. The employers' offer would have reduced the work year by 1.5 percent, the union demand by less than 2.5 percent. (In practice sick time and other social reasons have reduced the actual work week below the theoretical. If vacation time is added, the German steel worker already works less than 80 percent of all possible annual work days, computed on the basis of a five-day work week.)

The stumbling block was the union's insistence that the steel industry explicitly agree to consider the one-hour work-week reduction as the first step toward the introduction of the thirty-five-hour week. While the actual time period for introducing the shorter week was clearly negotiable, there was no doubt that the DGB unions were ultimately demanding the shorter week in the entire economy. On 9 November in a speech before the recently established European Concerted Action (*Europäische konzentrierte Aktion*, an exact copy of the equivalent German institution in which EEC union, business, and government leaders meet to discuss economic issues), the DGB president, H.O. Vetter—who was then also president of the European Trade Union Association—even demanded a 10 percent work-week reduction in all EEC member states over the next four years.[7] Since the German employers' associations strongly oppose a reduced work week, with or without forty-hour pay, the quasi-ideological differences between steel management and union negotiations were greater than the actual discrepancy between union demands and the best management offer. Faced by an unyielding union demand, in early November the employers declared any further discussion of work-week reductions as futile, and the unions responded by breaking off wage negotiations.

Unlike other German unions, the I.G. Metall has been unwilling to include automatic mediation provisions in its collective-bargaining agreements.[8] The next step for the union, therefore, was to hold the mandatory strike election. According to German law, 75 percent of the organized employees (not of those voting) must approve a strike.

The three-day election was a rousing tribute to the discipline and solid organization of the I.G. Metall. By 22 November 87 percent of the eligible 155,000 union members had voted to authorize a strike; 8 percent voted no, and only 5 percent abstained. The union negotiating team recommended to the I.G. Metall to authorize a strike. After several days of campaign oratory and nostalgic attacks on the no-longer-existing steel barons, the union leadership set 28 November as the strike day, the same day that the employer associations' suit against the 1976 codetermination law was to open in Karlsruhe.[9]

The union leadership, however, did not authorize a strike of all steel enterprises in the Ruhr; instead it chose several key firms with a total employment of 37,000 union members to be struck. These firms included the profitable Thyssen and Krupp operations, as well as plants that primarily produced sheet metal for the automobile industry. The enterprises were chosen so as to generate pressure on the steel industry negotiators from the automobile firms and the more profitable sector of the steel industry.

The I.G. Metall made the selection of key enterprises for strike action an integral part of its strike strategy. These tactical strikes (*Schwerpunktstreiks*), designed to place the maximum economic and political pressure on the opponents, were countered by the employers through lockouts. The I.G. Metall launched an antilockout campaign in Germany with the hope of intimidating employers to abandon this traditional and effective weapon. The steel employers, however, responded promptly by closing plants that were either dependent on the struck works or unprofitable, adding 33,000 employees to the I.G. Metall strike payroll.

On December 6, the two opposing parties agreed to permit a political personality to mediate. Chancellor Helmut Schmidt excluded himself and his cabinet members; the declaration of the regional strike leader Kurt Herb "that a mediator must recognize the union demand for a start toward the thirty-five-hour week" did not make the mediation effort easier, especially since the heated political atmosphere made it more difficult to settle this conflict without serious loss of prestige of either party. Already the I.G. Metall's Stuttgart district leader Franz Steinkühler had threatened sympathy strikes, which are illegal under German strike law and would have made the I.G. Metall liable to heavy fines.

Steinkühler's threats and the attempt of the extreme left to exploit the steel strike prompted Loderer and Herb to change their public pronouncements. While still organizing strike meetings and demonstrations, they rejected any talk about sympathy strikes and stressed the fact that union and management would have to cooperate once more after the strike was settled.[10] Moreover, the population as a whole had not been sympathetic to the I.G. Metall's strike demands. Except for the SDP left wing, there had been little support for the thirty-five-hour week, although 50 percent of Germany's employees were worried about the rationalization process.[11] Most of the German newspapers, including the prestigious liberal *Süddeutsche Zeitung*, seemed to have been dismayed by the ideological formulation of the union's demand. An early settlement in which the union would have obtained a 2.5 percent reduction in the work year, without calling it a "first step toward the thirty-five-hour week," seemed a possible solution, but was blocked by the union leadership. The fact that the I.G. Metall had failed to demand a shorter work week in its recent negotiations with the metal working industry, but agreed to extend vacations by three days, reduced the sympathy for the strikers among employees. The newspapers, moreover, emphasized that the actual work week in steel had been forty-two hours rather than forty because works councils and employees like overtime, and plant management finds a forty-two-hour week most efficient. Since there exists an acute shortage of skilled workers, works councils, employees, and managers prefer making overtime payments to hiring new workers.

By mid-December the attempts of Nordrhein-Westfalen's social services minister Friedhelm Farthmann to mediate seemed promising. An ingenious proposal, combining a 4 percent wage increase with extended vacations, paid nonworking shifts (*Freischicht*), and a shortened work week gave the unions virtually everything they had asked for except the statement that the work-week reduction was merely the first step toward a thirty-five-hour week. The employers accepted the Farthmann proposal, but the I.G. Metall negotiating committee rejected it, although, according to newspaper reports, Loderer pleaded for acceptance of the Farthmann model.

The failure of the mediation effort increased the intensity of the verbal attacks on the employers. Loderer no longer attempted to hold back the district leaders, Herb and Steinkühler, but openly advocated brief sympathy meetings in nonstruck steel mills, thus violating the peacekeeping duty (*Friedenspflicht*), the very essence of the German collective-bargaining process.

The radical rhetoric of the strike leadership was nourished, and was in turn reinforced, by tendencies in the Social Democratic party to become once more a labor party. In 1958 the Social Democratic party had repudiated its Marxist, class-warfare past in the so-called Godesberger Programm and had pledged itself to become instead a broad people's party. During the last ten years, and especially since 1974, the years of the Schmidt administration, the SDP had been successful in appealing to broader segments of the population until its structure had become virtually indistinguishable from the American Democrats or Canadian Liberals. At the same time, however, the party apparatus has shifted to the left as former Jusos (Young Socialists) and academic neo-Marxists slowly gained control of the local party machinery. Only a very small fraction of the SDP voters are enrolled party members, and the district leadership can be captured easily by a handful of dedicated militants. In Munich, for instance, the neo-Marxists gained control of the party, repudiated the popular moderate SDP mayor, Robert Kronewetter, and lost the 1976 mayorality election to the Conservatives (CSU), but have continued to dominate the party machine.

In a similar vein, Mayor Hans-Ulrich Klose of Hamburg, a moderate elected on Schmidt's coattails in 1978 by the conservative natives of Schmidt's home town, moved suddenly to the extreme left of the SDP after his election, with the gleeful approval of the party functionaries and the stunned surprise of the voters.

The SDP leadership of Chancellor Schmidt, majority leader Wehner, and party chairman Brandt was able to hold the warring wings of the party together, but Wehner is in his seventies and Brandt is ailing; both are close to retirement. The steel strike created the appropriate climate to strengthen the radical wing, which wished to disavow the Godesberg program and turn the SDP once more into a labor-union party. In turn, the DGB leadership Vetter, Hauenschild, and the militant union leaders such as Loderer increasingly identified themselves ex officio with the SDP. Vetter was elected as an SDP member to the European Parliament in 1979, the first time ever that a DGB chairman has been an SDP candidate during his tenure in office.

About a third of the DGB members are CDU-CSU supporters. Their leadership has viewed with increasing concern the identification of the DGB-Metall leadership with the SDP. Dr. Norbert Blum, leader of the CDU-CSU trade union members, considers the increasing identification of the DGB leadership with the SDP as a threat to the supposedly apolitical nature of the DGB as a unity union (*Einheitsgewerkschaft*) and fears the possible return to the conditions of the 1930s in which each major party had its own union.[12]

Although much of the ideological struggle later on subsided with the strike settlement, the intense union-management conflict in the steel industry not only displayed fundamental strains in Germany society but contributed to the radicalization of German politics. In a speech at the University of Bonn on 14 December 1978, Federal President Walter Scheel appealed to the nation to abandon ideological dogmas and return to a rational discussion of issues. The next few years will show whether the steel strike was merely an isolated conflict or the beginning of a new era of class warfare.

Montan Codetermination and the Political Economy of German Steel

Germany's rebuilt and modernized steel industry grew vigorously throughout the 1950s and reached its peak in employment and total output in the early 1960s. Although Germany was the most efficient and best-managed steel producer in Europe, excessive world steel capacity and the slow growth of the Western economies put heavy pressure on German steel management to shed obsolete plants and invest heavily in labor-saving machinery to keep its costs competitive. With the exception of the 1975-1977 period, German steel has generally remained profitable throughout the postwar years, even during the periodic troughs of the world demand for steel. The ability of the German steel industry to remain profitable in spite of mark appreciation and sharply rising costs has been due to the market orientation of its management. Unlike the nationalized steel industries of Austria, Great Britain, and Sweden, the German steel management, with the tacit support of the works councils and the unions until recently, strove for profitability rather than for employment maintenance.

Relying primarily on attrition and on shedding guest workers, German steel reduced its work force by nearly one-third since its peak employment year in 1961 (table 3-1).

Although segments of the German steel industry are owned by provincial and federal governments, there has been no difference in enterprise policy between private and nationalized firms. This uniform strategy is derived from the market orientation of German managers but is also partially due to the legal position of top management, which is relatively well insulated against pressures from owners, be they private or public stockholders. This independence of the Vorstand has played a significant role in both the steel strike and the constitutionality test of the 1976 codetermination law and undoubtedly has been a key factor in management's ability to follow a long-run policy of increasing productivity and diversifying markets.

The position of the German steel industry has been made more difficult by the unwillingness of its European competitors to adjust their production to market conditions. Above all, the policy of the European nationalized steel industries to maintain employment at all costs has resulted in wild dumping by the heavily subsidized state-owned industries. As a consequence of this dumping and the competition of low-cost non-EEC producers, for the first time steel imports gained more than 40 percent of the German market during the summer of 1978.

The Montan Union, the core of the European Economic Community, has been struggling for decades with the inherent overcapacity of the EEC steel industry (Sweden, Austria, and Spain are not members of the Montan-Union).[13] Germany's insistence that production and pricing agreements be compatible with market forces have generally clashed with the preference of the French employers for strong cartel arrangements even before Great

Table 3-1
Work-Force and Labor Costs in the German Steel Industry, 1961-1980

Year	Work Force	Increase in Annual Labor Costs	Annual Decline in Work Force
1961	366,000		
1960-1970		8.3%	1.79%
1970	300,000		
1970-1978		10.3	3.05
1978	250,000		
1980	200,000[a]		

Source: Adapted from *Frankfurter Allgemeine Zeitung*, 29 November 1978, p. 11.
[a]Estimated at the current attrition rate of 1,000 workers a month.

Britain joined the EEC. During the summer of 1978, Etienne Davignon, the EEC's industrial commissioner (a quasi-European minister of industry), was able to obtain the adoption of a steel crisis program by all Montan Union members. The program set immediate production quotas and minimum prices but postponed until 1979 any decision about the restructuring of the European industry, which meant reducing overcapacity by closing plants.[14]

The three-point Davignon plan provided for the modernizing of the entire EEC steel industry, the restructuring of regional capacity and product mix, and social adaption (redundancy payments in excess of the already high minimum separation payments required by law throughout the EEC). In a speech before the I.G. Metall-sponsored conference on the impact of the steel crisis on employees, Davignon emphasized that the European steel strategy could be implemented successfully only if it did not conflict with the social demands of labor. If, he declared, the international competitiveness of the EEC steel industry were undermined through excessive social demands, a permanent protectionism in each country would follow. Davignon therefore refused to accede to the I.G. Metall's demand to support the thirty-five-hour week. He did, however, concede that the anticrisis plan of the EEC would be successful only if the employers accepted their social responsibilities.[15]

Davignon's speech reflected on the three conflicting forces that face European, and especially German, entrepreneurs. On one hand, the rationalization measures already undertaken had reduced the EEC steelworkers by 76,000 between 1976 and 1979, and implementation of the Davignon plan would bring a further reduction of 100,000 to 140,000 by 1980, thus virtually forcing the EEC unions to search for policies to slow the decline in steel employment.[16] On the other hand, the expansion in world steel capacity, especially in the so-called less-developed countries (LDCs) and Eastern Europe, does not permit a slowdown in the rationalization measures. Furthermore the inherent long-run instability of the contemporary welfare state and its inflationary implication have made it impossible to count on overall growth in the economy to absorb the excess steel employment. The drastic shrinkage of the Montan coal industry in the 1950s was made relatively painless by the strong expansion of the steel industry during the same period.

An examination of the shift in international steel production explains the pressures on German and EEC steel producers. During 1978 world steel production recovered from the three- to four-year recession, but among EEC producers only the German industry as a whole had a profitable year. Its estimated annual production was 42 million tons, compared with an output of 53.2 million tons during 1974, the last previous boom year. The subsidized nationalized or quasi-nationalized steel industries of Great Britain,

Italy, France, and even Belgium within the EEC, and Sweden and Austria outside, generally failed to break even in spite of an average production increase of roughly 8 percent over the previous year.

World steel production as a whole set a new output record of roughly 700 million tons of crude steel during 1978 and maintained this level in 1979. Although the appreciation of the yen has removed Japan as the major competitor of the European steel industry, its place has been taken by the Communist bloc, whose share of world production increased from 30 percent to 35 percent, and the LDC's, who supplied 6 percent (4 percent in 1974) of world demand and are expected to increase their output once more by 50 percent between 1979 and 1982.[17]

The appearance of a modern, highly capital-intensive steel industry in Korea, Taiwan, and to a lesser extent, Brazil is perhaps of less significance to an understanding of the German steel strike than the sudden emergence of the once thoroughly inefficient steel industry of India as a worldwide competitor. The chronically overstaffed and badly managed Indian steel industry produced the most expensive steel in the world during he 1950s. Although little has changed, Indian raw material and wages have remained low while the steel labor costs of the countries belong to the Organization for Economic Cooperation and Development have been increasing at 8 percent to 10 percent annually. Indian steel workers earn eighty dollars a month, enabling the now-profitable industry to produce the world's cheapest steel. As the EEC countries cut back capacity, India was planning to increase its capacity by 150 percent during the 1980s.[18]

German export-oriented industry can compete successfully with the LDC's and the Communists only if it reduces its average labor costs through automation and technological leadership. Its comparatively favorable economic position in Europe and even its political stability at home is threatened by the eruption of a welfare-state protectionism that attempts to preserve employment levels at subsidized state enterprises by hiding behind trade barriers (often of the nontariff kind) at home and dumping its products in the relatively free American and Central European markets. Great Britain, Sweden, Austria, and, to a lesser extent, the Benelux countries are reaping now the consequences of decades of redistributive policies that discouraged work, saving, and capital investments. As long as previously established work habits and the secular growth forces of the post-World War II period provided steady economic growth, the rapid expansion of social services could take place unhindered. Although the welfare state requires that industrial productivity increase to finance the ever-growing public sector, its insistence on maintenance of work places, even in the short run, turns all rationalization effort into a threat to unions and government. Over the long run, welfare-state policies reduce productivity and saving and increase absenteeism, inflation, and

narrow parochial concerns. As one industry after another becomes unprofitable and approaches bankruptcy, the government intervenes and
through subsidies and nationalization saves jobs but prevents a necessary
reallocation of resources. The sick industries, especially steel, cannot be exposed to market forces, and they require the kind of help that postpones the
problem, at least until after the next election.[19]

Given the competition of low-cost producers and subsidized steel companies, it is quite clear that the German steel industry chose automation and
capacity reduction through elimination of obsolete plants as its survival
strategy. It is equally clear that sooner or later the union leadership had to
become concerned over the steady decline in the work force. Compared to
any other European or American steel union, it is remarkable that the I.G.
Metall waited until 1978 to slow this process. Unlike the British or Austrian
steel unions, the national I.G. Metall leadership has not demanded that the
prevailing employment be maintained but has continued to accept a further,
though reduced, attrition. Loderer expressed his position succinctly:

> If today's work force (50,000 less than in 1970) in the steel industry were to
> be maintained, the weekly work period would have to be reduced 16 hours
> by 1985—the one extreme. If the work week remains unchanged, the work
> force would have to be reduced by one-half by the middle 1980s—the other
> extreme. If the work period were reduced by five hours per week, the
> employment attrition until the middle 1980s would not be stopped but
> neither [would it be] speeded up.[20]

If the interest of the I.G. Metall in slowing the employment attrition
rate is understandable, the choice of a reduced work week over increased
vacation as an employment-preserving instrument is difficult to explain.
First, when the opportunity arose, works councils and employees in the steel
industry have been eager to choose overtime work in the past rather than
prompt management to hire new workers; and the actual average work
week in the steel industry has been forty-two hours rather than the straight
forty-hour-week for this reason. There is little chance that a one-hour
reduction of the work week would result in additional employment, certainly not as much as increased vacations could provide. Moreover, in spite
of the cutback in employment, the steel industry suffers from an acute
shortage of skilled labor, as does most of the rest of the German economy.
The rationalization program has changed the unskilled-skilled labor ratio,
and the industry's traditional apprenticeship program has not been able to
supply the necessary skills.[21] Reduction in the hours worked would only emphasize the lack of skilled workers and hence increase overtime work.

In view of the drastic reduction in steel employment, however, the scarcity of skilled labor cannot be explained totally by the changed skill mix in
the industry. Moreover, there is a scarcity of skilled labor and artisans

throughout the German economy, while supposedly one million unemployed are looking for work. German employers and newspapers have been wondering increasingly, therefore, how seriously many unemployed are actually trying to find a job. Both the less-desirable industries, such as the hotel, restaurant, and retail trades, and also the construction and textile industries have difficulty finding unskilled laborers and even apprentices. It seems that even Germany is entering the welfare-state stage, in which work generally, but especially manual work, begins to become less attractive to segments of the population. The emphasis on higher academic careers has created the condition in Europe where Social Democratic labor governments make manual labor undesirable, apparently fit only for guest workers. Germany seems to be joining Austria, Sweden, and other EEC countries in having too many teachers and sociologists, too few artisans and skilled workers, and too many unemployed youths accompanied by a shortage of labor, other than "guest workers," to perform the menial jobs of a wealthy society. The German government reluctantly has begun to recognize that many citizens have been misusing the unemployment benefits. As of November 1978, it required that job seekers must be willing to accept lower-paying jobs or even move to another town if work is offered elsewhere.

The question of how serious German unemployment really was further complicated the negotiations between I.G. Metall and the employers. Since there is an unchallenged scarcity of skilled workers and since unemployment appears to German managers to be a social problem as much as an economic problem, even the objective facts appear different to the two parties. Moreover, since a reduced work week in the view of employers and most outsiders would not help steel employment in the short run, the employers believed that the I.G. Metall was motivated primarily by political and ideological considerations and therefore urged steel industry negotiators to take their stand on the principles of sound market economics, since a thirty-five-hour work week at forty-hour pay would sharply affect the competitiveness of German industry in world markets.

Politics of the Steel Strike

The steel workers began their strike on the same day that the Constitution Court convened for the first time to hear the employer associations' challenge to the 1976 codetermination law. The strike leadership chose this day to remind employers that increased union militancy was the response of organized labor to the employers' efforts to scuttle the 1976 law and to draw the court's attention to the fact that after twenty-seven years of equal codetermination in the Montan industry, the adversary relationship between management and unions was still so strong that a disagreement on working conditions could lead to a strike.[22] This point is important, since the major argument of the employers before the court was that multiple codetermination on the shop floor, on the supervisory boards, and even on the management boards had destroyed the mutual independence of employers and unions, as required by the German constitution (the so-called *Tarifautonomie*) and gave the unions an overwhelming advantage in the industry-wide collective-bargaining negotiations, the fourth codetermination forum.

There is little question that the steel strike was a powerful testimony to the continued independencce of the Vorstand. After more than a quarter-century of Montan codetermination, which provided more codetermination rights to the union than did the 1976 legislation, the steel management board was not only willing to face a strike rather than accede to union demands but even retaliated by locking out 33,000 steel workers. The court challenge to the 1976 codetermination law specifically noted that the supervisory board's authority to appoint and reappoint periodically the top management would create a tendency among the Vorstand not to antagonize the union-employee half of the board. It is not surprising, therefore, that the attorneys for the defense (federal government and Parliament) pointed to the aggressive conduct of the steel employers (*Vorstände*) in the strike as proof that supervisory boards in the steel industry had never attempted to influence collective-bargaining negotiations.[23]

Those who believe that codetermination in Germany no longer furthers cooperation but rather introduces party politics and even class warfare into the enterprise retorted that in the steel strike case, the demands of the unions were so extreme in their long-run implications that no Vorstand charged with the legal responsibility for the profitability and competitive survivability (*Wettbewerbsfähigkeit*) could have failed to resist. Only time would tell, moreover, how many management board members would be reappointed when their contracts expired.[24]

In spite of the questions raised concerning the long-run implications of the steel strike for the careers of the steel executives, the occurrence of this bitter strike weakened the position of the plaintiffs before the court. On the other hand, a major argument in favor of equal codetermination was also weakened since the harmonious relations in the Montan industry had been cited continuously by the DGB unions and the SDP advocates as an argument for imposing the 1976 law and for strengthening the union position even further.

The change from harmonious and widely celebrated union-management cooperation to hard-nosed adversary bargaining in the steel industry was accompanied by increased political intraunion rivalry. The I.G. Metall old-guard executive committee of Loderer, Meyr, and Judith was increasingly challenged by the younger district leaders such as Herb and Steinkühler. Indeed rivalry among the second-tier district leaders, in the opinion of German newspapers, may have been partially responsible for the steel strike, since Herb supposedly felt compelled to show that he could run as tough a strike as Steinkühler had the previous spring in Stuttgart.

The appreciable addition of university graduates to the I.G. Metall bureaucracy has added a third factor to the internal union tensions. Certainly management fears that the neo-Marxist academicians will add to the ideological content of I.G. Metall's policy and will reduce the pragmatic stance of the leadership.

Whatever the conflict and motivation within the I.G. Metall leadership, the strike was fully supported by its members and was carried on with discipline and good humor. The strikers rejected all attempts by Jusos and Communists to turn a collective-bargaining impasse into a "revolutionary situation." Still one fact stands out: after twenty-eight years of equal codetermination in the Montan industry, about 80,000 steelworkers were either on strike or locked out. In spite of labor in the boardroom, unions and management could not agree on a common strategy to cope with the economic and political forces that threaten the survival of an economically viable steel industry in the West.

The Steel Strike Settlement

The failure of the initial Farthmann mediation condemned the strikers to a joyless Christmas. Although the well-disciplined strikers at the plant gates assured all reporters that they were willing "to keep the works closed until Easter," sympathetic bystanders—spouses, friendly journalists, local Social Democratic officials—increasingly questioned the wisdom of risking the economic future of the steel industry over an issue of principle: explicit management commitment to the gradual establishment of the thirty-five-hour week. The growing criticism of the I.G. Metall's strike leadership encouraged the provincial minister, Friedhelm Farthmann, to renew his mediation attempt. Since it had become increasingly clear that the I.G. Metall leadership had only reluctantly rejected the initial Farthmann proposal for internal political reasons, the new proposal submitted in early January was merely a reworded version of the previous Farthmann model.

Again the employer negotiation team accepted and again the central union bargaining committee (*Tarifkommission*) seemed ready to reject the mediation efforts, in spite of previous clear indications by the strike leader, Herb, that it supported the revised—or reworded—Farthmann proposal, which, at the request of the union leaders, had already been released to the press. To the consternation of the public, and presumably Loderer and

Herb, the bargaining committee rejected on January 4 the second Farthmann proposal by a vote of eighty-six to thirty-two.[25]

The press greeted the second rejection with dismay and disapproval; the evident inability of the I.G. Metall leadership to obtain approval of a compromise it had helped to arrange dimmed the hope for any settlement. Militant functionaries were quoted in the press as being ready to strike "even if it kills us." In spite of the fact that the German automobile industry began to purchase Swedish steel in order to maintain production, the strike leadership decided to call out another 20,000 workers in the Ruhr valley.

The mediator, Minister Farthmann, had become convinced, however, that the national I.G. Metall officers wanted the strike to end and were quite ready to accept his solution. The only question was how the leadership could save face since it had made the "first step toward the thirty-five-hour week" the principal goal of the strike. The general public condemnation of the bargaining committee's failure to accept the Farthmann proposals strengthened the hand of the national I.G. Metall officers. On January 6, Farthmann once more reworded the proposal with the approval of the steel industry's negotiators. This time the strike leadership officially accepted and obtained subsequently the approval of the negotiating committee by a vote of eighty-seven to thirty-eight.

Quite clearly German union negotiators are influenced by public opinion, since the third and final mediation proposal adopted was virtually identical with the previous one, which had been overwhelmingly rejected only two days earlier. The final agreement is only slightly different, and not at all more advantageous to labor than was the employers' offer that Farthmann submitted before Christmas. For that reason, and because the steel industry refused to accept the thirty-five-hour week explicitly as a desirable goal, the foreign and domestic press spoke of a union defeat.[26]

Such an impression, however, would be entirely due to the excessive rhetoric of the strike and national union leadership, which made obtaining the "first step toward the thirty-five-hour week" the test of success or failure. If this criterion is not used, the 1979 steel contract could be called a modest success for the union, which forced more concessions from the employers than they themselves had to make.

The union membership, however, had been sufficiently convinced by the strike leadership of the necessity of achieving the thirty-five-hour week to perceive the final agreement as a defeat. In the mandatory vote to approve the agreement, only 49.5 percent of the union members voted for contract approval; the rest voted for rejection or abstained. Since only a 25 percent "yes" vote is necessary to make the agreement effective, the lack of enthusiastic support did not impair the agreement.[27] For Germany's well-disciplined unions, however, a contract approval by less than 50 percent of the membership is a massive vote of no confidence in the leadership. Only the future will show whether this loss of support will push the Loderer-Meyr-Judith leadership into a more radical or a more conservative position.

The final collective-bargaining agreement provided for a 4 percent wage increase (management had originally offered 2.5 percent, the union had demanded 5.5 percent) and two extra days off for workers over fifty years of age during 1979 and 1980 and a third free day in 1981. Moreover, night-shift workers and swing-shift workers with weekend schedules were provided four paid "free shifts", that is, payment for shifts not worked, in 1979 and 1980 and six a year starting in 1981. All steel employees received two more paid holidays in 1979 and three in 1980; beginning in 1981, all steel industry workers will have six weeks of vacation. Except for the extra vacation days for employees over fifty, the last employer offer contained nearly the same vacation and free shift benefits, although packaged differently. Moreover, the union had to agree to a five-year contract on those aspects of the agreement that regulate work week, vacation, and time off (called *Manteltarif* by the Germans).

The wage agreement runs for fifteen months and is retroactive to November 1978. The president and spokesman of the steel employers' association, H. Weisweiler, called the compromise agreement "sympathetic but expensive"—sympathetic because the industry did not commit itself "to an introduction of the thirty-five-hour week," yet made the work process more humane for those steel workers who operate under the most adverse conditions, but expensive because the contract will increase industry wage costs by 7.075 percent, roughly 50 percent more than the industry had been willing to pay originally.

In spite of the bitterness of the forty-one-day strike, a settlement that increases total employment costs by merely 7 percent must seem like a dream contract by British or American standards. If Germany can maintain its current low inflation rate, the steel industry should be able to absorb the cost increases and remain highly competitive, in spite of the *Manchester Guardian*'s statement that the "German steel strike contradicts [the assumption] that ruinous strikes occur only in Great Britain." (The same issue of the *Guardian* reported a demand for a 35 percent wage increase by the British truck drivers, the closing of schools and plants in the south of England, and the beginnings of a railroad strike.)

The strike settlement, however, does leave several questions open. In the short run the question, as posed by the Social Democratic *Frankfurter Rundschau*, is whether the works councils will insist on more overtime work instead of using the decrease in the work year to increase employment.[28] Moreover, without the cooperation of the works councils, management will not be able to expand its apprenticeship programs to train the additional skilled workers who are needed if overtime work is to be avoided.

In the long run the crucial question is whether union-management cooperation in the steel industry can be reestablished. The answer will be known only when the contracts of the current Vorstand members expire. Will the union-employee representatives on the supervisory board punish an able executive, especially perhaps the Arbeitsdirektors, because they opposed the union demands, or approved the lockouts in the 1978 strike?

The answer to this question will determine whether the Montan codetermination and, indirectly, the 1976 codetermination law are compatible with free, unconstrained collective bargaining between union and management. Unfortunately for the German courts, however, the decisions on the contract renewal of current steel top managers will not be made for several years. For the short run, the vigorous conduct of the strike by the steel management, and its apparent victory over the unions, must have impressed the court. Certainly in the winter of 1978-1979, the independence of the steel-industry management from trade-union domination had been demonstrated, in spite of the unions' prominent role on the supervisory board.

The future is not only uncertain for the Ruhr steel management but also for the I.G. Metall leadership around Loderer, and the Ruhr district strike leader, Herb. In order to generate the necessary enthusiasm for the strike, the leadership felt compelled to fall into the class-warfare rhetoric of the 1930s and thereby earned the militant, though undesired, support of Marxist and Jusos groups.[29] It may be difficult for them to get rid of the spirits they called. After thirty years of codetermination, management-union relationships in Germany are on trial once more.

Notes

1. The previous stoppage in November 1928 was not a strike, as mistakenly asserted in the American press (for example, *Business Week*, 10 December 1978, p. 75) but a lockout by the steel industry, which had refused to accept a nonbinding arbitration decision (*Schlichtungsbefund*). The conflict was settled within a few days by the Social Democratic minister of the interior, Karl Severing, who prevailed upon the industry to accept the arbitrators' recommendation with minor reinterpretations. The history of the 1928 strike is important if the public pronouncements of the I.G. Metall national leaders Loderer, Meyr, and Judith and regional strike leader Herb are to be understood.

2. The German minister of labor, Walter Arendt, greeted the passage of the 1976 law by saying that he anticipated the beginning of a "new era of cooperation, without parallel in history." As it turned out, the unparalleled era of cooperation between management and unions that began in 1945 ended in 1976. An excellent report on post-1976 reality is Erika Martens'

"Kleinkrieg im Aufsichtsrat" [Guerilla warfare on the supervisory boards], *Die Zeit*, 24 November 1978, p. 17.

3. A crucial role in these negotiations has been played by the Arbeitsdirektor, the vice-president of industrial relations who, under the Montan legislation, must be a member of the management executive committee but cannot be appointed without the approval of the union leaders on the supervisory board.

4. There is a serious question, however, whether there is significant involuntary unemployment in Germany.

5. Steinkühler, who is vice-chairman of Daimler-Benz's supervisory board, startled the German public by first calling a strike prematurely, before contract negotiations had broken down, and then by exhorting the strikers with wildly radical speeches. Most observers found the radical posturing of Steinkühler extremely anachronistic; it is difficult to take nineteenth-century class-warfare slogans seriously when they are expressed by the well-paid vice-chairman of the board.

6. Virtually every employee in Germany has a minimum of four weeks' vacation. Siemens introduced a five-week vacation for most employees in 1976. The steel industry already has had twenty-seven annual vacation days (more than five weeks) for employees with at least ten years seniority.

7. This meeting was called by the European Commission in Brussels to consider the revival of investment as the necessary step to obtain steady economic growth, but it quickly turned into a discussion of unemployment. Especially the recent European phenomenon of balancing production increases through overtime rather than work-force expansion was noted glumly. The European Trade Union Association demanded lower taxes for lower-income groups, increased public and private investment spending, and expanded government services.

8. Most German collective-bargaining agreements include mediation (*Schlichtung*) provisions. Just when the steel negotiations broke up, a mediation commission prevented a strike in Hessen's synthetic fiber industry. As a result of mediation efforts, the I.G. Chemie and employers agreed on a five percent wage increase although their regular negotiation sessions already had been broken off. *Frankfurter Allgemeine Zeitung,* 20 November 1978 (hereafter cited as *FAZ*).

9. After the death of Alfred Krupp, the last steel baron, his ailing empire became the property of a nonprofit foundation; there is no Krupp on its supervisory board, whose vice-chairman, however, is Kurt Herb, I.G. Metall district leader, chief negotiator and leader of the current strike. There is no longer a Baron Mannesmann or Hoesch on the boards of Mannesmann or Hoesch, only Loderer as vice-chairman of Mannesmann. There is still a Graf Thyssen on the Thyssen supervisory board, primarily for sentimental reasons, since his family owns less than 10 percent of the shares

of the enterprise, which was once Germany's most patriarchal firm. Interestingly, Hans Meyr, I.G. Metall vice-president, and H.O. Vetter, DGB president, are also on Thyssen's supervisory board, which in the past has enjoyed particularly close union-management cooperation. The stockholders include 40,000 employees at Hoesch (out of a total of 230,000 stockholders) and 76,600 employees (out of a total of 230,000 stockholders) at Thyssen, which has been distributing shares among its work force since the turn of the century. *FAZ*, 6 December 1978, p. 13, quotes a Thyssen worker, who spent the strike period at Palma de Mallorca as observing that "basically it is silly that we are striking against ourselves."

10. In a December 3 radio address, Loderer implicitly deprecated the class-warfare rhetoric of the strike leaders by emphasizing that "after the strike peace must again prevail," in spite of the acrimonious nature of the current conflict. Loderer specifically denied any intention of extending the strike, thus contradicting the ultramilitant district leader, Franz Steinkühler, who announced before a Stuttgart shop steward meeting that sympathy strikes were being planned as an answer to the lockouts.

11. The prestigious Institüt für Demoskopie, Allensbach, Germany's counterpart to the Gallup Poll, questioned a random sample of two thousand employees during April and May 1978. Fifty-two percent agreed with the statement: "I oppose that more and more workers are replaced by machines," while only 31 percent approved of the statement, "Entrepreneurs have to rationalize, or our goods will be too expensive and can't be sold any longer, because foreign countries produce more cheaply"; 17 percent were undecided whether to agree with either statement.

12. See Günter Vetter, "Die Rolle der Gewerkschaften in der Demokratie" [the role of the unions in the democracy], *Die Zeit*, 24, November 1978, p. 3, and Jürgen Eick, "Auf den Weg zur Gewerkschaftspartei" [On the road to the union party], *FAZ*, 8 December 1978, p. 1.

13. The virtual irreversibility of the nationalized and/or subsidized industry's policies has been demonstrated by the inability of current non-Socialist governments in Sweden and Holland to impose market constraints on unprofitable operations. For example, after lengthy negotiations, the Christian Democratic government, shipyard management, and union agreed to maintain the Amsterdam shipyard operations, "though such a decision is economically irresponsible" according to Dutch economics minister Gysbert van Aardenne, a firm believer in a free market economy and a member of a government that had set itself the task of halting the "drift to socialism." *Amsterdam Handelsblatt*, 30 September 1978, and *FAZ*, 1 October 1978.

14. Most of the obsolete equipment is located in Great Britain, France—especially Lorraine—and Italy. German industry spokesmen state that only 85 percent of its 69 million ton capacity corresponds to the most

advanced state of the art. G. Klotzbach, *FAZ*, 11 November 1978, anticipated the replacement of one-half the obsolete plants by 1980 and the scrapping of the other half, thus reducing German capacity by 7.5 percent. Since by German standards more than half of the British or French equipment is obsolete, Germany's European competitors have the choice of a very heavy investment program, for which there are not sufficient funds, the scrapping of at least one-fourth to one-third of their plants, or an attempt to get by through a mixture of subsidies, proportional capacity restriction in the Montan industry, and talk about future economic growth. All indications are that at least the British will follow this procedure. The French government, which recently quasi-nationalized an inefficient privately owned industry, has decided to eliminate inefficient plants. After losing sixteen thousand jobs over the past two years, the French steel industry is now confronted with a restructuring program that would reduce employment by another twenty thousand during the next two years. See "Lorraine's Cross," *Economist*, 16 December 1978, p. 97. These cuts, though large, probably will not be sufficient to cut France's excess steel capacity.

15. Speech reprinted in *FAZ*, 8 November 1978.

16. Figures presented by Rudolf Judith, I.G. Metall vice-president, at the same conference.

17. *Economist*, 16 December 1978, p. 97.

18. Ibid.

19. A particularly good example of the quite sudden social transition from Calvinistic virtues to welfare-state sloth is provided by Holland. According to the *Economist*, a recent survey of foreign businessmen undertaken for the Dutch government discovered that Holland ranked last, even below Great Britain, among EEC countries in which to invest. High tax rates, enormous social costs, low labor productivity, and a threatening 24 percent tax on profits (to be distributed among employees and unions) currently under discussion by the Parliament, have made Holland an undesirable country for investment. Of special interest are the high sick benefits; a Philips executive stated that at any time about ten thousand of its eighty-five thousand employees call in sick. Only Sweden offers more dismal statistics.

20. E. Loderer, in a speech at an I.G. Metall strike meeting 17 November, quoted in the *FAZ*, 18 November 1978, p. 2.

21. The structural change in the work force is pervasive throughout Germany. The conglomerate Siemens, for instance, announced in 1977 that semiskilled and unskilled workers made up 32 percent of its nonprofessional employees in 1977, while it was still 39 percent in 1973. Similarly the proportion of skilled workers and technicians increased from 45 percent to 50 percent. Siemens, *Annual Report, 1977*, p. 17.

22. The 1978 strike is not only the first labor conflict in fifty years; it may well be the first organized large-scale steel strike since World War I.

The 1928 conflict was a lockout and not a strike; the previous general strikes occurred during the French-Belgium occupation of the Ruhr between 1923 and 1925 and were directed against foreigners; thus they cannot be referred to as labor conflicts.

23. Attorney Anke Fuchs, permanent under-secretary of labor, quoted in "Role Conflict for Employee Representatives (on Supervisory Boards)," *FAZ*, 1 December 1978, p. 4. An excellent report on the third-day testimony before the Constitution Court.

24. Although the Montan codetermination law was not challenged, the plaintiffs' attorneys specifically pointed to the vacillating attitudes of the Arbeitsdirektors as an impairment of the management boards' independence in wage negotiations. In the original joint session of the Ruhr steel executives, the Arbeitsdirektors voted unanimously against accepting the union's thirty-five-hour week demand. Next, meeting in a special session of the Ruhr industry Arbeitsdirektors—the only Vorstand members who belong to a separate organization—they then voted unanimously against the lockout, forcing the Ruhr executives to meet once more—sitting as the *Stahlverband* ("steel association")—to decide by majority vote to impose a lockout but then leaving the execution of each lockout to the Arbeitsdirektor. This situation, the plaintiffs' attorney maintained, cannot be taken as a proof of the Vorstand's independence from union pressures in the contract negotiations. See ibid.

25. Ibid., 5 January 1979, p. 1.

26. For example, "Steeling the Workers for Defeat," *Economist*, 13 January 1979, p. 64.

27. Note how heavily German strike legislation is weighted against strikes. A vote of 75 percent of the union members is necessary to authorize a strike, while merely an affirmative vote of 25 percent is necessary to approve a contract negotiated between a union bargaining committee and management.

28. *Frankfurter Rundschau*, 8 January 1979.

29. Striking was the use of military terminology by the union leadership which recalled the slogans of World War II and especially World War I. Loderer visited the "strike-posts on duty" (*im Einsatz*) and called for dedication ("*Einsatzbereitschaft*," a military term meaning, in effect, to be ready for combat duty), discipline, and "holding out until final victory" (*durchhalten zum Endsieg*), a verbatim quote of official World War I exhortations.

4 The Changing Nature of German Codetermination, 1972-1980

Despite the solid economic growth and exemplary labor relations of the 1950s and 1960s, the 1952 codetermination law (Betr.V.G., 1952) was a serious defeat for the unions, which they were not willing to accept. The political campaign to reform the 1952 law began as soon as Parliament had passed the bill and will end only if the Montan Mitbestimmung is extended to the entire country. Explicitly the unions demanded equal codetermination, the equal participation of capital and labor in the economic decisions of enterprise and society; implicitly they demanded a greater voice in the works-council selection and in management-works council relations.

The employers (actually the top managers) opposed the union demands and emphasized that the employees were not only satisfied with the 1952 legislation but had shown repeatedly their outright hostility toward the inclusion of outsiders (union functionaries) in the codetermination process. Moreover, the employers and the non-Socialist parties declared, in every survey, public testimony had demonstrated again and again complete employee disinterest in supervisory board representation. From 1951 to 1980, employers have consistently maintained that "equal codetermination is a demand of unions, not of workers."[1]

The unions disdained to defend or even acknowledge the discrepancy between the codetermination goals of union leaders and employees. The academic supporters of the DGB position viewed the lack of interest in equal codetermination as a consequence of poor communication since the "DGB has not yet succeeded in clarifying the issues to the masses."[2] The DGB leaders, however, emphasized the ever-changing social responsibilities of the trade unions, which had grown long ago beyond the original collective-bargaining function; it was no longer possible to reduce the DGB to a mere representative of the workers' economic interests, since it considered its curent social-political task to include the promotion of the entire society's welfare (*Allgemeinwohl*).[3]

The question whether individual employees wish to be represented by the national unions on the supervisory boards "fails to recognize the essence of representation," the DGB argument continued, "which requires neither personal relation with the individual nor [even] their authorization."[4] Since the economic policies of a large enterprise affect the entire society, the narrow interests of employee representatives must be balanced by the broad view of the union functionaries who can consider the interests of all employees since they can coordinate (*abstimmen*) their views with their organization (in this case, the DGB).

It was, however, precisely the fear that the DGB would evolve into a mammoth interlocking directorate by coordinating the confidential information and decisions of the union representatives on the boards of the big firms that caused serious misgivings throughout society. Such coordination would not only give the unions great monopolistic powers, it would also impair the allocative role of the market. Confronted with this unfavorable public reaction, the unions played down the possibility of using codetermination as an opportunity to coordinate the views of individual union directors, thus reversing their previous arguments. The unions, moreover, pointed out that a handful of key bankers have been sitting on the boards of the major corporations; hence the DGB delegates, the spokesmen for labor, would merely balance the banking representatives, the collective spokesmen for capital.

German business has been much more highly leveraged than North America's and has often depended on debt financing for even short-run investment projects. German banks (and other Continental banks in general) have a much greater influence on company strategies than do American ones, and the potential guidance that an interlocking banking directorate could exert has been a very controversial issue, at least since 1948.

Those sections of the German public that wished to protect the market economy from monopolistic forces were not reassured by the prospect of having two outside groups with questionable loyalties toward free competition represented on company boards. To quiet these fears, the union spokesmen declared, "Should under unexpected circumstances a sociopolitically threatening concentration of power arise, the basic standards of a free society would also have to be applied to the trade unions."[5]

This disclaimer, however, ignores the practical political difficulty of recovering from the trade unions powers previously ceded. The very fact that the Biedenkopf commission printed this union statement without any further comments indicates the weakness of parliamentary commissions. Biedenkopf himself, incidentally, had warned of the growing concentration of union power during the 1976 election.

This union view, however, is of great interest because it illustrates the DGB's attitude toward society and employees. It also requires a reexamination of the notion of industrial democracy that has been advanced by Anglo-American observers as the wave of the future generated by codetermination.

Regardless of the intellectual merits of the union's position, the first real opportunity for codetermination reform arose when the CDU government was replaced by the Social Democrat (SPD)-Liberal (FDP) coalition in October 1969. In his first address to the Parliament (*Bundestag*), the new chancellor, Willy Brandt, made the extension of codetermination one of the major goals of his government. Avoiding initially the more controversial issue of the supervisory board's role in codetermination, the new labor-liberal government was able to produce the Works Legislation Act of 1972 (*Betriebsverfassungsgesetz* of 1972, hereafter referred to as Betr.V.G., 1972) in relatively little time. Most Anglo-American observers have underestimated the significant, though subtle, qualitative changes that the new law prompted in the codetermination relationship among employees, unions, and management.

Significant Aspects of the Works Legislation Act of 1972

The Betr.V.G., 1972, has extended the role of the works council, strengthened the position of the union within the enterprise, and formalized definitions and procedures. The most noticeable impact has been the bureaucratization of works-council operations.

Senior Managers

The 1972 legislation introduces the term "senior manager" (*leitender Angestellte*), which refers to managers who operate one or two levels below the management board and enjoy special confidential relations with the Vorstand; most American vice-presidents would fall into this category. It also recognizes the existence of three employee classes: workers, salaried employees, and senior managers. The members of the management executive board continue to represent the owners and in the legislation are referred to as both employers and entrepreneurs, although attempts are made to distinguish between those two functions (sections 53 II, 106 I). Generally the senior managers are excluded from works-council jurisdiction; hence they can be promoted, transferred, or even discharged without works-council approval. The definition of senior manager is hazy, however, and has become an issue of controversy between works councils and management.[6]

Works Council and Union

The 1972 legislation continued the 1952 provisions that distinguished clearly between works council and union roles. The unions represent the employees in industry-wide collective-bargaining negotiations and hence act in an adversary role. The works council is concerned with the internal affairs of the enterprise and serves in a cooperative role. The 1972 legislation, however, requires that employer, works council, union, and employer association cooperate in a spirit of mutual trust (section, II). A union is considered to be represented in the enterprise if only one employee is a member.

Cooperation is demonstrated by union participation in works-council meetings, meetings between managers and works-council members, and so forth. In order to ensure this cooperation, the union officials have the right (*Zutritt Recht*) to attend these meetings. The role of the union within the enterprise is hence greatly expanded and becomes a quasi-corporate function, since the support of the employees is no longer necessary as long as at least one employee is a union member.

Moreover, and theoretically much more important, the Betr.V.G., 1972, significantly expands the rights of the union within the enterprise. Specifically this applies to the election of the works councils where the unions may submit a list of candidates without the necessary minimum requirement of supporting signatures, that other groups have to meet (either one hundred signatures or 10 percent of the employees, whichever is less), and the attendance of national union officials at factory meetings of employees.

Furthermore in order to enable the unions to prepare themselves adequately for the works-council elections, the 1972 law provides for such elections every three years, beginning in 1972 instead of every two years. The election procedures, size of works councils, and other details are supplied in the 1972 legislation, although the new law makes no significant changes from the 1952 legislation. Workers and salaried employees are still represented proportionally in the works councils, and the minority still receives special treatment, such as a minimum representation. In case of very large works councils, executive committees again must contain at least one worker and at least one salaried employee, regardless of the proportions involved.

The election procedures, as well as the election of the election supervision committee (*Wahlvorstand*), are incredibly complex and are designed to avoid controversy or manipulation. With the cooperation of the employer, the election supervision committee determines who is a worker, salaried employee, or senior manager. Senior managers have no vote in the selection of the works council. Salaried employees and workers continue, as in the 1952 legislation, to vote secretly in separate electoral bodies; the distribution of works-council seats among competing election groups (*Wahllisten*) is proportional to the vote according to the d'Hondtschen system which, again, gives a slight preference to minority representation (see figure 4-1). (The d'Hondtsche proportional voting system allocates additional representation to fractions that otherwise might not count. For instance, if ten votes elect one representative and party A obtains thirty votes and party B fifteen, A would obtain three seats and B would obtain two).

The 1972 legislation is extremely involuted and legalistic in defining operating procedures, especially in determining who can or cannot attend regular works council meetings. In essence, the German Trade Union Federation (DGB) or the German Salaried Employee Union (DAG), or both, may send national union functionaries to works-council meetings at the request of at least 25 percent of works-council members. Works-council

An enterprise has three hundred salaried employees and six hundred workers. Accordingly, a fourteen-member works council will be elected, composed of eleven workers and three salaried employees. Let us assume that three groups compete for works-council seats by presenting three candidate lists to the voters (ordinarily a candidate will appear only on one list). In the election, list A receives four hundred votes; B three hundred; and C one hundred fifty; fifty employees fail to vote. According to the d'Hondtschen proportional-election procedure, group A obtains five worker and two salaried-employee representatives; B, four worker and one salaried-employee representatives; C, two worker representatives. The newly elected works council will elect two of its members chairman and vice-chairman by simple majority vote; one of these two must be a worker, the other a salaried employee.

Figure 4-1. Example of Works-Council Voting Procedure

members rarely ask for outside help hence this provision is of little practical value, although the entire tone of the 1972 legislation may have been the first step in the increasing bureaucratization of the works-council mechanism.[7]

The Betr.V.G., 1972, requires that the employer supply the works council with the necessary clerical staff and library at the employer's expense. Similarly the full-time works-council member now becomes a professional personnel administrator who devotes his entire time, at company expense, to council business. An enterprise with, say, four thousand employees will have a twenty-three member works council, which might consist of eight salaried employee representatives and fifteen worker representatives. In accordance with section 38, Betr.V.G., 1972, at least five works-council members (three workers and two salaried employees) would have to be freed for full-time council activity, and more if works council and employer so agreed. The consequent Parkinsonian expansion is easily imaginable.[8]

Whatever the operational significance of the law, the 1972 legislation recognized for the first time officially that the DGB had lost its monopoly as the sole representative of German labor. The DAG had already begun to gain increasing support by 1972, and the Christian Union as well as other groups reappeared in the works-council elections in 1978.

Extension of Works-Council Jurisdiction

The 1972 legislation goes far beyond the much simpler Betr.V.G., 1952, (thirty-one versus thirteen pages) in redefining the works councils' right to information (*Informationsrecht*), consultation rights (*Beratungsrecht*), participation rights (*Zustimmungsrecht*), and codetermination rights (*erzwingbare Mitbestimmung*). The extended application of the enforceable codetermination rights in the 1972 legislation has resulted in considerable litigation to clarify the more obscure points. Operationally, however, nothing has changed. Enforceable codetermination still means that the agreement of both employer and works council is necessary to implement a decision. In the absence of an agreement, only binding arbitration can solve the impasse, although, of course, both parties can decide to drop the issue.

The information and consultation rights of the works councils were substantially extended in 1972, however, in order to involve the employee representatives in the early planning stages of all decisions that affect changes in capacity, technology, work place, personnel planning, and production processes (sections 27, 28, 90). Quite clearly this was an attempt to extend to all firms the smoothly working management-works-council cooperation of the most successful codetermination practices. It is difficult to legislate virtuous behavior, however, and so far there is little evidence that the mandated consultation has had a qualitative impact on employee participation other than to increase the number of meetings between management and works council. Most of the 1972 modifications of the 1952 legislation have had a negligible operational effect, but some provisions either extended the participatory role of the council significantly in practice or led to further bureaucratization and hence to a qualitative change in works-council codetermination.

Personnel Administration: The 1972 legislation defines the works councils' participation and codetermination rights in the personal affairs of the employees in much greater detail but does not affect the actual procedures for most enterprises. The bureaucratic framework of the 1972 legislation, however, manifests itself by devoting a half-page of fine print to the procedures that the works council may follow in objecting to the dismissal of an individual employee. The 1952 legislation, by comparison, merely states that the works council is to be consulted in each dismissal case.

The 1952 legislation, passed by a conservative parliamentary majority, assumed that both management and works council would cooperate to administer the personnel affairs of the enterprise in a rational, efficient manner; hence it was merely necessary to require that management and works council talk about each dismissal, without having to prescribe complicated, intensely bureaucratic procedures. The 1972 legislation still stresses cooperation between management and employees but, under union pressure, already thinks in ideological terms of the "participation of capital and labor in enterprise management," an entirely different matter. Moreover, a confrontation concept of works council-management relations begins to be acknowledged in the letter of the law, which makes it possible for the council to hold up any dismissal decisions.

So far the 1972 legislation generally has not altered the manner in which employees are hired, dismissed, and transferred. But if the works-council members were determined to exploit the letter of the law to the fullest, virtually no one could ever be dismissed in a German enterprise. The consequences for management authority and employee morale would be far-reaching.[9]

Economic Affairs: The 1952 law created the economics committee (*Wirtschaftsausschuss*) as an information forum in oder to further "mutual trust and cooperation." In the 1972 legislation the term "mutual trust and cooperation" was eliminated; in its stead is a detailed list of issues, twice as long, that require consultation between the economics committee and employer. The economics committee consists of three to seven members, including at least one works-council member, and is fully appointed by the works council. Operationally no changes have occurred thus far; however, the law again provides potential ammunition to a hostile works council to generate controversy and delay decisions.

The important sections on works-council rights in the case of mass layoffs and plant closings (section 72-73 in the 1952 law, sections 111-113 in the 1972 law) are operationally almost unchanged. They require maximum consultation and cooperation and provide for arbitration in the case of redundancy payments. The 1972 legislation, however, provides binding arbitration in case management and works council fail to agree on redundancy payments (referred to as the "social plan"). Because no instances are known in which management and works council failed to agree on a redundancy payment plan, the actual change in the 1972 legislation, the subject of hectic ideological debate, has had no operational consequences so far. It is important to emphasize that the works council still cannot prevent the actual layoffs but merely has to be consulted in advance.

Important Consequences of the 1972 Law

The government attempted to strengthen the role of the DGB and its constituent unions within the enterprise and may have been marginally successful in this attempt, at least for the period 1972-1976. Since 1976, however, the development of conservative rival unions and radical opposition groups within the DGB unions may have weakened the authority of the union federation.

The intention to broaden codetermination by extending the specific areas in which works-council participation is required had little operational impact in those enterprises in which works council-management cooperation had already advanced significantly beyond the letter of the 1952 legislation. In instances in which confrontation rather than cooperation had been the rule, the 1972 legislation led to the bureaucratization of codetermination. It is pecisely in these enterprises that management considers the 1972 legislation as an obstacle to its ability to act decisively.

The most significant consequences of the 1972 legislation, however, have been entirely unforeseen and unintended. By requiring employers to provide office space and clerical help to the works council and by enabling a larger proportion of works-council members to work full time on works-council business during regular hours, the employee-works council relationship has been drastically changed. As the works-council chairmen and full-time members become professional administrators, bureaucratization has replaced participation on the shop floor. The works council still represents the interests of the employees, who still routinely reelect most of their representatives, but for the individual worker the works council has become just another paternalistic hierarchy with which to deal.[10] Direct participation becomes the exception.[11]

The bureaucratization of the works council must have greatly increased the cost of codetermination except for those enterprises in which it performs routine personnel administration tasks.[12] The cost of works-council codetermination is virtually never discussed, however, and most codetermination participants are ill at ease when this subject is raised. There can be no doubt that the 1972 legislation increased the cost of works-council administration substantially, although council members merely receive the salary, plus increments, of the positions they held in the enterprise prior to election. Only the council members who are elected to the supervisory board receive the pay and perquisites of supervisory board members; these are quite substantial, however. The 1972 law dealt only with the works legislation and left the more controversial enterprise legislation unchanged.

In several instances—especially the steel and printing industries—strong national and local unions did succeed after 1972 in dominating the works councils in an unprecedented manner; the imposition of union guidelines on the already hierarchical work force-works council relationship further alienated employees from their representatives, however, and encouraged the formation of opposition groups that demanded the extension of industrial democracy to employee-union relations. The bitter intra-work-force struggle at Daimler-Benz (Mercedes) offers an excellent example for the ideological conflict between the advocates of direct democracy in union affairs and the authoritarian union leadership.

The Daimler-Benz Case

The Daimler-Benz Corporation, manufacturer of Mercedes-Benz cars, trucks, and buses, has been one of Germany's best-managed and most successful firms. In its relationship with its employees, the management has been eager to preserve as many of its management prerogatives as possible. Its relationship with its union, the I.G. Metall, has been correct but cool. No external union functionaries served on its supervisory board until 1 July 1978. Ninety percent of the workers (nonexempt employees) at its main plant in Stuttgart belong to the I.G. Metall. Encouraged by the 1972 works-council law, the national union took an unusually strong hand in selecting the union-supported candidate list (*Wahlliste*) for the September 1972 works-council election and disregarded the wishes of local union members. Two popular and respected shop stewards (*Vertauensmänner*, or union representatives) formed an opposition group—named the Hoss-Mühleisen Gruppe—which won 27 percent of the blue-collar vote and eight out of twenty-nine works-council seats.

The I.G. Metall reacted by expelling Willi Hoss and Herman Mühleisen from the union, though both had been active members and local officers for years. Within the Daimler-Benz plant, great pressure was brought on their supporters, in which, according to Hoss and Mühleisen, middle management cooperated with the I.G. Metall and the works-council majority. Both Hoss and Mühleisen had been members of the Communist party (DKB) until 1971, but both had left the party because of its lack of internal democracy. Although much of the group's early left-wing rhetoric may have annoyed middle management, the support for the Hoss-Mühleisen group among the conservative Swabians showed that the authoritarian attitude of national union and works-council leaders had created serious resentment among workers and employees.

The I.G. Metall, which on several occasions in 1978 and 1979 did not hesitate to include Stalinist Communist party members in its candidate lists in the Opel and Ford works, emphasized the New Left affiliations of several of the younger leaders in the Hoss-Mühleisen group. By 1978, however, the Hoss-Mühleisen group had abandoned much of its left-wing vocabulary, avoided affiliation with any political group, and emphasized its opposition to all forms of bureaucracies and its faith in direct shop-floor participation as the only acceptable form of industrial democracy.

The Hoss-Mühleisen works-council members refused to become professional council members and continued to work in the shop. They identified specific cases in which worker participation could be effectively extended and demanded extensive discussions with the work force before the works council attempted to negotiate with management the distribution of productivity premiums. Most surprisingly, seven of their sixteen candidates for the April 1978 works-council elections were foreign workers; though 30 percent of the Daimler-Benz hourly employees were foreigners, the I.G. Metall had only two guest workers on its list of thirty-five candidates.

In the April 1978 works-council election, the Hoss-Mühleisen group attained somewhat less than 30 percent of the blue-collar vote and elected once more eight of the twenty-nine works-council worker representatives, including its leaders Hoss and Mühleisen and a former student leader, Dieter Marcello.

The election results were soon overshadowed by the charge that I.G. Metall had manipulated the election by stuffing the ballot boxes. Subsequently the courts did determine that somebody had falsified and cast thirteen hundred invalid ballots. The courts declared the April election invalid and called for new elections on 29 September 1978.

The court case and the manipulation charges, virtually unheard of in Germany, brought the I.G. Metall considerable bad publicity, both at Daimler-Benz and nationally. The union admitted that its works-council members had lost touch with shop-floor workers and for the first time permitted the choosing of I.G. Metall candidates through direct election by the local union members.

Direct election (*Urwahl*) of the works council by the employees had been one of the demands of Hoss and Mühleisen and is always demanded by employee groups that object to external control by outsiders. In turn the DGB unions invariably oppose an Urwahl, whether it is the direct (preliminary) election of union candidates for the works council, the actual works-council elections, or the supervisory board members elections. The DGB unions have consistently preferred indirect elections by electors (*Wahlmänner*), as the political struggles over the codetermination legislation of 1950, 1951, 1972, and 1976 have shown. The I.G. Metall's concession to elect the union candidates for the September works-council election through a ballot of all its members therefore indicated its weakened position.

This direct preliminary election merely determined the candidate list for the subsequent September election, which then was to decide the composition of the works council by choosing among five competing lists: I.G. Metall, Hoss-Mühleisen, Christian Workers Union, German Employees Union (DAG), and Independents. According to the law the I.G. Metall could have asked for an election to compel workers and salaried employees to vote as a common electoral college, but it did not. If all the permutations possible had been played through between April and November, production would have suffered.

The September works-council election produced a sensational result that was a severe moral defeat for the I.G. Metall, which obtained 54 percent of the vote, barely a majority of the total vote cast (see table 4-1). Since only 68 percent of the eligible voters participated, the powerful I.G. Metall gained the explicit support of less than 35 percent of the Daimler-Benz workers and salaried employees, devastating results for Germany's strongest and most militant union, which has most consistently claimed to speak for all employees. With 70 percent (66 percent in April) of the eligible hourly workers voting, the I.G. Metall obtained fifteen (previously nineteen) seats with 52 percent of the vote, Hoss-Mühleisen obtained twelve (previously eight) seats with 30 percent of the vote, and the Christian Union obtained two (previously two) seats with 6 percent of the vote; the rest of the seats were distributed among splinter groups.

With 63 percent (52 percent in April) of the eligible salaried employees voting, the I.G. Metall obtained nine (previously ten) out of eighteen employee seats, DAG three (previously three), the Christian Democratic Employees two (previously two), and various independents four (previously three).

Table 4-1
Works-Council Composition at Daimler-Benz Stuttgart Plant, October 1978

Election List	Workers	Salaried Employees	Total
I.G. Metall	15	9	24
Hoss/Müuhleisen	12		12
Christian Union	2		4
Christian Democratic Association		2	
DAG		3	3
Independents		4	4
Total	29	18	47

Source: Compiled from *Frankfurter Allgemeine Zeitung*, 2 October 1978, p. 3.

The Daimler-Benz works council today is more fragmented than it was even during the most divisive days of the Weimar Republic, and the I.G. Metall has never had as much opposition; this case may be an exception, however. The local union leadership has been dominated by the I.G. Metall leadership to an unusual extent and, hence, by the rivalries among regional and national leaders. In particular the ambitious and supermilitant regional I.G. Metall leader, Franz Steinkühler, greatly influenced the behavior of the I.G. Metal local at Daimler-Benz, Stuttgart. Steinkühler, elected to the supervisory board in 1978, not only managed to combine the role of a Daimler-Benz director with that of a class-conscious radical union leader, he also managed to be an authoritarian union leader while publicly advocating industrial democracy for Daimler-Benz employees.

As a consequence of Steinkühler's ambitions, the I.G. Metall union has built a third in-plant bureaucracy with offices and full-time staff. It has not only dominated the works council but in many instances competed with the company personnel department and the works-council hierarchy in an effort to promote national union policies. At the same time the antibureaucratic sentiments in the work force were articulated particularly effectively by Hoss, Mühleisen, and Marcello, who also gained the confidence of the foreign workers. Moreover, the crude ballot-stuffing incident of the April election greatly damaged the I.G. Metall and probably distorted the election outcome. Altogether an unusual set of circumstances strengthened the anti-I.G. Metall-DGB sentiments among the Daimler-Benz workers. Greater sensitivity toward the work force's wish for local autonomy and a decisive voice in the nomination of its representatives should reduce the opposition to the national union leadership.

The 50 percent of the Daimler-Benz salaried employees' vote that the anti-I.G. Metall groups obtained was much more representative of the prevailing national trends, however, than the I.G. Metall's performance among the workers. During the 1978 enterprise elections, the national DGB unions only obtained 43 percent of the white-collar vote; as a consequence, today more than 40 percent of the total works-council membership belong to non-DGB organizations. This is a completely novel development that had not been anticipated during the preparation of the 1972 and 1976 legislation and its consequences cannot yet be fully assessed.[13]

The Fight Over Equal Codetermination, 1972-1976

The trade unions' persistent demand for equal codetermination as the necessary manifestation of the equality of capital and labor in the economy and society was an ideological concept that had five specific aims:

1. A greater role for the union within the enterprise and, particularly, greater union influence on the works council.
2. Allocation of 50 percent of the supervisory board seats to union-employee representatives, in accordance with the existing Montan law.
3. A dominant role for the DGB and the national unions in the selection of the enterprise's union-employee delegation to the supervisory board.
4. Establishment of a national, high-level union-employer committee to discuss and plan jointly total investment and other macroeconomic policies.
5. Appointment of a union-approved Arbeitsdirektor to the management board, along the lines of the existing provisions in the 1951 Montan legislation.

The 1972 legislation satisfied the trade unions' demands for a greater role in works-council deliberations. The establishment of the Concerted Action (*konzentrierte Aktion*) in the same year, a consultative management-government-union committee to discuss national issues, was meant to satisfy the unions' demand for a quasi-corporative forum within the existing political constraints. The unoins were far from enthusiastic about the Concerted Action, which lacked any real authority, but decided to participate to exploit all possibilities for national management-union consultation. The major union efforts, however, were directed toward obtaining—in trade-union rhetoric—"equal participation of Labor in economic decisions through the *sole true* representative of Labor," the DGB and its affiliated unions.

The question of equal participation led to a bitter and divisive controversy within Parliament and between employer and union spokesmen. The public remained rather quiet and uninterested; certainly there were no spontaneous meetings or resolutions among employees to demonstrate their support for the DGB leadership. If anything, the opposite occurred. Rival organizations, such as the German salaried employees' union (*Deutsche Angestellte Gewerkschaft*) and the Christian Union, began to gain strength, threatening the DGB's monopoly position for the first time since 1945.

The DGB demand for equal codetermination opened two distinct issues. First, should the employees obtain 50 percent of the supervisory board seats, and could such a reform be instituted without violating the constitutional guarantee of property rights? Second, should the employees continue to elect their board representatives, or should the unions have the right to select union officials as the appropriate board members?

The position on these two issues was quite varied, but generally the employer associations opposed both the allocation of half of the supervisory board seats to union or employees and the unions' dominant position among the employee representatives. The SDP generally supported the position of the DGB but wished to reduce somewhat the authoritarian role of the union in the selection of the employee delegation as contained in the DGB proposal. The CDU-CSU (conservatives) theoretically approved 50 percent employee representation on the supervisory board but opposed any special position for the unions. The selection mechanism of the 1952 Betr.V.G. was to be maintained for works-council and supervisory board members.

The FDP (liberals) opposed both equal codetermination and a special role for the unions. In this respect the FDP, the coalition partner of the Social Democrats, was to the right of the conservative opposition. The FDP did propose, however, to "make full use" of the Betr.V.G., 1972, in order to enable each individual employee to participate in internal decision processes.

The Protestant church (*Rat der Evangelischen Kirche*) was split on specific codetermination issues but generally favored extension, as well as some role for public interests. The Catholic church's position was close to that of the CDU-CSU: full cooperation of employer and employees through equal representation on the supervisory board, but exclusion of outsiders and no special role for the national unions.

Political Environment of the 1976
Codetermination Law

In July 1976 the West German Parliament passed the Mitbestimmungsgesetz of 1976 by a huge majority with the support of the SDP-FDP and most of the CDU-CSU. The 1976 law was a compromise between the conflicting views of the SDP and the FDP, which also took into consideration many of the CDU-CSU recommendations. The employers strongly objected to the legislation, and the unions also expressed their disappointment, although the DGB obtained much that it had asked for.

The assumption that the unions' disappointment with the 1976 legislation was mostly a political ploy was strengthened during the fall of 1977. At that time the two major employers' associations challenged the legality of the 1976 law before the German Constitutional Court (roughly equal to the U.S. Supreme Court) on the grounds that the 1976 codetermination law deprived the stockholders of their property by allocating to the union and employees the decisive role in the decision-making process.[14]

The DGB leadership, which until then had referred to the 1976 law as entirely unsatisfactory, reacted furiously to the employers' legal step and withdrew from the Concerted Action, expressing the futility of further "cooperation between 'capital and labor.'" The relationship between employers and unions had deteriorated slowly but steadily since 1972, and certainly since 1976; the 1977 challenge of the codetermination law of 1976, however, worsened the relationship further, and prompted even leaders like Vetter, Loderer, and Hauenschild (I.G. Chemie) to use rhetoric reminiscent of the 1930s. At the DGB Congress in May 1978, for instance, an unexpected resolution to nationalize the basic industries, banks, and insurance companies—a perennial call during the 1930s—was even passed by a decisive majority. The next day, however, the DGB leadership had the nationalization resolution reconsidered and then defeated, but the incident demonstrates the much more strident tone that prevails today in German union-management relations, as well as within the DGB.

Since the regsignation of Social Democratic Chancellor Brandt in 1974, the German public mood had steadily become more conservative. Although the string of provincial and municipal CDU-SCU victories had ended by the winter of 1978-1979, and although the Social Democrats regained some of their lost strength in the spring 1980 elections, the CDU-CSU has maintained its improved position and in 1980 governs the majority of the German Länder, and hence the Bundestag (the politically weaker German counterpart of the U.S. Senate). After several minor setbacks in the provincial elections during early spring 1979, the CDU-CSU showed its real strength by gaining the absolute majority of the German vote in the June 1979 European Parliament election in which Chancellor Schmidt could not help his party.[15]

The basic CDU-CSU strength has been undermined in national elections by weak leadership, internal feuding, and Schmidt's popularity. The dissatisfaction with the SDP left wing has been demonstrated, however, by the municipal elections of 1977-1979. Socialist bastions, such as Frankfurt (1977), Munich (1978), and Düsseldorf (1979) have elected CDU-CSU mayors for the first time since 1945; the CDU-CSU has lost some of its gains in spring 1980 by elections. Social Democratic victories in Hamburg

(June 1978) and Bremen (October 1979) were the result of Schmidt's popularity, although the neo-Marxist elements came close to capturing the party machinery in both city states.[16] The increasing power that strongly ideological functionaries have gained in both major parties (SDP and CDU-CSU) has led to a superficial polarization of professional politics, which effectively disguises the pragmatism and moderation of the electorate. Only Helmut Schmidt, who is thoroughly disliked by the SDP left wing, had been able to carry the SDP-FDP coalitions to a narrow victory in the 1976 elections, when the CDU-CSU had again become the strongest party, and he is expected once more to win the fall 1980 election for his party.

Precisely during this conservative period, however, the moderate DGB leadership rediscovered the class-warfare rhetoric of the interwar period. Simultaneously the employers' association publicly blamed the unions for virtually every economic problem and was ready to counter sporadic strikes with industry-wide lockouts at a moment's notice. As a consequence of the growing militancy, the printers' and metal-workers' strikes in 1978 were waged with unusual toughness by both sides. Admittedly the rhetoric was greater than the actual damage to social cooperation, and both strikes were settled with wage settlements that were well within government guidelines. It is important to recognize, however, that both the 1976 law, as well as the 1977 court challenge to it, and the 1976-1978 implementation period have put a heavy strain on German union-management relations.[17]

Prior to a discussion of the 1976 Mitbestimmungsgesetz, however, two points must be emphasized. First, the 1976 legislation is a poorly drawn-up compromise between the SDP and the FDP, which is more conservative on this issue than is the CDU-CSU.[18] Second, the codetermination reform had intended to unify German legislation and eliminate the special treatment of the Montan industry. In order to get a law passed before the 1976 election and keep the union leadership relatively happy, compromises had to be made, with the result that as of 1 July 1978, Germany had not two but three enterprise legislations. In the Montan industry the Montan Mitbestimmungsgesetz of 1951 continued to be in force. In the rest of the economy, companies with more than 500 but fewer than 2,001 employees were still governed by the enterprise legislation of the Betr.V.G., 1952. This means that employees continued to elect their representatives to one-third of the supervisory seats. And finally only corporations and limited-liability companies with at least 2,001 employees were subject to the new codetermination law of 1976.[19] This included about 650 firms, with 4.5 million to 5 million employees, or one-fourth of the work force, which produces 50 percent of the industrial output. Figures 4-2, 4-3, and 4-4 give a graphic presentation of the supervisory board composition under each enterprise legislation. Table 4-2 lists all existing German codetermination laws.

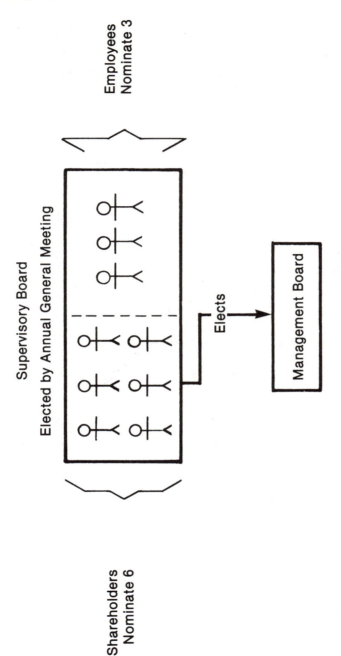

Figure 4-2. Companies with 2,000 or Fewer Employees (Works Legislation Act, 1952): Model for Nine-Member Supervisory Board

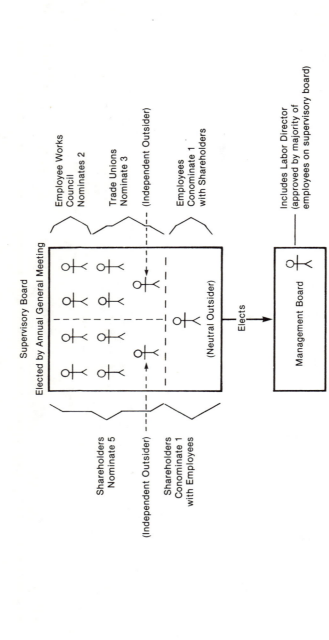

Figure 4-3. Coal Mining and Iron- and Steel-Producing Companies (Codetermination Act, 1951): Model for Eleven-Member Supervisory Board

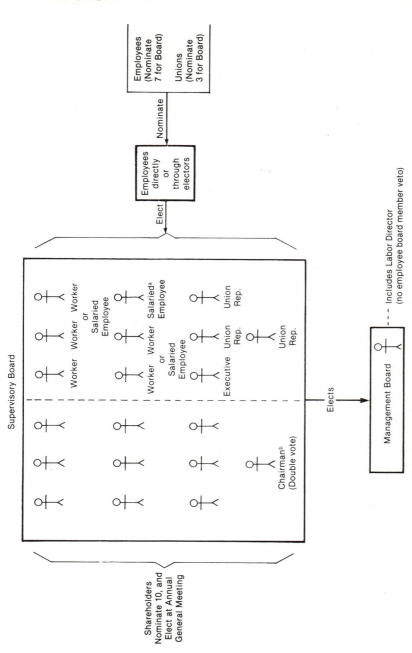

[a] At least one worker or one salaried-employee representative.

[b] Elected by board members, but normally the chairman is shareholders' choice. Chairman has extra vote to break a tie.

Figure 4-4. Companies with More Than 2,000 Employees (Codetermination Act, 1976): Model for Twenty-Member Supervisory Board

Table 4-2
Germany's Current Codetermination Laws

Year	Law	Applies to	Number of Employees Covered
1951	Montan Codetermination (*Montan Mitbestimmung*)	Montan industry firms with more than 1,000 employees	0.6 million
1952	Enterprise Legislation of Works Legislation Act (*Betriebs V.G., 1952 Drittel Parität*)	Small corporations and small limited-liability companies with more than 500 but fewer than 2,000 employees	0.6 million
1954	Civil servants personnel representation	Federal, state, and municipal employees	3.6 million
1972	Works-council component of Works Legislation Act (*Betr. V.G., 1972, Innerbetriebliche Mitbestimmung*)	All German firms with at least 5 employees	9.3 million
1976	Codetermination Law (*Mitbestimmungsgesetz*)	Corporations and limited-liability companies with more than 2,000 employees	4.5 million
	No works-council law	Small firms with fewer than 5 employees	3.4 million

Codetermination Law of 1976

Supervisory Board

All firms included in the codetermination law of 4 May 1976 that do not already have supervisory boards (such as privately held companies, in Anglo-American terminology) must form supervisory boards, which in turn will choose the Vorstand.

The supervisory boards, however, were not given specific tasks by the legislation. This lack prompted several enterprises to change their charter during the implementation period of 1976-1978 in order to strengthen the position of the Vorstand. Daimler-Benz, for instance, waived supervisory board approval of all investments below DM 3 million (previously DM 500,000).

Board Composition

The supervisory board of the enterprise is composed equally of stockholders and employee representatives. Each board will consist of twelve, sixteen, or twenty members according to the size of the firm. The employee representation on the board will be composed of employees of the enterprise and outside union functionaries in the following way:

1. A delegation of six employee directors will consist of four employees and two union functionaries.
2. A delegation of eight employee directors will consist of six employees and two union functionaries.
3. A delegation of ten employee directors will consist of seven employees and three union functionaries.

All employee delegations must include at least one senior manager (*Leitender Angestellte*).

The composition of the employee delegation was clearly a compromise. The unions did obtain the direct representation on the supervisory board that the 1952 legislation had not provided them, but while union functionaries comprised a majority of the employee delegations in the Montan Mitbestimmung law, the 1976 legislation allotted only one-third to one-fourth of the employee supervisory seats to the union. Moreover, the outside representatives were to be elected by the employees, and by 1978 the DGB had to compete with rival unions for the supervisory seats allocated to the unions, a development that was not expected when the compromise legislation was passed. No official tabulation of all supervisory elections has appeared, but various institutes, funded respectively by the DGB or employer associations, have presented differing versions.[20] Judging by the results reported in the newspapers, it seems that the trade unions affiliated with the DGB have won at least two-thirds but no more than three-quarters of the roughly seventeen hundred board seats available to union officials.

Election of Employee Directors

Employee directors are to be elected in accordance with the d'Hondtsche proportional voting system: directly by the employees if the firm has fewer than eight thousand employees but indirectly through electors if the firm has eight thousand or more employees. Both procedures can be reversed if the employees decide accordingly in a special election. Similarly workers and salaried employees vote as separate electoral bodies unless they decide otherwise in another special election. The senior manager candidates for the supervisory board seat are nominated by their peers and elected by all salaried employees. If all variations are used, four preliminary elections must take place before the main event.[21]

The nomination procedures for the two types of employee-union directors (internal and external) are complex and led to extremely involved and cantankerous elections in 1978. The nominations for the worker or salaried employee representatives must be signed by a fifth of the respective electorate (or by one hundred, whichever is less). Nominations for the senior manager seat(s) must be signed by either one-twentieth or by fifty of the eligible executives. Since in almost every case only one supervisory seat is to be filled by a senior manager, the proportional election procedure in this instance is replaced by a series of complex preliminary majority elections.

The nominations for the external board representatives (union directors) are made by the unions that are represented in the enterprise, or at least in a firm covered by the 1976 codetermination law. The insertion of this operationally unimportant clause, over the strong opposition of employers, at first seemed to be a great victory for the DGB, since it upheld its position that the trade unions' collective representation of labor's interests does not require majority approval or the consent of the individual employee. At the time this issue was discussed, the unions affiliated with the DGB held a near monopoly on employee representation, except for the small salaried employees' union (DAG). By 1978, however, the DAG and other rival unions had grown in strength and, using this provision, challenged the DGB unions in virtually every major election.

The actual elections of the union directors have been in accordance with the d'Hondtsche proportional voting system. In case only one nominating list has been submitted to the electorate, it must contain twice as many names as there are union seats available in the supervisory board. Although the unions did gain ex-officio representation on the supervisory boards, the individual employees have a much greater voice in the actual selection of the external union representatives than in the Montan industry.

This awkward selection procedure has been a compromise between the wishes of the union, which strongly preferred indirect, straight-majority elections, and the commitment of the FDP and CDU-CSU to direct, proportional elections, which would ensure minority representation and hence increased participation. The election procedure of the 1976 legislation did not give the union de facto veto rights over the selection of employee candidates, which the Montan Mitbestimmung has contained.

The internal employee-director delegation consists of blue- and white-collar workers in direct proportion to their numbers in the enterprise; at least one senior manager, elected by all salaried employees, must hold one of the salaried employee seats on the supervisory board. The FDP has supported this provision in order to soften management's opposition to the legislation, while the unions strongly opposed it. The guarantee of a supervisory board seat for senior managers was the price that the SDP had to pay in order to move a codetermination reform bill through Parliament before the 1976 fall election.

Election and Role of the Board Chairman

The supervisory board elects from its members a chairman and vice-chairman with a two-thirds majority. In case such a majority is not obtained, a second election takes place in which the stockholder representatives elect the chairman and the employee-union representatives elect the vice-chairman. Except for the appointment of the management executive committee, all supervisory board decisions require a simple majority. In case of a tie vote, the chairman of the board has two votes and can break the tie.

The supervisory board appoints the members of the management executive committee with a two-thirds majority. In case the majority is not obtained, a lengthy negotiation process is required before the supervisory board can select the Vorstand with a simple majority vote, in which the board chairman may cast a double vote to break a tie. This double vote, which reduces the employee-union representation to below 50 percent, has drawn most of the unions' fire and has been given most attention in the United States. But this provision may turn out to be less important than other less-publicized clauses.

Arbeitsdirektor

The management executive committee must include a vice-president for industrial relations. Unlike the Montan codetermination law, however, there is no requirement that the Arbeitsdirektor be approved by the unions.

The DGB has been particularly unhappy with the Vorstand's ability to appoint an Arbeitsdirektor without union approval. As a consequence union reinterpretation of the law has led to numerous court cases and controversies. Initially most controversies arose during the end of the 1976–1978 transition period when management boards occasionally assigned the Arbeitsdirektor's duties and title to one of their members. In each case, the DGB unions strongly objected and demanded that the Arbeitsdirektor appointment should be made by the new supervisory board, which was to be elected in accordance with the 1976 legislation.

In one instance, the labor court rejected the Arbeitsdirektor selected by the VFW-Fokker (aerospace) Vorstand and appointed the corporate works-council chairman, Gunther Hilbrink, in his place. Since the stockholder representatives had the support of the senior manager delegates, Hilbrink would have been removed from his court-appointed position even without the double vote of the chairman at the next meeting of the supervisory board. The I.G. Metall union was satisfied with a moral victory and advised Hilbrink not to accept the position. In turn the VFW-Fokker Vorstand decided to avoid further confrontation and finally appointed an Arbeitsdirektor who was acceptable to the union. The new Arbeitsdirektor, K.H. Jantzen, a well-known Social Democrat from Hamburg, had little previous managerial experience in the private sector.

In the case of the Ford works in Cologne, the I.G. Metall also strongly opposed the Vorstand's choice for Arbeitsdirektor. The Ford company, however, insisted on its rights and was willing to go through the lengthy election procedure until it finally could use the chairman's double vote to elect its candidate, H.J. Lehmann.

Although Lehmann's reputation as a particularly tough manager had given the union reasons to oppose his nomination, the I.G. Metall's opposition to the Arbeitsdirektor appointment at G.M.'s Adam Opel A.G. seemed to reflect the DGB policy to obtain through confrontation the veto right that the 1976 law had failed to grant it. In the Opel case, the union indicated that it would abstain from opposing the popular management candidate, W. Schlotfeldt, if it obtained concessions in other areas. This sort of negotiation was precisely the type of development that Adenauer had perceived in 1951 as a possible and unfortunate result of equal codetermination in the Montan industry.[22] In general, however, management did not hesitate to use the chairman's double vote or, more frequently, the support of the senior manager on the supervisory board, to gain a majority for its Arbeitsdirektor appointment.

Operational Significance of the 1976 Law

The codetermination law of 1976 has been a compromise. The unions did not receive parity on the supervisory board, nor a majority of the employee director seats, nor will they be able to dominate the selection of internal employee directors as they could under the Montan legislation. On the other hand, the new law does recognize the unions explicitly as a collective representative of all employees, even to the extent of requiring union functionaries as supervisory board members (directors) of nonunion enterprises. In addition, the employee-union representation on the boards has come close to the 50 percent limit, and even if the double vote of the chairman and the presence of a senior manager on the employee-director delegation give the management-shareholder representatives on the board an important edge, the employers have been fearful that, over the long run, the union influence on managerial decision making will not be significantly less under the new 1976 legislation than it has been in the Montan industry since 1951.

Under current social conditions in Germany, no major corporation would rely on the dual vote of its board chairman over the long run to carry out major policies against union-employee opposition. Moreover, most levels of management, especially in manufacturing and personnel, require the support and cooperation of the works councils in order to operate successfully. The ability to work smoothly and effectively with works councils and union officials has become a requirement for the successful career of a line manager. A reputation of being a demanding boss, with perhaps, well-known conservative opinions, may very well become a serious handicap to an ambitious junior manager; on the other hand, being known for one's progressive political views and one's ability to obtain union support may become a major asset.

The postwar years in Germany (and Western Europe in general) have shown that any political gains made by labor become almost irrevocable. Having obtained almost 50 percent of the supervisory board seats, many managers believe that labor will succeed in gaining full parity in another decade. The employers fear that all of the inducements and rewards for present and future German managers will be designed to encourage accommodations with union officials.

The only major obstacle that remains to the ever-increasing influence of the union leadership has been the sudden awareness that German union leaders and their allies among Social Democratic politicians are as easily corrupted by power as are others in similar positions. Since 1976 an unending series of major and minor scandals—concentrated in the Socialist citadels of the states of Hessen, Hamburg, and Bremen—have illustrated to the German public the dangers inherent in the web of influence (Verfilzung) connecting union leaders, union-owned enterprises, Socialist bureaucrats, and friendly businessmen. German public opinion has become less friendly toward the unions, and even the relationship between the current Schmidt administration and the key union leaders—Vetter (German Trade Union Federation), Loderer (Metal Workers), Adolph Schmidt (Mine Workers), and Hauenschild (I.G. Chemie)—has cooled. Moreover, German employers are considerably tougher than their peers in Great Britain or Scandinavia and lately have been unwilling to make any unwarranted concessions.

Still there is little, if any, change that the powers of the unions will be limited. Under the new 1976 codetermination legislation, German management, including the management of American subsidiaries, will operate with greater limitations on its freedom of action than ever before. Employee codetermination has been changed to union-employee codetermination, a quite different product.

The Briam-Frerk Case: A Tale of Two Personnel Directors

How different the new codetermination may turn out to be might be indicated by the case of Dr. Peter Frerk and K.H. Briam, the personnel vice-presidents and Vorstand members of VW and Krupp, respectively. Trained as a sociologist, with comparatively little management experience, Frerk had been chosen as a quasi-Arbeitsdirektor by the former VW president Kurt Lotz for his liberal political views, his closeness to the Social Democratic party, and the likelihood that he would be able to get along with the unions and above all, the VW supervisory board vice-chairman, Loderer, president of I.G. Metall. Frerk turned out to be an excellent manager who dispatched his duties without showing undue deference to Loderer, the works council, or I.G. Metall. His independence, however, seemed to have been his undoing, since his last contract was not renewed. He was replaced on 1 October 1978 by Karl-Heinz Briam, the Arbeitsdirektor of Krupp-Hüttenwerk A.G., a close friend and confidant of Loderer. Briam's managerial experience prior to his Krupp appointment consisted of editing the I.G. Metall journal, *Der Gerwerksschafter* [Union member], which many do not consider an appropriate background for an industrial-relations vice-president of a multimillion dollar steel enterprise.

From all indications, however, Briam's tenure at Krupp was quite successful, which might merely prove that executives and management schools alike overrate managerial experience and training. This, certainly, seems to have become the view of the Krupp-Hüttenwerk A.G. management, which will be replacing Briam with Otmar Günther, whose major qualification for the position seems to have been his most recent job—special assistant (*Referent*) to Eugen Loderer.

This case may be an extreme example. The Krupp-Hüttenwerk A.G. is in the Montan industry. Through historical accident, the I.G. Metall has an especially strong position at VW where Loderer has had and will have the support of the supervisory board.[23] Loderer, moreover, is an unusually aggressive union leader—by German standards, at least—who openly enjoys the acquisition and use of power. This case, however, does provide insight into the power exerted by key union functionaries and in the sincerity of their avowal to consider "only the best-qualified managers" for Vorstand nominations.

In the 1976–1978 implementation period, no significant changes in the supervisory boards' composition or in their relations with management occurred. The 1976 legislation had allowed for a two-year transition period, which most firms used to prepare the necessary elections of the new supervisory boards and to change, in many cases, their charters to increase the Vorstand's ability to act without supervisory board approval. The full impact of the 1976 legislation will not become clear for several years, although recent experience has given some indication to what extent the hopes and fears concerning the codetermination reform will be justified.

Codetermination and Union-Management Confrontation, 1976–1980

Since 1976 union-management relations in West Germany have lost some of their cooperative aura. The DGB leadership responded to the employers' association's decision to challenge the constitutionality of the 1976 codetermination law by threatening to reconsider the entire concept of social cooperation. Moreover, the I.G. Metall even threatened to resist a possible court decision against equal codetermination, and in at least one incident, a leading SDP politician, Rhein-Westfalen's minister of social services Farthmann, even threatened the court with the dire consequences of a general strike if it declared the 1976 law unconstitutional.

Although the court challenge was directed against the 1976 legislation, a decision that the provision for equal representation of employees on the supervisory board violates Germany's constitutional guarantee of property ownership could have applied also to the Montan codetermination.

In March 1979 the Constitutional Court upheld the constitutionality of the 1976 law, primarily because the compromise features introduced by the liberals (FDP) had preserved a stockholder majority on the supervisory board. The court decision seems to guarantee the status quo and to preclude further extension of union codetermination. It will take years, however, before union-management relations will return to the pre-1976 cooperation.

The growing confrontation between union and management spokesmen has been primarily rhetorical, although the 1978–1979 strikes in the printing, metal, and steel industries were, by German standards unusually long and divisive. The employers reacted with industry-wide lockouts to tactical walkouts in selected enterprises. In the end, however, the settlements were quite moderate and well within the government guidelines.

The pseudo-radical posturing of union leaders like Vetter or Loderer had several unexpected consequences. On one hand it prompted union officials, primarily in the I.G. Metall, to cooperate with the Communists; for instance, in May 1978 the I.G. Metal works-council election list at the Opelworks in Russelsheim included ten Communist party members, and at the Grundig A.G. (a television manufacturer) the Communist party (DKP) leader, Franz Braun, was elected to the supervisory board on an official I.G. Metal ticket. On the other hand, the reintroduction of class-warfare slogans enabled Left-Marxist factions to oppose the DGB unions in regular works-council elections, successfully in a few instances. Thus in West Berlin, representatives of Maoist-Trotskyite groups (*K-Gruppen*)in 1978 elected several works-council members in the Metall industry with the votes of the foreign workers. In Ludwigshafen the Communist (DKP) Otto Zimpleman overcame the opposition of the I.G. Chemie and won the preliminary election for the worker representative on the BASF supervisory board, but he was defeated in the final election.

The relationship between management and unions on the national level deteriorated as a consequence of the 1976 legislation, and intense political controversy emerged within the work force in several enterprises for the first time since 1933. Day-to-day relations between the works councils and management throughout the economy, however, seem to have been undisturbed by the worsening political and economic climate. Compared to the deepest recession period (1974–1975) when the works councils had to approve layoffs and redundancy plans, the actual working atmosphere on the lower levels may even have improved during the first half of 1979.

On the national level, however, management's and labor's conflicting, long-run expectations and aspirations have threatened the continued existence of social cooperation.

Management's Long-run View of Equal Codetermination

Management's expectations were clearly stated in its 1977 court challenge to the 1976 codetermination law's constitutionality. Management predicted that the unions would become the dominant force in the economy because they would exert their influence throughout the governing Social Democratic party on a national political level, through industry-wide collective bargaining on the economic level, through the codetermined board's selection of the Vorstand at the top-management level, and through the increasingly union-dominated works council on the middle-management level. The compromise safeguards added to the 1976 legislation would not count too much since the pressure to obtain consensus, typical for German enterprises, would prevent the supervisory board chairman from using his double vote in most cases.

The dominance of the unions in the economy, industry, and society, furthermore would undermine free collective bargaining since the unions would sit on both sides of the bargaining tables, which might result in higher wages than the enterprise could afford. Moreover, because of union power, strengthened by the presence of a handful of union officials on all key supervisory boards, young managers would decide that their careers demand accommodation with the unions and, ultimately, the Social Democrats. In the long run, the de facto superiority of the unions in the economy would threaten the constitutional guarantee of property rights.

Management also called to the court's attention that during the discussion over the 1976 codetermination legislation, the unions no longer fully denied that collective bargaining between two mutually independent opponents might be threatened, but often stated that if the equal representation of capital and labor undermines such bargaining, then the constitutional provision guaranteeing it should be changed.

The employers' attack on the 1976 codetermination legislation not only dealt with the long-run ideological aspirations of the DGB but also took issue with the immediate operational consequences of implementing the 1976 codetermination law. Only the codetermination specialists in the personnel department understood the complexities of the supervisory board election processes, but the entire organization clearly could anticipate the innumerable meetings and conferences among management, works councils, and union groups. Moreover, the conflicting ambitions of middle managers appearing in the candidate lists of various rival union and intra union groups could easily politicize the whole organization.

On the supervisory boards, the employers argued, the disciplined DGB union functionaries would either dominate the employee-union delegation, as they have done in the Montan industry, or feud with the non-DGB union representatives and the independent works-council members. In either case, a divisive factor would be introduced into the organization that would divert management and employees from their important tasks. Promotion and work allocation would be determined increasingly on a purely political basis. Inherent tendencies among many firms to accommodate themselves with the unions and to support them ultimately to reestablish shop discipline would be further encouraged and might culminate in the extinction of the entrepreneurial instinct within the firm.

Union's View of Equal Codetermination

The union leadership's testimony before the Constitution Court supported the constitutionality of the 1976 legislation by emphasizing the explicit restraints on union power that had been written into the law. These restraints, such as the double vote of the board chairman and the mandatory election of a senior manager to the supervisory board, had been vigorously opposed by the unions in the past. The intellectual difficulty of supporting a law by emphasizing the very aspects that had been attacked before forced the union spokesmen before the court to emphasize legal technicalities in their briefs that did not reflect, and perhaps even disguised, their long-run aspirations.

For the unions, equal codetermination on the supervisory board and in society meant primarily a guarantee for survival as a vital institution. High progressive taxation, inflation, a complete government welfare system with high pensions, extravagant vacations, and generous unemployment benefits have sharply reduced the importance of the unions; their role may be especially weakened when a Social Democratic government is in power and when a chancellor lays down wage guidelines that no union dares to break.

While the government's performance threatened to reduce the importance of the unions on a national and industry-wide level, the works council had threatened to supersede the unions within the enterprise; hence only equal codetermination similar to the Montan Mitbestimmung could ensure the survival of the unions as a powerful institution. The union leadership realized that equal participation could not be obtained without accepting equal responsibility; the unions would, therefore, be transformed into a different institution whose function would no longer be confined to wage bargaining.

Union ideologists such as Dr. Hans-Adam Pfromm, I.G. Metall's expert on codetermination, have emphasized the broad social responsibilities of the unions; they have developed from mere advocates of labor interests into the social conscience of the nation. The loss of Tarifautonomie, according to Pfromm, is no longer important in a society in which capital and labor participate equally in economic decision making, since the unions have outgrown their role as worker advocates. The DGB president, Heinz Oskar Vetter, went considerably further in a speech at the Hans Böckler Foundation in September 1978, when he viewed the 1976 codetermination law as merely a step toward the "control of power in the firm, the economy and the society."[24] Vetter's remarkable speech expressed a view that the DGB leaders did not present to the Constitution Court. Union and government spokesmen did emphasize before the court, however, that the constitution failed to specify an economic system. The transformation of capitalism into a cooperative system was therefore not excluded as a possible long-run consequence of extended codetermination practices. The unions' view of their future role in society is ultimately more compatible with a corporative state than with a free-market economy, the state of affairs that German management dreads.

The Court's Codetermination Decision

The employers' 1977 challenge of the 1976 codetermination law was taken up by the court during the winter of 1978–1979. The German Constitution Court, which consists of two circuits, has ordinarily followed a close literal interpretation of the constitution, which may have limited the reform enthusiasm of the Social Democrats, especially during the Brandt administration. In general, however, the court has been attuned to public opinion. Typical for German court procedures, the decision upholding the constitutionality of the 1976 codetermination law was handed down after a relatively brief four-week period of public testimony and judicial deliberation. The court attempted to meet each point made by the plaintiffs and defendants (government and Parliament) in explaining its decision in 113 clearly written pages.[25]

1. The constitution does not demand "extended codetermination," as asserted by the DGB's amicus curae brief, nor does the constitution require a particular economic system. The constitution does guarantee individual liberty, private property, and the freedom to pursue any vocation desired (*Berufsfreiheit*), including an entrepreneurial career. The entrepreneurial role is paramount and fully protected in small- and medium-sized enterprises, which are exempted from the 1976 law. In large-scale enterprises, the social aspects dominate, especially since the stockholders contribute their capital, without playing a managerial role. The constitution merely guarantees the narrow property aspect of a partnership between capital and labor. The legislators may develop any economic system, provided it satisfies the constitutional guarantees.

2. The 1976 codetermination legislation does not establish full parity, least of all "supra parity" (union dominance), in the enterprise as charged by the plaintiffs. The provisions of the law that enable the shareholders to elect the supervisory board chairman give the employer representatives an effective majority on the board. It is up to the employer to make use of the advantage that the law confers. (This point was made by the court at least five times in its decision.)

3. The court agreed that the mutual independence of employer and employee associations must be preserved but declared that the Parliament's optimistic prognoses about the continued existence of free, independent collective bargaining, as well as the continued operability of the enterprise, was reasonable (*vertretbar*). Should it turn out that the legislators' assumptions were wrong, its decisions will have to be corrected.

4. The codetermination law is based upon the loyal cooperation of employers and employees. If such cooperation exists, the ensuing codetermination will be quite different from one that develops in an atmosphere of mutual distrust and hostility. The view that codetermination legislation is based upon the full cooperation of employees and employers is reaffirmed in several places in the court's decision.

In summary, the court found that the codetermination law had been designed to improve the cooperation between the social partners, employers and employees. Should the desired cooperation not occur in all cases, the law gives the employers ample opportunity to prevail in cases of conflict. By implication, at least, the chairman's double vote, or the mandatory inclusion of a senior manager among the employee directors, strengthened the constitutionality of the 1970 law. This fact should make it difficult for the DGB to obtain full parity on the supervisory board over the next decade.

Consequences of the Court's Decision

The court decision was widely acclaimed by the DGB and government, but, after initial dismay, the employers did discover some consolation; the court made it clear that codetermination had gone far enough. In the explanation of its decision, the court constantly repeated that the 1976 legislation, purposely and consciously, gave the stockholder representatives a de facto majority on the board. Moreover, any use of this employer supremacy (Übergewicht) is entirely appropriate and within the intention of the law. The attempts to change the corporation charter to strengthen the role of the Vorstand further is completely legitimate, therefore, in spite of strong union opposition to this practice.

The clarification of the law's constitutionality and the simultaneous reaffirmation of the employer's ability to prevail in cases of a conflict with the employee-union directors reduced the existing tension between employers and unions. Although Vetter and other DGB leaders refused to abandon the goal of full parity on the supervisory board, they recognized that for the time being, the solutions of technological and structural problems had higher priorities.

The court's repeated emphasis on the essential cooperative nature of codetermination was immediately echoed by the government; Economics Minister Otto Graf Lambsdorff, especially, made strong efforts to revive the Concerted Action, the tripartite meeting of employer, government, and union leaders formed for the discussion of national goals and policies. The unions had withdrawn from these corporative meetings after the employers had challenged the codetermination law's constitutionality.

The unions had never been happy with the Concerted Action since this forum lacked any real power, and although Vetter and others expressed their willingness, in principle, to resume their participation, they also tried once more to change the nature of these meetings. In accordance with its fifty-year-old objectives, the DGB suggested immediately the creation of economic and social councils (*Wirtschafts und Sozialräte*) to develop investment and employment policies. The subsequent impasse was finally broken in September 1979 when key representatives of the employer associations, unions, and government met for the first time since January 1977 to reconsider the future format of a revived Concerted Action.

The court's emphasis on the cooperative nature of codetermination was balanced by its repeated observation that the legislators had not conferred full parity on the employee-union directors; hence management and stockholder directors are entitled (even obligated) to make full use of all of the advantages that the law provides. This aspect of the court decision strengthened further the determination of employers throughout the economy to use all existing management prerogatives and preserve, above all, top management's independence from union pressure.

The court decision seemed to have achieved the impossible; the clarification of the status and the meaning of the law has brought peace to German labor relations. The current mutual acceptance of the status quo is still quite different from the active employer-union cooperation of the 1950s and 1960s, and rising inflation (about 5 percent in 1979) and union militancy do not augur well for contract negotiations in the 1980s. The court decision and the inability to win a breakthrough on the thirty-five-hour week during the steel strike have channeled the union demands once more into bread-and-butter issues.[26]

Labor Relations in German Enterprises under the New Law

The court decision seemed to have enhanced employer-union relations on the macrolevel but has had little impact on the enterprises' supervisory board behavior. Eighteen months after the last supervisory board reorganized itself under the provisions of the 1976 codetermination law and eight months after the court decisions, relations between stockholders and employee-union directors have been sufficiently strained to cause concern among financial and economic journalists.[27]

Especially in the industries organized by I.G. Chemie and I.G. Metall, the working atmosphere within the supervisory boards has deteriorated perceptibly in key companies, with important consequences for the entire decision-making process.

Complexity of Legislation: The 1976 law not only created an awkward mechanism for supervisory board elections, it failed to redefine the responsibility of the directors, individually and collectively, and to circumscribe clearly the power relation among stockholder assemblies, Vorstand, and supervisory boards. Although German boards and managers are generally very reluctant to bring controversies before the courts, several issues have already been placed before the judiciary, thereby damaging severely the collegiality of the board as an institution.

Loss of Homogeneity and Polarization: In the opinion of the so-called stockholder representatives, the presence of external union officials has ended the basic consensus concerning the long-run objectives that had prevailed in the older boards, in which the employee directors almost invariable were drawn from the enterprise's work force.

The external union representatives on the board, however, have demonstrated that they are first of all the representatives of the union—or of labor—and only secondly the representatives of the enterprise's work force. The DGB, and especially the I.G. Metall leadership, have been making it very clear that they do not consider themselves bound by the director's oath of secrecy concerning the confidentiality of board meetings. Many union directors follow the policy that every board decision ought to strengthen further the position of the union in the firm, in the industry, and in the economy.[28] In enterprises in which particularly articulate union leaders are supervisory board members (such as BASF, Daimler-Benz, Du Pont Germany, Opel, and VW), every issue is considered not only on its merits but also on it implications for the union-stockholder equilibrium.

End of Free Board Discussions: The leaders of the DGB unions have attempted to force the employee delegates into presession caucuses, very much in accordance with the custom in the Montan industry. Although employee directors, as well as non-DGB union directors, have generally accepted the leadership of the DGB functionaries, controversies between employee and union board members (external versus internal employee directors) have occurred frequently in those caucuses, and increasing union militancy in election year 1980 may lead to further fragmentation in the employee-union(s) delegation to the supervisory board.[29] In the meantime, however, the presession caucuses have ended the free discussion of issues among board members since, in many cases, only the union functionaries present vigorously in the full board meetings the position previously determined in the caucus. With the exception of the senior manager, the employee delegates, especially the workers among them who are neither university nor Gymnasium graduates, remain quiet throughout the discussions, just as the Montan experience had already shown. Instead of an exchange of ideas, the supervisory board becomes a quasi-political forum in which attempts at persuasion are replaced by rhetoric. Unless the stockholder-management delegates are willing to use the double vote of the chairman frequently, they are almost forced to offer compromises that will be acceptable to the union delegates. In the view of management on many boards, substantive decisions have been replaced by political ones.

It is difficult to ascertain how long it will take before the changed conditions on the board will affect the quality of managerial decisions. Nevertheless several consequences of the 1976 law already have changed the chararacter of the DGB union.

The powerful role of the unions on the supervisory board—referred to as semisocialization by a German observer—has virtually turned the unions into employers on the national scene, a role that the steel and coal-mining unions have already played in the Montan industry. Union leaders such as Schmidt and Loderer appear as senior board members in key enterprises and have taken over, almost eagerly, managerial tasks.[30] They now carry responsibilities for both the success of specific enterprises and the industry.

The unions also have become the largest employment office for academicians who wish to become supervisory board members. Loderer alone has hundreds of open supervisory board positions. Young university graduates who have never worked on the shop floor have made sudden and lucrative careers as professional directors. The dominance of academicians in the central offices of the DGB and the large unions has been extended further. There is very little left of employee participation in the prevailing supervisory board codetermination, but the sudden prominence of upper-class academicians as union board directors will contribute further to the alienation of shop-floor and office employees from the national unions. This trend may well be a dialectical irony. The gain in union power on the supervisory boards and in the economy may strengthen even further the Left and Right anti-DGB groups among the employees. The Stuttgart Daimler-Benz election may have been the first sign.

Altogether there exists enough evidence to demonstrate that the 1976 codetermination law has begun to change management-union relations. Even if the relations between works council and management may not have changed perceptibly, codetermination as a whole has been quite different in 1978, 1979 and 1980 from what it was three, six, or ten years ago. Several of the actual and prospective changes in union-management relations were exposed in the events that surrounded the constitutional challenge to the 1976 codetermination law, the court decision, its interpretation by the various parties, and the immediate consequences. In the long run, however, the fate of codetermination will depend on the political atmosphere in which it operates.

The smoothly functioning day-to-day cooperation of works council and management, along with the pragmatic nature and common sense of the large majority of Germans, seem to promise that codetermination will remain a workable form of labor-management relations. On the other hand, the institutional momentum for survival will continue to generate union demands for more power. Moreover, the current generation of union leaders—Vetter, Loderer, Schmidt, Judith, and Hauenschild—will retire within five years, and the rising generation of labor leaders is generally more militant and has no memories of the failures of Weimar and the postwar era, which, in effect, have been responsible for promoting social cooperation in lieu of class warfare.

The last imponderable in the future of codetermination is presented by the Communist party's recent success in infiltrating the youth sections of the trade unions. The SDP establishment's nonchalant toleration of the cooperation of Jusos with Communist and Marxist groups in the universities has invited many complacent union leaders to ignore the emerging popular-front sentiments among various trade-union functionaries. When Horst Niggemeier, a spokesman for the mine workers, publicly warned against Communist infiltration of trade-union schools and youth groups, he was viciously attacked in April 1979 by a leading functionary of the wood and plastic (*Holz and Kunststoff*) union who rejected all charges of Communist influence as "grotesque nonsense," which merely attempted "to divert [worker attention] from the economic crisis."

By September 1979, however, the Communist party's success in establishing a strong foothold in the DGB's youth section could no longer be denied, and the leadership decided to fire the head of its youth organization, Heinz Hawrelink.[31] Hawrelink may take the blame for a situation that has much deeper roots. United fronts of Stalinist Communists, Maoist-Trotskyites, and Jusos have existed in most German universities since the late 1960s. These coalitions have dominated the student organizations, a corporate part of the university structure, in West Berlin, Bremen, Frankfurt, Hamburg, Heidelberg, and other universities. In spite of the fact that the united front of Marxist students frequently interfered with the academic freedom of non-Marxist professors and students, the German public, and especially the SDP and the SDP government—and even German society as a whole—has tried to ignore the entire situation, even though the Jusos violated the SDP ruling that prohibits cooperation with the totalitarian Left.[32]

Encouraged by the acceptance of united-front tactics in the unviersities, neo-Marxist or merely opportunistic middle-level trade-union functionaries have cooperated with local Communist party groups and indulged in class-war rhetoric that is incompatible with the social cooperation of Germany's codetermination laws. When fighting units (*Kampfeinheiten*) of young Communist trade-union youth groups and Jusos in September 1979 attacked Conservative party election meetings in the Ruhr and pelted the CDU-CSU leader, Franz Josef Strauss, with tomatoes and eggs, the whole country became alarmed, and SDP and trade-union leaders strongly reminded lower-level functionaries that cooperation with the totalitarian Left violated the spirit of democratic trade unionism.[33]

The future of German democracy and codetermination will depend on the attitude of the emerging new leadership in the DGB. If inflation, reduced growth, and possible political polarization lead them to forsake social cooperation and seek refuge in class confrontation, the SDP may go the way of the British Labour party. There exists a small but influential gray zone in the German Left, which extends from the Jusos to the Communist party to the K-groups (Maoists and Trotskyites) to the terrorists. Only the strong antitotalitarian democratic convictions of the current pragmatic DGB leadership has kept this "gray zone" from gaining significant political influence. Although the term *gray zone of the SDP* was coined by Franz-Josef Strauss, this concept is fully shared by moderate SDP leaders. The former trade-union leader and defense minister, Georg Leber, a vigorous advocate of codetermination, has just published a book in which he warns that democracy in Germany can survive only if "it is daily reconquered."[34]

Leber is optimistic about the future of German and Western democracy because codetermination and social legislation (*Arbeitsrecht*) have changed the nature of work in the Federal Republic and established social cooperation in the enterprises. It is worthwhile, however, to consider the worst-case scenario. In Great Britain the various Marxist groups gained control—or at least influence—in the trade unions in the 1960s and are now about to capture the Labour party. Until the character of the new trade-union leadership is better known, it is possible that Germany will experience a similar development when Vetter, Loderer, Schmidt, Hauenschild, and other labor leaders of this generation have retired. A militant, neo-Marxist trade-union leadership would change the nature of codetermination from social cooperation to permanent class warfare. The next few years will show whether the political climate in Germany will remain sufficiently pragmatic and nonideological to permit the survival of social cooperation in the enterprise and political cooperation in Parliament.

Notes

1. The earliest source for this statement seems to have been the *Der Arbeitgeber*, 15 March 1951, pp. 18–19.

2. Paul Fischer *Labor Codetermination in Germany, Social Research* (December 1951) p. 474 (My Italics). Although this quotation is typical for the union's official position over the next twenty-five years concerning the noticeable lack of membership support on this issue, no German DGB official would have been rash enough to use a hackneyed term like *masses*.

3. Kurt Biedenkopf et al., *Mitbestimmung Im Unternehmen*. Paliamentary Report, Bonn 1970, (hereafter cited as Biedenkopf report). Swedish unions responded in almost identical phrases when challenged on their social-political goals.

4. Biedenkopf report, p. 38 (my italics and translation).

5. Ibid., p. 45 (my translation).

6. "The subjective definition of a senior manager as an employee who enjoyed the special personal trust of the employer was discontinued with the Betr. V.G., 1972." Eberhard Witte and Rolf Bronner, *Die Leitenden Angestellten* (Munich: C.H. Beck, 1977), p. 113 (my translation). The authors list numerous objective measurable criteria that could be used to define senior managers but decide that no set of standards is completely accurate. As a consequence, negotiations between employer and works council result in a mutually acceptable list of senior managers; in some cases, the labor courts have had to decide whether a specific employee was a senior manager.

7. Visitors to BASF's Ludwigshafen plant, for instance, will immediately notice on entering the main gate an impressive building that is solely devoted to housing the BASF corporate (*Konzern*) works council and its large clerical and technical staff.

8. As part of the empirical research on codetermination, the highly competent works-council chairman of a German multinational firm was interviewed. During the conversation the chairman's wife called and said that her physician had prescribed a new medication. The works-council chairman had his chauffeur in his company car pick up the medication in the company infirmary and immediately deliver it to his wife. Clearly the works-council chairman had become an integral part of top management and did not hesitate to adopt all the perquisites due his position.

9. Even prior to the 1952 and 1972 legislations, dismissal of an employee had been difficult under German law. Upon joining an organization, each employee obtains an unlimited contract (*Arbeitsvertrag*), which can be terminated only for good reason. With each year the vested rights of an employee in his job grow, until after five years he virtually has tenure. The current unwillingness of management to expand employment, especially by hiring younger workers, has been partially explained by the difficulty with which employees can be fired.

10. The year 1978 seems to have been the first one in which several powerful works-council members were not reelected.

11. The 1972 legislation made a special effort to increase the participation of younger workers and women in works-council business (see part III, sections 60-73). In practice, the youth representation has merely generated an additional minor bureaucracy within the works council, with no operational significance.

12. The excessively legalistic-bureaucratic nature of the 1972 legislation has contributed to changing the nature of the works council and its relationship with the employees. An entire paragraph (section 41), for instance, merely tries to define when the works council can (and cannot) solicit funds for birthdays, wedding gifts, and funerals.

13. See H.U. Niedenhoff, "Die Betriebsratwahlen 1978" *Gewerschafts Report*, December 1978, p. 17.

14. The two major German associations, equivalent to the National Association of Manufacturers and the Chamber of Commerce in the United States, had at that time a common president for the first time in their history. He was Martin Schleyer, a successful and sophisticated entrepreneur who strongly believed that German management had to fight for retaining the management prerogatives necessary to carry out its responsibilities. In 1977 Schleyer was kidnapped by terrorists, tortured, and murdered.

15. In a parliamentary system, the voter cannot select the prime minister. Many independents usually vote Social Democratic merely because they prefer Schmidt as chancellor. This vote is lost, of course, in a "European" election, in which independents may vote for a different party. In the provincial elections of spring 1980, Schmidt's influence became particularly strong because the upcoming national elections in the fall of 1980 encouraged switch voters to vote SPD to strengthen the chancellor.

16. The FDP, which had been far to the left of the SDP in Hamburg, lost decisively and was virtually eliminated.

17. The moderation of German unions must not be overestimated, however. For instance, as a consequence of world excess steel production, the Klöckner-Werke have reduced their steel-making capacity by 8 million tons and have simultaneously invested heavily in automated systems. Since 1971 their employment was reduced by eight thousand people, at a saving of DM 300 million. Wage increases for the reduced personnel also equaled DM 300 million, however. Increases for 1978 were financed by a further reduction of sixteen hundred employees.

18. How much of a hastily put-together compromise it was—after years of discussions and testimonies—may be shown by the fact that it took the Parliament until June 1977 to decide how to define the term *Leitender Angestellte* (senior manager) for the purpose of the upcoming supervisory board election. The original provision in the 1976 legislation required binding arbitration if employer and works council disagreed, but most constitutional lawyers considered this clause unconstitutional. In general, "the legal election procedures for the codetermination elections are so complex, that it is doubtful . . . if the voter always understands what the purpose of the election is, and in which election he participates." Karl Lichtenstein, codetermination expert in I.G. Chemie, quoted in *Mannheimer Morgen*, 12 August 1977. For corporations with subsidiaries, the legal election pro-

cedures, mandated by Parliament, consist of 40 pages and 139 paragraphs.

19. The law applies to four different forms of shareholding companies: corporations (*Aktiengesellschaft* or *A.G.*), limited-liability companies (*Gesellschaft mit beschränkter Haftung* or *GMBH*), similar to privately held companies in the United States; a mixture of a limited-liability company and partnership (*Kommandit-gesellschaft auf Aktien* or *KgaA*), which exists only in Germany and Austria; and profit-making cooperatives (*Erwerbs-und Wirtschaftsgenossenschaft*).

20. See *Süddeutsche Zeitung*, 3-4 May 1978.

21. Four elections, because salaried employees and workers vote separately in each case. Majorities in both electoral bodies are necessary to change the dual election procedure into a common one, or to replace indirect elections by direct ones, or vice-versa. In addition, there is the nomination and election of the electors in those enterprises in which indirect election of supervisory board members occurs.

22. When mine-worker chief Adolf Schmidt attempted in 1976 to have his assistant, F.W. Kramer, appointed to the Preussag Vorstand as personnel vice-president, even the three internal employee directors voted with the stockholder representatives against the four union representatives on the board to reject an "obviously unqualified candidate."

23. The union-owned Bank für Gemeinwirtschaft is a major VW stockholder, and its representative on the supervisory board has been voting consistently with the employee-union representatives, giving Loderer, under the 1976 legislation, an eleven-to-nine majority; moreover, as long as the SDP is in power, Loderer generally can count on the two votes of another stockholder, the representatives of the federal government.

24. Quoted in *Frankfurter Allgemeine Zeitung*, 8 March 1979, p. 11 (hereafter cited as *FAZ*).

25. See Jürgen von Eick, "Schicksalsjahr 1978" [Fateful year 1978], FAZ, 18 May 1978.

26. In a speech in Osnabrücken on 8 September 1979, Loderer announced that the I.G. Metall would demand not only complete compensation for the inflation since the last contract (about 6 percent by September 1978) but also a share of the 4 percent productivity gain. Henig Markmann, director of the DGB's Economics Institute, warned the public that the 1980 contract renewal talks will be "especially tough; the social climate between the 'social partners' will be rougher than in the last two years." As it turned out, the I.G. Metall did obtain a 7 percent wage increase in February 1980. This is quite high for Germany, although idyllic for the United States or United Kingdom. FAZ, 10 September, 1979, p. 11. In September 1979, Schmidt and Economics Minister Lambsdorff met with union and employers' association leaders to emphasize the necessity of moderate wage increases in 1980 for the future health of the German economy. Ibid., 19 September 1979, p. 1.

27. Articles by financial writers Günter Götz, Jürgen von Eick (FAZ), Rainer Hahrendorf (*Handelsblatt*, Düsseldorf), Otto Schulmeister (Vienna's *Die Presse*), and Hans Christoph Leo (general counsel, Esso A.G., Germany) have been the basis for the following material. Recent personal discussions with the public affairs directors of American subsidiaries of major German firms and American firms with subsidiaries in Germany have also supplied information.

28. See "Director Conflicts," *Wall Street Journal*, 10 December 1979, p. 1.

29. A striking example of the growing union militancy was provided at the I.G. Metall's shop steward conference in Dortmund, October 1979. *Dortmunder Handelsblatt*, 29 October 1979, p. 13, and FAZ, 30 October 1979, p. 11. At this conference the union officials made the following points. (1) Works-council members and employee directors must not be prevented from spreading confidential information for the benefit of employees and union. The concept of proprietary information is a pompous, obsolete concept (*Popanz*). (2) Strategic enterprise data should be collected and stored centrally. Since the union has "friends in key positions," the I.G. Metall's headquarters obtains some information more quickly than do company managers. (3) Works-council representatives must resist the full partnership ideology (*totale Partnerschafts ideologie*) and attend union instead of enterprise training programs. (4) Legal questions are essentially power questions (*Machtfragen*). The union must create conditions that German labor courts can no longer ignore.

30. In July 1979, Vice-Chairman Loderer presided over VW's annual stockholders' meeting in place of the ailing chairman, Hans Birnbaum, to the consternation of many stockholders.

31. See "Der Gewerkschaftsbund trent sich von seinem Jugendsekretär," FAZ, 14 September 1979, p. 13. The defense of "loyal" Communist union functionaries by the wood and plastics union official, Detlef Hensche, triggered a vigorous discussion among union functionaries, which was generally highly critical of Hensche. FAZ, 2 October 1979, p. 4.

32. Interestingly enough the U.S. media have not reported on the undemocratic conditions at German universities. The systematic violation of even elementary academic freedom at, say, the University of Bremen, has never caught the attention of U.S. reporters.

33. Unfortunately former Chancellor Brandt and his close associate Egon Bahr were not among those who perceived a reemergence of the ghosts of Weimar. Displaying a selective devotion to free speech, Brandt and Bahr merely commented "that [the attack] has to be expected if one [Strauss] visits the Ruhr"; the similarity to statements by Nazi leaders that justified pogroms during the early 1930s was so obvious that virtually the entire press criticized Brandt strongly. The incident was not reported in the American press.

34. Georg Leber, *Vom Frieden* (Stuttgart: October 1979) Seewald Verlag. A preliminary edition, which contains only the chapter about Leber's construction union's (I.G. Bau-Steine-Erde) fight against Communist takeover attempts in the postwar years, appeared in August and generated considerable furor on the Left. Leber, long a bete noire of the SDP Left, was finally dropped from his position as defense minister by Schmidt in early 1979, ostensibly to mollify the public's indignation over repeated spy scandals in the defense bureaucracy. The fact that the dismissal of Leber was a convenient way to pacify the SDP Left probably was just as important a reason.

5

Management and Employee Behavior Under Codetermination: Case Studies

The previous chapters have presented a few brief case studies to illustrate how German managers and employees cope with particular codetermination phenomena. This chapter examines how codetermination has affected the behavior of management, employees, and unions over a longer period of time. These case studies should help show how codetermination works in practice. The Volkswagen case demonstrates the impact that a powerful and aggressive union leader may have on managerial behavior, while the BASF study looks primarily at the politics of union-works council-employee relations. The Siemens case illustrates the harmonious integration of the works council into the overall personnel structure of a well managed firm. None of the cases is truly typical for the industry involved or for the entire economy. Taken together, however, they strengthen the overall understanding of the operational nature of codetermination by presenting significant operational characteristics of German codetermination practices.

Decision Making at Volkswagen[a]

The decision-making process at the Volkswagen Corporation during the 1970s, but especially in the period 1972-1976, provides a unique opportunity to study the simultaneous effects of both codetermination and government control during a period of declining sales, rapidly rising costs, and a worldwide recession.

Postwar growth and prosperity may have concealed the potential contradiction inherent in codetermination and political control.[1] The serious difficulties that have confronted both VW and the organizations that have dominated its board of directors enhance the significance of this case study.

Legal-Political Situation at VW

The peculiar legal-political situation at VW is a result of its history. Established by the National Socialist government in 1937 to produce an

---

[a]An earlier version of this case study appeared under the title "Decision Making at Volkswagen 1972-1975" in the *Columbia Journal of World Business*, Spring, 1976, and is reprinted with the kind permission of the Journal's editors in a modified, up-to-date form.

inexpensive car for the people and reborn in 1948 under Heinrich Nordhoff's leadership, VW remained a state-owned enterprise until 1972.[2] The decision of the then Conservative-Liberal government to sell the VW shares to private stockholders was opposed not only by the Socialists but also by groups within the Conservative party (CDU-CSU). As a consequence, only 60 percent of the VW shares were sold to the public, 20 percent were allotted to the state of Lower Saxony, the home of the Wolfsburg plant, and 20 percent were retained by the federal government.

Until the implementation of the 1976 codetermination law on 5 July 1977, the VW board of directors consisted of twenty-one members, of which seven (one-third) were elected by the employees under the provisions of the *Betriebsverfassungsgesetz*, and the state and federal government each appointed two members, which left only ten shareholder directors.[3] Since the trade unions are very closely affiliated with the governing Social Democratic party, it has been popular to speak of the "red" board of directors at VW.

Seeds of the VW Crisis

The rapid growth of the German economy and the VW enterprise, as well as the strong, dynamic personality of Heinrich Nordhoff, the first VW chief, concealed the conflicting interests among the four groups represented on the VW board of directors after 1962: shareholders, federal government, state of Lower Saxony, and union. The shareholder representatives had the usual interest in growth and profitability expected from the typical board. Because the special VW shareholder legislation sharply limited individual stockownership (*Volksaktien*) and hence widely distributed it among 1 million owners, one could expect that someone who owned a few VW shares should have been more interested in annual dividends than in growth. If this was so, there is no evidence that the stockholder directors shared this viewpoint. On the contrary, they fully supported Nordhoff's expansionist policy, which, however, also resulted in good stock market performance. Nevertheless during periods of falling demand, shareholder directors can be expected to demand quick and vigorous cost and personnel reductions to preserve the profitability of the enterprise. They will also demand that the company strive to minimize worldwide production cost through optimal plant location, at home and abroad.

The federal government was, of course, concerned with the long-run growth and economic profitability of the enterprise and hence showed little inclination to interfere with the management, as long as its performance criteria were met and as long as VW was led by as strong a personality as Nordhoff. On the other hand all German governments since 1937 have used the VW works as a means to industrialize the underveloped areas of Germany. It is no accident that in 1937 the main plant was located in Wolfsburg, then a small hamlet of a thousand inhabitants in a poor agricultural area of north Germany, nor that the VW management subsequently chose the problem areas along the East German border and East Frisia as its new plant-location sites. The price for the hands-off policy of state and federal politicians during the years 1948-1968 was management's cooperation with the government's long-run regional development policy (*Strukturpolitik*). The reason why underdeveloped regions are underdeveloped, however, is that for good economic reasons they have not been attractive to industry, which explains the failure of massive regional development programs in Appalachia, northern England, and southern Italy.

Until 1972 the VW success story concealed the inherent contradiction between the demands of a long-run regional development policy and the market requirements of a profit-seeking enterprise. The location of VW plants in marginal areas affected not only the cost structure of the enterprise but made the newly industrialized areas dependent on the fortune of the VW company, a point that was to haunt VW management in later years.

The state government of Lower Saxony represents the third vested interest on the board. Although its long-run stakes in VW are quite similar to those of the federal government, its interests in using VW as a tool to industrialize its underdeveloped areas are perhaps even stronger, since it has fewer other means at its disposal. It is also even more motivated by short-run considerations than the federal government is, since the opening or closing of one factory will have a much greater impact on Lower Saxony than on West Germany. The Social Democrats governed Lower Saxony until 1976, and their representatives on the VW board generally followed the lead of the federal representatives but in turn demanded their support on matters of special state interest. For instance, when the VW management acquired the NSU automobile company in 1969 in a diversification move, the state representatives on the VW board demanded and subsidized the establishment of an entirely new plant in Salzgitter, on the East German border, to build the new NSU K-70 car. Although there seemed to have been no particular reason why the relatively short-lived K-70 could not have been built in one of the two established NSU plants, and none at all for building it in Salzgitter, the board majority supported its colleages from Lower Saxony and a $200 million plant sprang up a few miles from the border.

The seven employee-directors on the pre-1977 board had been dominated by the representatives of the trade union. Eugen Loderer, head of Germany's powerful metal union, has been a vice-chairman of the board of directors and has played a major role in VW decision making. The employees are, of course, interested in high wages and, in the long run, in the stability and growth of their company. The union has also been interested in using VW as a pacesetter in wages and working conditions and in supporting the industrialization policy of the state and federal governments. If these union policies should turn VW into a high-cost producer, then the interests of the union and the employees no longer coincide. Although both unions and employees will be strongly opposed to any layoffs during difficult times, it is not inconceivable that the employees might be willing to accept wage cuts in order to avoid mass work force reductions while the union would defend the existing wage level of a pace setter even at the expense of layoffs. As long as the union dominates the employee information media and as long as management, for its own reasons, is not interested in challenging this point, this real but hidden conflict between union and employees will not manifest itself openly.

The majority of VW's board of directors might have been tempted, at least in the short run, to subordinate the entrepreneurial aspects of the enterprise to their own priorities. As long as a strong management could satisfy the demand of union and government directors during boom periods, the board majority would show little inclination to interfere with the way management ran the business, thus abdicating the all-important controlling function of a German *Aufsichtsrat*. It could be expected, however, that a recession would reveal the conflicting interests represented on the VW board.

Crisis Management at VW, 1972-1975

Heinrich Nordhoff died in the spring of 1968, leaving his successor, Kurt Lotz, a highly profitable enterprise, whose major trouble seemed to have been finding ways to dispose of its huge surpluses. With perfect hindsight, however, we know today that VW suffered from three serious problems.

First, it was a high-cost producer. In Germany most wages are set by industry-wide bargaining. Since German automobile workers are, for the most part, represented by the I.G. Metall, their wages are set by the agreement between the union and the entire metal-fabrication industry. The industry-wide contract can be supplemented by individual agreements between a company and its local union. By 1968 VW wage costs already exceeded the average wages in the metal industry by 17 percent, not counting the VW fringe benefits, which always had been among the highest in the industry.[4] However, the modern plant facilities and extremely efficient production procedures kept the unit costs in control as long as the company maintained production near the 100 percent level.

Second, VW's product mix was narrow. When Nordhoff died, the VW product line consisted of the thirty-year-old "bug", its stretched-out version, the Variant, sold in the United States as VW 1500 and VW 1600, and the VW bus, all powered by the same reliable air-cooled motor that Ferdinand Porsche had designed in 1937. The new VW boss, Lotz, had already been haunted by the fate of Henry Ford's "Tin Lizzy," an equally reliable, no-frills car, which almost led the Ford Motor Company into insolvency when during prosperous 1927, the U.S. public suddenly wanted more than merely inexpensive and efficient transportation. Lotz considered the development of new models and new engines the most important task facing him, and he had no difficulty in convincing his colleagues and the board of this view.[5] By implication, at least, Nordhoff was held responsible for the crucial lack of diversification. Although undoubtedly Nordhoff had failed to realize the changing taste of European car buyers, who began to demand luxury and high-speed performance from their cars in addition to reliability, Americans must be surprised at some of the criticism advanced. At a time when Detroit was being severely attacked for wasteful model changes that either did not improve the automobile at all or added unnecessary and dangerous horsepower to cars that already possessed excess high-speed capacity, it was startling that the German press—from the leftish *Spiegel* to the conservative FAZ—had criticized Nordhoff for not having followed U.S. practices.

Lotz did not share this blanket criticism of Nordhoff. On the basis of lifecosts, operational economy, reliability, and maintainability, the VW beetle was still in 1968—and even in 1978 when the last one rolled off the Emden assembly line—a superior car.[6] The appropriate strategy, therefore, was to develop new medium-priced cars to compete with Opel and German Ford in Europe, while holding on to those customers who preferred the puritan beetle exactly in its existing form. Lotz was not only able to gain the support of all pertinent groups within the VW organization for this strategy, but all later VW chiefs adopted Lotz's long-run policy as their own.

The third problem was high export dependency. It became part of the conventional wisdom to cite VW's high dependence on export markets as one of the structural problems that the post-Nordhoff management had not been able to master. In 1968 VW did sell nearly 70 percent of its output abroad; over 700,000 units (almost 40 percent) were sold in the United States. Moreover, since 1960 VW has, on the average, sold two-thirds of its output abroad (until 1975 one out of every three cars in the United States). This high export proportion is not unusual for German firms, however. The machine tool industry, for example, exports over 60 percent of its production, with several individual machine-tool enterprises exceeding 75 percent. Similarly the foreign sales of the entire automobile industry also exceed 60 percent, an average reduced by the comparatively low U.S. sales of GM's and Ford's large German subsidiaries. What was unusual, however, was the high dependence of VW on a single foreign country. Hence the economic conditions affecting the VW's U.S. sales had to remain under constant management scrutiny, with contingency plans ready to defend the U.S. sales.

In 1968 Lotz was not equipped with perfect 1975 hindsight and therefore devoted his energy to the development of new models. Since VW had no plans for new medium-priced models ready, in 1969 Lotz bought a small but innovative German automobile company, NSU, and merged it with the Auto-Union, a former Daimler-Benz subsidiary purchased by Nordhoff in 1965. The resulting fully owned new company, Audi-NSU, was intended to become the producer of a wide range of medium-priced cars, which were to compete with BMW, Opel, and Ford in Europe and the luxury compacts of the big three manufacturers in the United States.[7] This strategy concept has been fully realized today, though the first Audi-NSU product, the K-70, was a failure. Apparently rushed through the design and production stages in incredibly short time by U.S. standards, the K-70 appeared with too many problems and had to be withdrawn after a few unprofitable years.

Similarly two new versions of the basic VW models, the Super-Beetle and the 411, a successor to the VW 1600, were not successful. Although Lotz could hardly be blamed for the failure of the two models that had been developed primarily under the administration of his predecessor and although the rapid production of the NSU K-70 was a calculated risk, apparently fully approved by the board of directors, the lack of success of the new models undermined his position. Serious quarrels broke out among cliques in the executive committee and the board, and Lotz was fired in September 1971, after only two and one-half years in command.[8]

First Attempts to Replace the Beetle

No acceptable explanation has been given for Lotz's forced resignation, though the lack of support among his senior managers may have been the real reason. The failure of the new models incurred losses; however, this was primarily the fault of the board majority who had passively permitted the directors representing the Lower Saxony government to convince the VW executive committee to build a new expensive plant in Salzgitter in order to produce the new K-70. The challenging combination of a new car built by a new work force in a new factory was one reason why the K-70 proved to be such a troublesome car. Without the DM 600 million spent on the Salzgitter plant, the K-70 today would count as merely a minor difficulty that had to be overcome in the successful development of a new product line.

Lotz can also be criticized for permitting a 17 percent wage increase in 1970, an unusually high figure for Germany and even for VW. Although

VW sales had reached an all-time high in 1970, profits had already dropped to 2.5 percent (they were 5 percent in 1969) of sales and to about 11 percent (in 1969 33 percent) of capital. The absolute profit, however, still amounted to DM 300 million in 1970 and to more than DM 1 billion over the three-year period 1968-1970.[9] Under these circumstances it would have been difficult for any new company head to make a significantly better bargain, especially if the board majority strongly supported the union's demands. U.S. managers will appreciate the situation if they imagine for a minute a Walter Reuther as vice-chairman of the General Motors board in 1970. At any rate, there is no record of any board criticism of management's wage policy during the Lotz years.

There was much talk that VW, under Lotz as well as under his successor, continued to expand production capacity at a time when the new glamour company Daimler-Benz had already reduced its annual investment sharply. If, however, we deduct the DM 600 million investment for the Salzgitter plant, VW's expensive gift to Lower Saxony's Social Democrats, we find that VW's capital expenditures actually declined during the years 1970 to 1971.

During Lotz's administration, VW correctly identified the product-mix problem, developed a long-run strategy still in force today, and acquired NSU, which turned into a major success by 1974. But Lotz acquiesced too readily in the board's Salzgitter Scheme, which turned the K-70 failure into a major loss. Lotz and the executive committee also permitted wage costs to rise more than necessary, but again with the full approval of the board.[10] Do German board directors then fire chief executive officers who do not have the good sense to oppose them? If the board majority is made up of a coalition of different interest groups, an individual director may be prevented from officially opposing a particularly questionable idea of his colleagues, though he may wish that the CEO would. Lotz's successor, Rudolf Leiding, did not hesitate to take on the board members, singly and collectively; he lasted an even shorter time than Lotz did.

Conflict on the Supervisory Board

To understand the atmosphere at VW, and hence the real reason for the failure of Lotz (and Leiding), we must look briefly at the behavior of successful management teams in the coal-steel industry where equal codetermination has prevailed since 1951. As we know, the real decision-making process in the Montan industry takes place in informal caucuses in which senior managers exchange information and explore alternatives with appropriate board and employee-council members.[11] Only when a consensus has been reached in these caucuses will a particular proposal be submitted to the executive committee or the board for final, pro forma approval. Controversial topics, therefore, seldom come before the board unless a compromise has already been reached.[12]

The same informal consultation process developed at VW after Nordhoff's death; only those topics on which agreements had already been reached came before the supervisory board. Although this caucus procedure may have worked reasonably well in the coal-steel industry, it delayed decisions and promoted conflict and personal vendettas in Wolfsburg. The absence of agreements on important issues not only kept the board from facing problems openly but also saved key members from publicly defending positions that they advanced privately, though vigorously, through unofficial channels. Individual VW executives, in turn, often seemed concerned primarily with seeking the approval of important board members and adjusted their behavior accordingly. The amiable board chairman, Josef Rust, was too weak to hold the board together and to keep individual members from interfering in management affairs, and Lotz had neither the strength nor the authority to hold his team in line and finally had to resign.

Lotz's successor, Audi-NSU head Rudolf Leiding, essentially accepted Lotz's assessment of the VW situation. Product-line diversification, with special emphasis on medium-priced models, had to remain the primary management goal. In addition, Leiding recognized the urgency of two other problems, which could no longer be overlooked: sharply increasing wage costs and the related sudden unprofitability of the U.S. market.

Automobile wages had advanced sharply in Germany, and especially at VW, which had continued to pay premium wages. Although Lotz had already been concerned about this development, he would not or could not prevent the drastic 17 percent wage increase in 1970, nor could he seriously influence the wage negotiations in 1971 that led to an 8.6 percent wage increase in 1972 and a 9.6 percent wage increase in 1973. Wage increases of 8 and 9 percent are not considered excessive by U.S. standards, but they were too much for a company whose profits had been steadily declining since 1968. Leiding's attempt to obtain employee cooperation in making VW wage costs more competitive did not gain much support from his colleagues on the management executive committee, but led to a conflict with the vice-chairman of the board, Eugen Loderer, boss of the powerfull I.G. Metall. Loderer believed, not without reason, that only during the last decade had German workers begun to obtain their share of the German prosperity, and opposed even a temporary withdrawal from the positions gained. His views were supported by several members of Leiding's management team.

It was not surprising, therefore, that Leiding did not have sufficient support within his own management. Too many senior executives were familiar with the views of the dominant board members and were unwilling to express unpopular opinions. Leiding finally decided to go directly to the employees, and in the spring of 1974 wrote a letter to each one, asking for the utmost restraint in the coming wage negotiations. Although the request was well received by many employees, Vice-Chairman Loderer considered the letter a declaration of war, and the already bad relations between the VW chief and the union boss deteriorated further. Wages rose 14 percent in 1974.

Leiding's discovery that the all-important U.S. market was in jeopardy led to similar internal controversies, which were also never resolved. The profitability of the U.S. market had originally been exaggerated by selling the Wolfsburg-built VW for overvalued U.S. dollars. Rising costs in Germany had to lead to price increases, which became serious when the dollar was first officially devalued and then continued to float downward in world exchange markets. In spite of a 15 percent price increase, 1971 was still a good year, with almost 550,000 cars sold. In 1973, a 31 percent price increase had more serious consequences and together with the oil crisis led to the sharpest decline ever in U.S. VW sales. Most frightening to Leiding, however, was that the 1973 price increases still did not account fully for the rising prices at home and the declining value of the dollar.[13]

The management of VW's U.S. subsidiary had long recognized the importance of the U.S. market and demanded the establishment of a production or assembly plant in the United States. In spite of the importance of the U.S. market, the views of VW's U.S. management had little impact in Wolfsburg—perhaps, as a cynic commented, because U.S. workers could not vote in German elections and did not pay German union dues. Leiding, however, shared the assessment of his U.S. managers and made preparations either for building a U.S. production plant or entering into a cooperative arrangement with a U.S. manufacturer.

Leiding first obtained the support of his management team and began only later to inform certain board members of his decision. In the summer of 1974 Leiding's U.S. project became known to the entire board and to the public at large, although no specific proposal had been submitted formally. The manufacture or even assembly of VWs in the United States was immediately opposed once Vice-Chairman Loderer and Lower Saxony's Socialist secretary of labor Greulich, began to contemplate the consequences of shifting one-third of the VW production overseas.[14] Carefully, but effectively, Loderer and the "Red Saxons" let it be known that they would oppose building a U.S. production center. Typically for VW's decision process, once Loderer's views became known, important senior executives began to shift their position and now attacked the American project either openly or in informal caucus sessions.

The informal policy-formulation procedure developed in the coal industry had been a disaster at VW. Rather than leading to converging assessment of the problems facing the company, the informality of the decision process enabled key board figures to let their positions be known without having to defend them in public. Senior managers, in turn, found it easier to intrigue against Leiding's projects in caucus sessions than confront him in executive committee meetings with well-reasoned position papers. Political rhetoric rather than rational discussions prevailed among key managers and board members, imposing a process of decision by default on the organization.

The New Models

If Leiding was thwarted in meeting the problems of rising costs and a declining U.S. market, he was amazingly successful in developing new models quickly, and should be credited with the resurgent VW sales in 1976, 1977, and 1978. Within two years five new models rolled out of the VW and Audi factories. Built according to the Detroit building-block concept that permitted the use of common components, the investment costs were sharply below the original estimates and also ensured substantial production cost savings, once the sales of the new models lived up to plant capacity. The oil crisis of early 1974 and the recession delayed the success of the new models. However, by the spring of 1975 Audi 80 (Fox), Passat (Dasher), and Golf (Rabbit) began to sell relatively well in the United States as well as in Europe and enabled VW to regain the top automobile manufacturers' spot in Germany, though the corporation still lost DM 157 million over the whole year worldwide.[15]

The success of the new models came too late for Leiding, and for VW, which lost DM 800 million in 1974 on top of its losses during the last quarter of 1973. The sudden precarious nature of VW finances finally forced the intervention of Germany's pragmatic Chancellor Helmut Schmidt in the fall of 1974. He obtained the resignation of the ineffective board chairman, Josef Rust, and replaced him with a successful manager, Hans Birnbaum, head of the Salzgitter A.G. As the CEO of a large steel manufacturer fully owned by the federal government, Birnbaum had developed a management philosophy that required managers to be able to work with union officials and politicians on supervisory boards but also demanded board nonintervention in management affairs. Although this view contradicts the caucusing procedure that has evolved in the coal and steel industry, for the short run it probably was correct for VW. Leiding had to leave in the fall of 1974, in spite of his outstanding managerial qualities, because he had not been able to live with the highly politicized board and had become anathema to Loderer.

New Management

The new chairman, Birnbaum, made it clear to board members and senior executives that he, and implicitly Chancellor Schmidt, would no longer stand for intrigues. The high VW losses, nearly a billion marks in two years, and the frequent management changes had become a political liability to the socialist-liberal coalition government in Bonn. Thus the new VW chief, former Ford executive Toni Schmuecker, had a board majority behind him whose overriding objective was, once more, the profitability of the enterprise.

Schmuecker saw the problems confronting VW in 1975 in the same way his predecessors had viewed them in 1972 and 1968. Since the product diversification already had been completed successfully, he could devote himself to the cost-reduction problem. He abandoned all attempts, however, to reduce individual wage and salary costs but looked toward production cuts, capacity reduction, and intensive automation as a means of reducing costs sufficiently to make a profit at prevailing prices. This is precisely the decision that American automobile manufacturers made in the mid-1970s when its price rises in the fall of 1974 led to a virtual buyers' strike. The decision to cut production and hence lay off workers, while maintaining the prevailing wage-salary level (including executive salaries), was accepted as the lesser evil by managers and unions, in Detroit and Wolfsburg, with or without formal codetermination.

The textbook response of oligopolists to sales declines has been to cut back supply and maintain price as far as possible. Interestingly the unions also prefer maintenance of established wages and benefits to sacrificing hard-won gains, even at the cost of significant unemployment. The common interest of corporate managers and unions in the automobile industry has added immensely to the rigidity of prices and wages, regardless of the form this de facto codetermination takes.

In the VW case, the demands of the market required a substantial cut in employment and the purchase of at least an assembly plant in the United States. Schmuecker finally convinced the board in April 1975 to approve a 25,000-worker reduction in the work force over the next twelve to eighteen months, from its current level.[16] Shortly thereafter he obtained board approval of initiating negotiations to acquire an American assembly plant. Although the union and especially its chief, Loderer, offered token opposition to this decision, they were, at this point, more concerned with the impact of the VW crisis on its demand for equal codetermination in German industry. For the next twelve months, at least, Loderer and the union delegates on the board chose a low profile.

The passage of the 1976 codetermination law strengthened once more the position of Loderer and the I.G. Metall; as long as the Social Democrats governed Germany, the union-employee faction on the supervisory board could count on eleven out of twenty possible votes on most issues, once the new supervisory board was elected. The nine union-employee directors and the two government officials could be expected to agree, especially on all personnel questions, including appointments to the management board.

The VW management quickly realized the implications of the new legislation and made every effort to court Loderer's cooperation and support. While other enterprises changed their charter to strengthen the position of the management board—for example, by increasing the size of investments that could be made by the Vorstand without supervisory board approval—VW did just the opposite.[17] Furthermore it rushed through the necessary elections to establish the new board on 5 July 1977, a full year before the deadline.

New Supervisory Board

The new board consists of twenty members, ten employee representatives and ten stockholder representatives. The ten employee-directors include one senior VW manager, six VW employees (each of them a works-council chairman in a VW plant), and three union officials (Eugene Loderer, president, I.G. Metall; Gerd Kühl, secretary, I.G. Metall; and Dr. A. Schunk, also I.G. Metall secretary). The stockholder representatives include two ministers of Saxony's conservative (CDU) provincial government, two senior civil servants representing the Social Democratic-liberal federal government, and six representatives elected by the shareholders, including VW's board chairman, Hans Birnbaum, CEO of the government-owned steel-iron enterprise, Salzgitter A.G., until his retirement in October 1979.

The VW management was fortunate that the attractive new models, designed and developed under Leiding, came off the assembly line just when the world economy recovered during 1976 and 1977. In Germany especially, strong automobile demand heralded the recovery and strengthened VW sales. In the United States (and Brazil) sales recovered but never again reached the volume of the early 1970s; even in 1978 and 1979, VW's total sales lagged behind the Japanese competition, especially Toyota. In most other countries, however, VW regained most of its former position, although the Japanese began to increase their market share even in Germany to 4.2 percent in 1978.[18] In Germany VW wage increases exceeded once more industry standards, and during 1976, 1977 employment grew by 15,000 over the low point in 1975 and reached 210,000 in 1979, still below the 1973 peak. In spite of the improved economic position of the company and Toni Schmuecker's conciliatory skills, relationships between key managers and board members remained tense.

During the stockholders' meeting in July 1979, Schmuecker presented the final, board-approved, long-run strategy: high wages at home, which create "a permanent competitive handicap" (*einen permanenten Wettbewerbsnachteil*), and an impressive investment program abroad, especially in the United States, Mexico, and Brazil, to remain cost-competitive.[19]

Over the long run, VW's global position has been saved by the excellent new models developed by Leiding, by the OPEC price increases, which sharply increased the demand for efficient small cars, and by the inability of America's automobile manufacturers to produce a competitive small car.

Conclusion

The political orientation of the supervisory board and the lack of appropriate leadership had made it possible for key figures at VW to exert authority without having to accept the responsibility for acts of commission and omission. In such a climate difficult decisions could be postponed until they came almost too late. At VW at least, the prenegotiations in caucuses did not contribute to an objective assessment of the situation. On the other hand the social and political considerations that made themselves felt in the VW decision process must be taken into consideration in any Western country, regardless of whether government and union are represented on the board.

The fact that during the mid-1970s the crucial decisions in Detroit have not been very much different from those in Wolfsburg is some evidence that the complexion of the supervisory board may be less crucial than managers or union officials think. If, however, the VW experience can be considered as a preview of managerial behavior under equal codetermination, it is reasonable to assume that a 50 percent union representation on the supervisory board will lead to delays in making unpopular decisions during recessions. It can be anticipated that top managers will be assessed as much by their ability to get along with the union as by their entrepreneurial qualities.

Industrial Relations at BASF

BASF (formerly Badische Anilin & Soda-Fabrik A.G.) has been one of Germany's best managed high-technology firms for well over a hundred years. Its heavy emphasis on pure and applied chemical research since the enterprise's inception in 1865 created the technical expertise that enabled the company to regain its leading worldwide position only fifteen years after its main plant and headquarters in Ludwigshafen had been completely destroyed during World War II, along with 80 percent of all housing in the Ludwigshafen-Mannheim metropolitan area.

Throughout BASF's history, the firm's sophisticated management board—which has borne a striking resemblance to Du Pont's executive committee between 1900 and 1940—has devoted nearly as much attention to its personnel and industrial relations as it has to strategic planning, research, and development.[20] From the beginning BASF's Sozialpolitik was at least comparable, if not superior, to the most comprehensive personnel welfare policies of the mid-nineteenth century Rhineland entrepreneurs. BASF worker and salaried staff housing rose and expanded simultaneously with the Ludwigshafen plant, later accompanied by medical services, sick-pay insurance, and private pension funds, in advance of and later beyond Bismarck's social legislation.

BASF's employee relations have developed smoothly from its highly paternalistic phase in the pre-World War I period to a full acceptance of employee codetermination in the post-World War II period. Since BASF has been paying consistently above industry-average wages and fringe benefits, one might safely assume that its industrial relations are among the best of Germany's successful enterprises. But, at least at its giant Ludwigshafen plant, BASF's management has had to cope with a fractious union leadership, a politicized, ideologically fragmented work force, and a works council that has taken an unusually strong adversary position in its dealings with plant management.

Management-Union Relations

The chemical workers' union, I.G. Chemie, has organized more than 90 percent of the chemical industry's production workers and has been one of Germany's more militant unions. Labor costs in the highly automated industry are relatively low, and the union has taken full credit for the high wages and excellent working conditions of Germany's most glamorous growth industry. The union, moreover, has been able to maintain a tighter shop-floor organization throughout the industry than have most other major German unions. Still, on an industry-wide basis, the relationships between union and top management, works council, and plant management have not been different from those in other industries. Although today the public attitudes of industry and union leaders no longer reflect the cooperative spirit of the 1950s and 1960s, actual shop-floor employee-management relations throughout the industry have not changed significantly. The chemical industry, in fact, has avoided the long and highly damaging series of strikes that plagued the metal-working, engineering, newspaper, and printing industries during 1977 and 1978, with damaging consequences for their labor relations.

The I.G. Chemie has recognized that the industry's amazing growth period has ended and has therefore set itself the twin goals of maintaining both its members' standard of living and industry-wide employment. This strategy clashes with the industry's efforts to rationalize, to expand abroad in order to avoid growing tariff barriers and to take advantage of lower wage costs, and to drop unprofitable products. Still this conflict of interest between employees and management is essentially short run and amenable to a rational compromise—in short, precisely of the type that German codetermination institutions have been able to settle smoothly.

Industry and union have agreed upon an industrial strategy that permits management to accomplish its rationalization and foreign investment goals as long as the existing work force maintains its level of living and the number of production workers is reduced by attrition only. The 18 percent drop in industry-wide profits during 1977, and an even sharper decline during the first two quarters of 1978, made such a compromise defendable to all but the most radical employee groups in spite of the subsequent recovery in 1979. The I.G. Chemie has a sophisticated, strongly anti-Communist president, Karl Hauenschild, a strong supporter of Chancellor Schmidt. However, it also has its share of middle-level functionaries who delight in camouflaging an essentially cooperative policy under militant class-warfare rhetoric designed to appease the various small but articulate K-groups and (Stalinist) communist cells, which have been particularly vocal in the Ludwigshafen-Mannheim area.

Politics of the Ludwigshafen-Mannheim Region

The German chemical industry is concentrated in relatively few areas and is therefore covered in great detail by local newspapers. The political maneuvering of ambitious second-level union officials and radical employees has been closely covered by the Ludwigshafen-Mannheim press, which has become especially sensitive to political activists because of its proximity to the radical students at nearby Heidelberg.[21] Labor relations in the chemical industry in general and the Ludwigshafen-Mannheim area in particular have received a worse press than is actually justified, but there is no question that strident class-warfare slogans, of the sort not heard in Germany since the 1930s, had been routinely expressed by candidates in the 1977-1978 works-council and supervisory-board elections.[22]

The radical posturing of I.G. Chemie officials and the activities of K-groups in turn have prompted the establishment of conservative Christian associations among both salaried employees and workers throughout the industry, but especially in Ludwigshafen, thereby adding to the conflict on the shop floor.

Why the BASF Ludwigshafen works has been one of the more cantankerous work places in Germany is difficult to explain. The reason most often given (but which I do not share) is the size of BASF's main operation. It employs about 50,000 people, one-fourth of Ludwigshafen's wage earners. Moreover the BASF works accounts for two-thirds of the city's taxes. This overwhelming presence of the company, according to Ludwigshafen officials, has created resentment in the population, especially among class-conscious union members, in spite, or perhaps because, of the particularly thorough corporate welfare programs developed by *die Badische* ("the company"). Moreover, during the pre-World War I and even during the interwar period, the paternalistic employers did not practice the current managment's noninterference policy with the political affairs of employees, city, and province.[23] Organizations have long memories, and the battles of the 1930s seem to be especially deeply etched into the collective minds of the DGB unions.[24]

This conventional explanation is not quite convincing. Bayer and Hoechst operations are almost as large in their respective areas and have a quite similar history. A better explanation might be that BASF's proximity to Heidelberg, a center of left-wing radicalism in Germany, has made it a convenient target for Communist penetration. Out of a total of 200,000 works-council members elected in 1978, only 0.4 percent (800) are Communists. These members are concentrated in the major enterprises, however, and "among the 22 largest firms—which includes BASF—21.7 percent of all works council members are Communist party (DKP) members, or belong to other extremist left-wing groups."[25] There is little doubt that the lopsided nature of Communist penetration is a result of party strategy. Activists enter firms as directed, excel as hard-working, loyal trade-union members, and seek election on their record as shop-floor activists, without disguising their party affiliation, however.

The prominence of the BASF Ludwigshafen works may also have attracted radical ex-students who took menial factory jobs in manufacturing industries in order to "revolutionize" the working class.[26] Neither the I.G. Chemie nor the BASF personnel department has taken the self-styled student revolutionary very seriously, even though the Revolutionary Union Opposition (RGO, for *Revolutionäre Gewerkschafts-Opposition*), the front organization for the K-groups, won a Ludwigshafen works-council seat in the April 1978 election and came close to winning two more.[27] The RGO failed completely, however, in its attempt to gain representation on the supervisory board.

1977 Supervisory Board Elections

A closer look at the December 1977 supervisory board elections in Ludwigshafen provides a good view of both the political issues that prevail at the Ludwigshafen plant and the often-unanticipated consequences for employer and union of the 1976 codetermination law. The December supervisory board election provides a better example than the April works-council vote, since it is relatively easy to obtain a seat on a fifty-nine seat works council under a proportional election system that tries to protect minorities. The supervisory board elections offer a better illustration of employee sentiment. They also provide an opportunity to observe the incredible complexity of the election process (see figure 5-1).

The BASF is a corporation with thirty-two subsidiaries and nearly eighty works, which, under the 1976 legislation, required the selection of nearly one hundred election committees and the establishment of voting lists for workers, salaried employees, and senior managers. According to the terms of the 1976 legislation, the election was to be indirect (a vote for electors) and to be held in two separate electoral bodies unless the employees decided otherwise (see figure 5-1). The anti-DGB-I.G. Chemie forces at the Ludwigshafen works asked for a vote to replace the indirect with a direct election, and the I.G. Chemie responded by demanding an election to eliminate the electoral distinction between salaried employees and workers (*gemeinsame Wahl*). The I.G. Chemie lost both preliminary elections, which came as a complete surprise in the case of the direct versus the indirect election. The trade unions invariably prefer indirect election because the selection, nomination, and election of electors (*Wahlmänner*) is more easily controlled by the union apparatus than in direct elections in which the proportional election system assures minorities of representation. The BASF supervisory board primaries demonstrated again that individual employees, though they may be good union members, do not want to delegate their codetermination rights to union officials, whether they come from within the enterprise or from the national office.

In the final election, the candidates of the I.G. Chemie faced the Employee Coalition BASF, which consisted of the German Salaried Employees Union (DAG), the Christian Union Chemie, and the Independent Employees Association. The RGO, having failed to nominate one of their own, quietly supported the I.G. Chemie. At stake were ten supervisory board seats, of which four were to be allocated to workers, two to salaried employees, one to a senior manager, and three to national union representatives. With only 53.4 percent of eligible employees casting their votes, the I.G. Chemie won all four workers' seats by a vote of 19,732 to 4,498, though the fourth seat by only a very slim margin (490 additional votes would have given the coalition one worker seat on the board), and it split the two salaried-employee seats with the coalition by a vote of 10,960 to 10,802. Most surprisingly, and most irritating to the DGB and the I.G. Chemie, the coalition even gained one of the three union seats by obtaining 18,055 votes versus 26,337 for the I.G. Chemie.[28] Including the representative of the senior managers, three out of the ten employee directors are not associated with the I.G. Chemie. The board met for the first time in July 1978 after the stockholder assembly chose its representatives. Although

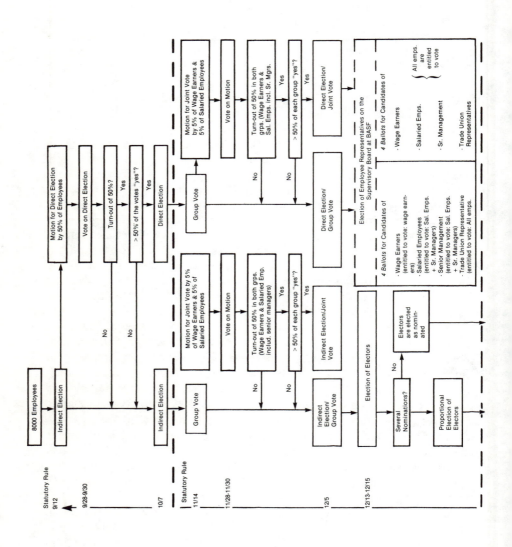

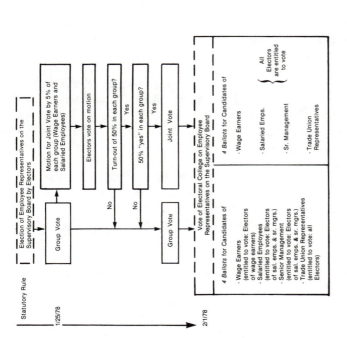

Source: Adapted from material supplied by BASF's Public Affairs Office in New York City.

Figure 5-1. Flowchart for Selection of Employee Representatives on BASF Supervisory Board

no one can say today how the division among the employee delegates will affect the functioning of the supervisory board, a few conclusions can be drawn from the BASF election.

1. A voting participation of less than 54 percent demonstrates that supervisory board codetermination is not an important issue to many employees.

2. The DGB has lost considerable support in one of the most highly organized industries in the country.

3. Many loyal union members will oppose the paternalistic attempt of the national union to dominate codetermination processes but will still support the union tickets in the final election. The BASF workers who did not obey union instructions to vote for direct elections in the end supported the union ticket by four to one.

4. The increasingly radical rhetoric of several union officials at both the national level and at the Ludwigshafen plant and, simultaneously, the development of conservative rival unions, may lead to internal strife within the work force and to a politicization of the works councils. The ability of the extreme left-wing group, RGO, to win representation on the BASF-Ludwigshafen works council during the April 1978 elections virtually guarantees such a development for Ludwigshafen.

5. The direct election cost to the BASF is estimated at nearly 2 million marks. The indirect costs will be much higher since both the BASF personnel department and the works council had to add more codetermination election experts to their staffs. Given the size of BASF, a few million marks will not make much difference, but the increasing bureaucratization of the works council very well may. In the BASF A.G. a total of eighty-three works-council members have been elected, of which thirty-six, nearly half, became full-time works-council officials. In addition, there are twelve hundred shop representatives (*Betriebsvertrauensleute*) who play an intermediate role between works council and employees and who therefore work only part-time on their regular jobs.

New Works-Council Leadership

By emphasizing the dissenting groups within both the I.G. Chemie and the Ludwigshafen work force, this case study has failed to give appropriate attention to the effective and pragmatic works-council members and shop representatives who are both good union members and loyal BASF employees and who are responsible for employee-management relations that would be considered as good anywhere but in Central Europe. The epitome of this cadre of conscientious union officials is Kurt Herrmann, the newly elected works-council chairman of the BASF A.G. in Ludwigshafen, a class-conscious skilled worker and a patriot, the very backbone of the Social

Democratic party, who does, however, exemplify a new and different codetermination process.

In an interview with the *Mannheimer Morgen*, Herrmann freely admitted that he is "authoritarian in the sense of authority" and believes that running a "tight ship" (*straffe Führung*) is a necessity if he is to convince the "all-mighty discussion partner" on the other side of the table.[29] He differs fromhis predecessor, Rudi Bauer, who had been works-council chairman and supervisory board member for over a decade, and from most works-council chairmen of the 1950s and 1960s by accepting an adversary relationship between employees and employer, works council and management. "I recognize the pluralistic society and represent specific interests, which, unfortunately, even highly educated persons [management] can't understand. There are [different] group interests and hence natural conflict."

On the other hand Herrmann does not admit that different group interests could exist among employees and rejects the fragmentation within the work force that was displayed by the most recent works-council and supervisory board elections. Herrmann condemns the "chaos seekers of the [extreme] right and left" (the left-wing K-groups; there are no right-wing extremists in Ludwigshafen) and pleads by implication with several I.G. Chemie functionaries for a sharper rejection of the pro-Moscow Communists.

In spite of the highly publicized success of the K-groups in the April works-council election, Herrmann does not believe that they will play a significant role at BASF, "though they are damaging for the work force since they throw dirt at the works councils and unions and oppose parliamentary procedures."

On the other hand, Herrmann expresses his regard for Professor Seefelder, BASF's CEO. He acknowledges his mental toughness and willingness to accept responsibilities, and he recognizes the fact that even Seefelder and the BASF management's room for decision is highly limited by objective constraints, but he wishes that BASF's top management would also understand the constraints that limit his maneuverability. Herrmann sees his task as maintaining as far as possible the existing wages and working conditions; he admits freely that economic "conditions have become worse" and does not oppose, in principle, technological change, but he rejects "rationalization at all cost." Herrmann, moreover, recognizes that works councils and unions have neglected the apprentices and young workers, who have drifted into extreme left-wing positions though he claims they are all "good Social Democrats" at heart. Herrmann is a good personification of the responsible, pragmatic union member and works-council official of the mid-1970s, who combines a moderate adversary position with an understanding of the economic constraints that require employee-management cooperation over the long run.

The BASF management has not been willing to admit that the conflict with the Ludwigshafen works council (not to be confused with the BASF A.G. corporate works council, which has also been meeting at Ludwigshafen) may well become the rule rather than the exception for employee relations in the 1980s.

For several years BASF has been publishing *Social Report* intermittently, which includes information on the structure of the work force, working conditions, employee relations, relations with the city and province, and economic data.

The "Social Report" *BASF Menschen, Arbeit, Geschäft '77* [People, work, business '77] appeared in May 1978 and emphasized the company's commitment to codetermination as a tool to achieve common tasks through close cooperation with the works council and employees. The regular 1978 *Annual Report* appeared in May 1979 and reflected on the economic environment in which BASF management operates. Taken together both give a good indication of BASF management's ability to cope with the economic issues of the period within the peculiar constraints imposed by the politics of works council-union relationships.

"Social Report"

The "Social Report" was addressed to the work force, the public, and the shareholders during a time when labor relations were exposed to considerable strain. BASF's top executives stressed, therefore, that

> in most [BASF] enterprises the relationship between plant management and works council was shaped by the recognition that the problems of the future will require even closer cooperation [literally, "joint action"]. . . . In general, [management and works council] succeeded in tackling common tasks without a strength-robbing conflict.[30]

The report continued, however, to acknowledge more in sorrow than in anger that in "the Ludwigshafen works the relationships between plant management and [local] works council were subject to strains, since the declining revenue made it impossible to satisfy all-works council demands and wishes.[31] Addressing the employees over the heads of union and works council, the report stressed:

> Economic constraint cannot be simply ignored. More than [ever] before, must [management and employees] short-run advantages be weighed against the long-run [economic] security.

> The limited financial possibilities of the enterprise force not only the [Ludwigshafen] plant management but also the works council to revise their thinking; additional [employee] gains in the future shall only be possible if the economic situation improves.[32]

The three key issues that separated BASF A.G. management and I.G. Chemie, Ludwigshafen works management and works council, were clearly and explicitly spelled out in the 1977 "Social Report's" discussion of employment security.[33]

The first issue was job security. Over the long run no enterprise, not even BASF, can afford to employ more personnel than are needed. Through attrition management reduced excess personnel, a strategy that will enhance long-run employment security. Although management planned to rely on attrition, the adaption of certain works to demand would require the transfer of personnel. Job security, according to the report, cannot be equated with the right to a certain individual job.

The second issue concerned rationalization and mobility. No enterprise can afford not to keep up with technological development. The report pointed out that technological change would accelerate further in the future, thus requiring every employee to be willing to learn new methods, perhaps in a different field, in a different location. (The union was also concerned with the decline in the worker-to-salaried-employee ratio, which the company acknowledged elsewhere in the report as an irreversible trend.)

The third area was foreign investments. Data provided in the report showed that foreign investments (especially in the United States, Canada, and Brazil) comprised 75 to 80 percent of total investment for the past five years. The company described these investments as necessary to defend its established markets and demonstrated that the investments had strengthened employment at home.[34]

If we compare the position of the BASF works-council chairman, Herrmann, and the company on the three crucial issues, it is not difficult to perceive an area of compromise that should enable management to accomplish its objectives over the long run. The question remains, however, to what extent the authority of the corporate works council and the I.G. Chemie has been weakened and to what extent the Ludwigshafen plant works council and work force will be able to resist further political polarization.

1978 Annual Report

The internal controversies created by the 1978 works-council and supervisory board elections subsided during the second half of the year. The annual report stressed, therefore, the tight profit picture that faced the company. Implicitly the high labor costs were blamed for BASF's inability to increase profits in spite of increased sales (see figures 5-2 and 5-3). BASF therefore continued its personnel shrinkage policy throughout 1978 and the first six months of 1979, in spite of verbal union opposition (see figure 5-4). The BASF works councils, however, quickly accepted management's personnel policy and willingly authorized overtime work during the summer of

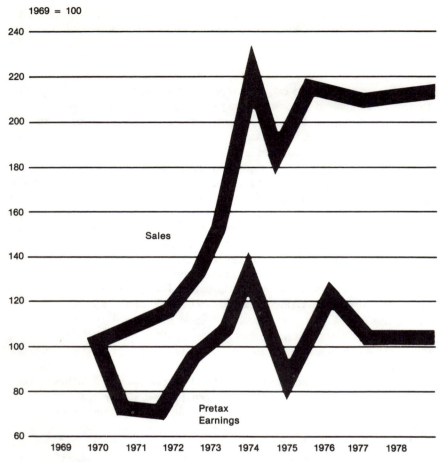

1969 = 100

Source: Adapted from BASF *Annual Report* (1978), p. 2

Figure 5-2. BASF Aktiengesellschaft: Pretax Earnings and Sales

1979, when economic conditions began to improve throughout the German chemical industry.

The rash of wildcat strikes that broke out in Germany during the early 1970s was often directed against decisions taken jointly by works council and management. The German liberal establishment in the universities and the communications media had encouraged attacks on almost all forms of authority. The success of the anti-DGB forces of the Left and Right during the 1978 works-council elections may have been the beginning of an attack on the only authority that has not been undermined so far: the DGB unions million DM

	1976	1977	1978
BASF Group	20,983	21,150	21,513
Germany	10,574	10,467	10,572
Outside of Germany	10,409	10,683	10,941
BASF Aktiengesellschaft	9,798	9,632	9,680
Exports	5,288	5,246	5,388
Share of exports	54.0%	54.5%	55.7%

Source: Adapted from BASF Annual Report (1978), p. 2.

Figure 5-3. BASF Group Sales, 1978

and the works council. Three years have passed since the divisive works-council elections of 1978. By all indications the new works-council cadres have quelled the internal opposition and reestablished reasonably good relations with management, at least until the next industry-wide recession.

Codetermination at Siemens

Throughout the twentieth century the Siemens A.G. has been one of Germany's largest, best-managed, and most resilient corporations. It has survived two world wars, the destruction of its former headquarters in Berlin, and the loss of facilities in Central and East Germany yet has become once

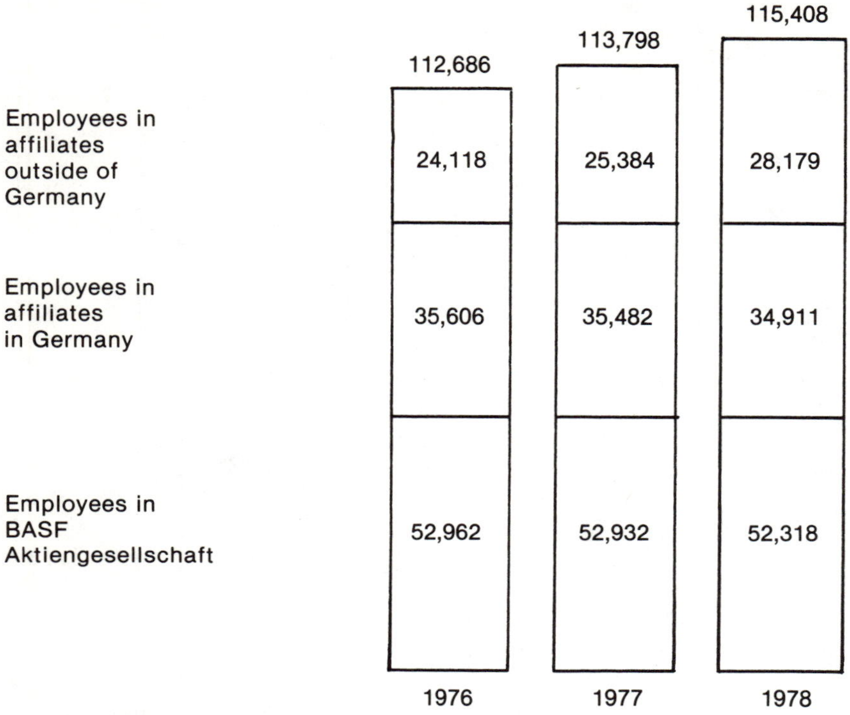

	1976	1977	1978
	112,686	113,798	115,408
Employees in affiliates outside of Germany	24,118	25,384	28,179
Employees in affiliates in Germany	35,606	35,482	34,911
Employees in BASF Aktiengesellschaft	52,962	52,932	52,318

Source: Adapted from BASF Annual Report (1978), p. 26.

Figure 5-4. BASF Group Personnel

more one of the West's most successful electrical manufacturers with worldwide operations. Although Siemens is substantially smaller than General Electric or Philips, Americans can conceive of its role in the German economy if they imagine a merged General Electric and Westinghouse with the successful, paternalistic personnel relations of IBM, another family-dominated giant enterprise.[35] (See table 5-1 and figure 5-5.)

Interwar and Postwar Labor Relations

During the golden age of German codetermination between 1952 and 1972, the works council was smoothly integrated into the Siemens A.G. personnel administration process, and top management successfully adapted to the constraints of the 1952 codetermination legislation. The exemplary labor relations at Siemens during this period become particularly noteworthy when we consider the naturally conflicting tensions that have existed between the house of Siemens—the feudal name given to the enterprise by the

v. Siemens and Halske families—and the militant I.G. Metall, which represents the Siemens workers.

Since the firm's inception, the Siemens management has taken great pride in innovating a web of employee benefit programs that were consistently ahead of both the social legislation of the day and even of the practices of most other paternalistic enterprises. (The term *paternalistic* is not used pejoratively in this context but merely implies that the Siemens family, very much like the Daimler-Benz, Hoechst, and BMW owners, considered its employees as coworkers, or *Mitarbeiter*, a German term that implies much closer personal relations than its English translation, rather than hired hands.) In practice the Siemens management accepted the workers' right to organize and bargain collectively even in the 1920s and 1930s, but it never abandoned its sense of responsibility for its "coworkers" or the right to address its employees directly, over the head of the union.

The 1952 codetermination legislation actually reinforced the house of Siemens atmosphere in which employees and management communicated with each other through works councils and the personnel department in a spirit of organic cooperation, without the intrusion of outsiders. The role of the I.G. Metall was restricted to negotiating with the employers' association over wages and working conditions for the union members. Siemens emphasized that the company voluntarily incorporated the collective-bargaining provisions in the individual contracts drawn up for all its employees, the less than 40 percent who are I.G. Metall members, and the more than 60 percent who are not.[36] The Siemens works councils, moreover, which, unlike the unions, represent the entire work force, have been successful in achieving working conditions that have been significantly superior to the standards set by the industry-wide collective-bargaining agreement.

Siemens's arms-length relation with the local union organizations has accompanied its strong efforts to assign a significant role to the works council in day-to-day personnel administration. As a consequence, key works-council members have achieved an importance in determining personnel policies that exceeds greatly the minimum requirements of the law. In

Table 5-1
Siemens: Comparison of Key Economic Variables

	1975-1976	1976-1977	1977-1978
Employees	304,000	319,000	322,000
Wages and salaries[a]	9,843	10,811	11,829
Sales[a]	21,885	25,932	29,048
Investment[a]	1,469	11,685	1,377
After-tax profit[a]	606	650	721
Percent of Sales	2.9	2.6	2.5

[a]In million DMs.

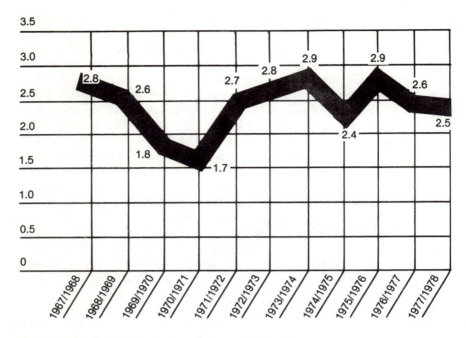

Source: Adapted from Siemens Annual Report (1978).

Figure 5-5. After-Tax Profits as a Percentage of Sales

return, the works councils have displayed considerable independence from local and especially national union leadership. With the possible exception of the Berlin plant, employee-works council-management relations have remained remarkably harmonious. The Siemens's personnel department has attempted to safeguard the cooperative atmosphere among its employees by rigorously enforcing the ban on party politics on enterprise premises, which had been written in the 1952 and 1972 legislation. Where other enterprises may have tolerated violations committed by state or federal ministers and union leaders, especially during the 1976 parliamentary election, Siemens encouraged political activities of its employees on their own time and outside company property, but kept its own grounds free of all partisan activities.

An Empirical Study of Siemens's Codetermination

The generally smooth cooperation between Siemens's works-councils and management, as well as the effective social integration of the work force, have been the subject of a thorough investigation by a team of sociologists under the leadership of Professor P. Fürstenberg (University of Linz). With the full cooperation of the Siemens management, Fürstenberg and his associates interviewed and surveyed employees, works-council members and chairmen, and personnel and works managers during the period December 1967-December 1968.[37] The results of this survey illustrate precisely how well the Siemens management adapted to the 1952 works legislation. Furthermore, the Fürstenberg study can be used as a benchmark to explore whether the house of Siemens succeeded during the 1970s in insulating its employee relations from the sharply deteriorating relationship between employers and the DGB unions (and especially the I.G. Metall).

Works-Council Organization: Siemens had 104 works councils in 1968 (117 after the works-council election in 1978) with a total of 1,287 works-council members (about 1,500 in 1978), of which 142 (11 percent) were fully released from their regular work (275 or 18 percent in 1978, an 80 percent increase in professional works-council members). The works councils, in 1968 as well as in 1980, are grouped into geographic regions, which elect delegates to nine intermediate conferences (*Verbindungskreise*) from their ranks; the 58 members of the Siemens central works council are then chosen from the membership of the 29 regional conferences (*Entsendungskreise*). The central works council selects from its membership an eleven-member executive committee (*Gesamtbetriebsausschuss*), which carries out the policies determined by the central works council. For the purpose of discussing key issues with Siemens's top personnel management, a five-member negotiation committee is chosen, which for most purposes constitutes the actual works-council leadership. This leadership is chosen through a system of indirect elections, in which, at each higher level, the electors are increasingly professionalized works-council members. This procedure determines the oligarchic nature of the works-council process, although it assures a homogeneous and high-quality leadership.

The indirect nature of employee representation at Siemens is reinforced by the election of employee and union supervisory board members by electors, who in turn are chosen by the employees. This indirect method of election is preferred by the unions because it reduces minority representation. The indirect-election process, together with the professionalization of the works council, led to a decrease of employee support for codetermination among Siemens employees.[38]

Works-Council Procedures: Although the negotiation committee may be instrumental in shaping Siemens's personnel policy, mainly it is concerned with settling grievances, like all other works councils. The joint meetings attended by the negotiation committee and Siemens's top personnel management constitute the last stage in Siemens's grievance procedures and attempt to resolve all issues that have not been settled at the two lower levels. In rare cases where no grievance resolution is achieved, the issue is submitted to arbitration on labor court procedure.

The vital task of supplying employees with relevant financial and marketing data has been assigned to the economic committee, which consists of twenty members of the central works council. As early as 1968, the Siemens's economic committee satisfied all of the additional information requirements imposed on management by the Betr.V.G., 1972. Top management supplies the committee with detailed reports on the competitive situation, production and sales goals, enterprise profitability, manpower plans, and possible cutbacks or expansions.

Siemens also has personnel staff units, which are either staffed jointly by management and works councils (committees for safety, and work evaluation) or entirely run by the works councils (committees on salaried employee problems, training, recreation homes, wage administration, employee improvement suggestions, and works news). The supervisory boards of two separate Siemens subsidiaries devoted to employee home building and the support and care of retired workers are staffed one third by the central works council and two thirds by the Siemens management board. On the top level the personnel department, works-council economic committee, and representatives of the supporting staff committees meet periodically and more frequently informally to formulate industrial-relations policy (see figure 5-6). The constant informal contacts between personnel managers and key works-council members have been very important in creating the implicit standard operating procedures for Siemens's employee relations. The longevity of Siemens's key works-council members help to maintain stable personal relations between key council members and personnel managers, although it reinforces the oligarchic, paternalistic aspect of Siemens's industrial relations.

Composition of the Siemens Works Council: German employees elect older, generally skilled, and personally respected colleagues with long service records to works councils. Fürstenberg supplies unusually specific data for the composition of the Siemens's works councils prior to the spring 1978 works-council elections.[39] As expected, the typical member is a middle-aged, male, skilled worker, although tenure and education are below the German norm. (See table 5-2.)

The major characteristics of the works council were not changed by the 1965 or 1968 elections, except for the remarkably large number of nonunion members elected in 1965. The same is true for the 1970s. In 1975 the I.G. Metall obtained 80 percent of all works-council seats but only 75 percent in the 1978 election. The profile of the Siemens's works-council member has remained amazingly stable throughout all elections since 1965 with a few minor changes.

The first change concerns age. The rapid expansion of Siemens's work force during the 1960s and subsequent stabilization during the mid-1970s tended at first to lower the age of works-council members. There are good indications that the last election (1978) increased the average age once more, although no survey has been taken so far.

Regarding union membership, since the mid-1960s, the I.G. Metall has tightened its shop-floor organization, and the percentage of new workers elected to the works council reflects the higher I.G. Metall membership on the shop floor. Among salaried employees, and to a lesser extent even among workers, rival unions gained strength in the 1978 election.

The third change concerns education. The efforts to Americanize the German educational system and to direct a larger percentage of the school population into the Gymnasia (or as in the Socialist Länder Hessen, Bremen, and some others, develop a nonselective, and mediocre, second-ary-school system designed to replace the Gymnasium in the future) has resulted in a larger number of young salaried employees with at least a six-year Gymnasium education in nonexempt positions. Furthermore, the number of foreign workers with minimal education has been reduced at Siemens, as well as throughout Germany. We can be certain, therefore, that the educational profile of works-council members in 1978 is different from the 1968 survey.

These surface changes, however, do not disguise the overall stability in the composition of the Siemens's works councils throughout the years.

Evaluation of Works-Council Activity: Numerous surveys since 1952 have disclosed the German employees' generally favorable attitude toward works-council codetermination. The Fürstenberg study successfully analyzes nuances of employee and management evaluation of works-council ac-tivities that have not been included in previous macrosurveys.

One question concerned the qualities that works-council candidates should possess (table 5-3). The answers generally are very much in line with previous and later surveys, although the low importance of union member-ship is primarily a characteristic of Siemens.

The answers to the significant questions concerning the personal cooperation between works council and works management, as well as works council and first-line supervisory, displayed a high assessment of existing harmony (table 5-4).

Questioned on what they expected from the central works council, 43 percent of the employees answered counsel and information, 36 percent answered help in solving general problems, and 10 percent for assistance in dealing with top management.

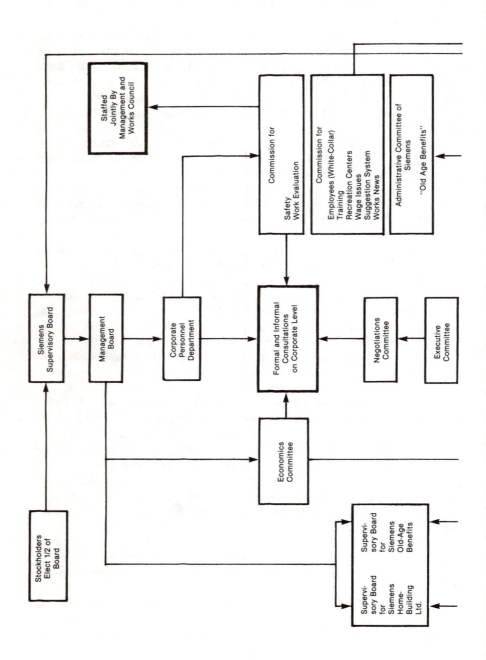

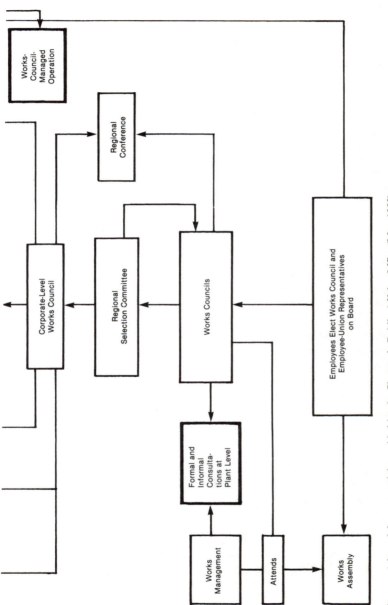

Source: Adapted from material provided by the Siemens's Public Affairs Office (May 1980).

Figure 5-6. Siemens Works-Council and Industrial-Relations Structure, 1978

Table 5-2
Profile of Siemens Works Council, 1968

Age: Over 40		75%
Sex: 84% male (64% of work force male)		
Education		
More than 8 years primary school		75
Completed university or postsecondary training		9
Training		
Skilled workers or employees		51
Semiskilled workers or employees		20
In-house or external vocational training program (beyond apprentice training) completed		23
Employment longevity		
Joined company before 1945 (at least 23 years tenure)		28
Joined company 1945-1955		45
Joined company 1956-1965		27
Career		
Promoted to supervisory position		21
Promoted from hourly worker to salaried employee		10
Employment status		
Workers (hourly employees)		62
Unskilled or semiskilled	13	
Skilled	49	
Masters	3	3
Salaried employees		38
Technical assignments	14	
General administrative assignments	15	
Specialists	6	
Tenure as works-council member		
More than 8 years		29
New member (elected in 1965)		33
Full-time works-council members		11
Union membership of works council (1965-1968)		81
Percentage of newly elected works-council members in 1968 who did not belong to a union		41

Source: Friedrich Fürstenberg, *Die Anwendung des Betriebsverfassungsgesetzes in Hause Siemens*, Siemens A.G. (Munich 1970), p. 11.

[a]The uncharacteristically large percentage of works-council members with less than 10 years longevity was a consequence of the rapid growth of the enterprise during the late 1950s and 1960s.

Table 5-3
Question: What Qualities Should a Works-Council Candidate Possess?

	Work	Answers From Works-Council Member Interviewed	Plant Management
Personal qualities			
Generally good character	33%	56%	50%
Strong social conscience	30	18	3
Skilled in human relations	20	7	15
Leadership qualities	9	6	12
Intelligence	6	9	20
Political convictions		2	
No personal qualities necessary	2	2	
Substantive qualities			
Professional skills	11	53	41
Appropriate training (for works council)	27	22	23
Works experience	45	7	27
Union membership	3	13	1
Member of certain crafts	5	1	
No substantive qualities necessary	9	4	8

Source: Adapted from Fürstenberg, *Die Anwendung*, p. 13.

According to these answers, the works council serves both as a social-welfare agency and a tool of worker participation. There is no evidence that this attitude toward the works council has changed over the last twelve years.

Works-council members were also questioned on their relations with the union; 75 percent expected primarily training and information from the I.G. Metall, while only 15 percent awaited active policy guidance.

Work-force and works-council members were asked to evaluate works-council activities (table 5-5). The table shows that the works management assessed the effectiveness of the works council even higher than did the latter's members. The work force, though generally favorably inclined toward the works council, was much less enthusiastic over its activities. Industrial-democracy advocates interpret the lack of enthusiasm as a consequence of the integration of works council and personnel department, but a more reasonable interpretation might be that a well-established, smoothly working institution may be taken for granted.

Table 5-4

Question: How Do You Judge the Personal Cooperation between Your Works-Council Member and . . .

	Good	Adequate	Bad	No Answer or Not Applicable or Don't Know
Answers of employees surveyed				
. . . Your works management	36	17	7	40
. . . Your immediate boss	31	13	9	47
Answers of works-council members interviewed				
. . . Your works management	65	22	11	1
. . . Your personnel section	58	25	6	11
. . . Your immediate boss	53	25	21	1
Answers of interviewed works managers				
. . . Your works management	93	6	1	0
. . . Your personnel section	69	13	3	15
. . . Your immediate boss	66	30	1	3

Source: Adapted from Fürstenberg, *Die Anwendung*, p. 18.

How little the individual employee is affected by the works council is shown by the next question addressed to the work force: "Have you ever asked the works council for help or advice?" Seventy-four percent answered "no." Similarly when employees were asked, "Have you ever had the opportunity to discuss with someone in the works personal or substantive difficulties?" only 5 percent mentioned the works council, 54 percent a superior, and 12 percent colleagues. (It is the opinion of employment specialists at Schenectady's General Electric Company that a much larger percentage of American employees would have chosen colleagues.)

Employees questioned about whether they would obtain help from the house of Siemens if they had run into difficulties gave the company a rousing vote of confidence by answering overwhelmingly in the affirmative (table 5-6). Similarly impressive is the answer to the question, "Do you have the impression that the works management pays attention to the opinion of the employee?" The answers of the employees are presented in table 5-7.

The answers to the questions posed by the survey team show a high degree of social integration of individual employees and an effective cooperation between works council and works management. The general decentralization policy followed by Siemens management has provided the framework for effective works management-works-council relations within the overall guidelines set by top management. The close personal relations

Table 5-5
Question: How Do You Judge the Activities of the Works Councils?

	Workers	Salaried Employees	Total
Work-force rating			
Good	40%	30%	37%
Satisfactory	26	32	28
Not satisfactory	12	13	12
No opinion	22	25	23
Works-council members' rating			
Good	74%	76%	74%
Satisfactory	25	22	24
No opinion	1	2	2
Works-management rating			
Good	80%		
Satisfactory	18		
No opinion	2		

Source: Adapted from Fürstenberg, *Die Anwendung,* p. 21.

between managers and key professional works-council members created even in 1968 the danger of bureaucratization and even the formation of oligarchies at various levels. These trends that Fürstenberg noted were strengthened by the 1972 works council act. On the other hand even Siemens has been affected by Germany's recent deteriorating union-management relations, and the political fragmentation of the works council may have rekindled a certain adversary relationship between personnel departments and works councils. Fürstenberg stated in 1968 that a precondition for the successful operation of the works councils was the absence of strong union-management conflict. In 1978 the relationship between I.G. Metall and the employer associations had become antagonistic, although by 1979 some improvement in the overall union-management relations on the macrolevel could be noted.

The DGB unions, however, strongly opposed management's attempts to weaken provisions of the 1976 codetermination law through changes in the corporation charter. In the spring of 1979 I.G. Metal chose to challenge Siemen's charter revisions before the courts in a model suit (*Musterprozess;* the closest American equivalent would be a class-action suit). The fact that the I.G. Metall chose Siemens as the object of its suit had been interpreted as an indication of the existing animosity between I.G. Metal leadership and Siemen's top management.[40] Both company and union officially reject this view.

Table 5-6
Question: Would You Obtain Help from Siemens?

Yes	74%
Would not ask for help	2
Don't know	14
No	10

Source: Adapted from Fürstenberg, *Die Anwendung*, p. 26.

Siemens proceeded along two different paths to cope with the 1976 legislation. First, it reinterpreted (or revised) its charter to assure that the second vice-chairman of the supervisory board who is elected by the entire board had to be a stockholder representative (this issue was mute before 1978, since employees selected only one-third of the supervisory board). The second vice-chairman, together with the chairman and the first vice-chairman elected by the employee and union members of the board, form the executive committee (*Präsidium*), thus giving shareholders a two-to-one majority in this forum. Siemens is the only German company with two vice-chairmen. Second, Siemens's supervisory board changed its procedural rules (*Geschäftsordnung*) to give the board chairman the opportunity to cast his double vote on all board committees when necessary.

On January 16, 1980, the Munich district court (*Landesgericht*) rejected the plaintiff's challenge to Siemens' charter and procedural rules. The court upheld specifically the charter provision that gives the board chairman a double vote on all board committees in case of a tie vote and rejected the contention that the executive committee had to consist of an equal number of employee-union, and stockholder representatives. (The plaintiffs, two I.G. Metall representatives on the Siemens board and one I.G. Metall functionary, had maintained that the chairman's tie-breaking double vote could only be used in meetings of the full board.) The court, however, did strike down Siemens' charter provision that reserved the second vice-chairman position for stockholder representatives. Both parties appealed the decision;

Table 5-7
Question: Is Management Sensitive to Employee Opinion?

Yes, very sensitive	55%
In certain cases	30
No	13
No opinion	2

Source: Adapted from Fürstenberg, *Die Anwendung*, p. 27.

it is expected that the next court session will take place in the late fall of 1980.[41]

Inspite of the court case, Siemens management and works councils have been able to maintain their cooperative relationship in most, but not all, forums. The decades of skillful adaption to the codetermination laws should enable the house of Siemens to continue its exemplary employee relations even during a period of revived union militancy and impaired cooperation on the supervisory board.

Notes

1. VW, the epitome of the German *Wirtschaftswunder*, owes its existence to two Austrians, Adolf Hitler, who conceived the idea of a "people's car," and the legendary engineer, Ferdinand Porsche, who designed the "bug."

2. One of the major stockholders is the labor-union-owned Bank für Gemeinwirtschaft. Its representative on the supervisory board, Walter Hesselbach, has voted with the seven employee-union members, giving the union-Socialist bloc a twelve-to-nine majority. In 1977 Hesselbach became the CEO of the BGAG (Beteiligungsgesellschaft für Gemeinwirtschaft, A.G.), the fully DGB-owned conglomerate, which controls DM 2.2 billion of assets.

3. In January 1976 the Socialist-Liberal state government of Lower Saxony was defeated and replaced by the Conservatives. The new minority government has been represented on the VW board since April 1976. Since the Conservatives needed the support of Liberals, its representatives played a low-key role. In June 1977, the VW supervisory board was restructured in line with the codetermination law of 1976, one full year before the deadline. On the new board, the union-employee delegation, if supported by the vote of the union-owned bank representative, has a majority.

4. The paternalistic Nordhoff pioneered in developing exemplary benefits in the 1960s. VW was the first, for instance, to grant not only four weeks paid vacations but also supplied its workers with an additional vacation pay (*Urlaubsgeld*). Today many large companies, including Siemens, follow the same procedure.

5. Though VW total sales in Germany peaked in 1970, its market share had been dropping from almost 45 percent in 1960, to 33 percent in 1968, and to 26 percent in 1972. Since then it recovered again and reached almost 31 percent in 1974, and has been around 30 percent ever since. It reached 33 percent in the first half of the 1979. *Frankfurter Allgemeine Zeitung*, 5 July 1979, p. 13 (hereafter cited as *FAZ*).

6. The VW beetle is still produced by VW-Mexico but can be purchased outside of South America only with great difficulty.

7. Actually VW owned only 60 percent of Audi-NSU in 1969, but slowly increased its share to 75 percent, and finally purchased the remaining 25 percent in 1970 for DM 500 million. There had been much criticism of this transaction, which seemed to have been motivated by a surplus of ready cash and trouble with independent stockholders.

8. The abrupt dismissal of a CEO is a very rare event in Germany; Lotz's dismissal is still a controversial subject matter.

9. For comparison purposes it is best to value the mark at thirty-three cents for the period 1968-1975 and at forty cents for the period 1976-1978. This seems to correspond to its purchasing power, regardless of the widely fluctuating mark-to-dollar exchange rates, which have been at less than two-to-one for the last four months of 1978 and throughout 1979.

10. VW wage costs have exceeded the metal industry average by about 14 percent during the last ten years. In 1969 and 1970 the VW differential rose to 17 percent and 23 percent, respectively.

11. Kurt H. Biedenkopf et al. *Mitbestimmung im Unternehmen,* Parliamentary Report, Bonn, 1970, p. 36. The Biedenkopf report uses the German term Willensbildung, for which no good English translation exists. "Corporate policy formulation" comes closest but is too awkward; hence my translation is "decision-making process."

12. Ibid., p. 126.

13. In 1970 a VW sold for $3,000 and earned almost DM 11,000. By 1972 after the mark revaluation, the same $3,000 earned about DM 10,000. This dropped to DM 7,500 after the dollar devaluation and to DM 6,900 in March 1975. It is fairly certain that in the first half of 1975 VW lost money on every car sold in the United States if the car were valued at average costs. VW's U.S. dealers talked of a DM 10 million loss from the sale of 53,000 Rabbits. *Wirtschaftswoche* 18 July 1975, p. 60.

14. Socialist Helmut Greulich, who represented the state of Lower Saxony on the VW board of directors until 1976, actually carried the title minister of social affairs, but his assignment was comparable to the head of the state labor department in New York or California.

15. The small cars, Audi 50 and its VW version, Polo, have not been sold in the United States so far, but the sale of Audi 80 and especially the Golf (Rabbit) did extremely well in early 1975. By the summer of 1975, VW sales began to drop again, however, and total sales for 1975 amounted to only 267,000 units, 53 percent of the 1970 high of 569,000. Sales recovered substantially between 1977 and 1979.

16. The layoff of excess production workers in Germany cost VW several hundred million marks according to Schmuecker, since German firms are required by law to make layoff payments. The average total employment during 1975 was 118,000 for VW-Germany.

17. Point four of the VW charter has been changed to extend the super-

visory board's control over investments. *Report for the Year 1976* (3 May 1977), p. 4.

18. "The Japanese Threaten," *FAZ*, 29 March 1979, p. 12.

19. See *FAZ*, 5 July 1979, p. 13.

20. See Alfred D. Chandler, *Strategy and Structure* (Garden City, N.Y.: Doubleday & Company, Anchor Books edition, 1966), chap. 2.

21. Heidelberg University was terrorized by radical Marxists during the late 1960s and early 1970s. The most famous group of ultras, the Heidelberg "patient collective" (the name is an allusion to the "sick capitalistic world"), has become the breeding ground for terrorist gangs. The universities of Heidelberg, Frankfurt, and Berlin have supplied the cadres for both the German terrorist scene and the K-groups, which have been infiltrating industry.

22. In a note to the author, a BASF codetermination specialist maintained that "it is incorrect [to assume] that remarkably many Communists are active in BASF's Ludwigshafen works, or that they influence its [political] atmosphere. There are, however, within the I.G. Chemie functionaries who represent ideological tendencies which please the Communists." This statement still leaves the question open why a major mainstream German union, historically closely associated with the reformistic trade-union wing of the Social Democratic party, develops functionaries whose ideological posturing pleases Communists. This question becomes even more intriguing if we consider that Ludwigshafen-Mannheim, with a conservative Catholic population, is located in the deeply Catholic, Rhineland-Palatinate region, the heartland of the CDU.

23. In 1925 Germany's three leading chemical (dye) companies, BASF, Bayer, and Hoechst, were merged into the giant trust I.G. Farben, at least partially in response to protective U.S. policies. I.G. Farben was dissolved in 1945 by the Allies, and its original components were reconstituted in 1952. Today each one of its successors is larger in terms of sales or capital invested, measured in 1932 marks, than I.G. Farben was at its peak.

24. Residents of Schenectady, New York, and other company towns have expressed similar attitudes. The hourly workers among GE's thirty thousand employees have managed to be simultaneously proud and loyal employees and strong supporters of the militant social-democratic International Union of Electrical Workers, or (IUE). In the November 1978 IUE election, the mainstream local officers were opposed unsuccessfully by an opposition more to the left and even by a "Revolutionary Worker" group, a Maoist group that obtained fewer than 50 votes. The main difference is that the press did not cover the election campaign closely and has ignored the Schenectady radical unionists.

25. See *Die Zeit*, 7 September 1979, p. 20. The German version of the FBI (*Bundesverfassungsschutz*) routinely monitors works-council elections and activities and reports on the extent of subversive activities.

26. Often former student militants were helped in their decision by their

inability to get better jobs. Since West German universities still permit their students the feudal privilege of "not studying," many radical students who have been matriculated for many years have never obtained their degrees. Moreover, a high percentage of left-wing students who did complete their studies majored in sociology and political science, subjects in which German students receive inferior training. It is not surprising, therefore, that the universities graduated many more social scientists than industry could accommodate.

27. During the spring 1978 elections, the RGO also won works-council seats in the Berlin Siemens works (primarily through the votes of the foreign guest workers whom the RGO courted), and about a half-dozen other plants of major manufacturers. The RGO obtained 34 percent of the workers' vote at the steel manufacturer, Hoesch Union, in Dortmund.

28. See *Die Rheinpfalz*, 17, 19 December 1977; *Mannheimer Morgen*, 17 December 1977.

29. *Mannheimer Morgen*, 9 May 1978.

30. *BASF Menschen, Arbeit, Geschäft, 1977* (Ludwigshafen: BASF A.G., 1978), p. 22 (my translation).

31. Ibid.

32. Ibid., pp. 22, 23 (my translation).

33. Ibid., p. 10.

34. Ibid., p. 12.

35. In the 1979 list of West Germany's One hundred largest corporations, Siemens ranked second, with 1978 sales of DM 29 billion and a worldwide work force of 304,000. The steel-coal-chemical conglomerate VEBA is number one, with DM 31 billion sales. *FAZ*, 1 September 1979, p. 13.

36. In a 2 January 1979 memorandum to me, a Siemens personnel manager noted that Siemens has "no trade-union membership statistics" but estimates that 40 to 50 percent of the workers and 10 to 15 percent of the clerical employees are I.G. Metall members.

37. See Friedrich Fürstenberg, *Die Anwendung des Betriebsverfassungsgesetzes im Hause Siemens* [The application of the works legislation in the house of Siemens] (Munich: Siemens A.G., Personnel Department, 1970), pp. 9, 10 (hereafter cited as *Fürstenberg*). In addition to the interviews and surveys, Fürstenberg and his team examined minutes of meetings between works councils and works management for the period 1958-1967 at three different locations.

38. In the 1975 election the I.G. Metall won 80 percent of the works-council seats but only 76 percent in 1978. About 50 percent of the eligible votes were cast in each election.

The relationship among the I.G. Metall, rival unions, and independents was clearly expressed by the January 1978 supervisory board elections. Of the three trade-union seats, the I.G. Metall won two, the rival DAG one, with a 2,697-to-1,003 electoral vote ratio. The I.G. Metall won all four worker (hourly employee) seats with a smashing electoral vote of 1,874 to 56 but won only one out of the two employee seats with 823 electoral votes versus 627 electoral votes for nonunion independents, 326 electoral votes for the DAG, and 11 votes for splinter groups. It is difficult to predict whether I.G. Metall external functionaries and internal employee representatives will vote as a unit but one can expect that the Siemens board will lose its homogeneous nature.

39. *Fürstenberg*, p. 11.

40. "Musterprozess der I.G. Metall gegen Siemens," *FAZ*, 21 March 1979, p. 11. See also the editorial in *Handelsblatt*, 22 March 1979, p. 2. Actually the I.G. Metall did not appear as the plaintiff but acted through several union officials, either in their capacity as shareholders or as board directors.

41. Details of the court case have been made available to the author by Mr. Werner Osel of Siemens's public information office.

6

The Development of Union-Management Codetermination in Sweden

Swedish labor-management relations have attracted the attention of North American academicians, journalists, and labor-relations specialists for several decades. During the past ten years, however, the perception of Swedish conditions has lagged consistently behind reality. Few American managers were aware of the sharply deteriorating employer-trade union relations in the early and mid-1970s, and even fewer realized that industrial relations improved once more during the late 1970s. The moderate wage settlements of 1977, 1978, and 1979 played a major role in reducing Swedish inflation. Still, collective bargaining's sociopolitical environment has been changed so drastically since 1945 that Sweden may no longer fit the description of a capitalist society.

Renowned Harvard economist Joseph Schumpeter believed that the very success of capitalism in raising the standard of living weakens the institutions necessary for its survival. Ultimately capitalism will be replaced gradually by a highly bureaucratic and centralized, though democratic, form of socialism, which will exploit the productive capacity that had been created by corporate enterprise.[1] Sweden may very well be the outstanding example of the Schumpeterian thesis, which certainly was not impaired by the election of bourgeois governments in 1976 and 1979.

Until the 1970s, legislation had played a much smaller role in shaping labor relations in Scandinavia than in Germany or the United States. Once collective bargaining had become well established in the early 1930s, both unions and employers made every effort to keep the government from restricting their freedom to negotiate. But in the 1970s, and especially during the last years of the Palme administration (1973-1976), union and employer federations frequently failed to agree on a series of new union demands. Government legislation has given the trade-union leadership what they could not obtain at the bargaining table (table 6-1).

In the early 1920s, the Scandinavian labor movements showed some interest in establishing works councils, and especially the Norwegian and Danish unions proposed unsuccessfully legislation to extend industrial democracy along the lines laid down in the Weimar constitution.[2] During

An earlier version of this chapter appeared as "Union-Management 'Codetermination' in Sweden" in the *Journal of Social and Political Studies*, Vol. 4, No. 2, Summer, 1979, pp. 147-173. The material has been brought up to date and included in this book with the kind permission of the editors of the *Journal of Social and Political Studies*.

Table 6-1
Important Events in Swedish Labor-Relations History

1889	Swedish Labor Federation (*Landsorganisationen i Sverige, LO*) founded; originally consisting of crafts unions, LO adopted industrial organization in 1912.
1902	Swedish Employers' Confederation (*Svenska arbetsgivareföreningen*) founded. Mostly relatively small businesses; comparatively little political influence; government hands-off policy established early.
1906[a]	LO and SAF agree on management prerogatives and on workers' right to organize. Henceforth every collective-bargaining agreement contains a clause reemphasizing employers' right to hire, fire, and allocate work, and establishes nonunion shop; this clause, now called article 32, was included as article 23 in the SAF statutes in 1905. In return for LO's acceptance of article 23, the SAF recognized the workers' right to organize and bargain collectively. The 1906 agreement determined Swedish labor legislation until the 1970s.
1909	General strike called by LO and lost.
1920	Mediation Act. Established government mediation service, available on demand.
1928[a]	Collective Agreements Act and Labor Court Act are passed over strong union opposition. Resembling the Taft-Hartley Act, the Collective Agreements Act required the union to live up to the agreements made and, in turn, forced employers to abide by collective-bargaining contracts. Disputes over interpretation were to be adjudicated before Labor Court. Under the peace obligation of this act, no strike or lock-out could be called during the existence of agreement. The Labor Court, similar to the German model, was comprised of two labor and two employer members and three labor court judges; actually little used.
1936	Act on the Right of Association and Collective Bargaining. A Wagner Act type of legislation, it was enacted by the Social Democratic government primarily to help the white-collar workers to organize.
1938[a]	Basic Agreement between LO and SAF (also called *Staltsjöbaden* agreement after resort where this document was negotiated) to pledge themselves to strive for peaceful cooperation. Forestalled government action to regulate labor relations and prohibit strikes that threaten national interest. Expressed forcefully the LO-SAF view that "the State cannot be justified . . . in forcing upon Swedish employers and workers a regulation of working conditions." In return, both parties pledged themselves to "be responsible" and consider national interest. The Basic Agreement epitomized Swedish labor-management relations until 1976.
1943	Confederation of Swedish Professional Associations founded (*Sveriges akademikers centralorganisation, SACO*). Politically neutral.
1944	Confederation of white-collar unions (*Tjänstemannens centralorganisation, TCO*). Social-democratic federation of white-collar unions; jurisdiction today overlaps both LO and SACO. Organized with sections dealing with government (TCO-S), municipal (TCO-K), and private employers (PTK). PTK, federation of salaried employees, represents today also some SACO unions in industry-wide negotiations.

1946	Works-council legislation. Enabled unions, if they so desired, to negotiate the establishment of advisory works councils. Little interest in works councils among union leadership.
1956	Solidarity wages policy adopted explicitly in LO-SAF national wage agreement; remains as guideline for centralized LO-SAF wage negotiations during the next twenty years.
1966	Civil servants obtain right to strike; applies to municipal and national government.
1969-1970	Wave of wildcat strikes against union-employer wage policy; often by skilled workers, professionals, to protest narrowed wage differentials.
1970	Beginning of fundamental shift in LO policy and consequent abandonment of Basic Agreement. LO obtains through government legislation rights previously reserved to management.
1971	Strike by SACO-SR (SACO federated union of high government and military employees) broken by government legislation, ordering employees back to work.
1972	Experimental law providing for union representation on board of directors. Amended in 1973; two representatives chosen by unions on all boards of firms having more than 100 employees.
1974	Act on Security of Employment; sharply restricts employer's right to fire set forth in Basic Agreement. Also applies to municipalities and government.
1976[a]	Right of Employees to Collective Agreements on Participation in Decision-Making. Nullifies article 32 of SAF statutes, adopted as basic agreement by LO-SAF in 1906 and 1938, and also replaces the fundamental labor laws of 1928 (Collective Contracts Act) and 1936 (Act on the Right of Association and Collective Bargaining). Makes all aspects of management decision-making negotiable. Sets minimum limits of union codecision-making rights in absence of collective agreement. Greatly increased union power in plant and office. Became effective 1 January 1977.

[a]Especially significant legislation.

the early 1930s Social Democratic parties came to power in Norway, Sweden, and Denmark, and although they have dominated Scandinavian politics ever since, or at least until 1976, they have shown little interest in establishing works councils.[3]

Under the benevolent neutrality of the Social Democratic government, the Swedish trade unions' policy of relying on industry-wide collective bargaining had become the most effective device to advance the interests of Scandinavian workers. Consequently the pragmatic Swedish trade unions became the most influential force in molding Scandinavian labor strategy, at least until the early 1970s.

Collective Bargaining on the National Level, 1933-1970

In Sweden, labor relations and wage negotiations had been dominated for over forty years by an alliance of big business and big labor, which had been institutionalized in the macrocollective bargaining between the Swedish Employers Association (SAF) and the Confederation of Trade Unions (LO). Until 1975 the Swedish federation of white-collar unions (Central Organization of Salaried Employees, or TCO) has generally followed the labor-market policy advocated by the LO, while the Confederation of Professional Associations (SACO), the only federation not closely tied to the Social Democratic party, has been politically too weak to affect the long-run egalitarian trend of Swedish wage negotiations, although the counter-revolution began with a strike of SACO unions against the government in 1971, and again in 1975.[4]

The 1971 strike was defeated by the Social Democratic government, which passed legislation ordering the strikers back to work. The TCO members, and the Swedish middle class generally, sympathized with SACO's strikes against Sweden's egalitarian wage policy, and several TCO-PTK (civil-service) unions joined briefly in the SACO walkout. The fact that the TCO managed to keep its membership in line, however, demonstrates the docility of individual union members and of the local union leaders.

The local trade unions and employer associations, organized along parallel industrial lines, are under the complete control of the national organizations, which in turn have ceded much of their authority to quasi-corporate bodies, the SAF and the LO, called "roof organizations" by the Swedes. Since 1956 the SAF and LO have concluded nationwide agreements that promoted uniform wage development and served as a framework for subsequent industry-wide bargaining. If the various national unions and employer associations have comparatively little voice, the individual employee or employer has none. Swedish social institutions in general prefer to deal with the group and its leadership rather than the individual, and the labor legislation of the 1970s very explicitly favored the organization rather than the individual.[5]

The Swedish trade-union federation had used the centralized negotiations as its major tool to implement its social and wage policies. Known as the solidarity wages policy, the LO has successfully narrowed pay differentials among industries and within firms since 1951.[6] The long-run goal of the LO leadership, however, has not only been to equalize income but also to change the economic nature of Swedish society.

Although the LO wage policy has remained constant for over twenty-five years, at different times different economic and political models have provided different arguments in its support. From the days of the first Social Democratic prime minister, Hjalmar Branting, to the latest Olof Palme, the theory of functional socialism has provided both the long-run ideological goals and the justification for short-run class cooperation.[7] This peculiar Swedish mixture of ideology and pragmatism has kept both Marxist intellectuals and practical labor leaders in one party, in spite of the constant tensions that have existed between these two interest groups.

The functional-socialism doctrine grew out of the investigations of a committee, appointed by Branting in 1933, to consider socializing the means of production. The committee took a sophisticated institutional view of property relations and found that ownership was not important, since it was not necessarily related to control.[8] Through legislation and fiscal and monetary policy, the Social Democratic government could acquire the functions that traditionally had been reserved to the owners of capital. The term *socialism* was broadly redefined as a "political-economic policy carried out in the interest of the masses."

Although the Scandinavian Social Democratic parties have accepted the doctrines of functional socialism since the 1930s, for a long time their actual quasi-Keynesian policies had been quite indistinguishable from those of the American Democrats.[9] Until the 1970s, functional socialism differed little, if at all, from the liberal, reformistic policies followed by most governments in North America, Australia, and Central Europe. During the late 1960s and early 1970s, however, functional socialism did provide the platform to express the increasingly radical and egalitarian sentiments of the LO and party leadership.[10]

In the 1950s the LO's solidarity wage policy was designed to accomplish two pragmatic goals: end the government's incomes policy imposed during the war, together with the remnants of the direct wage and price controls of the 1940s, and keep Sweden's economy internationally competitive by preventing excessive internal wage increases as a consequence of the world economy's Korean War inflation. The employers endorsed the LO's goal enthusiastically because it promised to end government interference. By

1954 Swedish Parliament and Swedish society had accepted the idea that "the government should not intervene in wage formation."[11]

In return for the SAF's support of the LO's solidarity wage policy, the union leadership reaffirmed once more its acceptance of article 32 of the Swedish Employers' Federation, which defined the nonnegotiable management prerogatives. The LO's willingness to exclude from collective bargaining all topics pertaining to management's right to hire, fire, direct, and allocate work was the price it had had to pay for gaining management's recognition in the basic agreement of 1938 and to obtain the SAF's help in ending the government's incomes policy in 1954.

Solidarity Wages Policy and Structure of Swedish Industry in the 1970s

During the 1960s the LO's solidarity wages policy had the primary goal of prompting structural changes in the Swedish economy by eliminating small, internationally noncompetitive firms and encouraging the migration of labor into the export-producing sector of the economy. The SAF, in which the large, internationally known firms dominated, offered little resistance to the LO's program and may even have drawn short-run benefits from it. The by-product of this policy led to the further centralization of wage negotiations and consequently strengthened the LO and SAF headquarter's bureaucracy.[12] The solidarity wages policy successfully accomplished its purpose of restructuring industry in the 1960s and probably was responsible for both the success of the Swedish economy during that decade and the crises of the mid- and late 1970s. In the 1970s, however, the solidarity wages policy seemed to serve primarily ideological purposes since the LO demanded once more the reduction of the already narrow differentials among professional, skilled, and unskilled labor. Belatedly the SAF began to object to the further extension of the LO wages policy and in addition decided at last to resist numerous new LO demands that would have weakened management prerogatives severely. At this point a virtual revolution occurred in Swedish labor-management relations. The LO abandoned its acceptance of article 32 as the basis of union-management relations, discontinued its decades-old working arrangement with the SAF, and gained the help of the government in obtaining its demands through a series of unprecedented labor laws, which are enumerated in table 6-2.

Swedish employers, the spokesmen of the so-called bourgeoisie parties, and foreign observers have held the radicalization of Swedish labor and SDP party leaders responsible for this sudden change in LO policy.[13] It is difficult to accept this viewpoint, however, since the LO adopted the solidarity wages policy in 1951 merely as a component of a carefully laid-out program that was designed to lead to an egalitarian, socialist society—a

Table 6-2
Recent Swedish Labor Laws

1972	Act Concerning Employee (union) Representation on Board of Directors: Entitles union to choose two representatives for board of directors.
1974	Security of Employment Act: Increases difficulty of dismissing or laying off employees.
1974	Promotion of Employment Act: Supplements the Secuirty Act and provides for consultation with municipal and regional authorities in case of large-scale layoffs.
1974	Act Concerning Status of Shop Steward: Legalizes existing LO-SAF agreements but makes the position of shop steward very secure.
1976	Amendment to Worker's Protection Act of 1949: Strengthens the influence exerted by employees on the design of the work place. Gives employees priority of interpretation of collective-bargaining agreement (in case of controversy, employees' views prevail until courts or arbitrators decide case).
1976	Act on Employee Participation in Decision Making.
1977	Working Environment Act: Replaces Worker Protection Act of 1949, considered as a framework for further regulation of working environment by National Board of Occupational Safety and Health and through collective-bargaining agreements. Extends definition of working environment to social and technical development in society.

socialist society, however, that was to be dominated by the labor union and its leadership rather than by the functionaries of a Social Democratic government. The LO bureaucracy, which negotiated wage settlements in line with the pragmatic, short-run goals advanced through the 1950s and 1960s hardly cared that its policies were merely an aspect of functional socialism. The intelligentsia in the LO and SDP, however, have recognized that the "total result of all these changes at the micro level would ultimately lead to a drastic transformation in the economic life of the country."[14]

Rehn Model

This transformation in the economic life of the country was the goal of the economic policy adopted by the LO in 1951 in its Trade Union and Full Employment (TUFE) statement.[15] This statement in turn was based upon an economic-growth model developed by the LO economist Gösta Rehn during the 1950s.[16] The Swedish economy, Rehn postulated, consisted of two different sectors: manufacturing export industries, subject to international competition and hence comprising large-scale, efficient, profitable, capital-intensive enterprises, and domestic service industries (including agriculture), which were generally labor intensive, protected from foreign competition, and hence less efficient, and also less profitable. In order to maintain full employment at the weakest segments of the Swedish economy,

orthodox Keynesian policy would have required an inflationary level of effective aggregate demand, with very high wages and profits in the export
sector, and hence, Rehn feared, an ultimate revival of an incomes policy
that eventually would lead to the demise of the labor movement. In order to
maintain full employment, price stability, and free collective bargaining,
the solidarity wages policy proposed to reduce the wage differences among
and within industries but set the level sufficiently high to eliminate the
smaller firms in the domestic sector that could not carry the costs of the national agreements. The Rehn model is quite compatible with Marx's model
of a two-sector producer and consumer-goods economy and would promote
through union-wage policies the transformation of prices into values, as
well as the equalization of profits that Marx postulated.[17]

The SAF, dominated by big business, had been a willing partner in the
implementation of the LO wages policy. Consequently industries in which
small firms dominated, such as textiles, clothing, and footwear, were
especially hard hit by this structural policy, which did encourage a shift in
the labor force and in capital investment toward large-scale, capital-
intensive, bureaucratic enterprises.

The solidarity wages policy and the restructuring of the economy were
only two components of both the Rehn model and the TUFE program. A
sharp increase in indirect taxation was also advocated, and implemented by
SDP governments, in order to reduce the extra purchasing power gained by
the high wage policy. Moreover, Rehn postulated, a high level of indirect
taxation would prevent industry from escaping increased wage costs
through price increases. In the short run, increased unit costs would—and
did—prompt Swedish industry to increase its efficiency by rationalization,
but in the long run it would make it more and more difficult for Swedish industry to generate future investment funds out of retained earnings. A
fourth component of the Rehn model, therefore, was the development of a
public-sector investment fund as the primary source of the capital needs of
Swedish industry. Moreover the collective public-sector savings were supposed to reduce an unequal income distribution and increase the government's control over the economy.[18] In fact the government-controlled national pension schemes, introduced by the SDP governments in 1958 and
1964, have become the major source of public-sector investment capital.[19]
By 1970 the National Pension Fund supplied about 40 percent of available
investment credit.[20]

The profit squeeze on Swedish industry became noticeable in the 1960s,
but its consequence, in the short run at least, was masked by the ready
availability of public-sector investment funds during a global period of
economic growth. In my opinion, the separation of investment decision
from actual enterprise profitability and future profit expectation has been
responsible for the enormous overcapacity of Swedish industry in the mid-

and late 1970s and the painful shrinking process of disinvestment that the non-Socialist governments have been forced to undertake since 1976.[21]

Sweden's functional socialism had disdained nationalization as unnecessary; during the 1970s, however, both Socialist and non-Socialist governments have been forced to take over, fully or partially, large firms in the shipbuilding, mining, and steel industries to avoid bankruptcy of the overexpanded firms. The state-owned NJA steel works has been absorbing formerly privately owned firms, and in November 1977 the non-Socialist government became half owner of a new steel conglomerate, Svenskt Staal AB. The large shipbuilding firm, Kockum, was nationalized in March 1979 and incorporated into the state-owned Svenska Varv, whose losses were 2.6 billion kronen (about $500 million) in 1977 and 2.1 billion kronen in 1978. In August 1979, several large steel wholesalers were purchased by Svenskt Staal since the company "could not operate profitably without its own sales organization."[22]

Sweden's low unemployment figures mask a sizable underemployment: "Around 70,000 Swedes are registered as unemployed, 170,000 are employed in retraining, public relief work, etc. . . . . In addition 50-60,000 people threatened with lay-offs are kept on . . . subsidised by the government."[23] By February 1978, unemployment increased by another 40,000. Swedish unemployment has been a relatively low 2.5 to 2.7 percent (equal to about 4.0 to 4.2 percent by the American definition), but hidden unemployment, about 4 percent by early 1978, reached about 6 percent by fall 1978, accompanied by an inflation rate of over 14 percent, and dropped back to 5 percent during 1979. The high 1979-1980 budget deficit, close to 12 percent of the GNP or 25 percent of total expenditures, should increase inflation, especially since oil-price increases had not been fully passed on to consumers by June 1980. Swedish nationalization thus is a consequence not of ideology but of living beyond its means during the first half of the 1970s; during that time wages increased by 40 percent and consumption grew at an average 2.4 percent, while the gross domestic product grew at less than 1.5 percent and investment dropped drastically.[24] The fact that the government has not been able to reduce expenditures in spite of an 1979-1980 interest burden equal to almost 4 percent of GNP (18 billion kronen) shows that the bourgeois governments have not been able to prevent Sweden from living beyond its means during the second half of the 1970s. (See figure 6-1.)

Swedish industry's inability to self-generate investment capital is being used as an argument by Socialist theoreticians and LO leaders to hasten the death of Swedish (Scandinavian) capitalism. Socialist theoreticians such as Mogens Lykketoft and Bö Södersten reason that the major historical purpose of capitalism has been its capability to generate capital. If Scandinavian capitalists can no longer perform this task, they say, they should be replaced by the trade-union federation in the management of the

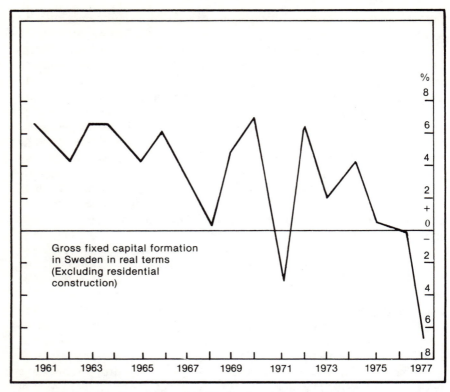

Source: Adapted from Boston Consulting Group, in *Economist*, 24 November 1979, p. 109.

Figure 6-1. The Decline in Swedish Investment

enterprise.[25] Although Scandinavian, and especially Swedish, labor unions had long opposed labor codetermination and profit sharing, the growing interest in the German experience among Europe's intellectuals prompted a reevaluation.[26]

Industrial Democracy

The lurch to the left in the Swedish Social Democratic party under Olof Palme has encouraged the rise of pseudo-Marxian rhetoric and the demand for broad popular participation in social decision making in Swedish society. The popularity of the former German chancellor Willy Brandt among Swedish intellectuals had led to a timely reevaluation of the German codetermination experience. The change in Swedish and Scandinavian perception of the German experience prompted the trade-union leadership to abandon their previous opposition to employee codetermination and to adopt the New Left rhetoric by extolling worker participation in economic decision making.[27] In the hands of the LO bureaucracy, however, worker participation became the domination of corporate decision making by national union functionaries.

The LO leadership's rather sudden interest in employee participation was not prompted only by the popularity of participatory democracy. There were also valid pragmatic reasons why the LO had to embark on a new strategy if it was to survive. In the 1950s the LO leadership had realized that functional socialism could develop in Sweden under Social Democratic rule into a government-dominated society with no place for strong unions. If Keynesian full-employment policies were accompanied by a tough incomes policy that would include price, wage, and profit control, trade unions would lose their reason for existence, as the Eastern European experience has demonstrated. The LO's answer to this threat had been the Rehn model, which made the unions rather than the government the vehicle for social change. By the 1970s "high wages, excellent social benefits and high taxes . . . reduced dramatically the marginal utility of wage increases."[28] If demands for further improvements in wages, benefits, and working conditions had lost their appeal, the LO was once more threatened with becoming an appendix to the Social Democratic party.

Prompted by both New Left rhetoric and fears for its survival, the LO leadership suddenly adopted the cause of industrial democracy and in the early 1970s repudiated its decades-old acceptance of SAF article 32, and demanded a larger voice in enterprise decision making for its members. Although the LO's press releases on codetermination emphasize the right of the employee or labor to share equally with the owners or capital in the management of the enterprise, any discussion of the implementation of the LO's version of codetermination showed clearly that only union functionaries would participate in the decision process. It is very important to keep this issue in mind, since the rhetoric of the socialist LO theoreticians may be misleading.[29]

The TCO congresses of 1970 and 1973 and the LO congress of 1971 provided the forum for launching the industrial-democracy issue. The LO adopted a working paper, "Democracy in Companies," which emphasized that "industrial democracy must be regarded as one part of the democratization of society as a whole."[30] Democracy was defined as the complete equality of labor and management "in all types of questions that employees are interested in."[31] Very much like German unions, the LO and TCO leadership considered the union as the appropriate representative of labor and the professional LO and TCO functionaries as the voice of the unions.

Unlike the Germans, however, the LO rarely discussed the actual implementation of employee participation—not in the proposals submitted to Parliament and certainly not in the journal articles cited, in which the concept but never the process of employee participation has been discussed. This cavalier treatment of the implementation of industrial democracy is especially significant if we compare it with German codetermination legislation. German law prescribes not only the election mechanism that chooses employee representatives in great detail but also the actual participatory structure. Even the German union federation leadership, which has demanded an increasing role in the codetermination process, has always included in its proposals a detailed presentation of the selection system, which afforts employees, at least theoretically, an opportunity to reject unpopular union candidates.

From the beginning, the Swedish unions have been ambivalent in their interpretation of industrial democracy. Whenever the concept was discussed, the official statements referred to employees or labor. But when actual implementations were considered, invariably local or national union officials were the hierarchically appointed instruments of the participatory workplace democracy.[32]

Union Codeterminatrion through Legislation

Since the union leadership recognized that the SAF would not agree to bargain collectively over work-place issues or accept the local union official as the personification of industrial democracy, LO and TCO abandoned their fifty-year-old strategy of relying on collective bargaining and called on the government to give them through legislation what they could not hope to obtain at the bargaining table. The 1971 LO report specifically called for legislation to abolish legal and institutional practices that had been created by labor's past acceptance of article 32 of the SAF constitution.

To complete this revolution, the 1971 LO Congress affirmed that, in principle, legislation is preferable to collective bargaining if it leads to faster results. Since labor through its unions would henceforth participate in managerial decision making, the employees had to obtain first-hand knowledge of economic issues and top-management decision making. The LO and TCO therefore revised their previous opposition to collaboration with management and demanded union representation on the boards of directors. The LO congresses even adopted the rhetoric of the German union leadership by referring to labor's right to share with capital in enterprise management.[33] (German unions used this phrase to demand equal board representation, defined as 50 percent of the seats; the LO Congress did not specify the exact share but implicitly demanded only minority representation.)

Several left-wing (pro-Communist) labor leaders still maintained the traditional Swedish trade-union view, which feared that the loyalty of individual members would be lost if the union attempted to maintain simultaneously its adversary position against management and participate in managerial decision making. The LO and TCO congresses rejected these views decisively, however. Since the minority view at these two congresses reflected not only the previous attitude of the Scandinavian labor-liberal-SDP coalition but also the views of most Western European and British trade unions, the decision of the Swedish LO and TCO leadership to demand a participatory role in decision making was striking, and it indicated the beginning of significant changes in European labor-management relations. In 1980 with the exception of Great Britain, only Communist unions and labor leaders still refuse to strive for codetermination. This does not mean that the Scandinavian, Benelux, and French unions have become more collaborationist; far from it. The socialist unions are striving for a gradual, although drastic, change in the existing industrial system, while the Communist unions typically cling to the orthodox sixty-year-old Leninist view of the revolutionary role of radical trade-union leaders.

Labor's new demand for industrial democracy was transmitted in 1971 to the Swedish Parliament by the Lo president, Arne Geijer, who was also a leading SDP member of Parliament. As a consequence, in December 1971 the SDP government appointed the Special Commission on Labor Law to study the democratization of the work place and suggest new legislation, which "should be based on the premise that questions connected with the right to direct work should be regulated in collective bargaining agreements.[34]

The labor law commission consisted of representatives of the governing Social Democrats, the three opposition parties (Liberals, Center, Conservatives), and the LO and the TCO. The minutes of law commission meetings show that the "bourgeois" party leaders were more worried about appearing "intransigent and reactionary" than interested in representing the electorate (the Conservatives shortly thereafter changed their name to Moderates). They also show and SDP leadership that is quite pragmatic and much less enthusiastic in the support of the LO-TCO position than would have been expected and an LO-TCO delegation with well-prepared maximum and "nonnegotiable" minimum demands, which does not hesitate to ally itself with the opposition parties on specific issues if its interests warrant it.

Generally the government representatives supported the LO-TCO contention that labor-union officials are the appropriate instruments of employee participation, while the bourgeois members of the commission attempted to reserve for individual employees some codetermination prerogatives along the lines of the German works-council legislation. On the other hand, the LO-TCO members gained, surprisingly, the support of the opposition members in their attempts to gain equal treatment of public- and private-sector employees. It was not quite clear from the minutes whether this position was taken merely to annoy the government or whether the bourgeois parties really believed that employee codetermination in the public sector might have a decentralizing effect on the Swedish bureaucracy. The possibility that union participation in the decision making of public agencies might encroach on the democratic process or the domain of elected officials seemed to worry the SDP more than the opposition members. On other questions, the socialist government was cast as the defender of management prerogatives. For instance, the trade-union representatives wanted to give local trade unions the "main priority of interpretation," which meant that in case of controversy, the union prevails until a decision is made by an arbitrator or labor court. The unions were supported on this issue by the Liberal and Center bourgeois parties but opposed by the SDP and Conservative party representatives.

The LO and TCO members of the labor law commission filed a thirty-point minority report, when the committee presented its findings to the Parliament. Both majority and minority, however, were equally determined to eliminate all legal and institutional obstacles to employee or, actually, union participation in managerial decisions that affect the work place and job security.

The most significant barrier to employee participation had been article 32 of the SAF constitution, which emphatically stated that allocation of work, hiring, promoting and firing, supervision, work environment, and similar areas were management prerogatives and must not be subject to collective bargaining. As a consequence, Swedish employees had considerably less control over their working conditions than did American and German workers, and Swedish shop stewards, even after the 1974 legislation, have played a much less significant role than their American counterparts. The government bill on employee participation in decision making submitted to Parliament therefore provided primarily a legal structure that nullified the SAF's article 32. In line with both minority and majority recommendations, the government bill contained a clause that created the foundation for the right of employees to participate in decisions concerning the work place. By design or accident, this particular clause turned out to be another "article 32," that is, article 32 of the new law on participation in decision making on the labor market. While the old article 32 of the SAF constitution had defined the management prerogatives, the new article 32 of the government bill stated:

The contracting parties to collective agreements on wages and general conditions of employment should, *if the employee side so requests,* also sign collective agreements on the right of employees to participate in decision-making on matters concerning the direction and allotment of work, the inception and termination of employment agreements or other management matters.

It is important for the understanding of this Swedish legislation to compare article 32 of the government bill with the original right-of-negotiation clause in the report of the labor legislation committee:

It is the duty of the employer to negotiate with his counterpart at the local level on all matters concerning the relationship between the employer and an employee who belongs to the trade union concerned. *This duty applies as soon as the trade union has requested negotiations. . . .* This proposed new right of negotiations applies to all matters which today are unilaterally determined by the employer. It is applicable both to individual cases and to matters of a more general nature, e.g., matters concerning production, business and management. The right of negotiations applies to matters at all levels in business enterprise and the public service.[35]

The original committee report specifically mentions the trade unions as the initiator and medium of employee participation, while the government bill refers to the employee side. The difference is merely rhetorical, however. Whenever the term *employee* is used, we ought to replace it by *union* or *union leadership* to provide the appropriate meaning.

During much of 1976, the Swedish middle class was becoming increasingly disillusioned by the SDP government. An ever-increasing tax burden, a high-handed, insolent bureaucracy that considered an attempt at tax avoidance a much more serious crime than mugging or robbery,[36] and a growing absentee rate among employees created a climate in which the radical rhetoric of the Palme government generated a strong opposition to any attempt to weaken further the last remaining bastions of the bourgeoisie.[37] Moreover, the growing purge of non-Socialists in key ministries and the promotion of loyal Socialists to university chairs turned even the vacillating Liberals into opponents. The proposed act of employee participation therefore became more controversial outside Parliament than inside. The lack of any particular grass-roots movement in favor of codetermination and the widespread misgivings about tampering with the existing Swedish management structure did prompt the opposition parties to examine more closely the justifications for the act. Still, Prime Minister Palme had little difficulty in having an only superficially amended law passed by a Parliament in which the SDP and the Communists together held exactly 50 percent of the seats.

The 1976 Act of Employee Participation in Decision Making—Palme's last success before losing the election—differs from the German model by vesting all participation rights in the trade unions. The most important aspect of this law is not its prescriptive provisions but rather the declaration that all managerial decisions were henceforth subject to collective bargaining. Rather than giving employers mandatory directions to obtain employee approval in specific areas, the Swedish legislation makes it possible for the trade unions to obtain codecision rights through the collective-bargaining agreement. By rooting codetermination in the collective agreement, employee participation is delegated to the union leadership, even if the word *employees* is used in the appropriate passages.[38]

Should employers and unions fail to agree on codetermination issues in the collective agreements, the law provides a minimum level for participation. In fact, it forces employers to consult with union leadership on topics previously excluded from collective bargaining regardless of the provisions of the existing agreement.

The participation law provides local unions a primary right to negotiate on all important business matters. Employers must consult the employee side (which means union leadership) before making any significant managerial decision, and they may not implement a decision before the negotiations are concluded. This means that management can no longer make marketing or investment decisions without union approval.

Employers also must inform employees about all important matters pertaining to the business and must assist unions in carrying out investigations of the firm in order to gather pertinent information if the trade union deems it necessary.

Employees are given a preference in interpreting collective-bargaining agreements. If a disagreement arises between union and management, the union view prevails until the dispute is tried and adjudicated by the labor court. In subcontracting relationships, the trade unions are entitled to prohibit employers from farming out work if the union perceives that subcontracting will undermine the participation law or the collective agreement.

Most importantly, perhaps, the Employee Participation Act establishes only the minimum level of union participation. The Swedes consider contractual agreements more desirable than legislation. The new legislation encourages collective agreement on employee participation that should go beyond the minimum standards provided in the law, which become effective only if union and management cannot agree. Unions have the right to strike in pursuit of their participation aim even if existing agreements disallow strikes over wages.

Codetermination, Profit Sharing, and Management Behavior, 1977-1980

The employee-participation law became effective 1 January 1977. There is little evidence, however, that the actual changes in the work place or in union-management relations have been noticeable so far, although the LO leaders have been using the class-warfare rhetoric of the 1930s in their public pronouncements.[39]

In the spring of 1977, Bo Södersten wrote:

> The . . . result of all these changes at the micro-level will be a drastic transformation in the economic life of the country. These events [the participation law] mark the labor unions' new readiness to assert themselves. They point toward a much more direct employee influence over . . . the operations and progress of the individual firm in the future.[40]

Like many other observers, Södersten underestimated the decades-old institutional working arrangements that had been developing between pragmatic local union leaders and local management. If we can judge by the German experience, employees and local union officials are not very interested in top management decisions that do not affect job security. On the work-place level, mutually acceptable procedures had been developing over decades, which so far seem not to have been changed significantly. There is also little evidence so far that the union representation on the board of directors has had a significant impact on the firm's decision process.

The union leadership's lack of interest in exploiting or expanding its foothold on the board of directors is explained by its ambitious plan to gain control of the Swedish industry through an employee profit-participation scheme. In the autumn of 1975 the German-born LO economist, Rudolf Meidner, advanced a proposal (subsequently called the Meidner plan) to channel company profits into a trade-union-administered wage-earners' investment fund, which would have made the LO-TCO bureaucracy the majority stockholder of all incorporated Swedish firms within twenty-five to thirty-five years.[41]

Meidner Profit-sharing Plan

The major long-run goal of the Meidner plan was to "change the Swedish political and economic system" and to establish the LO as the dominant institution; in the short run the employee investment fund was designed to achieve the following objectives:

1. Complement the solidarity wage policy by eliminating the "high profitability" of the most efficient firms that are prevented by the egalitarian industry-wide agreements to pay higher wages than their less effective competitors.
2. Eliminate the "concentration of wealth," which, supposedly, stems from industrial self-financing.

3. Create a public investment fund to provide to Swedish industry the necessary capital that it can no longer provide itself as a result of the high tax and high public-expenditure policy of the last decade.
4. Increase the employees' influence by the collective co-ownership of productive capital.

Points 2 and 3 are obviously contradictory. It is, of course, quite accurate to note that the ability of Swedish industry to generate investment capital has been severely impaired. Although the compulsory collective savings of the pension funds have generated adequate funds, its investment in socially desirable projects has inflicted upon Sweden heavy excess capacity in steel, shipbuilding, coal mining, and other areas and has funded the disastrous policy of the Palme administration to insulate the economy from the world recession by stockpiling inventory and thereby maintaining employment. (In spite of a successful devaluation and sharply increasing export sales, Swedish GNP in 1978 dropped because industry had to run down excess inventories before it could increase production. The devaluation, supported by moderate wage settlements in 1978 and 1979, enabled exports to increase and led to a 5 percent GNP growth in 1979).

Efficient firms have used internally generated funds primarily for labor-saving investments; the depressed Swedish stock market has made certain, however, that the owners have not benefited from this rationalization policy.[42]

The Meidner plan appeared initially as a technical report on "employee influence on capital formation" and did not gain much attention. In 1976, in the midst of the election campaign, the LO congress adopted a slightly revised Meidner plan as its major political objective. Almost immediately the Palme government appointed a commission to prepare the necessary legislation, thereby badly misjudging the mood of the country. The prospect of an economy dominated by the centralized LO leadership outraged even many supporters of the government—an opinion poll showed three out of four union members opposing the Meidner plan—and undoubtedly contributed to the defeat of the government.[43]

The popular repudiation has not deterred the LO leadership, however; for ideological and pragmatic reasons the LO is seeking a wider role in society. In 1976 Gunnar Nilsson, LO president, exclaimed, "With or without employee investment funds an inexorable change is taking place in the part to be played by the trade unions."[44]

The 1977 LO congress rejected the contention that the Meidner plan had contributed to the SDP defeat and once more emphasized that employee participation in "the profit they create" would be the major LO goal. Since the LO normally gets what it wants, a brief glance at the Meidner plan is warranted. Moreover, the LO's demand has gained the attention of other Western European unions; hence profit participation may become the labor-relation issue of the 1980s.

The most important features of the revised Meidner plan, as adopted by the 1976 LO conference and reformulated in the fall of 1978, follow:

1. Incorporated enterprises with more than fifty employees shall issue annually special stock certificates equal to 20 percent of pretax profit. These certificates would be deposited into a collective employee fund as employee shares.
2. The employee shares would not be distributed to the firm's employees, as proposed by the Danish LO, but would be held collectively by an industry-wide wage earner fund.[45]
3. The dividends paid on the employee shares will flow into a central clearing fund and be collectively owned and managed by the trade unions.
4. The administration of the industry wage earner funds would be carried out by the individual national trade unions in collaboration with the LO.

Depending on the profitability of the Swedish economy, the LO would become the majority stockholder of three-fourths of the Swedish private economy within twenty-five to thirty-five years. The more profitable an industry, the quicker the LO would become its owner. The major purpose of this revolutionary proposal was its objective "of achieving employee power over industry and society."[46] The most striking feature of the Meidner plan, however, is the complete neglect of the individual employee. The LO bureaucracy, not the individual worker, and not even the local union would become the owner of Swedish industry.

If the Meidner plan were ultimately legislated, Sweden would be converted into a highly centralized corporate state, governed by and for the trade-union functionaries. Enough Swedish voters feared such a development to convince the SDP leader, Olof Palme, and the LO president, Gunnar Nilsson, to drop this issue temporarily. At a press conference in July 1978 Palme promised to delay any further consideration of compulsory profit-sharing ideas until the 1981 SDP party congress, regardless of the outcome of the 1979 election. This meant that Parliament could not pass a version of the Meidner plan until after the subsequent election in 1982.[47]

In the meantime, the SAF has advanced a counterproposal to pay 1 percent of the annual wage bill into decentralized regional funds, along the lines of the Danish LO proposal. These funds would invest the shares of the entire Swedish industry, very much like American mutual funds. After five years, each employee could cash in his shares and either spend the money or invest it in regular Swedish stock certificates. If the SAF were able to implement its proposal, it might become a major obstacle to the Meidner plan. Since such a far-reaching measure could not be carried out without the approval of the LO, an unlikely event, the SAF profit-sharing proposal will remain an academic proposition, though it seemed to have gained some popularity among Swedish employees.

The nature of the Meidner plan is best demonstrated by several sentences drawn from Meidner's 1978 article in *Working Life in Sweden*.[48] Initially Meidner conceded that his profit-sharing plan "in an almost revolutionary way would change the Swedish economic and political system," but he then reassured American readers by adding that "such a change would remain within the limits of the 'Swedish Model,' which is a mixture between market economy and state planning." The "reassurance" is quite disingenuous, however, since the "Swedish model" has had very little macroplanning other than Keynesian fiscal policy; moreover, what planning there had been has been carried out by an elected government rather than by LO functionaries.

Work Environment Act of 1978

In Sweden, worker participation has taken the form of increasing the power of the union leadership on the macrolevel. Until recently much of the transformation into a quasi-socialist (actually corporative) society has taken place with the active cooperation of big business, motivated by short-run, opportunistic reasons. The SAF's recent realization that they have actively abetted in the strangulation of capitalism may have come too late. Three years of nonsocialist governments have done little to change the sociopolitical environment in which management operates; particularly the labor-market policies of the previous SDP government have been continued by both Fälldin's coalition government (1976-1978) and Ola Ullsten's Liberals (1978-1979).[49] Burdened by the history of the mass unemployment that existed in the early 1930s under a bourgeois government, the nonsocialist governments relied on nationalization of ailing industries and enormous employment subsidies to keep overt unemployment low.

In order to emphasize its basic commitment to the welfare state, the Fälldin government, moreover, proceeded in the fall of 1977 to replace the Worker Protection Act of 1949 (amended 1974) by the new Work Environment Act, which was motivated by the concept that "work must be fun." In order to accomplish this goal, the act required a satisfactory "working environment . . . in relation to the nature of the work and social and technological developments."[50] Although the act is full of hortatory statements—for example, "Work [must] be arranged in such a way that the employee himself can influence his work situation" and "working premises must be arranged in such a way as to provide a suitable working environment"—it has had little impact on Swedish factories and none on the high absenteeism rate.[51]

The Work Environment Act was passed by a new government that had pledged to reduce Swedish bureaucracy; its only achievement, however, was the creation of a huge new government agency, the National Board of Occupational Safety and Health, which is charged with administering the act. Since the working environment had been made safe through previous legislation and is closely regulated through collective-bargaining agreements, the new act and the new bureaucracy primarily affected the operating costs of small family-run businesses, especially in agriculture and tourism. These were the very strata of society, however, that had supported Fälldin's Center party in the 1976 election and subsequently chose to vote for Bohman's Conservatives in 1979.

Swedish Trade-Union Behavior under Non-Socialist Governments, 1976-1980

On the whole, the economic policies of the two nonsocialist governments between 1976 and 1979 were quite successful. The rate of inflation had been reduced by the winter of 1977-1978, and price levels remained stable until inflation throughout Europe was revived by OPEC price increases in the fall of 1979. The devaluation of the currency stimulated exports, lowered imports, restored the profitability of Swedish export industries, with the exception of steel and shipbuilding, and achieved a 5 percent GNP growth during 1979. Of particular importance for the revival of the Swedish economy were the moderate wage agreements reached between the LO and the SAF employer association in 1978 and 1979.

It may have been the shock of the SDP defeat in 1976 or the absence of a friendly SDP government to provide the appropriate atmosphere, but by mid-1978 the LO leadership seemed to have returned to its pre-1970 pragmatism. Even during the 1979 elections, LO president Gunnar Nilsson's public pronouncements were quite subdued and far less ideological in nature than Palme's Marxian election rhetoric.

The employer's federation, on the other hand, seemed to have regained some vigor. In the spring of 1979 the SAF opened an aggressive public-relations campaign against the "imminent danger" of the "full socialization of the Swedish economy." A mobile SAF exhibition, which crisscrossed Sweden for several months, attacked three "imminent dangers":

1. The trade union federation's "latent" demand for union-managed employee profit-participation funds, which would transfer the control of the Swedish economy to trade-union functionaries.
2. The oppressive taxation system, which forced the Swedish average income recipient to pay 64 percent of earnings, through direct and indirect taxes, to the government.

3. The increasing tendency of most Swedish politicians to attract votes through ever-expanding subsidy programs.

In order to "get Sweden moving again" the SAF proposed two measures: to return to the payment of performance wages, to make it worthwhile again for employees to work vigorously, and to gain permission for enterprises to earn a profit again; increased productivity, capital formation, and hence new jobs will be provided only by a profitable economy, not by union funds (figure 6-1).

Olof Palme attacked these proposals as "asocial," and the LO vice-president, Lars Westerberg (who emerged as the hard-hitting LO spokesman during 1979 while Gunnar Nilsson adopted a restrained attitude) viewed the SAF campaign as an effort to "intimidate" the unions. Questioned by German journalists during a press conference in April 1979, Westerberg admitted, however, that the controversial profit-sharing funds should lead, over the long run, to a change in enterprise ownership.[52]

The controversy generated by the SAF campaign could have led to a full examination of the major socioeconomic issues in the subsequent 1979 election campaign. Unfortunately, for the most part, the political parties chose to avoid all important issues and bored the apathetic public with idle slogans. On the Left, Palme, running virtually a one-man campaign, occasionally even attacked the government for its massive increase of the public debt and for its nationalization of the steel and shipbuilding industries. For the most part, however, he relied on pseudo-Marxian phrases to create a class-warfare atmosphere. He succeeded with his slogan "egoism versus solidarity" in isolating the Conservatives and frightening the Liberal and Center parties into reaffirmations of their dedication to the welfare state. It was left to Gösta Bohman, the Conservative party leader and finance minister in the Fälldin administration, to call attention to several fundamental problems: the deplorable state of public education, the ever-rising crime and drug addiction rates, the high absenteeism and low productivity of labor, and above all the continued growth of an expensive and imperial Swedish bureaucracy, which administers the 64 percent of GNP the government spent in 1978-1979, the highest public expenditure-GNP rate west of the Iron Curtain.[53]

The Social Democrats and the Center and Liberal parties avoided a discussion of these issues, however, and a bored electorate returned the non-Socialist parties with a reduced one-seat (1976, five-seat) majority over the Socialist-Communist opposition. Within the new government coalition, Bohman's Conservatives were the big winners, while the Liberal and Center parties were the major losers in the 1976 election.

There is little likelihood that the weak bourgeois majority that formed a second Fälldin administration will initiate any significant social and economic changes.[54] There has been and will be further minor reforms of existing legislation, however, that affect the working environment. The Center party, agrarian in origin but currently attracting romantic urban middle-class intellectuals, is basically hostile to the industrial society and is eager to return to a simpler, less-materialistic way of life. Its dedication to the improvement of the quality of life resulted in the Work Environment Act of 1977 (which became effective on 1 July 1978), an essentially empty but expensive gesture. Of greater importance is the Center party's opposition to atomic energy, which had led to the collapse of the first Fälldin administration in 1977.

Atomic energy has become a divisive factor in Sweden's political and economic life, and it cuts right through the traditional party line-up. Sweden, which has neither oil nor coal, is greatly dependent upon atomic energy, which had been strongly expanded and supported in the past by the Palme administration. The wave of antinuclear sentiment, however, that spread through Western Europe after the Three Mile Island events in the United States has also affected the middle-class intellectuals in the Social Democratic party. Operation of existing nuclear plants and further expansion of atomic industry are favored today by the trade unions (especially the LO), Swedish industry (SAF), and the Conservatives. Palme himself has begun to vacillate on this issue, while the Center party is passionately opposed to both the expansion and even the retention of atomic energy. It is supported in this position by the Swedish Communist party, which made unrelenting opposition to nuclear energy its major election issue. The Liberals also generally oppose the extension of nuclear energy but are sufficiently pragmatic to accept the necessity of operating existing nuclear plants. The atomic energy referendum in the spring of 1980 authorized the government to continue to operate existing nuclear plants and to complete the atomic energy installations currently under construction.[55]

Atomic energy has replaced the Meidner plan as the most controversial issue of the day without, however, achieving a reorganization of political forces to supply a new working majority. It is extremely unlikely that the second Fälldin administration will last for the entire three-year legislative period, and Sweden may very well be governed by another minority government before 1982. During a period of economic uncertainty and weak government leadership, the SAF and LO had been expected to return to a policy of pragmatic nonideological cooperation in order to aid the Swedish economy. The high balance-of-trade deficit, the renewed inflationary pressures in the wake of the 1979-1980 OPEC price increases, and soaring foreign indebtedness forced the coalition government to make every effort to reduce expenditures and to keep wage increases below the inflation rate.

Swedish society, and particularly the segment represented by middle-class civil-service unions, rebelled, however, against government attempts to impose a 5 percent reduction in living standards. During collective-bargaining negotiations in early 1980, Swedish public and private managers remained firm. In following the informal government directives on wage settlements, public employers offered a 5 percent wage increase—a de facto 5 percent cut in real wages—while the SAF at first wanted to keep wages at the current level and later offered a 2.3 percent raise. The LO rejected any wage settlement that would fail to keep up with the inflation rate, thus demanding, in effect, that the unorganized segments of the work force pay for the inflation induced by the OPEC price increases.

The LO broke off the wage negotiations and, imitating the I.G. Metall's tactic during the German steel strike of 1978-1979, ordered 100,000 workers in key plants to walk off the job. The SAF also adopted the tactic of its German counterparts and locked out 700,000 production workers in response. By mid-May 1980, strikes by police, nurses, and municipal employees had increased the number of idle workers to over a million, a quarter of the total work force. The most severe labor conflict since the 1909 general strike brought the country to the edge of chaos and forced the government to abandon its hands-off policy and to persuade the SAF employers association to accept the mediation proposal of a 6.8 percent wage increase; similarly, the Swedish press, with few exceptions, urged the LO to end the strike and be satisfied with the 6.8 percent increment.

The 6.8 percent figure was arrived at by splitting the difference between the LO demand for an 11.8 percent increase and the SAF offer of a 2.3 percent raise; due to the pressures on them, the LO and the SAF reluctantly accepted the mediation-board settlement. Both SAF and LO, as well as the Swedish public realized that this conflict had no winner. The Left-leaning mass-circulation paper *Expressen* correctly called the strike a "war without victors, only losers."

The Swedish assessment of the strike's consequences seem realistic. In the short run, the *Expressen*'s judgment that the strike produced only losers was widely accepted; but as it became clear that one of the major strike aims had been the overthrow of the government and that the weak, vacillating Fälldin coalition government had not only survived but seemed to have been actually strengthened, the opinion grew that Olof Palme and LO president Gunnar Nilsson had lost more than had the SAF and the bourgeois parties.

The political objectives of the massive strike had been clearly stated in the trade-union paper *Aftonbladet*: "The working class must fight such a bourgeois government vigorously and consistently; this government has gained power through trickery. We shall force it to resign."[56]

The misuse of the strike weapon for political purpose was a severe break with Swedish tradition and was criticized by both the public and the press, which ordinarily would have supported the LO. When Palme subsequently introduced a vote of no confidence in the Parliament, the coalition parties, surprisingly, closed rank and maintained their one-vote majority. The strike had helped to cement the coalition, which only a few weeks before had failed to elect the speaker because two Liberals had supported the Social Democrats.

There seems to be a growing consensus in the country that Sweden, like Denmark, has been living beyond its means and that at least a 5 percent cut in the country's standard of living will be required to reverse Sweden's enormous balance-of-payment deficit ($2 billion in 1979 and about $4 billion in 1980) and consequent foreign debt (see table 6-3). There exists serious doubt, however, whether a non-Socialist government will be able to obtain the cooperation of the unions to reduce real wages. The blatant use of union power to reverse the outcome of an election and the inability of the governing Danish Social Democrats to gain effective trade-union support for its deflationary measures may have given the second Fälldin administration another lease on life. It is not clear whether the Swedish system will be able to generate the political realignment necessary to curtail the welfare state or replace the current market system with a union-dominated command economy.

Scandinavian Epilogue: Recent Labor-Relations Developments in Denmark

The issues of industrial democracy and union-employee profit participation have emerged suddenly in Denmark as the trade union demands that toppled governments, destroyed coalitions, and prompted new elections.

The Swedish trade unions' restraint in concluding moderate wage settlements in 1978 and 1979 emphasized the LO's return to a pragmatic policy of social cooperation with employers. During the same period the Danish trade-union federation (also the LO) became ever more adamant in pursuing the increasingly militant-ideological policy first adopted in the mid-1970s. The establishment of a trade-union-administered profit-participation fund has become the foremost political objective of the Danish LO leadership. The pronouncements of Denmark's LO president Thomas Nielsen between 1977 and 1979 took on the same class-warfare rhetoric that his Swedish colleague Nilsson had abandoned since 1977.

The economic disequilibrium that has engulfed the Scandinavian welfare states has had particularly severe consequences for Denmark.[57] Persistent inflation, accompanied by large budget and international-payment deficits, has led to a decline in investment in the export-industry sector, while high public and consumer expenditures maintained excessive domestic demand. Since early 1976, various Social Democratic minority governments had launched repeated stabilization campaigns, without any success. In

Table 6-3
Swedish Balance of Payments, 1968-1978
(millions of kroner)

Year	1968	1969	1970	1971	1972	1973[a]	1974	1975	1976	1977	1978 (est.)
Sweden	−562	−1,019	−1,367	1,094	1,271	5,312	−4,213	−6,702	−10,497	−14,750	−15,000

Source: Adapted from OECD, *Economic Surveys, Denmark and Sweden* (1978).

[a]OPEC price increase in 1973-1974.

order to broaden his parliamentary base, the Social Democratic prime minister, Anker Jörgensen, formed a coalition government with the liberal Venstre party in the fall of 1978. (The Venstre, "Left," was originally a "liberal," small-landholders' party but has broadened its appeal since the 1950s.) Denmark has more than a dozen political parties represented in Parliament, and even the Social Democratic-Liberal coalition was not assured of a firm majority.

The LO leadership bitterly opposed the SDP-Venstre coalition and accused Jörgensen of betraying the working class. The government's attempt to enforce its wage-price guidelines prompted it to mediate the annual employer-union federation wage negotiations during March 1979. The LO demanded an 11 or 12 percent overall real wage increase, while the employers asked for a 3 percent wage cut and a three-year wage freeze. The Venstre supported the wage freeze, while the parliamentary SDP suggested that a small increase in the already indexed wages would be reasonable. LO president Nielsen responded by calling the coalition government "a lackey of the bourgeoisie" and by adding the demand for a "clearly definable worker's share in the means of production" to the collective-bargaining agenda.[58]

In March employer and union negotiators broke off further negotiations, and only the intervention of the government mediator prevented a strike lockout of more than 300,000 private-sector employees. The 700,000 public employees, "from [Lutheran] pastors to professional [army] officers to police to municipal employees," demonstrated throughout the country for higher wages, a thirty-five-hour week, and a minimum five-week vacation. Although the size of the 1978-1979 Danish budget deficit (DK 8.5 billion, or about $1.5 billion) and accumulated foreign debt (DK 50 billion, or about $8.8 billion) made the demands of Denmark's civil servants seem outrageous, still public-sector wages had not been indexed, and most public employees had lost 10 to 20 percent of their salaries to inflation over the past four years.

At the last minute, the government mediator produced a fragile settlement that gave the Danish unions a 3.5 to 5 percent wage increase, additional holidays, and, most importantly, preserved the indexing of private-sector wages. The coalition government barely survived this settlement and lost considerably in voter support during the elections for the first European parliament in June 1979.

By the fall of 1979 Denmark's economic crisis seemed to have deepened. A higher discount rate (11 percent) and a 3 percent devaluation of the currency had failed to help the export industries, had further increased inflation through higher import prices, and had reduced the profitability of the export-intensive agrarian sector. The seventh stabilization program since 1976 had failed. The coalition government could not agree on an effective stabilization policy because the unions strongly opposed a "wage-price stop" and demanded a "first step" toward economic democracy. The LO president Nielsen vehemently attacked Jörgensen and asserted that no stabilization policy could succeed without LO support.

During the last three decades no Danish government has survived an entire legislative period, and the two coalition partners were reluctant to dissolve Parliament.[59] Jörgensen tried to achieve a compromise by accepting a mild profit participation fund if the unions in turn would support a wage-price freeze. The Liberals (Venstre) objected and accused the SDP of being dominated by the "authoritarian" LO leadership, which, they charged, was emerging as a quasi-"super government."

In September 1979 Prime Minister Jörgensen reluctantly dissolved the Parliament and called for an election on 23 October, the eighth in fifteen years. The communications media blamed the trade unions for the fall of the coalition government, and most observers predicted an election defeat for the Social Democrats and gains for the bourgeois parties. The Venstre party leader, Henning Christophersen, managed to form an election coalition of four non-Socialist parties and waged a "union-bashing" campaign that promised an end to wage indexing, cuts in public expenditures, and restoration of price stability. Christophersen's election strategy resembled the decision of British Prime Minister Edward Heath to exploit public resentment against the coal miners and call an election in 1974 in order to determine "who governs the country." The surprising answer in Great Britain had been "the unions." The Labour party won that election because the voters feared that a Tory victory would have caused a bitter class warfare between government and trade unions.

The SDP leader, Jörgensen, drawing on the British experience, pleaded that wage-price stabilization policies could be effectively carried out only in cooperation with the unions. Enough Danes agreed with Jörgensen to give the Social Democrats a moral victory in the October election; the SDP won four additional parliamentary seats and increased their popular vote from 37.1 percent to 38.3. They now hold 69 seats out of a total of 179, far short of a majority.

As anticipated, the Liberals and the Conservatives also improved their parliamentary and popular standing (the Conservatives with seven additional seats were the real winners of the election), but their gains were almost completely offset by the losses of their two small allies, the Center Democrats and the Christian People's party. Altogether the bourgeois bloc now holds 55 (53 in 1977) seats in the new Parliament; it is too weak to form a government but too strong to permit the Social Democrats to take effective measures.

The 1979 election may have made Denmark a shade less ungovernable according to *Economist*, but the difference will not be noticeable.[60] Since the election failed to produce a workable coalition majority, the Social Democrats decided to form a minority government and to obtain the necessary support for specific bills on an ad hoc basis either from the two Marxist parties on the Left (total of 16 seats) or the two liberal parties (Radicals, 10 seats, Venstre, 22) in the Center.[61]

When the new Parliament opened in November 1979, Prime Minister Jörgensen submitted the toughest incomes-stabilization policy since 1940 in order to overcome the chronic economic crises and generate an export-led boom. In an effort to obtain union support, Jörgensen included a tax reform and the establishment of a union-administered, employee profit-sharing fund in his program.

Most of the Western governments today face problems similar to Denmark's. It should be quite illustrative, therefore, to see how a trade-union-supported Social Democratic government intended to cope with the consequences of the very policies that it has administered over the past thirty-five years. Anker Jörgensen's economic program is useful to examine in this regard. His program consisted of three parts:

1. A short-term freeze of wages, prices, rents, and dividends until January 1980 to give the government time to work out a two-year incomes policy that will have union and employer-association support.
2. The establishment of a union-administered profit-sharing fund that would receive 10 percent of corporate after-tax profit annually
3. An income-redistributing tax reform that would increase corporate income taxes from 37 percent to 40 percent, eliminate tax-free investment funds, and end the 10 percent tax allowance for investment in machinery and equipment.

Because Denmark, like almost all other Western countries, suffers from business's inability to invest, Jörgensen's deflationary policies seem guaranteed to lead to a collapse of business activities. The promised profit-participation fund did not convince the unions to support the entire Jörgensen package. It is important, however, to note the self-defeating concessions that a labor government will have to make to the trade unions in order to pass an income policy. Jörgensen had been interested, above all, in breaking the inflationary impact of indexed wages and current account deficits (see figure 6-2).

In order to obtain trade-union approval of a wage freeze, however, Jörgensen had to "broaden the area of 'industrial democracy' " by promising the LO the profit-participation fund, and hence, the prospect of ultimately owning Danish industry, as well as by attempting to increase further the redistributive nature of the tax system. Jörgensen's deflationary budget was decisively rejected by the Parliament in January 1980. The profit-participation fund, especially, was overwhelmingly defeated with the

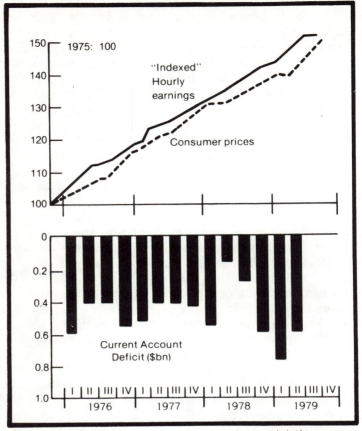

Source: Adapted from *Economist*, 10 November 1979, p. 90.

Figure 6-2. Denmark's Dilemma

combined votes of the radical leftist parties, the center parties, and the conservative parties. Faced with a foreign debt equal to 20 percent of the GNP
and a $2.83 billion balance-of-payment deficit that exceeded 40 percent of
the GNP, the government finally persuaded the unions to accept a 10 percent ceiling on wage increases and succeeded in obtaining additional
nuisance taxes from the Parliament. None of these measures will solve Denmark's severe crisis. As long as the Unions insist on profit participation as
the price for cooperation in an effective stabilization policy, Denmark's
problem will remain unsolved.

One hundred years ago, employee participation in the decision-making
processes emerged as a movement to overcome class differences and to

strengthen the organic nature of society. By 1980 codetermination had become a divisive force in northwestern Europe, especially in Denmark, Sweden, and the Netherlands, and it has seriously undermined social cooperation and the willingness to compromise.

Notes

1. J. Schumpeter, *Capitalism, Socialism and Democracy* (New York: Harper & Row, 1941).

2. An experimental works-council law was passed in Norway in 1922. The increasing radicalization of segments of the Norwegian labor movement—a large splinter group even joined subsequently the Fourth (Trotskyite) International—created a political climate in which a works council designed to overcome class conflict could not function. The "Center-Right" coalitions that governed Norway during the 1920s permitted the works-council law to expire.

3. Actually the Social Democratic parties governed more often than not with coalition partners. In Sweden only from 1940 to 1944 and from 1968 to 1976 did the Social Democratic party govern by itself, although from 1968 to 1976, as in the 1940s and 1950s, it required the cooperation of the small Communist party to stay in power and pass legislation. In 1976 a non-Socialist coalition came to power in Sweden, while Social Democratic governments have come and gone in Denmark during the last three years. The Danish Social Democrats have never had a majority in the country or in the Parliament but have managed to hold office in twenty-three years out of the past thirty. Anker Jörgensen, the Social Democratic prime minister until August 1978, won 37 percent of the vote in what by Danish standards was a landslide victory in 1975, giving him 65 out of the 179 Folketing seats, which are divided among 11 different parties. Since the Liberal, Paul Hartling, had run the country during 1974 with only 22 seats at his disposal, Jörgensen—who retired briefly from politics in 1978—was in a rather strong position. He subsequently governed with the support of the Liberals until October 1979 and has once more been the head of a minority government since that time.

In Norway the 1977 election showed that the country was again equally divided between Socialists and non-Socialists, although the non-Socialists showed strong gains in fall 1979 in municipal elections. Intellectually, however, the Socialists are now on the defensive throughout Scandinavia, especially since the enormous tax burden and ever-increasing bureaucracy have begun to alienate liberal middle classes, which generally had supported the SDP in the past.

4. Neither the SACO nor the TCO has been as centralized as the LO.

SACO is a federation of professional (university graduates) associations, which continue to speak for their members. For negotiating purposes, TCO is split into three agencies that represent state, municipal, and private salaried employees. TCO represents the interests of its members to other pressure groups, while each agency bargains for its members.

5. See the Industrial Litigation Act (1974), for instance. The law assumes that an employee's case will "usually be pleaded on his behalf by the union to which he belongs. *An employee may only plead his own case* if his union-organization does not wish to do so." Swedish Ministry of Labour, *New Labour Laws* (n.d.), p. 28 (my italics). There is no provision in the Industrial Litigation Act for an employee to sue his union for unfair practices. In 1972 an experimental law reserved two board of directors' seats for union functionaries if the union decided to take advantage of this legislation. The local union, not the employees, decided; the union leadership, not the employees, chose the representatives.

6. At the 1951 LO congress, the leadership submitted a report, "The Trade Union Movement and Full Employment," which contained the outline of the solidarity wage policy.

7. Actually the first Swedish Social Democratic government was formed in 1921, but it lasted only a short time and had little impact on society.

8. Roughly at the same time, Thurman Arnold in his *The Folklore of Capitalism* (New Haven: Yale University Press, 1937) as well as Adolf Berle and Gardner Means *The Modern Corporation and Private Property* (New York: Macmillan, 1930) expressed strikingly similar views in the United States.

9. In Sweden, the Swedish school (Knut Wicksell, David Davidson, Bertil Ohlin, and Erik Lindahl) provided the intellectual foundation for precisely the same policies that Keynesians advocated in the Anglo-American countries. K. Wicksell (1851-1926), an anti-Marxian middle-class radical, knew Hjalmar Branting well and in spite of several disagreements with the Social Democratic leadership, probably had a more lasting influence on the pre-World War II Swedish labor leaders than Marx had. Certainly the lasting concern of Scandinavian Socialists with population control and egalitarian income policy is due to Wicksell, who considered himself a Malthusian. Wicksell's marginal-productivity theory imputed appropriate functional shares to the factor of production, which would be "optimal only if the income distribution were reasonably equal." Bertil Ohlin, who became the leader of the Liberal party, opposed the Social Democrats in the 1950s when they added high indirect taxes to their Keynesian-type fiscal policy in order to weaken the allocative tasks of the labor market.

10. The relation between the union and the Social Democratic party leadership has always been close and may have become even closer between

1972 and 1977. For example, the LO chairman, Gunnar Nilsson, has been a member of Parliament and a leading Social Democratic politician for years. In May 1977, Nilsson brought the country to the brink of a general strike over some technical labor-relations issues and supported, for tactical reasons, the excessive wage demands by the civil-service unions, very much against the wishes of the LO membership. Nilsson believed that a general strike would help return the Social Democrats to power in 1979. See "Brinkmanship," *Economist*, 28 May 1977. Once it became clear that Nilsson's use of trade-union power to achieve political ends antagonized broad segments of the electorate, the strike issues were quickly settled. In the spring of 1980, the LO and TCO finally called their general strike, but the government survived.

11. Assar Lindbeck, "Theories and Problems in Swedish Economic Policy in the Post-War Period," *American Economic Review* (June 1968):70.

12. See Gösta Edgren, Karl-Olof Faxen and Clas-Erik Odhner, *Wage Formation and the Economy* (London: George Allen & Unwin, 1973). This is an English translation of an excellent 1972 study of the short-run economic impact of the solidarity wage policy and macroeconomic bargaining in the late 1960s by the economists of, respectively, the SAF, the LO, and the TCO. It is significantly different in tone from *Wage Policy: A Report to the 1971 Congress of the Swedish LO Confederation* (Stockholm: LO, 1972). *Wage Policy*'s radical rhetoric conveys the LO leadership's ideology.

13. In the Scandinavian and German-speaking countries, all non-Socialist parties commonly have been referred to as bourgeois (*bürgerlich*). This form of reference has disappeared in Germany since the 1970s but is still in use in Austria, Switzerland, and Scandinavia.

14. Bö Södersten, "Industrial Democracy Present and Future," *Scandinavian Review*, no. 2 (1977):73. Södersten attempts to show that the SDP and LO have been following a careful long-run strategy of overcoming capitalism with almost Leninist perseverence. This view is nonsense, but the SDP's Socialist theoreticians have been able to make use of each gain to prepare for the next demand that would further weaken capitalism. Since a weakened capitalism could no longer produce the necessary profit to provide investment capital, a union-administered wage-earners' fund will ultimately replace the function of the capitalist. See Mogens Lykketoft, "Toward Economic Democracy: Wage Earners' Funds," *Scandinavian Review*, no. 2 (1977):40. Södersten describes how "employee participation will increase the efficiency of the firm (as workers obtain managerial control). Under a capitalist system of profit maximization social controls are absent—if a worker shirks he will 'steal' only from the capitalists, by lowering their profits." This was written in 1977, as absenteeism has become a

major problem in the nationalized and private sector alike, when the nationalized Swedish iron-mining firm LKAB lost $115 million in 1977 and when the nationalized Swedish shipyards were rapidly reaching British dimensions in their inability to compete. See *Economist*, 31 December 1977, p. 84.

15. Swedish Conference of Trade Unions, *Trade Unions and Full Employment* (Stockholm, 1951). Generally referred to as the TUFE report.

16. The so-called Rehn model consists of a series of papers and memoranda produced by Gösta Rehn and his colleage Rudolf Meidner, who attained international prominence by advocating a profit-sharing plan in 1976 that would have made the LO the owner of most major Swedish firms within twenty to thirty years. The significant point is that the Meidner profit-sharing plan of 1976 is a logical consequence of the Rehn model of the 1950s and the TUFE program of 1951. Two English-language articles by Gösta Rehn are ''The Problem of Stability: An Analysis and Some Policy Proposals,'' in *Wages Policy under Full Employment*, ed. R. Turvey (London: William Hodge & Co., 1952), and ''Swedish Wages and Wage Policy,'' *Annals of the American Academy of Political and Social Sciences* (March 1957). Neither article gives the full ideological flavor of the Rehn model, which is more apparent in the TUFE report of 1951.

17. See Finkelstein and Thimm, *Economists and Society* (New York: Harper & Row, 1973):137ff.

18. Rehn, ''Problem of Stability,'' pp. 46-54.

19. The highly controversial national pension plan of 1958 was passed by a one-vote margin. In a special election, called by the SDP on the pension issue, the SDP and the Communists obtained 50 percent of the parliamentary seats, the three non-Socialist parties the other 50 percent. The SDP needed the continued support of the Communist party, and, on some occasions, of several Liberal members of Parliament until 1968, and again from 1973 to 1976.

20. The growth and consequences of the politics of pension schemes were analyzed by Björn Molin, *Tjänstepensionsfragan: En Studie i Svensk Partipolitik* (Goteborg: Akademie for Laget-Gumperts, 1967).

21. In 1976, the last year of the Palme government, only 30 percent of Swedish industry operated near capacity *Economist*, 27 August 1977, p. 67. In spite of past rationalization efforts, the seminationalized Svenskt Staal A.B. still had 25 percent more employees than needed in 1977, and an absymal productivity of 160 to 180 tons per man year, compared to 400 to 450 tons in the Japanese industry; its 1978 losses were 669.5 million kronen (about $134 million). The non-Socialist government coalitions, in power since 1976, have not been daring or successful in pruning excess manpower throughout Sweden's swollen industries. The Norwegian Labor party (minority) government has been much more hard-nosed in combating inflation, trade deficits, and overstaffing. In September 1978, the Norwegian

Parliament overwhelmingly approved its two-year deflationary policy of public spending cuts, incomes and price freezes, planned work-force reductions in the national sector, and withdrawal of subsidies to "lame ducks" in the private sector.

22. *Svenska Dagbladet*, 1 March 1979, p. 1; FAZ, 27 August 1979, p. 12.

23. "Sweden: The Model Loses Her Glamour," *Economist*, 27 August 1977, p. 66.

24. See *Economist*, 7 January 1978, p. 76; *Wall Street Journal*, 10 October 1978, p. 17; *Svenska Handelsbanken*, (October 1978).

25. See Lykketoft, "Toward Economic Democracy," and Södersten, "Industrial Democracy." Lykketoft, a Danish economist, considers that all Scandinavian countries are in the process of "overcoming capitalism," although perhaps at different rates. Both Lykketoft and Södersten are leading Socialist theoreticians within their respective parties.

26. Typical of the disdainful, patronizing manner in which the Scandinavian Socialist establishment has viewed the German codetermination model is "Industrial Democracy, Yesterday and Today," by I. Logue, M. Peterson, and B. Schiller, *Scandinavian Review*, no. 2 (1977):4. According to Logue, Peterson, and Schiller, American influence "strengthened" German capitalists and hence enabled the Adenauer government to "impose" codetermination in the coal and steel industries; the authors believe that the limitations of German codetermination were exposed by the 1969 wave of wildcat strikes in the steel industry against the codetermination boards.

Actually the German wildcat strikes in 1969 were not directed against the supervisory boards but rather against the industry-wide wage agreement. During 1969-1970, however (and again in 1979), Sweden experienced a much more significant series of wildcat strikes, which were directed at the egalitarian union-SDP wage policies, "demonstrating that the authority and legitimacy of the unions . . . had been eroded." Andrew Martin, "Worker's Participation," *Scandinavian Review*, no. 2 (1977):17. As far as the frequency of strikes was concerned, Germany's and Sweden's have been equally low. Of the time lost annually because of strikes (measured in days lost per 1,000 employees), Germany and Sweden both had only 43. The United States, by comparison, lost 1,247. Great Britain lost 633; and France lost 277. Only Norway lost fewer—11. LO Fackförenings, Rörelsen, no. 3, 1975.

27. As of 1972 unions have been able to place two labor directors on the boards of companies with more than one hundred employees; however, up to 1976, local and even regional union leaders had viewed board-level participation with little enthusiasm and had only bothered in 60 percent of all possible cases to nominate employee-directors. The employee-directors, in turn, kept a low profile in board meetings.

28. Logue, Peterson, and Schiller, "Industrial Democracy," p. 11.

29. See Lykketoft, "Toward Economic Democracy"; Södersten, "Industrial Democracy"; Rudolf Meidner, *Coordination and Solidarity* (Stockholm: LO, 1974), chap. 1. An especially good example is Bernt Schiller "Industrial Democracy in Scandinavia," *Annals* (May 1977):63. Not once does Schiller show that employee participation in both decision making and profit distribution would be administered through national and local union officials. Schiller, however, does provide a glimpse at the implementation of worker democracy in LO fashion in "LO, paragraf 32 och företagsdemokratin," *Trisma* (1974):84-105. Similarly Rudolf Meidner refers consistently to "employees" or "employee representatives" in "Employee Investment Funds and Capital Formation," *Working Life in Sweden* (June 1978). In fact, however, it is the union functionaries and not employees who would administer the Meidner investment funds.

30. *Industrial Democracy Programme Adopted by the 1971 Congress* (Stockholm: LO, 1972).

31. Official terms of reference for the commission quoted in Lennart Förseback, *op. cit.*, p. 54.

32. See especially Meidner, "Employee Investment Funds," pp. 5-7.

33. The terms *labor* and *worker* have generally been replaced by *employee*. The sudden reappearance of *labor* in the LO proclamations of the 1970s is an indication of its ideological shift.

34. *Proposals for an Industrial Democracy Act*: *A Summary of the Proposals of the Labour Legislation Committee, Ministry of Labour* (1974), p. 7.

35. Ibid., p. 4 (italics added).

36. The growing Swedish crime rate has become a serious problem. Although the number of actual incidents is still below American levels, the sharply accelerating increase in robbery, theft, and similar crimes has been disturbing to Swedish society. Similarly the ease with which narcotics use has spread among university students has been unsettling to middle-class parents.

37. The deteriorating morale of Swedish employees has caused special alarm. "As affluence becomes pervasive the willingness to work and especially to cooperate closely is fading out. . . . With the able-bodied eligible for social benefits unprecedented for mankind, and the difference between working and not working in Sweden amounting to amere $2.50 daily, there is very little incentive left." Curt Nicolen, chairman of the SAF, at the European Management Forum quoted by *Wall Street Journal*, 6 February 1978, p. 10. Volvo, for example, has had a 25 percent absenteeism rate, forcing management to hire five workers for every four needed.

38. See sections 1, 6, 11-13, "Act on Employee Participation in Decision Making," referred to as "Act on the Joint Regulation of Working Life," reprinted in *Toward Democracy at the Workplace* (Stockholm: Ministry of Labor, 1978), pp. 19, 88.

39. *Neue Züricher Zeitung*, 23-24 September 1978, viewed with amusement the "revolutionary pretentions" of Swedish functionaries, who raised their "manicured fists" to sing the "Internationale" at the September 1978 conference of the Swedish Social Democrats, while *FAZ*, 25 September 1978, in its coverage of the conference, commented on the pictures of Marx, the class-warfare rhetoric of Palme, who comes of a wealthy, aristocratic family, and the enthusiastic reception of the South West African and Rhodesian terrorists.

40. Södersten, "Industrial Democracy," p. 74.

41. The 1971 LO Congress authorized a study on the impact of the solidarity wage policy on profits, income distribution, and capital formation. This task was assigned to an LO economist, Rudolf Meidner, who previously had been a major contributor to the Rehn model. The Meidner plan differs substantially from a profit-sharing plan for individual employees advanced by the Danish LO in 1973, since it was designed to deliver the control of Swedish industry to the LO leadership. Meidner, who emigrated to Sweden in the 1930s, claimed that his plan expressed the thinking prevailing among German union leaders at that time; actually there is no evidence for this statement. German radical thought in the 1930s conceived of worker self-government at the lowest level of industry, not of a centralized bureaucracy command economy. Today the German New Left is particularly hostile to the DGB bureaucracy and favors direct democracy in union and plant affairs. "Die 'Gruppe Hoss' wirbt gegen die Gewerkschaft" [Gruppe Hoss agitates against the union], *FAZ*, 27 September 1978, p. 10.

42. All quotations are from Meidner, "Employee Investment Funds," June 1978, p. 8.

43. Cf. Heikki Konkola, "Can Employers Live with Industrial Democracy," *Scandinavian Review* (Summer 1977):49.

44. Gunnar Nilsson, "News from the 1976 LO Congress," mimeographed (Stockholm: LO, 1976), p. 16.

45. The latest revision of the Meidner plan (Meidner, "Employee Investment Funds" June, 1978) merely increases the role of the local union in the administration of the fund.

46. Schiller, "Industrial Democracy," p. 71.

47. See *Economist*, 8 July 1978, p. 79.

48. R. Meidner, "Employee Investment Funds," June 1978, p. 8.

49. During 1977-1978 the cost of labor market policies (primarily employment subsidies) amounted to 2.5 percent of GNP; by comparison, the German government spent 0.5 percent on employment-creating activities, although it had 4 percent unemployment. See "Sweden before the Election," *Die Zeit*, 15-16 September 1979, p. 18; see also *Svenska Handelsbanken* (September 1979).

50. *The Working Environment in Sweden* (Stockholm: Ministry of Labor, August 1977), p. 9. The Labor Ministry booklet describes the new

Work Environment Act and the agency set up to enforce it, the National Board of Occupational Safety and Health.

51. Work Environment Act, chap. 2, sections 1, 2.

52. FAZ, 26 April 1979, p. 11.

53. German journalist Werner Adams reported on a visit to Stockholm's major shopping center, Sergels Torg, where drugs are sold openly, drunks and drug addicts lie in corners, and gangs of youthful rowdies roam the subterranean passages. "Far from Paradise," *FAZ*, 15 September 1979, p. 3.

54. See Curt Golsson, "Sweden—An Economic Approach," *Wall Street Journal*, 12 October 1973, p. 20. Also note Gunnar Biörck, Conservative member of Parliament, in *Svenska Dagbladet*, 8 August 1979, which attracted significant attention in the Swedish press but was generally ignored by both Social Democrats and Liberals. Biörck attacked the "bureaucratic terrorismus," which, removed from parliamentary control, forces judges, school administrators, small businessmen, and civil servants to adhere to the bureaucracy's ideological party line and to comply with "badly written, poorly spelled, unbearably lengthy, and unsubstantive regulations." Biörck was particularly caustic about the separation of teaching and research at the universities.

55. In the atomic-energy referendum, Swedish voters had three choices: support the Center party-Communist position and abandon nuclear power production immediately; follow the Conservative party and expand atomic energy; or vote for the Social Democrat alternative and express the aim to abolish atomic power sometime in the future but in the meantime use and expand existing nuclear facilities.

For practical purpose, there was no difference between the SDP and Conservative party positions, though the Social Democrats in the last week of the referendum managed to place themselves rhetorically closer to the opponents of nuclear power. In the end the opportunity to declare oneself opposed to nuclear power while simultaneously benefiting from its existence and growth proved the most popular choice for the Swedish electorate. Proposition II, supported by the Social Democrats, obtained a majority and assured that, for the present century, Sweden would continue to draw heavily upon nuclear energy.

56. *Aftonbladet*, 2 May 1980 (my translation).

57. See *Economist*, 9 June 1979, p. 56, and 19 November 1979, p. 90; *Berlinske Tidende*, 28 September 1979, pp. 1-2; *Wall Street Journal*, 12 October 1979, p. 20.

58. Literal translation: "A lackey government under the command of the bourgeoisie." See *Berlinske Tidende*, 21 February 1976, p. 2; *FAZ*, 23 February 1979, p. 12.

59. The position of the Social Democratic party has been weakened

slowly but steadily in all Scandinavian countries. See "Scandinavia's Socialists," *Economist*, 9 June 1979, p. 56. Even with the support of the Communists in Sweden, the alliance with radical Leftist splinter parties in Norway and the operational coalition with Left-Liberals in Denmark, Scandinavia's Social Democrats are today in the minority.

60. See "Ungovernable Denmark Turns a Shade Less So," *Economist*, 27 October 1979, p. 51.

61. Norway's parliamentary procedures are the opposite of Denmark's; there are no by-elections, nor can the Parliament be dissolved prematurely. The current Social Democratic minority government of Odvar Nordli faces four non-Socialist parties, which are just one seat short of a parliamentary majority. During the last municipal elections in September 1979, the Social Democrats received only 36 percent of the vote (42 percent in 1977), the Conservatives 30 percent (25 percent in 1977), and the four non-Socialist parties together 56 percent. In spite of the absence of a popular or parliamentary majority, Nordli has governed firmly, though not entirely successfully. The North Sea oil revenues have not generated the export-led expansion that had been anticipated, but they have heated up an already inflationary consumer economy. The Norwegian trade unions have shown little interest in profit participation so far.

7 Codetermination in Western Europe

The relationship between employees and entrepreneurs in Western Europe has been shaped by the conflicting forces of social cooperation and class conflict. The euphoria of the immediate post-World War II period strengthened the forces of social cooperation on the continent, and by 1950 most Western European countries had introduced some form of works-council legislation as a step toward worker participation in plant management. The opposition of the traditional trade unions to works councils in particular, and social cooperation in general, however, condemned most forms of codetermination to operational ineffectiveness, in spite of the support of the Christian Democratic parties that governed most of Western Europe from 1945 into 1970.

During the 1970s the radicalization of sections of the socialist parties and their affiliated unions, as well as the success of German codetermination, prompted many union and socialist party leaders to take a further look at codetermination, but for quite different reasons. Legislative proposals that would greatly increase union power and change the existing economic system considerably have been under discussion in France, Great Britain, the Netherlands, and the Common Market (EEC). The defeat of the British Labour government in 1979 and the election victories of moderate right-of-center groups in France, Belgium, and the Netherlands in 1977 and 1978 condemned some of the more radical proposals to an early, though perhaps only temporary, death. There is little doubt that some form of codetermination will emerge in most Common Market countries during the 1980s. A brief look at the codetermination controversy in the key countries will permit some informed guesses about future developments and also illuminate the political-economic conditions that will shape future codetermination legislation.

The Netherlands

Labor-management relations in the Netherlands are particularly important for an understanding of West European trends because they illustrate clearly the significant ideological changes in attitudes that have occurred during the 1970s among key Western union leaders and socialist intellectuals.[1] Until the late 1960s the Dutch economy operated under an industrial-relations system in which employer associations, unions, and government cooperated to set price- and incomes-policy guidelines within which industry-wide collective-bargaining agreements were negotiated. The key organization of this corporate structure was the Social Economic Council, a tripartite organization on which the trade-union federations, employer associations, and the government were equally represented. The council was established in 1950 as an advisory committee to the government on a broad range of social and economic topics. It originated most of the price-wage policy of the next fifteen years.

The government representatives on the council were considered public representatives, since outstanding personalities, frequently academicians, were appointed to this committee to represent only themselves. For our purpose, however, the term, *government* is quite appropriate, since the Netherlands has been ruled by a relatively small elite of politicians, senior civil servants, and university professors who have held key decision-making positions. The frequent changes from Center-Left to Center-Right governments merely disguise the fact that the same handful of people have been governing Holland, decade after decade. Given the broad consensus that has prevailed among this elite, at least until the early 1970s, it is appropriate to refer to the Social Economic Council that dominated the Dutch economy until recently as a corporate, tripartite government-labor-capital institution.

In purpose and operation the Social Economic Council strongly resembled the national economics council that the much stronger German unions have been demanding in vain since 1919. The powerful position of the Dutch labor unions in national economic decision making, in contrast to their relatively weak position in the firm, is a peculiar Dutch phenomenon that may explain the postwar successes and the current difficulties of the industrial-relations system.[2]

Structure and Ideology of Dutch Unions

The Netherlands trade unions are organized on an industry-wide basis but have been divided along ideological, denominational, and, most recently, social lines. Yet they have managed to cooperate in industry-wide collective bargaining and generally coexist peacefully. The once Social Democratic and now Socialist union federation (*Nederland Verbonds van Vakverenigingen*, NVV) has been the largest and generally the most class-conscious and aggressive organization. Until the early 1970s the NVV was quite comparable to the German union federation, the DGB, though lately it has become much more motivated by socialist ideology.

The second largest union federation—over the years roughly two-thirds the size of the NVV—has been the Catholic Workers' Federation (*Nederlands*

Katholiek Vakverbond, NKV), which until the late 1960s had been less militant and had favored social cooperation explicitly. The most conservative union federation that has emphasized most strongly the need for social cooperation between employers and workers has been the Protestant Workers' Federation (*Christelijk National Vakverbond, CNV*), which since World War I has had a membership about one-third of the NVV's.

In January 1976 the NVV and the NKV merged into a superfederation, the Federation of Netherlands Trade Unions (FNV), to coordinate policy and prepare for a full-fledged merger of their member unions some time in the future. Roughly at the same time, and as a reaction to the penetration of FNV cadres by neo-Marxist groups, the independent and white-collar unions grew perceptibly in membership and influence and became almost another union federation. Opposition to the federation with the NVV among the more conservative Catholic white-collar employees, as well as the leftward lurch in the NKV leadership, may very well lead to further shifts from the NKV to the independents.

In spite of the recent revolutionary rhetoric of Dutch union leaders, the history of the Dutch trade-union movement has been one of social cooperation with employers and government to an extent unparalleled even in Germany and Austria. There are many indications, however, that a more acrimonious climate may prevail in the 1980s.

From Social Cooperation to Economic Controls

The participation of the trade unions in economic decision making occurred primarily on the national level in both the prewar and, especially, the immediate postwar periods. To the extent that this cooperation took place in tripartite forums, close personal relationships developed among a handful of trade-union leaders, managers, and senior government officials.

The strength and importance of the unions on the national industrywide level have not been reflected in their position within the firm. Organized on a geographical basis, as once were America's Knights of Labor, the unions lacked even basic local organizations in plant or enterprise until the 1970s. Therefore the Christian Social movement, strong among both Catholic and Protestant workers, did not have to overcome the opposition of Socialist unions at the plant level in order to advance its ideas of social cooperation in lieu of class warfare or unbridled capitalism.

Worker participation in enterprise and society had its roots in the Netherlands almost entirely in the Christian Social movement. Although there were many striking similarities between sociopolitical conditions in the Netherlands and Bavaria-Austria, the quest for a reconstruction of the social order, which would lead to a just Christian cooperative society, came to Holland from France after the end of World War I. The Dutch Christian Social movement, under the leadership of a liberal Catholic, J.A. Veraart, was concerned mainly with developing joint industry boards staffed by worker and employer representatives, not only to set wages and working conditions but to develop a total management strategy for the industry. The parallels to both Roosevelt's National Recovery Act and Mussolini's corporative state are obvious, although, of course, Veraart preceded both.[3]

The industry-wide board was charged with advising the government on economic policy, although the exact links were not defined. The entire system was referred to as PBO (*Publiekrechtlijke Bedrijfsorganisatie*, or "industrial organization under public law") and under this acronym was debated for more than a decade.[4] In 1931 Parliament passed a watered-down version of Veraart's PBO system, the Law on Industry Boards (*Bedrijfsradenwet*), which authorized but did not require the establishment of industry-wide, union-management boards to consider jointly production and marketing policies, as well as wages and prices. In the opinion of J.D. Windmuller and other observers, these industry-wide boards, which mainly emerged in nonmanufacturing industries, had relatively little impact other than providing the foundation for the much more effective and tougher postwar PBO.

Although the Netherlands Christian Social movement was concerned primarily with the corporate cooperation of capital and labor on the national level, some consideration was also given to worker participation in enterprise. The Netherlands had lacked Germany's relatively broad pre-World War I experience with works councils, but the French ultramontane movement had prompted also several paternalistic Dutch employers to sponsor employee representation forums during the last quarter of the nineteenth century. After World War I there were, however, no demands for works councils by socialist intellectuals or union leaders such as there had been in Germany and Austria. During the early 1920s, the Christian Social movement's advocacy of worker participation created some interest in employee participation in enterprise decisions, which was called *medezeggenschap* (codetermination).[5]

The ambivalence of the socialist unions toward employee codetermination, the general weakness of all unions at the enterprise level, and the opposition of the employers' associations, which preferred to deal with unions on an industry-wide level, all precluded any works-council legislation. Several quasi-works councils were established, however, either through collective-bargaining agreements or voluntarily by the employer (Philips was one). These councils had only advisory functions, however, and resembled more the American personnel representation plans of the 1920s than the German works councils of the interwar period.

Cooperative Economic Planning

The Netherlands experienced in the immediate post-World War II decade a most successful implementation of a revitalized PBO system—tripartite cooperation among government, employers, and unions to achieve economic growth with stable prices—accompanied by a mild attempt to increase worker participation in the enterprise.[6] A web of government legislation established de facto price and wage control as well as industry-wide production planning, administered through both bipartisan labor-management industry-wide boards and national quasi-corporate forums (Social Economic Council, Foundation of Labor), in which government, employers, and unions were equally represented.[7] During this period, economic decision making in the Netherlands became highly centralized and technocratic. Not only the national unions and employer associations lost considerable power to the top federation bureaucracies, but so did Parliament and the political parties, since the significant discussions and compromises occurred among labor, management, and government leaders either in the two national forums—the Social Economic Council and the Foundation of Labor—or in special summit meetings.[8]

The Dutch succeeded in combining a loose form of central planning and price-wage control to achieve a fifteen-year period of stable economic growth, labor peace, and expanding social benefits without injuring the basic democratic nature of society.[9] The technocratic, apolitical centralized decision making did tend to lessen the importance of the traditional democratic process, however.

During the same time, and under very similar political conditions, the Swedish trade unions had feared that a government income policy accompanied by a vigorous expansion of the welfare state would deprive the labor movement of any useful purpose. The Dutch trade unions, on the other hand, welcomed their acceptance by government and employers as the spokesmen of labor and responsible corporate partners of capital in the macroeconomic decision process. Although the top labor-federation leaders seemed willing to sacrifice short-run worker interests to long-run national welfare and although the national unions lost in importance during this period, the relative and absolute membership of all three labor federations grew significantly in the two postwar decades but has remained rather stable since, comprising today about 40 percent of the work force.[10]

Emergence of Works Councils

The union leadership seemed to have been sufficiently gratified by its national prominence that it did not attempt to strengthen the union organization at the plant level or to press strongly for plant-level worker participation. An agreement that seemed to have developed during the postwar decades led the employers to expect the unions not to interfere at the plant level in return for their acceptance as equal partners on the national level. There developed, however, quite spontaneously considerable demand throughout society for the extensions of the democratic process to the work place. This movement found support primarily among Catholic and Protestant intellectuals, the confessional parties, and segments of the Socialists.[11] The sentiment for more industrial democracy was also strengthened by the German example, and in late 1950 a Works Council Act (*Wet op de Ondernemingsraden*, or "Enterprise Council Law") was passed as a companion legislation to the PBO law.

The Dutch works councils were designed primarily "to contribute . . . to the best possible functioning of the enterprise and to strengthen social cooperation by increasing the two-way flow of information and consultation between employer and employees.[12] The employer (company president) or his representative was the ex-officio chairman of the works council and had the primary responsibility to supply the council, and indirectly the employees, with all necessary information to broaden their understanding of economic issues. Only in the areas of personnel policies and fringe benefits did the council have some participatory opportunity, which was greatly extended in a few firms (Unilever, Dutch Shell, and Philips) and neglected in most medium and small firms. Works councils had to be formed in every firm with at least twenty-five employees, but no sanctions existed for failures to obey the law. Hence many small and medium-sized firms never established the councils, and only about 50 percent of all eligible enterprises abided by the law.

Unions represented in the enterprise, as well as independent groups of employees, could nominate a list of employees for the council. The actual allocation of seats followed proportional voting procedures. The works council was supposed to be representative not only of the various union and nonunion groups in the enterprise but also to reflect age, sex, and religious distribution. The unions, especially the NVV, had fought very hard to obtain the exclusive nomination right for council elections but had little chance to have such an alien concept accepted by Parliament, especially since the Labor party (PvdA) has been much weaker than its Austrian, German, and Swedish counterparts.

The weak position of the trade unions in the enterprise was thereafter revealed by the works-council elections, which elected a surprisingly large number of nonunion members, especially in firms with a large percentage of white-collar employees.[13]

In spite of such apparent mild interest in the council and in spite of the apparently innocuous role assigned to it, Dutch opinion polls have consistently indicated that roughly three-quarters of all employees approve of works-council codetermination. This is even a somewhat larger percentage of approval than German and Austrian surveys have shown, which might indicate that the actual process of employee participation is more important than its scope.[14]

Rise of the New Left

During the mid-1960s, various intellectual and economic factors that emerged began to challenge both the spirit of social cooperation and the income-price policy administered by a centralized, technocratic bureaucracy.[15] The atmosphere engendered in the universities by the widespread hostility toward the Vietnam war nourished an antiestablishment ideology that developed from a frivolous radical-chic movement into a definite neo-Marxist renaissance.[16] The entire concept of social cooperation met increasing criticism from a relatively small but influential group of academicians, union officials, and journalists.

The Dutch unions, like the German unions, have a relatively large group of academicians among their top leaders. Moreover, the university graduates, especially economists, in the research departments of the three major federations have often exerted considerable influence on union strategy. For example, in 1973, the young economist and trade-union official Willem Kok was elected president of the NVV. During the late 1960s and early 1970s, left-wing groups within the NVV and the NKV were particularly influential. The tendency of a centralized-income policy designed to maintain the existing income distribution drew the fire of the New—and not so new—Left, which demanded the "abolition of privileges" and the reduction of wage and salary differentials.

In spite of the new respectability conferred upon the post-Stalin Soviet Union by the anti-anticommunism of the New Left, the dismal performance of the Soviet command economy was still sufficiently discredited to prevent any enthusiasm for central planning. Hence the attack from the New Left on the government income policy was accompanied by proposals to dismantle authoritarian structures throughout society and to replace them through participatory mechanisms. The possibility of obtaining industrial democracy through a major works-council reform rekindled interest in different forms of codetermination.

The trade unions as well as the management of several larger corporations had become increasingly opposed to centralized controls by 1960. The success of the free German and Belgian economies, the abandonment of postwar economic controls by most European countries, and the beginning of a European labor market all combined to strengthen the demands for change. Attempts by the Center-Right governent of that period to relax controls without abandoning effective wage guidelines merely seemed to increase the bureaucratic complexity in which industry-wide bargaining agreements had to meet the approval of layers of committees.[17] By 1967, after a short-lived Center-Left government had fallen, the Socialist NVV federation openly opposed further controls on collective bargaining. As the macroeconomic cooperation between employer and trade-union associations began to fall apart, greater attention was accorded to the works councils as instruments of employee-employer cooperation. An opinion survey carried out in 1966 by the Social Economic Council registered broad approval of the works council by both employers and workers, although particular aspects of the participatory procedures were criticized.[18]

As a consequence of the rekindled interest in works councils among intellectuals, unions, employers, and government, a parliamentary commission, generally referred to as the Verdam commission, was appointed in the early 1960s to investigate the structure of the enterprise, the role of the board of directors, and the effectiveness of the works council. The report submitted in 1965 proposed the reorganization of the board of directors into a German-type supervisory board with employee directors, as well as expansion of the works council's authority and functions. Although there seemed to be general agreement, in principle, that the Verdam report pointed in the right direction, specific proposals generated considerable controversy, especially among and within the trade-union federations.

The right-wing (Social Democratic) officials within the Socialist trade-union federation, as well as the majority of the Labor party, simply wanted to adopt the entire German codetermination legislation. They favored a strong works council with specific codetermination rights and employee-union representation on the board. The Protestant trade-union federation, and segments within both Protestant parties (especially the Anti-Revolutionary party), held similar positions, although they seemed to be less concerned with the details of board representation. The right-wing minority within the NKV also favored a German-type codetermination and corporation law.

The various employer associations generally approved of the expansion of the works council but insisted, for the most part, that the employer should retain his position as works-council chairman. Virtually all employers' associations, except the Protestant VPCW, opposed employee representation on the board.

The left wings of the NVV and the NKV also opposed both employee representation on the board and the concept of the works council as an instrument of social cooperation. Moreover, they recognized that in view of the weak union organization at the shop level, the works council could and would become a dangerous competitor. They advocated an explicit adversary relationship between unions and employers that would preclude the union officials from accepting the responsibility of employee-directors. The election of nonunion employees to the board of directors was, of course, completely unacceptable to the unions. The various ultra-Marxist splinter groups within and outside the NVV and NKV rejected the Verdam report in even stronger terms.

Dutch Codetermination in the 1970s

After lengthy debate the Dutch Parliament in 1971 passed a revised corporation law and a new works-council law. The new legislation was the result of many compromises but did expand the potential for employee participation considerably. The competence and potential influence of the works councils were further expanded in the 1978 reform of the 1971 legislation.

Dutch Corporation Law: Although the concept of limited liability has been effectively used by Dutch companies since the seventeenth century, with the exception of a few well-known multinationals most companies in the Netherlands were closely held, highly patriarchal family enterprises until World War II. Prior to 1928 most Dutch firms operated under an administrative council (similar to the nineteenth-century Prussian *Verwaltungsrat*), in which the owners or majority stockholders set company strategy and hired the operational managers. The company law of 1928 permitted Dutch firms either to adopt the German supervisory board-management board system or to maintain their administrative council, which by that time had become operationally quite similar to the Anglo-American board.

The 1971 company legislation required all corporations and private limited-liability companies with an equity of more than 10 million guilders and a work force of more than one hundred employees to appoint a supervisory board by July 1973. The new Dutch supervisory board has been modeled after the pre-World War II German *Aufsichtsrat*. Under the 1971 legislation, the supervisory board appoints the top management committee and periodically reviews its performance for the stockholders. As under the German system, major investments, mergers, or retrenchments required supervisory-board approval.

The selection method of the reformed Dutch supervisory board has been quite unique, however, and was the result of an ingenious compromise designed to satisfy both employers and codetermination advocates. Existing supervisory boards were instructed to appoint new members with the approval of shareholders and works councils whenever an opening occurred.

In those companies that had operated under the old administrative-council system prior to 1971, the stockholders would elect the initial supervisory board. As new openings arose, however, subsequent appointments to the board would require works-council approval. No employee of the firm or official of a union represented in the enterprise was eligible for election to the supervisory board.

If the supervisory board is unable to obtain the approval of both stockholders and works council for its nomination, it may either search for a more acceptable candidate or appeal to the tripartite Social Economic Council, which may approve or reject the board's nomination. There have been virtually no instances in which a supervisory board has made use of the appeal procedure.

The functions of the Dutch management committee (*Bestuur*) also have been virtually identical with the German Vorstand. The Bestuur legally is the company and is considered to be the employer who manages the firm in accordance with its professional competence. Although the approval of the supervisory board is necessary for major corporate changes, including mass layoffs or hiring, the board is not allowed to give directives to the management.

In practice the supervisory boards, especially in the large corporations, have remained self-perpetuating bodies. The pool of possible board members may have been reduced by the new requirement that the works councils as well as the stockholders approve new appointments. The new board structure has been in operation for seven years, without, however, having changed Dutch management processes in any significant way to date. Both employers (top management) and works-council members have been in agreement for a long time that employment stability and working conditions are among management's top priorities. In fact the main criticism of the reformed supervisory boards has come from union and socialist officials who have deplored the passive behavior of works-council-approved directors who, in their opinion, are too easily manipulated by management. This view is heatedly denied by both works-council members and managers; especially the latter have praised the competence and objectivity of the new directors.

As time passes, however, and as more and more older stockholder directors are replaced by new board members whose selection will have to be approved by the works councils, a new kind of supervisory board might emerge. Such an eventuality became even more likely after the 1978 works-council legislation reform. The new works council, no longer chaired by the enterprise's CEO, might adopt a more militant position, which, in turn, could affect the selection of the new directors.

Works Council Law of 1971: The works-council legislation of January 1971, an amended version of the 1965 Verdam commission report, made works councils mandatory for all corporations and private companies with more than one hundred employees, although it exempted multinational companies with more than 50 percent of their total employees serving abroad. For the most part, however, the multinationals operating in Holland, such as Dutch-Shell, Hoogovens, Philips, and Unilever, have had a well-established participatory system for a long time, which has conferred on the works council a status that exceeded the mandatory provisions of the 1950, 1971, and perhaps even the 1978 works-council legislation.

Although opposed by the Catholic and Socialist trade unions, the 1971 works-council legislation still retained the employer (actually the chairman of the management committee) or his representative as the chairman of the works-council committee, but it specifically recognized the works council as the advocate of employee interests. (The trade unions finally succeeded in removing the enterprise CEO from the works-council chairmanship in the 1978 law.) The 1950 clause, instructing the works council "to promote the best interest of the enterprise," has been retained, however, in both the 1971 and 1978 legislation. The works council has remained an instrument of social cooperation.

Works-council members are elected through a proportional voting system for two-year terms. The employees decide whether to vote as workers or salaried employees in two separate electoral bodies or as one common constituency. The unions have maintained their preferred status as being able to submit lists of candidates regardless of the size of their membership, while employees need the signatures of a third of the work force or thirty supporters (whichever is smaller) before their nominating lists are recognized by the enterprise's electoral commission. In spite of the relative weakness of the local union organizations, about three-fourths of the works-council members have been members of the three major union federations, although not necessarily all of them have been elected on official union lists. The rest are primarily members of independent white-collar and academic-staff unions. The 1971 legislation continued to require the individual enterprise to pay works-council expenses and to supply office facilities, which, however, are not nearly as lavish as those in German firms.

The 1971 legislation followed rather closely the German codetermination law of 1952 (Betr.V.G., 1952) in defining the works council's rights of codetermination, consultation, and information. The codetermination rights applied primarily to the social-personnel area; all decisions pertaining to profit sharing, working hours, overtime, vacations, shift work, pensions, retirement, and health programs require council approval. In case of disagreement, the bipartisan union-management industry boards, set up originally in the Betrijfsradenwet of 1933, are the final arbitrators. Since the national union officials represent the employees on the industry board, the unions' influence on the works councils should have been greatly strengthened over the long run. The economic crises of the late 1970s and government austerity programs, however, reduced the influence of the industry boards.

The consultation rights of the works councils have played a much greater role in the Dutch codetermination legislation than in the German. All personnel issues of interest to employees must be brought before the works council for advice and comment. These personnel matters include recruitment, promotion, dismissal, transfer, training procedures, job evaluation, and wage administration. The works council, moreover, must be given the opportunity to comment on major economic issues, including approval of the annual report, dividends, mass layoffs or recruitment, and temporary or permanent plant shutdown. In other economic areas, mergers, takeovers, and expansion or contraction of product lines, the council has the right to be informed in advance unless management believes that disclosure of its intention would jeopardize the project. This provision generated more controversy than it deserved, since management, especially in large corporations, generally did not take advantage of the escape clause, which was eliminated in the 1978 reform law.[19]

In practice, the works council has also taken on the tasks of monitoring the industry-wide collective-bargaining agreements. This has occurred, above all, in those enterprises in which the unions have been able within the last few years to build up a grass-roots organization, centered around a union shop representative (*bedrijfs contact man*).

The 1971 codetermination legislation strengthened the position of the works councils in the smaller and medium-sized firms that had previously disregarded the 1950 legislation. Moreover, the functions of the council were extended and had become more clearly defined. Yet employee participation in the decision process of the Dutch firm was still primarily advisory, though quite effective. There is ample evidence that the excellent works council-management relations in the larger enterprises had not been affected in any way by the 1971 legislation. It is perhaps surprising to recognize that during the 1965-1975 decade when segments of the Catholic church, the Socialist and Catholic union leadership, and the intellectual establishment had moved considerably to the left, harmonious relationships between enterprise management and works councils remained intact.

From Social Cooperation to Adversary Bargaining, 1974-1980: By 1974 the leadership of the FNV, the newly merged superfederation of Catholic and Socialist trade unions, had abandoned its previous ambivalence toward employee-union directors on the supervisory boards. Supported by the Labor party and left-wing Catholics, the FNV leadership demanded essentially the adoption of the German Montan industry codetermination legislation by the Dutch Parliament, as well as the introduction of a modified Meidner profit-sharing plan.[20]

The union demands threatened to end the Dutch consensus tradition, without strengthening the FNV unions in the enterprise. On one hand, conservative salaried employees, craftsmen, and right-wing Catholics were sufficiently antagonized either to leave the established unions and join new, independent, employee organizations or to form internal opposition groups that strove to elect antifederation candidates to the works councils. On the other hand, the radical rhetoric of the FNV leadership did not prevent young militant leftists from forming Marxist-Leninist-Maoist cells in unions and enterprises that were subsequently responsible for the wildcat strikes in 1969, 1970, 1975, 1976, and 1979. Although the actual incidence of these strikes was very low by British or American standards, they alarmed the Dutch public. The European recession of the early 1970s, aggravated by OPEC oil-price increases, further strained the cohesiveness of Dutch society and encouraged simultaneously an unaccustomed union militancy and management intransigence.

The 1971 laws had been passed after six years of debate with the approval of the social partners and a broad parliamentary support. The two laws represented the very best in Dutch consensus politics and under ordinary circumstances should have determined Dutch labor relations for many years without further amendments. The very nature of Dutch politics in which Center-Left coalition governments replace Center-Right administrations, yet the same handful of personalities reappear, does not make it likely that compromises agreed upon after years of discussion fail almost immediately. The unwillingness of the FNV leadership, under pressure of infiltrated Marxist militants, to give the 1971 legislation time to prove itself therefore was a significant indication of the changing nature of the Dutch union movement.

During the mid-1970s, a left-of-center coalition of independent Socialists, the Labor party, and the Protestant and Catholic parties under Joop den Uyl (1973-1977) had made an effort to return to a modified form of social cooperation within the framework of a government incomes policy. In 1974 the FNV and the CNV (Protestant Trade Union Federation) agreed to accept an incomes policy in return for a further expansion of the works councils and a mandatory profit-sharing plan (*Vermogensaanwasdeling*, or VA), which would have primarily benefited individual employees in line with CNV thinking. Although the profit-sharing plan discussed was quite different from the original Meidner-type plan proposed by left-wing leaders within the FNV, employers as well as segments of the middle class opposed it strongly.

The real issue, however, was not the specific content of the profit-sharing plan, or even specific provisions of the FNV-supported expansion of works-council authority; it was the changed political ideology of the FNV, which flatly rejected the view of the works council as a cooperative agency. The FNV leadership believed during the early 1970s that the works council should exclusively represent the employees' interests without concerning itself with the broader goals of the enterprise.[21] The works council, therefore, should have an opportunity to examine all managerial decisions rather than participate in the decision process. In order to protect the employees, however, the works council must be able to veto any decision that it considers harmful to employee interests.

The debate over codetermination and profit sharing served to emphasize the ideological incompatibility of the parties in the Center-Left coalition government of the mid-1970s, which could not agree on an amended codetermination legislation that would have been acceptable to its various constituencies.

In May 1977 the Labor party won a decisive victory, at least by Dutch standards, which made it the strongest party in Parliament, with about 38 percent of all seats. Paradoxically the newly found strength made it more difficult for the Labor party leadership to form a new coalition government, since leftist party and union leaders demanded the full adoption of the party program, including the controversial profit-sharing plan and codetermination reform. The leaders of the Christian Democratic party, relatively eager to renew the previous coalition rule, were unable to pledge the support of their party for these radical reforms, and for six months the Netherlands was without a government while various Labor party stalwarts took turns attempting to form a government.

In October a Christian Democrat, Dres Van Agt, suddenly obtained a two-vote majority for a Christian Democrat-Liberal right-of-center coalition government.[22] Subsequently provincial elections in March, local elections in May 1978, and the European Parliament election in June 1979 showed a strong and growing support for Van Agt, who has been governing with a relatively strong hand. The Van Agt administration promised to reduce inflation and government controls and reverse the drift toward a socialist economy. Although the administration seemed to show little interest in the further extension of codetermination legislation, it considered minor revision in the 1971 works-council legislation as a possible bargaining chip to keep the Christian Democratic party's left wing in line.

By 1977 the Catholic trade-union leaders affiliated with Van Agt's party had become as militant in their support of further works-council reform as were their Socialist colleagues in the FNV. In order to demonstrate the support of Catholic trade-union leaders for a broader codetermination law, we shall consider briefly the so-called compromise version of the original FNV-sponsored codetermination reform proposal, which came close to being adopted by the Parliament in 1976. The compromise version was drawn up by the Christian Democratic social affairs minister, Jaap Boersma, in an attempt to keep the Center-Left coalition together and to reintegrate the FNV leadership into the establishment.[23] Since the bill was a compromise, it contained parts that would have brought the Dutch works-council legislation in line with current German law. In other aspects the Dutch management still would have enjoyed much greater authority. Several clauses, however, would have strengthened the authority of the Dutch works council beyond anything available to its German counterpart.

Boersma's Proposed Codetermination Bill of 1974: The first provision was that the works council must be consulted before an appointment to the management committee was made by the supervisory board. (The original FNV proposal gave the works council a veto; Boersma's compromise required only consultation.) In practice this might have meant, however, that only a top management acceptable to the works council would be appointed over the long run. In the 1978 law the works council merely has to be informed.

Second, all important decisions affecting the interest of the employees, including major investment and disinvestment projects, could be taken only after prior consultations with the works council. In case of disagreement over important issues, the works council could appeal to the courts for a decision. (This clause was included in the Works Council Reform Act of 1978.)

Third, the works council would receive full codetermination rights on all social-personnel issues. In case no agreement was reached, management would be required to drop the matter unless an arbitration procedure was agreed upon.

Fourth, the works council, including its chairman, would consist only of elected employee members. However, a new consultative committee, composed of management and works-council representatives, would have been added.

Boersma's compromise did not deal with changes in the composition of the supervisory board or with the establishment of a union-dominated profit-sharing plan. We can assume, however, that these issues would have been raised by the FNV and the Labor party's left wing once the compromise works-council legislation had been accepted. It was precisely the view that any compromise might only be a platform for further demands that brought about the breakup of the 1974 coalition and prevented the Labor party in 1977 from forming a coalition government after its election victory.

The Van Agt administration opposed fundamental changes in the Dutch labor-relations system but did not object to strengthening the works council. The Christian Democrats continued to favor worker participation in enterprise decision making and also viewed a strong works council as an instrument to oppose the ideological influence of the FNV leadership. In the opinion of many observers, the opposition of the country's works councils to the radical FNV proposals in 1974 may have been the crucial factor in forcing the Netherland's most radical government since 1946 to resign.[24]

The government's austerity program and Europe's economic stagnation caused considerable unrest among trade unions and their supporters in Parliament. In order to keep its slim majority in Parliament, the Van Agt administration permitted the reintroduction of a works-council reform bill that strongly resembled Boersma's previous codetermination proposal. After relatively brief discussion, the Works Council Reform Act was passed by a strong majority in both chambers during the late fall of 1978.[25]

Works Council Reform Act of 1978: The reform act applies to all firms with more than one hundred employees and requires works-council approval on all matters affecting employment and personnel practices, including hiring procedures, new investments, mergers, mass layoffs, intercompany production, and marketing agreements. In case management and works council fail to agree, the issue comes before the Social Economic Council for final settlement.

The introduction of the Social Economic Council (SER) into the works council-employer relationship is a reaffirmation of social cooperation and represented a significant victory for the Christian Democrats. Assuming a continued chain of moderate coalition governments for the next decade, the SER can be expected to consider the economic welfare of society in mediating possible works council-management disagreement on strategic enterprise policy.

The new works council consists only of elected members, chosen from the work force. It will vary in size from seven to twenty-five members and will elect a chairman from its midst. The enterprise CEO will no longer chair the works council but will be expected to meet with the council at least six times a year.

Consultation between enterprise management and works council is compulsory in all areas in which the works council has consultation or codetermination rights. Moreover, management or works council may request advice from each other that will be rendered in subsequent consultation meetings.

In this area of composition and jurisdiction, the reform act was another compromise between Left and Right. The price for permitting the SER to resolve works council-management disagreements was the elimination of the employer from the council. Under the 1978 legislation, the Dutch works council becomes almost identical with the German. The employer no longer presides or participates in the deliberations of the council unless specifically invited. Eliminating the employer from the works council had been demanded by the Left for a long time, but it is very doubtful that this step will have any practical consequences under contemporary conditions.

The 1978 act extended the area of works-council consultation rights. Management must ask advice from the council whenever important economic decisions are under consideration. Specifically, the council has consultation rights with respect to important investments, large loans, large-scale recruitment, mergers and takeovers in the Netherlands, and liquidation of domestic subsidiaries.

Management is in no way required to accept the council's advice. Although the 1978 law is more specific than its predecessors, in fact very little has changed in practice since the management of most larger Dutch enterprises has always consulted with its works council on major economic issues. When major economic issues are concerned, however, the works council can appeal to the courts if its advice is not taken, and management must justify its actions. Management must now inform the works council whenever it intends to appoint or dismiss a senior manager. This appeals aspect of the information rights goes far beyond German works-council legislation.

The number of issues that require works-council approval before management can act have been increased substantially. The works council has codetermination rights in establishing or revising factory regulations, pension plans, profit-sharing plans, savings plans, working hours, vacations, wage administration, and job evaluation. The council also has such rights in regulating safety, health, and welfare issues; appointment, promotion, and discharge policies; and training and appraisal of personnel.

The 1978 law also extends the right of the works council to be informed of the economic status of the enterprise (annual report) and budget and investment plans. This extension affects primarily small and medium-sized firms, which have been rather secretive in the past.

Dutch Labor Relations since 1978: The major issue raised originally by the FNV in 1974 had not been the extent of works-council participation or even industrial democracy but rather the replacement of a political and labor-relations system based upon harmonious social cooperation by an adversary policy of confrontation and class warfare. In response, there emerged a growing number of social democrats in the Labor party and the Christian Democratic party who believed that in the name of industrial democracy a relatively small but influential group of labor leaders and intellectuals had endeavored to impose its values upon Dutch employees. This view was certainly corroborated by the attempt of the works councils of several major firms during 1974 to form a national association of works councils to oppose before Parliament and the public the radical "adventurous" proposals of the FNV.

During the mid-1970s when the leftist Joop den Uyl's government abandoned its support of the trade-union-sponsored codetermination laws, the efforts to form a national association of works councils to oppose the FNV leadership were dropped, since most works-council members were—and are—loyal union members who do not relish fights with their national and federation functionaries. At the same time it is obvious that, as in Germany, the advocates of reforms that would change the nature of the system did not speak for rank-and-file employees or for the works councils. Whatever the merits of their proposals, they had very little to do with industrial democracy. Indeed they might have been interpreted as attempts to thwart whatever industrial democracy had developed.

Currently there are few indications about how the new 1978 law has affected labor relations in practice. The breakdown in the Netherland's system of national wage bargaining in the spring of 1979 and the sharp rise in wildcat strikes during the summer of 1979 were consequences of the growing influence of Communist cells in strategic waterfront unions, economic crises, and government austerity policy. Certainly no one could or did blame the reformed works councils for the ideological militancy of the FNV trade-union leadership. If it can be assumed that FNV leader Wim Kok and his associates are not representative of Dutch workers during the late 1970s, and, as many observers believe, "the radicalization of Dutch society" has ended, works-council behavior will not be changed by turning its consultation rights into enforceable codetermination rights.

During the 1970s management only rarely made a significant personnel decision without works-council approval. The militant strikes of 1977 and 1979 often protested company retrenching decisions that had been approved by the works council. The spirit of social cooperation still distinguishes Dutch work force-employer relations and will change only if the FNV can capture the works council and impose its confrontation strategy on its members.

The continued good working relationships between management and works councils on the enterprise level in most industries contrast sharply with the increasingly adamant adversary relationship that has existed on the macrolevel between trade union and employer association representatives since 1978. Centralized tripartite wage talks have ensured labor peace since 1945, although the entire negotiating machinery has shown increasing signs of breaking down ever since the early 1970s. Even the pro-Labor Joop den Uyl government (1974-1977) had not been able to revitalize it or to reestablish the cooperative spirit of the 1950s and 1960s.

During 1976 and 1977 the FNV had developed a clever tactic to accompany statesmanlike but meaningless discussion on the highest national level with selective strikes of key enterprises or sectors. In 1977 the union's selective-strike policy forced the employers to abandon their demand for an end to the costly wage indexation, although the government had quietly supported such an anti-inflationary arrangement.

Faced by recession and inflation (see table 7-1), the trade unions demanded, generally unsuccessfully, job-security guarantees and prior union consultations on rationalization investment during the tripartite wage negotiations of 1977 and 1978. (Note that enterprises already consult the works councils; obviously this was not sufficient for trade union leadership.) In 1979 the FNV demanded a thirty-five-hour week without prior consultation with the major national unions (metal trades, building trades, and printing unions). The employers opposed the demand vigorously, citing not only the cost of a reduced work week but also the serious shortage of skilled labor and technicians, which would be aggravated. The employers emphasized once more that as a consequence of the 1974-1977 period, the once-flourishing Netherlands had become the country with the highest wages and highest social costs in the Common Market (labor costs are 35 percent higher than EEC average) and the largest loss of international markets because of reduced competitiveness.[26]

The government's Central Planning Bureau (roughly equivalent to the U.S. Council of Economic Advisers) supported the employers' contentions and predicted higher unemployment if the reduced work week were implemented. The continued rise in the Netherland's balance-of-payments deficit, another large 1979 budget deficit incurred by a supposedly conservative administration, and the pessimistic economic outlook for 1980 convinced the country at large that a reduced work week would add to the nation's economic difficulty. The major unions, led by the metal workers, the country's largest, quickly disassociated themselves from the FNV and settled with the employers on a compromise basis that kept the forty-hour work week but also preserved the inflationary wage indexing.

The chastened Wim Kok, president of the Socialist-Catholic FNV,

Table 7-1
World Stability Ranking, June 1979

	Inflation	Unemployment
Japan	2.6%	2.5%
Switzerland	2.9	0.4
Austria	3.3	2.4
Germany	3.7	3.4
Netherlands	4.1	4.1
Sweden	6.0	2.0
France	10.0	5.9
United Kingdom	10.1	5.2
United States	10.4	5.2
Italy	13.8	7.8

Source: Adapted from *Die Zeit*, 29 June 1979, p. 24.

promised to confer with the individual unions in the future before proposing social reforms. The permanent staff of the Social Economic Council proposed to return to the practice of the 1950s and 1960s and hold advanced talks prior to the annual wage negotiations in the hope of developing a five-year "rolling collective-bargaining agreement." The employers are primarily interested in simple two- to three-year wage contracts to avoid the annual strain and uncertainty, but most likely would agree to a five-year rolling plan.

It is very questionable, however, if the current ideological complexion of the FNV federation would permit such a return to a cooperative form of union-management codetermination. A brief sketch of the FNV's young charismatic leader Willem Kok may provide a better understanding of the doctrinaire nature of the trade-union federation's leadership.

Kok's career can serve as a vivid example of the changing nature of Dutch trade unions. The forty-year-old Kok comes from a bourgeois family, studied economics at the well-known Netherlands School of International Business (NOIB), and after a brief period of work for an export-import firm, became a functionary in the international-affairs office of the Socialist building-workers' union. He advanced quickly to the trade union's executive office and from there to the managing executive committee of the Socialist trade-union federation, NVV. In 1973 at the age of thirty-three, he was elected president of the NVV without ever having worked a day with his hands and subsequently, also became the president of the merged superfederation of Dutch Socialist and Catholic trade union federations, the FNV. Ambitious to establish himself as a European personality, he managed to win election as the president of the European Trade Union Federation in May 1979. In this position he succeeded H.O. Vetter, the perennial president of Germany's DGB, whose strong anti-Communist stance had maintained the pro-NATO, social-democratic position of the European Trade Union Federation.

It is far from certain that Kok will maintain Vetter's rejection of all types of popular-front cooperation with Communist trade unions and causes. His public statements reflect a socialist vision in which the trade unions obtain fundamental social and economic changes in Europe. In order to achieve the "Europe of the working people," Kok expounds a set of slogans and demands that puts him close to Olof Palme's position and far to the left of Central European trade-union leaders. For Holland and Europe, Kok demands further expansion of public investment, the early announcement by private enterprises of all major investment strategies, joint investment planning by "employees and employers," and reduction of unemployment through shorter work weeks, longer vacations, and earlier retirement.

Most important from an operational view is Kok's hostility to multinational concerns, which he expressed in his presidential address at the 1979

Munich conference of ETUF (European Trade Union Federation). The European trade unions, he asserted, "must no longer accept legal or other obstacles to international [union] solidarity actions" but must obtain a "code of conduct" for the multinational concerns that explicitly permits international-solidarity strikes to support the specific demands of any given national union.[27]

It is highly unlikely that Kok will actually persuade, say, German Ford workers to strike in order to prevent further transfer of engine production from England to Germany. The international solidarity of European trade unions has never been able to overcome their national interests. Kok's remarks are of interest primarily becuase they illustrate the socialist ideology that will dominate the Dutch trade-union federation during the 1980s, a sharp reversal of the pragmatism of the 1950s and 1960s.

Holland's deteriorating economic condition provides little leeway for trade union or employer maneuvering. In June 1979 the Van Agt government persuaded Parliament with great difficulty to adopt a deflationary austerity program, which made it even more difficult for unions or employers to reach an agreement in their collective-bargaining conferences of spring 1980. The government is determined to cut the current account deficit and public spending 5 percent by 1981 and reduce unemployment by 25 percent, while maintaining the guilder through high interest rates as much as possible at the June 1979 level to keep import prices low. Of particular importance to the economic future will be the government's success in reversing the underlying economic factors that have converted an international-payments surplus of $2.8 billion in 1976 to a deficit of $1.3 billion in 1978 and over $750 million in 1979. Only a revived atmosphere of social cooperation could create a social climate in which the austerity program could succeed.

All the evidence is to the contrary. Strains between trade unions and government, as well as trade unions and employers, are increasing. The weak government majority and the close association between the Christian Democratic party's left wing and the Catholic sector of the FNV has forced the Van Agt administration frequently to depart from its austerity program and increase government spending to keep inefficient enterprises alive. Moreover, a coalition of Socialists and left-wing Christain Democrats defeated the government in an advisory vote on Dutch NATO policy in November 1979 and again raised the question whether the most pragmatic Dutch government of the 1970s may survive until the end of the legislative period in 1981.

Conclusion

The radicalization of the FNV leadership and the segments of the Labor party has antagonized many of their former supporters. In spite of an apparent breakdown of the national consensus policy, the Dutch industrial-relations system has remained intact on the operational level, regardless of a growing, although still relatively small, number of strikes in 1976-1977 and again in 1979. Worker participation functions well on the works-council level, although it is still primarily advisory and consultative in spite of the new codetermination rights. Management, however, values works-council cooperation and will continue to avoid decisions that do not have council support, regardless of the implications of the most recent legislation.

If Dutch society continues to move to the left or if the FNV is successful in its effort to purge the works councils of all members who do not consider themselves as national representatives, the era of harmony will come to an end. The adoption of the 1978 works-council law could make it very difficult for management to make rational economic decisions if an adversary attitude replaced social coalition among Dutch employees. Should a major change in works-council attitude be accompanied by adoption of the FNV profit-sharing plan and by the allocation of 50 percent of the supervisory seats to union officials, the entire nature of Dutch society would be changed.

It is very unlikely that all of these measures would be adopted within the next few years. It is not entirely impossible that much of this legislative package will be implemented step by step over the next fifteen years by an intellectual establishment that tries to avoid confrontation with the FNV and is very eager to be considered progressive. Whether the October 1978 reform bill will become part of this tactic is difficult to assess at this time. Much will depend on how long the Van Agt government will remain in power and how successful its efforts will be to strengthen market forces and deflate the economy without creating high employment.

Worker participation in the Netherlands currently is overshadowed by the dismal economic situation in which the country finds itself after five years of socialist-egalitarian measures, which left it in 1979 with the same number of work places it had in 1950. The Netherlands in 1977 lost 6 percent of its share in world trade through a decline in exports and lost another 2 percent in 1978. Unemployment remained above 4 percent (equal to about 5.8 percent by U.S. definition), although inflation was reduced also to 4 percent, only slightly higher than Germany's (see table 7-1) but still too high for the Dutch trade unions. Moreover, even J. Stavinga, the Communist leader of Rotterdam's wildcat harbor strike during August 1979, sounded an antiwelfare-state theme when he explained why the well-paid harbor workers (who average about $22,500) refused to return to work: "This is a strike of discontent with a welfare situation in which a worker earns well, but through taxation and welfare payments actually gets too little in his outstretched hannd—even though he is part of the ideal Dutch system which takes care of him from the cradle to the grave."[28]

The discussion about the union-employee profit-sharing plans proposed by the socialist NVV has caused a sharp decline in investments and discouraged long-run planning. The entirely changed atmosphere in which business operated in Holland since 1975 is striking and illustrates how quickly well-established labor-management situations can change. The current administration of Dres van Agt is determined to reverse the march toward socialism. If it is successful and business responds through increased investments, labor relations may return to their previous stability. Interestingly, Van Agt has the full support of the German Social Democrats.[29]

Luxembourg *Janice R. Bellace*[a]

The small size of Luxembourg and the narrow range of its economic base have greatly influenced its pattern of industrial relations. Less formal than the models found in neighboring countries, the Luxembourg model of worker participation consciously aims to establish worker-representation mechanisms tailored to the size and nature of the enterprise.

The influence of trade unions is felt most keenly in the coal and steel industries, which are crucial to the economy of the country. There are two major union federations: the socialist CGT (*Confédération générale du Travail*) and the Christian LCGB (*Letzeburger Chreschtleche Gewerkschaftsbond*), which together have approximately forty-five thousand members. The unions affiliated with these two federations are composed entirely of blue-collar workers. The independent trade union, the FEP (Fédération des Employés Privés), organizes white-collar employees.

The major components of the Luxembourg model of worker participation are hybrid forms of other systems. The personnel delegates (*délégués du personnel*) perform a function that combines some of the duties of a works councillor with the grievance-processing tasks of a shop steward. The mixed-enterprise committee (*comité mixte*) in a small firm is analogous to a works council, and in a large firm, it is similar to a supervisory board.

Joint Management-Worker Committees

The law of 6 May 1974 instituted joint management-worker committees in small and modestly sized private-sector firms. This statute also mandated

[a]The section on codetermination in Luxembourg has been taken from Janice R. Bellace's *Codetermination in Germany, The Netherlands, and Luxembourg*, prepared for the Multinational Industrial Relations Program of the Industrial Research Unit, The Wharton School, University of Pennsylvania, 1976. Copyright © 1976 Trustees of the University of Pennsylvania. Reprinted with the kind permission of the coyright owner and the author. Janice R. Bellace is an assistant professor of legal studies and management, and a senior faculty research associate, Industrial Research Unit, The Wharton School, University of Pennsylvania.

board-level worker representation in large, limited-liability companies. Although these two bodies are similar in some respects, the composition of the worker representation and its function differ.

Structure of Mixed-Enterprise Committees in Small Firms: The 1974 statute mandates a mixed-enterprise committee for all firms employing at least 150 persons. The committee, which ranges in size from six to sixteen members depending upon the size of the work force, is composed of an equal number of management and worker representatives. The company's chief executive serves as chairman of the mixed-enterprise committee. The employer may select the management representatives by a method of his own choosing.

The worker representatives are elected by secret ballot of the company's personnel delegates. Worker seats on the mixed-enterprise committee are divided among white- and blue-collar workers on a proportional basis. Lists of candidates are drawn up by the personnel delegates. Any employee with one year's service with the company may be elected a worker representative for a four-year term.

Mixed-enterprise committees primarily serve in a consultative capacity although some powers of codetermination are accorded them. There is no absolute right of information.

Article 7 of the 1974 statute lists six general subject matters on which such committees have the right of codetermination: (1) the introduction or application of employee-performance rating schemes; (2) the introduction or modification of health and safety measures; (3) the establishment or modification of criteria concerning hiring, promotion, transfer, and termination of employment; (4) the establishment or alteration of criteria for employee assessment; (5) the setting or alteration of workshop regulations; and (6) the granting of employee merit awards.

Where the worker and management representatives fail to reach an agreement on a proposed change, either party may submit the issue to the National Conciliation Office. If conciliation fails to secure an agreement, the National Conciliation Office will act as an arbitrator.

Article 9(1) states that the mixed-enterprise committee must be informed of and consulted "on any economic or financial decision which might have a determining incidence on the structure of the enterprise or on the employment level." Although the statute contemplates prior consultation, this need not occur if management believes consultation "would endanger the carrying out of a projected operation" (article 9).

Articles 8 and 10 oblige the company manager to inform and consult the mixed-enterprise committee on various social and economic issues, such as the introduction, improvement, or modification of production facilities, machinery, production procedures, and methods and staffing requirements. Twice yearly the company manager must report on the economic and financial state of the firm.

Structure of Board of Directors in Large Companies: Although not specifically requiring a two-tier board, the 1974 statute contemplates the existence of a dual structure in joint stock companies (*sociétés anonymes*). The law covers all limited-liability companies employing at least a thousand persons, all companies in which the government has a 25 percent interest, and all companies that benefit from a government concession.

The 1971 law amends those provisions of the law of 10 August 1915 dealing with the board of directors. If a company operates with a unitary board structure, one-third of its directors must be worker-representatives. If a company has voluntarily chosen a two-tier system, one-third of the supervisory board must be worker-directors. In either case, the board must consist of at least nine directors.

Similar to the system operative in small firms, the worker-representatives are elected by a secret ballot of the personnel delegates according to the principle of proportional representation for white- and blue-collar employees. To be nominated, a candidate must have two years' service with the company. Worker-representatives in the coal and steel industries receive special treatment. Trade unions in these firms may designate three of the worker-representatives. These directors need not be employees of the company.

The term of office for worker-representatives is the same as that for shareholder-representatives. Article 30 of the 1974 statute provides worker-representatives with protection from dismissal during their tenure on the board unless so authorized by a court.

Worker-representatives have the same rights and responsibilities as the shareholder-representatives on the board. As such, they are subject to the same duty of acting in the best interests of the firm.

The range of issues that a worker-director considers depends upon the board structure of the company. If a company is operating with a unitary board structure, the range of issues could be broad. If the company is operating with a two-tier board, as is more likely now that worker representation is mandatory, the matters before the supervisory board could be quite narrow. The day-to-day management of the company would be placed in the hands of the management board. Since Luxembourg does not yet have a statute requiring a dual board structure, there is no mandatory division of functions between the supervisory and management boards. In all likelihood, companies voluntarily instituting a two-tier system would also be motivated to create a framework that places the supervisory board in a consultative and advisory capacity.

Personnel Delegates

The primary level of worker representation in Luxembourg is provided by the personnel delegates. Although their function is similar to that of works councillors, personnel delegates as a group do not operate along the lines of a works council. Statutes requiring personnel delegates have existed for over sixty years, most recently updated in 1962 and 1979.

The 1962 statute requires a delegation representing blue-collar workers (*délégation ouvrière*) in every firm that employs at least fifteen blue-collar workers on the average. A white-collar delegation (*délégation d'employés*) must be established in every firm employing twelve white-collar employees on the average. The language of the 1979 statute is, in many instances, either very broad or simply not specific. When the employer and the employees' committee disagree on the meaning of the statute, such disputes are referred to the minister of labor for resolution.

Election of Personnel Delegates: Any employee of the firm may be nominated for the position of personnel delegate. The lists of candidates are drawn up by the appropriate trade unions, while the number of personnel delegates to be elected varies according to the size of the firm. The number of delegates representing blue-collar and white-collar employees is determined on the principle of proportional representation of the work force. Delegates are elected for four-year terms by secret ballot of all employees.

Role of Personnel Delegates: Personnel delegates have the responsibility of protecting and promoting the interests and well-being of employees in the area of social matters. In carrying out this responsibility, personnel delegates communicate information and proposals directly to management.

Personnel delegates may seek to process individual grievances through direct contact with management. The delegates are required by statute to pursue grievance settlement through conciliation. Any attempt to organize a work stoppage in support of a grievance, without having first taken the issue to the National Labor Court, is prohibited.

Delegates serve in an advisory capacity when changes in workshop rules are contemplated. They also have a supervisory role relating to the administration of health, safety, and welfare measures.

Conclusion

The relatively recent introduction of mixed-enterprise committees makes evaluating the effects difficult. The trade unions, regardless of political allegiance, are dissatisfied with the present law, claiming that worker directors should hold more than one-third of the seats on the supervisory board of large companies. The present Christian-social/liberal coalition government is unlikely to make any changes in the present scheme, but if the socialist-liberal coalition returns to power, some changes are likely, particularly a move to introduce parity codetermination in the steel industry.

Belgium

The struggle of the Flemish people for a greater role in Belgian society and the recognition of their language has affected all political and social events in Belgium since World War II. It is impossible to separate labor-relations issues from the "language war." Moreover, since codetermination or worker participation has not played a great role in Belgium's free-enterprise society, I have not included a discussion of Belgian labor relations.

France

Although the first employer-sponsored works council on either side of the Rhine appeared in the nineteenth century as a result of the French ultramontan movement, worker participation in the decision processes of the firm has not yet become an important factor in the French economy. Catholic social movements have provided the only important ideological support for worker participation in France for the past hundred years. French politics is extremely old-fashioned, to the extent that neither Marxists nor anti-Marxists have been willing to admit that contemporary economic institutions may have changed somewhat since the days of Karl Marx or Jean Baptiste Say. In such an atmosphere there is little room for social cooperation.

The tense class warfare of the interwar period culminated in abiding suspicion and hostility between employers and workers and helped the Germans to destroy the Third Republic.[30] Such class hostility was hardly conducive to fostering worker participation as an expression of social cooperation, although Pius XI's encyclical, *Quadragesimo Anno* (1931), did have considerable impact on Catholic intellectuals, on the Left as well as on the Far Right.[31] The Catholic workers' movement on the Left was heartened by the encyclical's attack on materialistic capitalism and its support of cooperative production. The Catholic Right was influenced primarily by the encyclical's section, "The Reconstruction of the Social Order," which praised the "principle of subsidiarity," the admonition that it was unnatural and harmful for larger organizations to acquire functions that could be performed more efficiently by smaller organizations. The principle of subsidiarity led conservative Catholics to oppose large corporations as well as centralized government bureaucracies, and through the support of artisans, peasants, and small family enterprises led to the advocacy of social cooperation.

The practical impact of Catholic social thought on French labor relations in the interwar period was hardly noticeable and is mentioned here only to show the intellectual origin for the post-World War II codetermination legislation.

Structure and Ideology of French
Union Federations

Since 1945, as well as during the interwar period, the French labor movement has been divided into Communist, Socialist, and Catholic union
federations that have been concerned mainly with national and ideological
issues. They have neglected the individual worker and in many cases have
lacked the local organization to represent the economic interests of the
enterprise's employees. Although the major union confederations have
cooperated more frequently since 1945 than in the interwar period, especially in the negotiation of industry-wide contracts, they have continued to
view each other with the utmost distrust.

The General Confederation of Labor (*Confédération Générale du
Travail*, CGT) is the largest, oldest, and most powerful French union. Led
by a Stalinist bureaucracy since the 1930s, it has been closely tied to the
French Communist party and has faithfully followed the party line. The
CGT is interested in maintaining the revolutionary, class-conscious élan
among its working-class members and professes that only a revolutionary
change in the structure of society will free workers from exploitation. The
rather striking improvement in the living standards of French workers may
have sharpened its interest in immediate, short-run issues that promise further gains, at the expense of its commitment to distant revolutionary
changes. In response to the shifting attitudes of the manual workers, and to
meet the competition from the other federations, the CGT has taken a
greater interest in bread-and-butter issues during the last ten years and also
has been willing to cooperate with the other unions. The CGT, however, has
not wavered in its opposition to all forms of worker or union participation,
on either enterprise or national levels.

The relatively newest union federation, which has become the second
largest trade-union group, is the Confederation Française Democratique du
Travail (CFDT), which is close to the left wing of the current (Mitterand's)
Socialist party. Moderately Marxist in its ideology, it has broad support
among skilled workers and resembles the Dutch socialist trade unions
(NVV) in its advocacy of worker self-management and its opposition to
centralized, bureaucratic command economics, although, unlike the Dutch,
it still demands the nationalization of key industries. Opposed to social
cooperation with the ''class enemy,'' the syndicalistic bent of the CFDT has
permitted the participation of its members in local works council.

The Workers' Force (Force Ouvriers, FO), until the split with the CFDT
the second largest confederation, has been close to the old (pre-Mitterand)
anti-Communist Socialist party, currently the right wing in the Mitterand
party. Essentially social-democratic in nature, it draws its support primarily
from state and municipal civil servants. The FO has, in principle, supported

the German model of worker participation, as has the French Confederation of Christian Workers (CFTC) and the General Confederation of Salaried Employees (CGC). With Giscard d'Estaing's victory in the spring 1978 election, it has become entirely possible that these three reformistic confederations may merge. If they do not, codetermination will remain a weak force in France.

The local unions of each federation gain legal recognition by the employer as employee representatives if they have sufficient members. This may force an employer to deal with four to five unions in one firm, which is not as bad in practice as it may seem because the important bargaining agreements are negotiated on an industry-wide basis and because most of the internal issues are handled through a works council, whose members may or may not be union members.

At the end of World War II, both the de Gaullists and the French Christian Democrats (MRP) advocated legislation to encourage employee participation as a means of ending the alienation of the French worker and to replace class warfare with social cooperation.[32] Although the Communist and Socialist unions have consistently opposed all attempts to soften the adversary relationship between employers and employees, several weak, voluntary works-council laws were passed during the immediate post-"liberation" period 1945-1948 when all classes and parties pledged everlasting cooperation.

Formation and Operation of Works Councils: In 1945 General de Gaulle's provisional government introduced the first works-council legislation, which was adopted by the first postwar Parliament in 1946. Worker participation in France was strongly influenced by the experience of the Dutch enterprise councils of the interwar period. All French firms with more than fifty employees that were organized as a corporation (*société ánonyme*, or SA) had to form works councils (*comité d'enterprise*). The absence of sanctions in the legislation and the lack of interest among employees has prompted one-half of the firms required to establish works councils to disregard the law. Works councils have been established, however, in all major companies, just as in the Netherlands.

The works council was to be elected by the employees biennially to represent proportionally a cross-section of the various unions recognized by the firm. The legislation assigned to the council the dual role of both representing the interests of the employees and assisting management in improving the economic performance of the enterprise through the exchange of advice and information. The employer, in return, was required to provide the comité with pertinent financial information, such as balance sheets and income statements, which are routinely published by American enterprises but in France are considered confidential material that a true *patron* (employer) would never divulge. Furthermore, the employer was supposed to inform the works council of major planned investments, mergers, or any other import decision that would affect the employees' job security. Although the large French organizations, and especially the multinationals, have generally provided the information required by the 1945 legislation, the typical medium-sized French firm seems to have been able to disregard it frequently.

SAs with more than fifty employees also have been required to allocate two nonvoting seats on the board of directors to works-council members (*délégués du personnel*). In 1972 the number of nonvoting employees was increased to four, primarily to assure adequate representation of salaried employees. In the natonalized industries (especially petrochemical, oil, automobile, and transportation) the employees have held one-third of the board of directors' seats and have frequently supplied the vice-chairman of the board.

Virtually no empirical material exists concerning the effectiveness of the employee-directors in the natonalized industries, nor is there much material, beyond anecdotes, on the role of the nonvoting works-council director in the private sector. One can infer, however, that the employee-directors in the nationalized sector have behaved very much like their German counterparts; they have enthusiastically supported management through the expansionary cycles and have played a restraining role during retrenching periods.

The effectiveness of the works council seems to have varied greatly among industries and even within different plants of the same enterprise, in accordance with the personalities of the délégués du personnel, the strength of the various unions at the plant, and the attitude of management. For the most part, the works councils became preoccupied with processing grievances during normal times and with restraining layoffs during periods of economic decline. French labor laws, very much like Germany's, make it difficult and costly to dismiss personnel. Collective-bargaining agreements, rather than the weak works-council legislation, have determined the works council's participatory role in preparing redundancy programs.

During the May 1968 student revolutions, the manual workers and the major unions played a restraining role. Still there were many incidents of wildcat strikes and vandalism, often generated by a handful of ultra-Marxist sectarians. The leaders of the union federations, including the CGT, were surprised by the weakness of their local organizations and, without serious employer resistance, managed in 1968 to appoint union stewards to represent the national union on the plant level. Employers are required to free union stewards for their necessary duties and supply them with office space. Although the union stewards are charged primarily with strengthening the local union organization, the layer of union stewards representing different unions, on top of the works councils, has not added to the peacefulness of the shop atmosphere or made the life of French personnel managers easier. Moreover, the rate of union membership among French employees is still the lowest of any other Common Market country—less than 30 percent—and has not changed significantly. Still, with the exception of a few highly politicized industries—the Renault works, coal mining, the longshoremen, and the Lorraine steel industry since 1978—industrial life in France is quite peaceful, especially if compared with England or Italy.

Profit-sharing Plans: The peculiarly French institution of mandatory profit sharing may have been a factor in maintaining workable French industrial relations, although there is little evidence for or against this assumption. In view of the historical opposition of the French Communist and Socialist unions toward employee-union participation in enterprise decision making, de Gaulle urged in 1945 the adoption of profit-sharing plans as an expression of the cooperation of capital and labor. For the next fifteen years various profit-sharing plans were adopted unilaterally by French companies, although primarily in medium-sized firms. In 1959 the legal and tax foundations were laid for an extension of voluntary profit-sharing schemes, without prompting a significant increase in participatory enterprises. The large Gaullist majority in Parliament passed a second, mandatory profit-sharing law in 1967, which applied to all firms with more than one hundred employees that had no previous effective profit-sharing schemes. Critics of the 1967 legislation maintained that the profit-sharing bonuses have been figured into the price lists of the major firms and hence have been inflationary, while they have reduced available investment funds for medium and smaller firms.

On the ideological front, the profit-sharing plans have neither met the hope of the advocates nor justified the fears of the Marxist opponents. Since the plans do not recognize the contribution of each employee or his work group but depend primarily on annual pretax profits, the individual has become neither a true partner in the firm nor a minicapitalist who will cooperate in his own exploitation. In medium and small plants, however, in which good management-employee relations had been established previously, the 1967 profit-sharing legislation may have strengthened existing ties. During the spring of 1980, the profit-sharing legislation was further expanded, though without changing the fundamental shortcomings.

Expansion of Works-Council Prerogatives, 1966-1974: Alongside the profit-sharing legislation, the Gaullists passed a series of laws through the 1966-1969 period that extended the consultative and advisory functions of the works councils in the areas of job security, working conditions, safety, and training. Although the French works councils did not gain full codetermination rights, the obligation of the French management to inform the comité de'enterprise in advance of all important employment decisions and consult with the council about its implementation are virtually the same as in Germany. French management, in theory, can proceed without works-council approval; but in practice, the French employer may be even more limited in his freedom of action, since the French system does not have the effective arbitration procedures of the German, nor has French management integrated the works council in the enterprise as thoroughly. The patronat has continued to deal with the works council at arms length, although greater efforts have been made to obtain its cooperation since the 1968 union steward legislation strengthened the unions' position within the plant. Management in larger enterprises has begun to realize that the works councils have had a generally good influence on work morale and productivity and have protected the enterprise from the often irrational and demagogic posturing of the national union leaders, whose influence is now more quickly transmitted to the shop level by union stewards. The works council has become the instrument through which the silent majority can deal with management.

Although unions, management, and works councils have established an uneasy three-cornered relationship, it would be wrong to conceive of the union-works council interaction as entirely antagonistic. Most works-council delegates are union members and, most likely, have been elected on union election tickets. The council members are, however, primarily interested in bread-and-butter issues, employment security, and better working conditions and have been unwilling to risk the survival of the enterprise in order to demonstrate their revolutionary ardor. During periods of relative political tranquility, on the other hand, the works council often cooperates with the unions in obtaining management's approval of council recommendations.

In spite of the fact that French works councils have been more rational and cooperative than the British shop-steward committees, French employee participation in managerial decision making has had the characteristic of continuous, although restrained, confrontation rather than codetermination and cooperation. As a consequence, the works councils have not become part of the management process, and employee participation has been restricted to ameliorating decisions already made.

President de Gaulle realized that employee participation in French enterprises had not reached the level necessary to reduce the alienation of labor and after 1968 once more urged the Gaullist majority to consider fundamental enterprise reforms (réforme de l'entreprise).[33] Management responded primarily by experimenting with new work-place designs that encouraged job enlargement and the establishment of self-directing working groups. The two major Marxist unions displayed very little interest in these experiments, however, and the experiments did not reap significant successes.

After de Gaulle's resignation in 1969, the Pompidou administration abandoned all efforts to make fundamental changes in the enterprise structure and seemed satisfied with several minor extensions of works-council jurisdiction during the next five years. Economic growth was to be the answer to all socioeconomic problems.

Enterprise Reform and Codetermination

With the election of Valery Giscard d'Estaing in May 1974, an administration came to power that had pledged itself to reform and modernize French society. As a first step, Giscard's prime minister, Jacques Chirac, appointed the Committee for the Study of Enterprise Reform to prepare proposals that would be supported by the widest possible coalition of employers, employees, and unions. Chaired by Pierre Sudreau, a former minister, the twelve-member committee was supposed to represent employers, unions, and the public, but it met the predictable opposition of the two Marxist unions, the CGT and the CFDT. Invited to have their representatives join the Sudreau committee, both union federations restated their view that a true enterprise reform required first the replacement of capitalism by socialism. The CGT and CFDDT managed, however, to combine their rejection of the enterprise reform in principle with specific demands for giving works councils and union stewards far-reaching authority to veto management decisions. To the surprise of many, furthermore, CGT and CFDT leaders agreed to testify before the committee.

In the end Sudreau obtained the cooperation of the three moderate unions, the employer association (Le Conseil National du Patronat Francaise), key technocrats, and university professors. Meeting over a five-month period (September 1974 to January 1975), the commission attracted as much attention as the Biedenkopf committee did in Germany five years earlier, and the report submitted to Giscard d'Estaing in February 1975 was as well written and as widely read as its German predecessor.[34]

The Sudreau report has not resulted in enterprise-reform legislation so far. Discussed extensively for many months, it obtained the support of the government technocrats and the modernists of the political center (Independent Republicans, Catholics, and Social Democrats). It was strongly opposed by the Communists and, less forcefully, by the left wing of the Socialist party, as well as by many employers. The political animosity between the Gaullist leader Chirac and President Giscard, however, may have been the main reason why action on the Sudreau report was delayed until growing unemployment, inflation, and the approaching 1978 election precluded legislative action. Giscard's surprising, although convincing, election victory in March 1978 made it quite likely that many aspects of the Sudreau report will be implemented in the 1980s. A closer look at the Sudreau report therefore is appropriate.

Sudreau Report: The Sudreau committee, very much like the Biedenkopf commission, devoted the first part of its report to a discussion of the philosophical-political context of worker participation and enterprise reform. In the Biedenkopf report, however, the presentation of the political-ideological environment of codetermination legislation served merely as a background to a rather pragmatic assessment of the impact of worker participation on economic performance. After considering several reform alternatives, the Biedenkopf report culminated in a fairly detailed set of recommendations that were divorced from any strong ideological framework. In the Sudreau report, however, the philosophical-ideological postulates of the first part are closely reflected in the proposals of the second part, which were designed to reorder society rather than merely extend employee participation in the management of the enterprise. Since there are many different ways to reform French society, the Sudreau report frequently did not make a specific proposal but suggested different ways in which a particular problem of a technological society could be solved. For instance, the Sudreau committee strongly believed in extending the individual employee's control over his work process and, particularly, in abolishing unskilled, monotonous labor. In order to accomplish this goal, it suggested various procedures that seemed to combine the Volvo Company's experience in abandoning the assembly line, with contemporary American job-enlargement techniques and *Quadragesimo Anno*'s "principle of subordination" of centering authority on the lowest possible level through decentralization.[35] This eclecticism extended to most of the enterprise-reform proposals discussed.

The proposals in the Sudreau report were to be implemented over a period of time in many steps, each designed to gain the support of a broad consensus of emloyees, employers, and technocrats.

The first significant proposal concerned redesigning the work process. Indeed the major goal of the Sudreau committee was to end (or minimize) the alienation of the worker, which has been a consequence of the industrial revolution.[36] Consequently it recommended the participation of each employee in the design of his work, as well as the development of evaluation standards to make the entire work process more challenging. The intent of the Sudreau committee was not to increase enterprise efficiency or profitability but rather to transform the individual manual worker from a mere employee into a responsible, participating coproducer. Even if in the short run, or in a particular firm, the improvements in the work process or in working conditions were not cost-effective, society would benefit from the changed status of the worker by replacing class warfare with social cooperation. This proposal alone reveals the truly revolutionary intentions of the Sudreau committee.[37]

The second major area concerned reform of the enterprise structure. The Sudreau report's most specific proposals were designed to change the legal structure of the French enterprise to make it, simultaneously, more responsive to society, employees, stockholders, and unions. In the sections dealing with reforms in French company law, the committee repeatedly avoided the major issue: how management-union or even management-employee cooperation can flourish if the two major representatives of manual workers reject all forms of social cooperation as a betrayal of the working class. The CGT and the CFDT not only insist on the continued adversary relationship of union and employer but interpret the consequent confrontations not merely as a battle over the division of the system's profits but as a form of continuous class warfare that must end with the expropriation of the exploiters.

The international liberal establishment has decried the fact that French management has not accepted the trade unions as responsible partners, and sentiments to that effect appear, implicitly at least, throughout the Sudreau report.[38] Yet no one has discovered a way, so far, to turn an opponent who wants to remain an opponent into a partner. Employee participation in top-management decision making will become feasible only if the hold of the CGT and the CFDT on a broad section of the working class loosens. The Sudreau committee was quite correct in emphasizing the participation of individual employees in the decisions that concern his work, his work place, and his direct relation to his immediate supervisor as a necessary first step in enterprise reform.

Suggestions of the Sudreau report to link reorganization of the company with a reform of the profit-sharing system seem more workable than its suggestion for union-management cooperation, since they could be adopted, possibly with government encouragement and support, by medium-sized and smaller companies in which the CGT is not very strong. Under this proposal profit sharing would be limited to stock sales to employees who in turn would gain an increasing representation on the board of directors. The employee ownership of enterprises on a quasi-Yugoslavian model has been strongly advocated by the Gaullists and even more strongly opposed by the Communists. The French patronat also has not been eager to implement employee ownership, although a few steps along this line have been taken.

The mandatory establishment of social indicators, as advocated by Sudreau, seems more designed to gain the approval of the Giscard administration and *Le Monde* than of the employees. Data on absenteeism, turnover, training programs, accidents, and similar areas would provide an indication of the social health of the enterprise, which would help the government to undertake measures to integrate enterprise objectives with national goals. Only those who favor government intervention in the economy (dirigism) and distrust market forces will be impressed by the social-balance-sheet proposal; there certainly has been no demand for such indexes from the work force.

The Sudreau committee's proposal to allocate one-third of the board-of-director seats to employee representatives has gained the widest publicity in the domestic and foreign press, although it seems least likely to be implemented.[39] Representation of union officials on the board has been demanded by sections of the CFDT and the Socialist party; hence the Sudreau committee failed to make specific recommendations on the selection process for the employee-directors but merely indicated that these could continue to be chosen by the works councils, the employees, or the unions. The report advocated the gradual, although mandatory, allocation of board seats to employee-directors but urged that employee representation on the board in smaller companies (those with one thousand to two thousand employees) should be voluntary. The opposition of the CGT and sections of the patronat to this recommendation has stalled any further action on this proposal.

The third major area concerned reform of the works council. The Sudreau committee attempted to integrate the comité d'enterprise in the management process by defining its advisory role more explicitly, by strengthening its legal rights to information, and by adding subcommittees to deal with specific management issues. Of greatest interest are two additions: the establishment of an economic subcommittee, virtually identical with the *Wirtschaftsausschuss* of the German codetermination law of 1972, and the mandatory strategic planning report to employees to be required of multinational corporations. The economic subcommittee would analyze all economic information submitted by the company and discuss with the management representative the short- and long-run consequences of major investment, merger, or disinvestment plans. Neither the subcommittee nor the works council would be able to veto the management proposals but conceivably could exert considerable pressure if they were to oppose specific decisions.

In a similar vein, the commission proposed that foreign-owned multinational corporations appoint a representative to deliver annually to the works council a report on worldwide corporate strategy and its impact on the French subsidiary. It is highly unlikely that such a law would be enforceable if passed, unless a government used it as a potential tool to force foreign corporations to sell their French affiliates.

The works-council proposals are, perhaps, the weakest section of the report. The intentions were to strengthen social cooperation, to change the atmosphere in which the management and works council operate, but this cannot be done, as the commission recognized, by several comparatively minor changes in the body of the works-council legislation. For this reason the commission recommended against giving full codetermination rights to the works councils until they had become true social partners in the firm.

The Sudreau report recognized that full employee and works-council participation could not be obtained without fundamental changes in French society but that fundamental changes awaited a true reform of the enterprise. The only way to break into this seemingly closed loop was by concentrating immediately on the individual employee's working conditions and by slowly and gradually changing the existing enterprise structure through improved profit-participation mechanisms. Allocation of one-third of the board seats to employees does not seem to be very important in this context.

Implementation of the Sudreau Recommendations: So far the implementation of the Sudreau proposals has followed closely, although perhaps accidentally, my analysis. Since 1975 the Giscard administration has concentrated primarily on making manual work financially more desirable—for example, through early retirement for workers in strenuous jobs—or by encouraging changes in the work process through legislation or financial support of innovative programs. The March 1978 election precluded any major changes in the company laws throughout 1977, and the discovery of an unfettered price system's benefits by the postelection Giscard-Barre administration makes major codetermination legislation unlikely.[40] Still the Independent Republican-Gaullist coalition has been urging companies to install a social audit voluntarily and to strengthen the position of the works-council representatives on the supervisory board unilaterally.[41]

The government also continued its efforts to strengthen employee ownership of the enterprise and prepared a bill to require companies listed on the Paris stock exchange to distribute about 3 percent of their capital stock to their employees. Only those firms would be affected that had made a profit during two of the last three years (about eight hundred companies with 2.5 million employees), and the government would reimburse the owners by issuing government bonds redeemable over a ten-year period. The employee shares would be equivalent to "regular shares" and participate in all dividends issued. Not surprisingly, both the French Communists and the patronat opposed this bill. Unless the stockholders are willing to share ownership with *individual* employees, however, they will be replaced by trade union officials and state bureaucrats. The bill was presented to the Council of Ministers in November 1978, and was to have taken effect on January 1, 1980. In order to insure the passage of the expanded employee profit-participating law in April 1980, the government seemed to have postponed quietly the mandatory implementation of the employee owner- ship legislation.

Giscard has until 1981, the next presidential election, to modernize French industry by dismantling the mercantilistic system of government subsidies and "dirigism."[42] A gradual implementation of the enterprise reform advocated in the Sudreau report almost certainly will be part of this modernization process. In the view of the current French government, broader employee ownership of the enterprise, and expanding profit par- ticipation seem to be the safest paths to overcome worker alienation. Should Giscard also be able to divert the post-Mitterand Socialist party from its suicidal alliance with the Communists, French worker participation in management decisions may begin to resemble German codetermination.[43] The narrow margin (little better than fifty-one to forty-nine) that separated the supporters of the current administration from its Marxist enemies at the last election cannot be reassuring to foreign and domestic investors, yet for the immediate future at least, France may well be on the way to developing true worker participation on the shop floor, where it really counts, without creating additional levels of bureaucracies.

Great Britain

Codetermination as a mandatory form of joint management-employee deci- sion making in a spirit of social cooperation is nonexistent today in Britain and unlikely to develop in the foreseeable future. There is, of course, employee participation in decision making concerning work place and working conditions, and, of course, trade-union participation through industry-wide bargaining. How much employee participation is involved in industry-wide bargaining is difficult to determine because the national union leaderships' frequent discouragement of grass-roots support is matched by the general disinterest of individual members in union politics. In the vigorously fought May 1978 presidential election in the Amalgamated Union of Engineering Workers, in which moderate social democrats suc- cessfully defeated a fellow-traveling candidate and his Marxist ticket, only 32 percent of the members voted, in spite of a mail ballot and in spite of broad newspaper coverage.[44]

The vigorous adversary union-management relationship that has been carefully nurtured at the industry-wide and national levels, as well as the often-capricious confrontation strategy followed by the shop stewards at the plant level, make employee-management codetermination based on social cooperation an impossibility in Great Britain. The organization of the British work force into narrow, mutually suspicious crafts unions, moreover, would even turn the syndicalistic worker self-management model, advocated by the Dutch and French socialist unions, into a forum for intramural warfare.

Structure and Ideology of British Trade Unions

Much has been written over the past twenty years about the chaotic labor conditions in British industry. The actual conditions, however, have been better than the domestic and foreign newspaper reports have led one to believe. There are chaotic conditions at the Leyland (now nationalized) and Ford automobile factories; there are strike-happy dockworkers and stolid shipyard workers at Tyneside and the lower Clyde who would rather not work than tamper with their work rules; and there are all-powerful mine workers who paralyze the country and bring down governments when their demands are not met.[45] But labor relations in most medium and small firms, and even larger ones (including Imperial Chemical, Rolls Royce Motor Division, and British General Electric Co.) are not unmanageable. Although Great Britain has the second worst strike record in Europe (the worst one has been held by Italy since 1960), except for 1972 its working days lost per 1,000 employees due to industrial action have been consistently less than those of the United States.

British workers participate in determining their working conditions through the electorate shop-steward grievance procedure at the local level, and in a much more indirect manner they can influence their wages, hours, and job security through the collective-bargaining agreement that the union negotiates. Worker participation in union affairs has been notoriously low in Great Britain and has suffered even further by the infiltration of Communist and Trotskyite groups into the union movement during the 1965-1977 period. Especially in the giant Transport Workers Union and the Amalgamated Union of Electrical Workers, left-wing Labour party followers (the so-called Tribune group, named after the Marxist weekly) collaborated with the ultraleftist sects in electing Jack Jones (Transport Workers president until 1977) and Hugh Scanlon (AUEW president until Spring 1978), together with a Far-Left governing body. Low grass-roots participation has made it easier for the national union bureaucracy and for small, disciplined groups to disregard the silent majority among its members.

With the exception of the radical decade (1967-1977), the British trade unions and their Trade Union Congress (TUC) have followed a wholesome adversary policy in which they hope to obtain the maximum benefits from the existing system, very much as the American unions do. The TUC represented accurately the class-conscious attitude of its members, who

refused to consider enterprise management as part of their business and
therefore reject any responsibility for the economic consequences of
collective-bargaining agreements. It was the union's task to obtain the best
possible pay and working conditions for its members, and it was management's job to sign agreements that would permit them to make a profit. Except for the 1967-1977 period and, perhaps, the 1979 Labour Party Conference, the TUC leadership, and most of the leaders of its affiliated
unions, traditionally have supported the social democratic wing of the
Labour Party and its social reform policies but have opposed any form of
government interference in collective bargaining. Although the TUC had
been forced to accept an incomes policy from 1974 to 1979 in order to keep
the Labour government in power, it has been able to prevent any state interference in the collective-bargaining process.

Industrial Democracy and Trade-Union Power

During the mid-1960s, the intellectuals in the Labour party's left wing
discovered the cause of industrial democracy. Disappointed that the nationalization of key industries had not created new working relations, the
supporters of industrial democracy turned to the Yugoslav worker self-
management system for a new model to end authoritarian and bureaucratic
processes in private and state capitalism. (*State capitalism* has become the
term for nationalized enterprises among the left wing of Europe's socialist
parties.) Although second thoughts on nationalization did not keep the
more traditional Marxists of the Tribune group from demanding the nationalization of most industries, Labour party leftists joined the Institute
for Workers Control to develop books, programs, and strategies to enable
the extension of industrial democracy.[46]

At the same time the abysmal state of British labor relations and the obvious success of the German codetermination system prompted the political
center—social democrats, the Liberal party, and the Tory left wing—to
consider the adoption of the Central European employee-participation
scheme as a way to reform the collective-bargaining process. In 1966 the
Labour government appointed the Royal Commission on Trade Unions and
Employers' Associations (Donovan commission) to propose a strategy for
the restructuring of industrial relations in the United Kingdom. The
Donovan commission had an acute sense of the political feasibility of
several reform alternatives and seemed to have concluded early in its
deliberations that industry-wide collective bargaining in Great Britain
worked reasonably well and also reflected the reality of contemporary
union-management relations. As long as both sides felt most comfortable in

a highly ritualistic adversary position, any scheme requiring cooperation and shared responsibility was bound to fail.[47]

The Donovan commission therefore decided to consider primarily the reform of industrial relations on the plant level, where the most chaotic conditions prevailed. Once the commission had rejected the establishment of works councils, implicitly for the good reason that the trade unions strongly opposed works councils as potential competitors, there were not many concrete proposals left over, except for a few recommendations to establish various levels of union committees to reduce jurisdictional disputes and to strengthen the local union organization in order to control the shop stewards. Although the Donovan commission came up with no startling recommendations, it did contribute to the reexamination of British labor relations. A white paper entitled "In Place of Strife," issued by a Labour party government, made official that the demand to replace class warfare and confrontation with cooperation on the industiral front was not merely a policy for class collaborationists.

In the developing national mood, even the TUC seemed to abandon its hostility toward codetermination. In 1973 the TUC's research staff submitted a report.[48] In the opinion of at least one observer it "broke sharply with the rather xenophobic tradition of the unions by proposing what was, in considerable part, the European framework of industrial democracy."[49] In fact, nothing could be further from the truth. Although some of the union officials suddenly but eagerly demanded equal representation on boards of directors, the TUC report, as well as all subsequent statements by TUC leaders, completely rejected the works council, the only common European worker-participation institution, and refused to accept TUC responsibility commensurate with its powerful position in industry and society. Without an acceptance of responsibility for economic consequences of decisions made with union approval, no employer-union cooperation is possible, and without the works council as a focus of employee participation, no industrial democracy can develop. In fact, not the slightest concern with rank-and-file industrial democracy has ever been apparent in any TUC statement on participation.

The trade-union leadership quickly realized that union representation on corporation boards would greatly enhance its power and its ability to control corporate and macroeconomic decisions. A labor leader has been quoted as expressing these sentiments precisely: "Participation is about power; Industrial Democracy will lead to a socialist society."[50] Such a fundamental shift in power was what Industry Minister Tony Benn, the Labour party left wing, and the TUC leadership wanted.[51]

While the Labour party government continued discussing worker participation, the union leadership clearly and bluntly pointed out that its view of union codetermination precluded any form of individual employee participation.[52]

TUC Proposal on Union Participation: The proposal urged the passage of a new company act to replace Britain's Anglo-American board of directors with a German-type supervisory board; 50 percent of the board members would be union representatives, and 50 percent would represent the shareholdres. Management would be excluded from the supervisory board. Although the proposed legislation was to apply only to private-sector firms with more than two thousand employees, there were no reasons why nationalized enterprises could not be included.[53]

Union representatives would be elected through an undefined union election process, to be decided by the union organizations. Subsequent TUC statements have made it clear that the unions wanted to leave it up to the shop stewards how the elections should be conducted, which prompted the *Economist* to comment: "Do not expect them [the shop stewards] to organise secret ballots of all the workforce. The unstated TUC preference is that the directors be elected by the joint shop stewards' committee in each company—enough to terrify even the most progressive employer."[54] Nonunion members, furthermore, would not be permitted to participate in the election, nor could any union not recognized by the TUC represent the workers on an enterprise board.[55] Any union not wishing to participate in board codetermination would be free to abstain. The reformed company act would still apply, but the workers' seats would remain unoccupied.

The union members on the board would not share joint responsibility with the stockholder representatives as under German law but would be merely accountable to their constituency, the unionized workers of the enterprise. How this specialized responsibility would affect the issue of confidentiality of information was barely touched in TUC statements, although union officials in Germany, the Netherlands, and even Sweden went to great length to assure owners and managers of the discretion of employee-union directors.

Board participation of union representatives would be accompanied by extending collective bargaining to all issues that could affect the work force. In this case the TUC anticipated article 35 of Sweden's 1976 labor-relations reform bill and demanded that all major decisions on such issues as investment, location, takeovers, and mergers be subject to collective bargaining.[56]

The TUC's new demand for boardroom participation received its first limited official approval during the negotiations that preceded the so-called 1974 social contract between the Labour government and the Trades Union leadership. Threatened by double-digit inflation, unemployment, and a huge payments deficit, the TUC leadership agreed reluctantly to submit voluntarily to an incomes-policy in exchange for a series of promises, which entailed primarily the removal of all legal restraints on union behavior (realized subsequently in the Trade Union and Labour Relations Act of

1974) and the establishment of quasi-union codetermination in cases of mass layoffs (realized in the Employment Protection Act of 1975).[57] The Wilson government also promised to strive for union representation on enterprise boards as part of its social contract but did not seem particularly anxious to see such a measure implemented. In 1975, however, a Labour party member of Parliament, Giles Radice, a member of the left-wing Tribune group, introduced a bill into the House of Commons to give labor equal representation on the board of directors.

The Bullock Committee: Union Codetermination without Democracy: To defuse a lengthy and divisive national debate at a time when domestic and foreign management's confidence in the British economy was already at a very low level and in order to satisfy the TUC, the government set up a committee to inquire into the "radical extension of industrial democracy" through employee representation on the boards of directors. The commission was further charged with considering the TUC's study, *Industrial Democracy*, as well as the experiences of other European countries with codetermination and their economic consequences.[58]

Unlike the Brandt and Giscard administrations, which gave their commissions a free hand, the Wilson government restricted its committee of inquiry to considering solely the representation of workers on boards of directors in the context of the TUC proposal. It was quite clear to many proponents of industrial democracy that whatever the merits of the TUC proposal, it had absolutely nothing to do with that issue. Especially the Liberal party, which though quite small, is very influential in the universities, demanded that worker participation must involve individual workers and that any contribution to industrial democracy ought to contain a modicum of democracy. Adopting the same position as their German counterpart party, the British Liberals insisted that worker-directors be elected directly by the employees without allowing a special role for the unions. Moreover, worker participation had to start at the grass-roots level and be based upon works councils, which had to develop the cooperative atmosphere that would make codetermination on the board level operative.

The very narrow charge to the commission made it difficult for the government to assemble a distinguished panel, and it took a good deal of pressure to obtain the participation of the Confederation of British Industry (CBI), the major employer association.

In December 1975 after five months of searching for a prominent chairman, the government named an Oxford historian, Lord Alan Bullock, a Labor peer, to head a committee, which was joined by ten academicians and union and employee association representatives.[59] The testimony and statements submitted to the Bullock committee demonstrated that the British "center" (social democrats, Liberals, and Heath Conservatives) favored some form of employee participation in the management of the enterprise but opposed the TUC proposals, while the CBI and the mainstream of the Conservative party gave some lip-service to the principle of worker and profit participation but opposed both the TUC proposal and the German-type codetermination favored by the Liberals.[60] The Labor government supported the TUC proposal, but the thought of further strengthening the unions did not appeal to Prime Minister Wilson. Mr. Callaghan, who succeeded Wilson as prime minister in 1976, was much more enthusiastic about worker participation, and had urged Sir Alan to complete his report by December 1976.

Several Far Left unions and union leaders, as well as several Marxist groups inside and outside the Labour party, continued their opposition to any form of cooperation, however, even of the type favored by the TUC report, while several social democratic unions favored the extension of collective bargaining to include all managerial decisions over board participation, since the unions could not prevent sharing responsibility for the decision-making process once they became part of management.[61]

Management itself, primarily through the articulate and influential British Institute of Management (BIM), questioned the impact of union directors on the management process. The BIM feared delays in the decision process, confrontations, and political infighting on the boards, and an increasing reluctance of the best university graduates to enter business.[62]

The deliberations of the Bullock committee occurred during a time when the zeitgeist strongly favored some form of worker-participation scheme. The Bullock committee's visit to West Germany, and long conferences with Chancellor Schmidt, further convinced politicians and union leaders that Mitbestimmung was the key to Germany's economic success. But Bullock seemed not to have considered that Central European codetermination has been firmly anchored in social and legal institutions that had slowly developed over sixty years. Also the majority of his committee ignored the fact that German-Austrian boardroom participation was the capstone of a many-layered codetermination system based upon the works councils and accompanied by an orderly and rational collective-bargaining process.

The overwhelming weight of the testimony submitted was hostile to the TUC proposal. Still Sir Alan was determined to recommend to the government that offering the unions representation on the boards of directors was the only way to improve Britain's labor relations. Faced with an inflexible TUC faction on his committee, which, with the resignation of John Methven (representative of the BIM) had a six-to-five majority, Bullock slowly moved to the virtual adoption of the entire TUC proposal. Lord Bullock had hoped, however, to submit a report that reflected the consensus of his committee, and he hesitated to ignore completely the views of the employers' representatives. In response to the pressures of the chairman and afraid of being considered "rigid and inflexible" by "world opinion," the committee's anti-TUC faction had already moved far beyond the official position of the CBI in accepting minority union representation on the board but still resisted the TUC election mechanism and union-stockholder parity on the board.[63]

The hope that boardroom participation might make British unions more responsible was very strong in England even though the danger of further strengthening union power scared virtually everybody. This ambivalent attitude was most articulately expressed by the *Economist*, which urged the Bullock committee to come up with a sensible board participation scheme but simultaneously demonstrated how unprepared Great Britain was for any form of codetermination:

> [British] employers and unions mean very different things by "participation." At the extreme the authoritarian boss thinks participation is a lot of trendy nonsense. . . . At the other extreme is the union leader who will brook no compromise with capitalism. If he can't have a socialist paradise and workers' control, then he'll stick to the present system of industrial conflict.
>
> The tragedy for Britain is that both organized labor and capital come even now perilously close to these caricatures. The Confederation of British Industry . . . sees participation in terms of consultation without sharing power. The TUC . . . will only have it as part of the road to socialism.
>
> The other British problem is lack of practice. The TUC wants 50% control for its members who have 100% inexperience. The CBI wants plenty of participation on the shop floor yet only a handful of managers have ever dabbled in it. . . . Both the TUC and CBI rank and file are less than enthusiastic. All the more reason to start small—but fast.[64]

The *Economist* neglected to tell the Bullock committee how to start small in view of its charge and the inflexible attitude of the TUC faction. In the end the irreconcilability of the different views on the Bullock committee, and the unwillingness of the TUC lobby to compromise on any issue, forced Sir Alan to submit in January 1977 a report that did not represent a broad committee consensus.

The Bullock report had three basic points:

1. It recommended worker representation on the board, but the minority opposed parity of stockholders and union representatives and insisted that only employees of the firm could become worker-directors.[65]
2. The worker-directors were to be chosen through existing union machinery, with some safeguards for nonunion employees to be added.
3. The legislation to create worker-directors was to apply to all companies with more than two thousand employees. Worker-directors, however, were to be elected only in an enterprise if the local unions chose to participate.

Although the Callaghan government had hoped to pass a law in 1977-1978 implementing the Bullock recommendations, the opposition of the CBI, the misgivings of influential segments of the public, and the weakened position of the government through defeats in numerous by-elections deferred any serious attempt to submit a bill on worker participation. As the session of Parliament progressed, the Callaghan government's increasing dependence on the Liberal party for its very survival assured the death knell for the Bullock recommendations.

The government, however, did instruct managers in the nationalized sectors to prepare worker-participation programs, which revolved primarily around the election of union representatives to the board and encouraged demonstration projects. The one experiment that has had the longest run and has received the most publicity has been British Leyland's participation scheme. Since 1975 the government-owned Leyland works has had a three-level participation scheme at its troubled automotive group, which is under the control of the shop stewards. Plant committees to solve current problems are selected by the shop stewards. (If the shop stewards cannot agree on the selection, elections are held, a threat designed to keep even the most refractory shop steward committee in line.) The plant committees send representatives to the three divisional committees (cars, trucks, and buses), which in turn send delegates to the group committee, which discusses model changes, major investments, and profit-center performance. These committees have consultative but no codetermination rights. Management has professed that it has been happy with the cooperation of the three committees, which probably have added to the extrahierarchical flow of information.

Not surprisingly the "scheme has not led to an upsurge of participatory fervor among the work force."[66] It was, in fact, designed to discourage participation and protect the dominant position of the shop stewards. More importantly, and again not surprisingly, the Leyland participation experiment has had no impact on working morale, productivity, or shop steward behavior. Those plants that already had rather good productivity and labor-relations records continue to perform adequately, and the unmanageable plants have remained unmanageable.

Throughout the country the opportunity for improved employee-employer cooperation may have advanced somewhat during 1977 and 1978. The precarious existence of the minority Labour government, and its dependence on Liberal party support, enabled Jim Callaghan to keep Tony Benn and his supporters in the cabinet quiet and left the Tribune group in party and Parliament with no choice but to support the generally social-democratic policies of the prime minister, whose fatherly, forthright appearance strengthened his personal popularity, as well as the position of the party, at least until the chaotic strike wave of the winter of 1978-1979 undermined the Labour government.[67]

In the trade unions, the moderate groups have regained positions in most key unions, with one or two major exceptions (miners and salaried employees), and the proposed merger of the electricians (AUEW) and engineers would create a powerful social-democratic union of skilled workers, which would be the largest (over 2 million) member of the TUC, and, incidentally, opposed to worker-directors.[68] During early 1978, the moderate unions indicated that they would once more accept "stage four" of the government incomes policy, originally instituted four years ago by the Wilson administration to last for only eighteen months. The stage four incomes policy would have permitted wages to rise 5 percent.[69] The new and unaccustomed aura of TUC responsibility encouraged the government to launch in May 1978 its new white paper on worker participation, which not only put the ghost of the Bullock report to rest but recognized the serious criticism of the 1973-1974 TUC proposal, which had been expressed by representatives of most sections of British society.

1978 White Paper on Worker Participation: Under the able chairmanship of the education secretary, Shirley Williams, the cabinet committee that drafted the white paper emphasized voluntary participation schemes, to be introduced through collective bargaining, but proposed a minimum level of mandatory participation if intracompany negotiations should fail.

The white paper recommended two statutory provisions:

1. Companies with more than five hundred employees must establish a joint representation committee (JRC) on which all trade unions in the enterprise are represented, presumably but not explicitly through the shop stewards. All major policy decisions—investment, disinvestments, mergers, and layoffs—must be discussed by company management with the committee before they are implemented. The JRC will have consultative but no codetermination rights.
2. After four years of operation, JRCs in companies with more than two thousand employees will have the right to representation on the board of directors. Unless management voluntarily agrees to broader representation, the workers will appoint one-third of the directors. The company will have the choice of adopting the German supervisory board scheme by removing the managers from its unitary board or maintaining the Anglo-American board. The selection process by which the workers will appoint the worker-directors was left open; neither did the paper define what it meant by *worker*.

The 1978 white paper did not solve the question of how worker-directors could be democratically elected in the prevailing British shop climate without conflict with the shop stewards, nor did it provide the basis for effective employee participation on the shop floor. Still it was a drastic improvement over the Bullock report and might have improved union-management relations by improving information flow and permitting each side to understand better the constraints under which the other operates.

The Conservatives' 1979 election victory ensured that the white paper will be forgotten, at least for the next three years. The Labour party has been going through a difficult reorganization process in which the Tony Benn left wing may succeed in dominating the party. If a Marxist Labour party, purged of all social democrats, ever won an election in Great Britain, codetermination would become a moot point.

European Economic Community

The European Economic Community (EEC) has been considering legislation to develop a uniform European worker-participation model for the past ten years. The progress has been glacial, and nothing of any importance can be expected until at least two necessary conditions have been satisfied:

1. The establishment of a legislative agenda for the first European Parliament that had been elected by direct vote in 1979, and the consequent strengthening of the EEC institutions.
2. The convergence of existing worker-participation legislation in the member states.

Judging by the performance of the European parliament so far, no European legislation can be expected before 1981. Although possible legislation may have a rather insignificant impact unless the EEC regains the political influence it has lost since the end of the Adenauer-De Gasperi-Schumann period, it is interesting to consider briefly the worker-participation bills that had been under consideration by the EEC because it throws a light on European attitudes.

In line with the attempt to standardize economic and legal institutions, the previous European Parliament in Strasbourg and the European Commission in Brussels—the legislative and administrative branches of the EEC—had undertaken the drafting of a European corporation bill designed to reconcile the Anglo-American board with the German supervisory board. Since in Germany and many other European countries employees elect representatives to the supervisory boards, the issue of worker participation was first introduced to the community by the attempt to design a European enterprise. Subsequently the success of German codetermination prompted separate efforts among community technocrats to draft a union European codetermination bill.

Faced with the conflicting attitudes toward shop-floor codetermination among the representatives of the Conservative, Socialist, and Communist parties, the European Commission affirmed that employee participation at the work place could be obtained through works councils, profit sharing, employee ownership, and collective bargaining.

Having sidestepped the issue of direct worker participation, the European Commission had been concentrating on alternative schemes to ensure employee representation on the board level as a means of obtaining a European corporation law that was compatible with the legal environment of the member states.[70]

In its various working papers, the European Commission covered once more the entire discussion about the pros and cons of employee participation, without reaching the clarity and pragmatism of the Biedenkopf report. The only interesting feature of the EEC green paper was its implicit acknowledgement that the cooperation of labor and capital in a modern version of the corporate state might be against the interests of consumers and economic efficiency.[71]

In response to the very real threat that the cooperation of labor and capital might exploit the public, the green paper suggested that a third of the director seats be allocated equally among public representatives, labor, and capital. The inability to define public representatives stymied further discussion of this point, especially since German employer associations objected that the stockholders would retain only one-third representation under such a scheme.

Ultimately the drafting committee attempted to solve this problem by recommending that stockholder and employee directors jointly elect the public representatives. By that time, however, the direct election of the Strasbourg parliament had been agreed upon, and since neither the Sudreau nor the Bullock report had led to codetermination legislation in France or England, the European Commission resolved to delay further consideration until 1980 or 1981.

The EEC discussion concerning the addition of public directors was a major contribution, however, because it raised the issue that close employee (union)-management cooperation may not always be in the common interest, especially if it is accompanied by short-run government policies to maintain employment at all costs. The action of the socialist Austrian, British, and non-Socialist Swedish and Dutch governments to maintain inefficient companies in business through huge subsidies at the taxpayers' expense will meet the approval of the employees and managers concerned but will prevent the reallocation of resources necessary for an efficient restructuring of the economy. There can be little doubt that the taxpayers and consumers of Britain and Austria are not served by maintaining inefficient shipyards on the lower Clyde and unneeded, costly coal mines in Fohnsdorf. Since the European Parliament might be less sensitive to parochial pressure, it is quite possible that its further discussion of a European corporation law may lead to a discussion of the side effects of employee participation that have not been explicitly considered so far.

Notes

1. No one can discuss Dutch labor-management relations without acknowledging J.D. Windmuller's superb and definitive book *Labor Relations in the Netherlands* (Ithaca, N.Y.: Cornell University Press, 1968). Although we are primarily interested in the events since 1968, the reference point for assessing recent changes and future development must be Windmuller's book.

2. The term "industrial relations system" was coined by Windmuller in ibid., esp. pp. 83-86, to describe the web of legal and extralegal ties that associated employers, union officials, and government leaders into a net of mutual understanding and cooperation. "They [union officials] kept their traditional position as spokesmen for their members, but imperceptibly they added an important new function . . . of disciplining the labor force." Ibid., p. 84.

3. J.A. Veraart's first work, *Beginselen der economische bedrijfsorganisatie* [Elements of the economic organization of industries] (Bussum: Paul Brand, 1971), advocated the substitution of a new cooperative society for "chaotic capitalism." In his second major work, *Medezeggenschap en bedrijfsorganisatie* [Codetermination in industrial organizations] (Tilburg: Gianotten, 1971), Veraart defends himself implicitly against the comparison of his cooperative system with Mussolini's corporative state by emphasizing the role of free unions on his industry boards. His proposed system, however, would have punished strikes and lockouts.

4. See Windmuller, *Labor Relations*, p. 70. The translation "industrial organization under public law" is Windmuller's and, though awkward, the best there is. Although the Dutch word *Bedrijf* is akin to the German *Betrieb* ("works," "plant"), it actually means "industry" and cannot be translated by "works" without creating a wrong impression. Thus the 1933 legislation *Bedrijfsradenwet* (literally "works-council law") had nothing to do with works councils but instead authorized industry-wide boards for labor-management consultations. Similarly the national unions are called *bedrijfsunies*.

5. *Medezeggen* is somewhat milder than the German term *mitbestimmen*, which has been translated properly as "*codetermine*."

6. The technical term for setting macroeconomic targets has been indicative central planning. In the Netherlands indicative central planning

consisted primarily of setting broad macroeconomic targets—employment, gross capital investment, export balances—and supplementing them through structural policies. The modernization and extension of the Rotterdam wharf and harbor facilities during the 1950s and early 1960s helped in reaching macro export and employment targets.

7. The Extraordinary Decree on Labor Relations (BBA) of 1945 authorized a governmental mediation board to examine all wage scales, whether or not they were obtained through collective bargaining. After consultation with the corporate representatives of labor and capital, the mediation board imposed mandatory wage guidelines. The Industrial Organization Act (PBO) in 1950 set up the tripartite Social Economic Council—closely resembling the still-existing Austrian economic *Beirat*—to advise the government on socioeconomic issues and, more importantly, to supervise the establishment of labor-management industry boards with broad authorities for wages, prices, and production, quite similar to the NRA boards of the 1930s in the United States.

8. In the forty-five-member Social Economic Council, the three union federations held fifteen seats, employer associations fifteen seats, and public representatives appointed by the government also fifteen. By comparison, in the equivalent Austrian Beirat, the government is explicitly and actively represented through the chancellor and appropriate ministers.

The Foundation of Labor, which also resembled contemporary Austrian and prewar German institutions, represented industry, small business, agriculture, and the labor unions. See Windmuller, *Labor Relations*, p. 116.

9. In retrospect, the economic success of the PBO system during the period 1950-1960 has not been sufficiently recognized abroad. Among the best comments on this period are Stanislaw Wellisz, "Economic Planning in the Netherlands, France and Italy," *Journal of Political Economy* (June 1960):252-282; J.P. Windmuller, "Postwar Wage Determination in the Netherlands," *Annals of the American Academy of Political and Social Science* (March 1957):101-122; and Centraal Planbureau, *Scope and Method of the Central Planning Bureau* (The Hague: Centraal Plan Bureau August 1956). The disintegration of the PBO system during the mid-1960s emphasizes once more, however, that price-wage controls cannot work indefinitely in a democratic society.

10. Union membership in three federations grew from about one-third of the work force (800,000 members) to 40 percent (1.5 million) within the two postwar decades; however, the independent unions have slowly gained a larger share during the last decade. By 1977 the merged superfederation, FNV, had somewhat less than two-thirds of the total union membership, the independents a little more than 20 percent, and the Protestant unions about 15 to 17 percent. There has been no significant change since then.

11. The Dutch Social Democratic party (SDP), exactly like its Austrian and German counterparts, attempted to shed its Marxist, antireligious image in the immediate postwar period and to become instead a nonideological, liberal people's party. Unlike the German SDP, the Dutch party changed its name to Labor party (PvdA) and did attract a considerable liberal middle-class vote at the small cost of losing a few votes to left-wing splinter parties. During the past ten years the party has moved once more to the left; however, the PvdA had been a harmonious member of the numerous coalition governments that governed the Netherlands with the aid of the PBO system until the mid-1960s when the increasingly egalitarian policies (a quasi-solidarity wage policy) of the PvdA were no longer acceptable to its former partners. In order to participate in further periodic Center-Left governments, the Labor party had to forget about some of its more ideological reform plans when it was in power. The discrepancy between the relatively pragmatic behavior of Labor party ministers and the radical party platform was a confusing feature of Dutch politics during the early 1970s. In opposition for the past four years, the PvdA has been guided by its ideological functionaries, who have become increasingly hostile to NATO. In December 1979 the Dutch Socialists obtained the support of a parliamentary majority in rejecting the deployment of NATO nuclear missiles on Dutch soil and in the spring of 1980 on several occasions came close to overthrowing the government on questions of NATO rearming.

12. Article 6, paragraph 1 of the Works Council Law (1950), quoted by Windmuller, *Labor Relations*, p. 412.

13. No estimates exist for the percentage of nonunion works-council members during the 1950s; a guess that at least 25 to 30 percent nonunion representatives were elected seems conservative.

14. P. Drenth, "Overleg en ondernemingsraad: resultaten van sociaal-wetenschappelijk onderzoek," *Mens en onderneming* (January 1968), presents an overview of polls and research on employee attitude toward the works council and provides a brief though excellent summary of Dutch opinion surveys on codeterination issues during the mid-1960s.

15. Both Windmuller, *Labor Relations*, p. 440, and the "British Galbraith," R.L. Marris, "The Position of Economics and Economists in the Government Machine," *Economic Journal* (December 1954), commented on the extraordinary role that economists and their Keynesian econometric models played in determining Dutch incomes policy. To demonstrate the complete faith of the 1960 technocrats in their models, it is worthwhile to quote Tinbergen's defense of "econometric wage determination": "But why should we give up the best method of wage policy to give the unions something to do? Merely to give them something to do at the expense of the best method makes no sense. How about concentrating their attention, for example, on job classification, training, improvement of mobility through

better . . . information about . . . vocational opportunities.'' Quoted by Windmuller, *Labor Relations*, p. 440. It is striking that the Social Democrat Tinbergen would allot to the labor unions the same role allocated to them in the Soviet command economy. Obviously if Keynesian models or scientific socialism can determine the optimum wage, there is little left for unions to do. Tinbergen's remarks in 1962 seem to justify the policy of the Swedish LO, which feared such a turn of events.

16. Old Stalinists, within the Dutch Communist party and especially within various ultra-Marxist groups that emerged between 1965 and 1973, may have played a significant role in influencing various elite groups and forging, for a brief time at least, a new "anti-American united front." The Dutch Communist party was not a "study in futility" during this period. See Frits Kool, "Communism in Holland: A Study in Futility," *Problems of Communism* (September-October 1960).

17. See P.I. Drenth and J.C. van der Pije, *De Ondernemingsraad in Nederlande* [The enterprise council in the Netherlands] (The Hague: COP, September 1966).

18. Actually, however, it had been precisely the Dutch and Dutch-British multinationals (Philips, Unilver, Dutch Shell) that had smoothly working works councils with considerable authority long before the 1971 legislation.

19. Confidentiality of business information plays a much greater role in Dutch companies than in the United States. To safeguard secret agreements, the 1971 legislation gave management the option to state that prior consultation with the works council on certain sensitive economic issues would not be in "the best interest of the enterprise." Under these conditions management has to announce the decision to the works council as soon as it has been made and thereafter consult the council on dealing with the consequences. The 1978 works-council law removed this stipulation.

20. It has been difficult to determine the intellectual originator of the Dutch profit-sharing plan. It seems to have emerged from the NVV research department in response to criticism of the Meidner plan as overly bureaucratic and centralistic and has been adopted by Willem Kok, the youthful FNV president, as a personal issue. The current version of the profit-sharing plan permits individual employees to benefit from capital gains incurred by their company. Further payments would be made to regional and national (industry-wide) union organizations.

21. A Loderer or a Vetter would say that such a task is impossible because the long-run success of the enterprise affects all interested parties. It is precisely because the unions (and the works councils) will be held responsible that they must be able to share in the decision making.

22. The Dutch liberal party is to the right of the Christian Democrats. The Christian Democrats emerged from a merger of Catholic and Prot-

estant parties. The left wing of the Christian Democrat is more radical than the Labor party right wing.

23. The word *establishment*, although overused, is appropriate in this context to describe the self-renewing elite of party leaders, technocrats (such as Tinbergen), and academicians who have been governing the Netherlands honestly and often effectively since 1945.

24. See Wil Albeda, "Between Harmony and Conflict: Industrial Democracy in the Netherlands," *Annals* (May 1977):81. Albeda has been the social-services minister in the current Christian Democratic-Liberal government since 1977.

25. The Dutch Employers Association (VNO, for Verbond van Nederlandse Ondernemingen) published a hastily translated English summary of the 1978 law. *Summary of the Bill to Amend the Works Council Act* (Gravenhage: VNO, November 1978), is the only English version of the 1978 law.

26. Quoted and freely translated, from "Bummelstreiks künftig europäisch," *Frankfurter Allgemeine Zeitung*, 21 May 1979, p. 21 (hereafter cited as *FAZ*). See also *Amsterdam Handelsblatt*, 19-20 May 1979, and *Economist*, 28 April 1979, p. 94, 30 June 1979, p. 81.

27. FAZ, 21 May 1979.

28. Quoted in *Business Week*, 24 September 1979, p. 73.

29. See FAZ, 10 May 1978, p. 13.

30. In line with the Hitler-Stalin pact, the Communists opposed the French war effort and exhorted their followers to desert. German planes dropped copies of a speech by Russian foreign secretary Molotov over the French lines in November 1939 that urged French workers to "resist the imperialistic war."

31. The best-known intellectuals in this group were François Mauriac who received the 1952 Nobel Prize in literature, Charles Maurras who later supported the Vichy government, and P. Mauritain.

32. The Mouvement Républican Populaire (MRP) died with the Fourth Republic and has been absorbed today into the Gaullist and Independent Republican party. It had a distinguished career during its short life and through its leaders, Schumann and Monnet, played a major role in developing the Common Market. For an excellent discussion of the MRP, see Mario Einandi's *Christian Democracy in Italy and France*, (Notre Dame, Ind.: University of Notre Dame Press, 1952) pt. 2.

33. The term *réforme de l'enterprise* ("enterprise reform") covers the entire discussion over worker participation that has been carried on during the last fifteen years. The term may have received its wide use as a result of an important book, *Pour une réforme de l'enterprise* (Paris: Editions du Seuil, Paris, 1965), written by François Block-Lainé, a high-ranking French mandarine. In his réforme, Bloch-Lainé advocates the adoption of a co-

determination system modeled closely after the German 1952 legislation, with added recommendations for the redesign of the work place.

34. *Rapport du Comité d'Etude pour la Réforme de l'Enterprise* (Paris: La Documentation Francaise, 1975) (commonly called Sudreau report). An English translation of the Sudreau report was published in 1965 by the Industrial Research Unit of the Wharton School, University of Pennsylvania.

35. Peter Drucker, *The Practice of Management*, (New York: Harper and Row, 1954), effectively translated the principle of subordination into organizational procedures by advocating decentralization, delegation of authority, and lowering decision making to the lowest possible level. His concept of "every man a manager," first advanced in 1954, was strongly reflected in the Sudreau report.

36. Marx believed that worker alienation was a consequence of the capitalistic system, which separated the laborer from the ownership of his tools. The record of nationalized enterprise in Western Europe and of state enterprises in even the most liberal Eastern European countries (Hungary and Poland) has convinced all but the most conservative Marxists that ownership has little to do with alienation. Although today sociologists may consider even in the Soviet Union the phenomenon of worker alienation, the CGT and the French Communist party still think of nationalization of industry as the key factor in social reorganization.

37. See James Furlong, *Labor in the Boardroom*, (Princeton: Dow-Jones Books, 1977), pp. 103-106. Furlong, like most other Anglo-American observers, has been overly concerned with the Sudreau report's proposals on supervisory board codetermination, which admittedly were indefinite and far from novel. This, I believe, misses completely the spirit of the Sudreau report, in which the whole is certainly larger than the sum of its parts.

38. Especially the third and ninth chapters of pt. 2.

39. French companies have either a board of directors, similar to the Anglo-American model, with management representation and a board chairman who is the chief executive officer, or a German-type supervisory board that appoints the enterprise's chief executive committee but consists only of outside members.

40. An example of the new wind that is blowing now in France is the refusal of the government to subsidize the bankrupt textile companies of M. Marcel Boussac, one of France's best-known industrialists. There is virtually no other government in Europe today that take such a hard-nosed attitude.

41. The Independent Republicans are now called Union pour la Démocratic Francaise, and the Gaullists are the Rassemblement pour la République.

42. For an elaboration of these comments, see "Giscard Unchained," *Economist*, 1 July 1978, p. 11.

43. The views of Michel Rocard, one of the more promising new leaders of the Socialist party, are quite compatible with Giscard's views on participation and enterprise reform. If the Giscard-Barre administration is moderately successful in directing France's economy, the unlikely coalition of social democrats with utopian ultra-Marxists, which comprises the French Socialist party under Mitterand, cannot last. A Rocard-led Social Democratic party would ensure the success of Giscard's enterprise reform.

44. Since left-wing Marxists have been advocating various syndicalistic schemes during the past five years, it is important to point out that the use of the postal ballot in union elections has been bitterly opposed by Communists and Marxists in the trade union movement, including Jack Jones (former transport worker president) and Hugh Scanlon (former left-wing AUEW president). See "The Engineers' New Scanlon is a Right-Wing Duffy," *Economist*, 6 May 1978, p. 19.

45. The dock workers were rewarded for bringing the United Kingdom close to bankruptcy during the mid-1970s by the 1976 Dock Work Regulation Act, in which all overmanning and restrictive practices carefully grown and nurtured over decades were confirmed by the Labour government. The Callaghan government once more gave in to the Transport House (home of the Transport and General Workers' Union) by attempting to protect the dock workers from the competition of container shipping through the establishment of local dock boards that were to regulate work rules. This piece of legislation did not pass Parliament, but it did give an idea of the kind of legislation a Labour government would have produced had it won the 1979 election.

The most obsolete shipyards of Britain's inefficient shipbuilding industries were merged in July 1977 into the government-owned British Shipbuilders Corp. (BSC). Heavily subsidized by the National Enterprise Board (NEB, the state holding corporation), the BSC in 1977 was able to obtain substantial orders from the Polish government, under the condition that the new ships were to be delivered on time. In order to accept the contract, the BSC management asked the eighteen crafts unions for a pledge to accept mandatory overtime work. The unions refused to make any promises, the Polish order was lost, and the NEB was forced to lay off workers. In 1978 BSC was estimated to have lost £45 million, not counting the £80 million in subsidies received from the government.

46. See K. Coates and T. Topham, *The New Unionism: The Case of Workers Control* (London: Peter Owen, 1972).

47. A minority on the commission, however, wanted the government to encourage experiments in board-level union-management codetermination. Although throughout the Donovan report and the subsequent white paper,

In Place of Strife (London: Her Majesty's Stationary Office, 1969), the term "worker-director" appears, it refers invariably to a union official, appointed by the union, unless other selections methods are mentioned specifically. The TUC itself was not ready at that time for full-fledged participation but drew a distinction in its evidence between the "negotiating function of the employer" and the "overall tasks of management."

48. Trades Union Congress, *Industrial Democracy* (London, 1973 and 1974).

49. Andrew W.J. Thompson, "New Focus on Industrial Democracy in Britain," *Annals of the American Academy of Political and Social Science* (May 1977):35.

50. Unidentified TUC leader, quoted by *Economist*, 4 September 1976, p. 78.

51. See the two Labour party manifestos of 1974.

52. TUC, *Industrial Democracy*, passim.

53. The British Steel Corporation, a nationalized holding company, has had union worker-directors on its constituent enterprises since 1968, although without affecting in any way either management or union or employee behavior. In 1977 BSC again lost £443 million, and its management reluctantly decided to close the Bilston works, one of the most unprofitable plants. Although the worker-directors approved, the BSC trade unions (about twenty) threatened to strike, and management backed down immediately. The BSC's losses for 1978-1979 were expected to be above 400 Million. *Economist*, 8 July 1978, p. 88. This expectation proved to be correct.

54. *Economist*, 4 September 1976, p. 80.

55. In case anyone believes that the blatant disregard of the individual employee's wishes were merely a characteristic of the TUC radical phase (1967-1977), one might consider the difficulties that various salaried employees' unions had in being recognized in 1978. In spite of the fact that these unions had the support of 79 to 86 percent of eligible employees in several recent cases, the salaried employees' unions had to go to court to overcome the joint opposition of the TUC and the government conciliation service, ACAS. ACAS's excuse for refusing to recognize the professional staff unions was its "duty of promoting the improvement of industrial relations." Since the TUC unions threatened to strike if the salaried employee associations were recognized, ACAS reasoned that its mission prevented it from recognizing the "staff unions." See "One in the Eye for ACAS and Friends," *Economist*, 8 July 1978, p. 90.

56. TUC, *Industrial Democracy*, pp. 34, 35.

57. The 1975 Employment Protection Act gives the union, at the industry and enterprise level, some of the information and consultation rights possessed by German works councils. In case of mass layoffs, transfers, and

plant closing, management has to inform the union in advance and consult with the union on redundancy pay and other issues. Although the union has no codetermination rights, strike threats give it often a de facto veto, especially in the nationalized industry. For instance, decisions to close the BSC's Shelton plant were held up by a controversy over the redundancy pay.

58. "Accepting the need for a radical extension of industrial democracy in the control of companies by means of representation on boards of directors, and accepting the essential role of trade union organisations in this process, to consider how such an extension can best be achieved, *taking into account in particular* the proposals of the Trades Union Congress report on industrial democracy as well as the experience in Britain . . . and other countries. Having interest to the regard of the national economy, employees, investors and consumers to analyze the implications . . . for the efficient management of companies and for company law." Charge to committee by Secretary of Trade Peter Shore in "Mr. Peter Shore Announces Membership of Committee of Inquiry on Industrial Democracy" (London: Department of Trade, 3 December 1975), also quoted in *Economist*, 4 September 1976, p. 91.

59. The Bullock committee consisted of the following members:

Pro-TUC: Jack Jones, left-wing general secretary, Transport Workers (TGWU); Clive Jenkins, militant general secretary of the salaried employees' union (ASTMS); David Lea, TUC's chief economist; Professor George Bain, Industrial Relations Department, Warwick University; Professor K.W. Wedderburn, London School of Economics.

Pro-CBI: Norman Biggs, industrialist; Sir Jack Cullard, industrialist; Barrie Heath, industrialist; Nicholas Wilson, solicitor (corporation lawyer); and John Methven, a professional manager, who resigned in July 1976 to become the director-general of the CBI. Methven's resignation left a pro-TUC majority in control of the Bullock committee, which explains much of the committee's performance.

60. Except for the TUC and CBI representatives on the committee, few had any experience in industrial relations or line management. Bullock's qualifications seemed to rest primarily on his biography of Ernest Bevin, the great British labor leader and statesman.

61. The mine workers' leadership suggested the election of a twelve-member supervisory committee by the employees of each mine operation. The supervisory committee in turn would appoint the professional managers. This syndicalistic model is interesting, since the coal mines are nationalized and union officials have been sitting on the National Coal Board, the government holding company, for thirty years. Neither nationalization nor worker-directors seem to have made the coal miners less alienated. This result ought to lay to rest once and for all the notion that

nationalization and union representation on boards of directors have any impact on the life of miners or factory workers.

The necessity of finding a solution to the perennial obstreperousness of the British coal miner has prompted the Conservative party's policy group to recommend the establishment of worker cooperatives at coal pits. *Economist*, 27 May 1978, p. 21.

62. The historic reluctance of top-university graduates, especially from Oxford and Cambridge, to enter industry undoubtedly has been one of the causes of Britain's economic decline. If the graduates' preference for government over business careers had been prompted for a long time by feudal class bias, the higher government starting salaries and better pensions have provided good rational reasons more recently. From 1968 to 1975, the proportion of university graduates entering business has fallen from a low of 50 percent to an abysmal 36 percent.

63. A member of the British embassy in Vienna defined world opinion as the views expressed in the editorials of the *London Times*, the *New York Times*, and *Le Monde*. "The *Süddeutsche Zeitung* also used to be part of 'world opinion,'" he added, "until it moved to the right and supported Helmut Schmidt and balanced budgets. There is no room in 'world opinion' for budget balancing."

64. *Economist*, 4 September 1976, p. 79.

65. The Bullock majority recommended a $2x + y$ formula for allocating seats, where $2x$ = worker plus stockholder representatives, and y is the number of public representatives to be chosen by worker and stockholder directors. If, say, a company decided to let $x = 4$, and $y = 3$, the board would consist of 4 stockholder directors, 4 worker (union) directors, and 3 directors chosen by the other 8.

66. *Economist*, 4 September 1976, p. 81.

67. Callaghan had the full support of Chancellor Schmidt, who despised his predecessor, Wilson. After a particularly bad performance by Wilson, Schmidt is supposed to have quipped, "Britain has now the most incompetent Socialist government in Europe, after having had the worst Conservative one."

68. The "over 2 million" figure would be obtained if the Engineers (AUEW) merged not only with the Electricians (EEPTU) but also with the Boilermakers, Sheetmetal Workers and Metal Mechanics, as currently planned. This giant skilled-trades union would have about 2.1 million members, and exceed the 2 million members of the Transport Workers (TGWU).

69. By October 1978, the TUC had changed its collective mind once more and at its annual conference in October decisively rejected the government's plan for a 5 percent limit on wage increases during "phase four."

70. *Employee Participation and Company Structure, Bulletin of the European Communities* (Brussels: European Communities Commission,

1975). This was a working paper designed to draw comments and provide the basis for further discussions.

71. See the statement of the National Consumer Council to the Bullock committee in 1976, quoted by the *London Times*, 25 March 1976.

8 Postscript or Prologue? Cooperation between Capital and Labor in Austria and Switzerland

We have seen that Central European codetermination is shaped by the conflicting pressures to accommodate employee participation in the decisions that affect his work place with the union leadership's drive to assert its role in enterprise and society. The Austrian experience is an excellent example of formal, bureaucratic, union-dominated codetermination, while the individual employee's participation in the decision processes of firm and union has produced an informal, though effective, industrial democracy in Switzerland.

Austria: The Corporative State in Socialist Disguise

For the past sixty years, most of the problems and fashions of the twentieth century have reached Austria from Germany only after considerable delay. It is quite possible, however, that Austria's union-management-government codetermination system is a preview of the next stage in the socioeconomic development of Germany and the Common Market. Two potential trends in German codetermination that could change the entire nature of society, are already fully developed in Austria: the macroeconomic cooperation between the national corporate representatives of capital and labor, and the web of entanglements that connects the top union leaders with party, government, municipal, business, and even cultural interests.[1] These two phenomena have epitomized Austrian codetermination.

Growth of Austrian Codetermination

The medieval role of the estates (*Stände,* today corporate organizations called chambers, of employers, artisans, employees, peasants, and free professions), still well preserved in the Netherlands, Switzerland, and southern Germany, is most influential in Austria, where the various chambers send representatives to a price-wage commission that establishes national guidelines. The amazing price and employment stability that Austria has enjoyed has called attention to the peculiar coexistence of a Socialist government, corporative institutions, neomercantilistic policies, and a rampant nepotism, a coexistence that in the view of foreign observers might be as uniquely Austrian as a Strauss waltz. If several peculiarly Viennese characteristics of the Austrian Mitbestimmung are overlooked, we do recognize that the social cooperation between Austrian management and unions provides an understanding of possible further codetermination developments in Europe.

Austrian codetermination operates on two levels: a body of codetermination legislation that invariably has followed (or paralleled) the German experience, and a series of agreements among the employer association, the employers' chamber (*Wirtschaftskammer*), the Austrian Union Federation (*Österreichischer Gewerkschaftsbund*, or ÖGB) and the employees' chamber (*Arbeiterkammer*).

Very much like Germany, Austria, or rather the German-speaking parts of the Austro-Hungarian empire, had experienced voluntary forms of works councils in the nineteenth century.[2] In 1919 Austria adopted the German works-council and codetermination legislation with minor changes.[3] The Austrian works-council law existed until 1934, and under a different terminology, until 1938. The Austrian works council operated exactly like its German counterpart, and the two works-council representatives on the supervisory board were perhaps even more effective in Austria than in Germany.

After World War II, Austria nationalized its basic industries (coal and iron mines, steel and chemical industries) in order to keep them out of the hands of the Russians and also provided for equal codetermination on the supervisory boards of most nationalized enterprises, thus developing its own equivalent of the German Montan industry. Works-council laws of 1952 and 1961 further extended the codetermination role of the works council along the lines of the German model. The Austrian legislation, however, left the number of employee representatives on the supervisory board at the 1919 level of two. In 1973, however, the Austrian parliament approved unanimously the new *Arbeitsverfassungsgesetz* (literally "work constitution law," better translated as "work organization law") which allocated a third of the supervisory seats to employee representatives and, following closely the German Betr.V.G., 1972, extended further the participatory functions of the works council. There are, however, several significant differences between the German and Austrian legislation.

The employee-directors in Austria are not really full-fledged supervisory board members but rather additional board members, who serve without pay and cannot ordinarily influence the selection of the Vorstand, since a majority of the stockholder representatives is required for its appointment.

The Austrian works council may call a strike rather than appeal to an arbitration board if no agreement is reached with management in those areas in which the council has a "compelling codetermination right" (*zwingende Mitbestimmung*).

The Austrian works councils may also raise additional wage demands with enterprise management and thus actually supersede the unions. Minimum wages and industry-wide average wages are, as in Germany, negotiated nationally between the union and the industry, except that Austrian enterprises and employees have a little more flexibility in making adjustments, provided they do not conflict with the informal national guidelines established by the *Partitätische Kommission* ("Parity Commission"), the Austrian version of the Dutch Social Economic Council, which consists of union, employer, and government representatives.

The Austrian works councils can dispose of even greater institutional barriers to individual dismissals or mass layoffs than their German counterparts. As a consequence individual Austrian employees operate under a virtual tenure system and enjoy greater job security than do American civil servants. During recession periods, the works councils have readily approved the dismissal and repatriation of guest workers and, much more reluctantly, accepted long-run redundancy plans for native employees. In general, Austrian employers rely on natural attrition to make necessary work-force reductions. Works-council members enjoy by law super-tenure protection, a typically Austrian feature. In cases of enterprise liquidation "the works council members are the last to be dismissed."[4]

These discrepancies between West German and Austrian legislation, though relatively minor, illuminate several specifically Austrian features of Germanic codetermination. At first glance, the much weaker position of the employee representatives on the supervisory board is surprising, since the ÖGB has organized a much larger percentage of the work force than the DGB, its leaders are even more closely integrated in the governing Socialist party, and hence its influence in Parliament and society is stronger than that of the German unions.[5] Although the official reason given for the weak employee representation on the supervisory board in the 1973 law was the lack of a parliamentary Socialist majority, the real reasons were both the strong opposition of the employers and the relatively mild union pressure for additional worker-directors.[6]

Employer opposition was considerably strengthened by the fact that it included the two nationalized banks, Creditanstalt and Länderbank, which own or partially own about 65 percent of the so-called nonnationalized, private sector, including most of the larger enterprises such as Semperit (tires, industrial rubber), Vöslau (textiles), and Austria Hotel A.G. (the largest hotel chain).[7] Much of Austrian industry is greatly overstaffed, and neither the government nor the two, almost fully state-owned banks desire to make management's task to rationalize the private sector more difficult by increasing employee participation on the supervisory boards.

Codetermination in the Nationalized Industry

In the nationalized industries, efforts to adapt the production programs to changing world markets by closing inefficient old plants and shifting fabrication to the newer factories had been delayed severely by the employee-union-dominated supervisory boards, which have been primarily concerned with employment maintenance. In 1967 two consulting groups—one American, one Austrian—recommended, for instance, a changed product mix and a modernization program for the nationalized coal-steel industry, which would have required an immediate capacity reduction to guarantee stable and profitable employment in the long run. Although both government and top steel management accepted the plan in principle, the actual adoption has been slow.

In 1977 the senior union representative on the Alpine-Montan—the oldest and second largest coal-iron-steel enterprise—bluntly urged the government to accept the fact that the Austrian steel industry will be competitive and profitable only during the boom years of the world steel market. By implication this meant that the government and taxpayers would have to maintain employment through subsidies during recession years. Although this view is, of course, not shared by the Austrian government or by the nationalized industry management (ÖIAG), neither can afford to disregard the views of the union-employee directors, who not only hold 50 percent of the supervisory seats but together with the socialist directors form a working majority.[8] Important issues are, therefore, never discussed on the supervisory boards but settled by trilateral discussions among government, ÖGB, and enterprise management.

How difficult it is to implement necessary but unpopular measures in a state-owned enterprise that has equal codetermination is demonstrated by the case of the notorious Fohnsdorf coal mine in Styria, a high-cost enterprise with the deepest shafts and the longest portal-to-portal transportation in Europe. Since the early 1960s, the closing of this coal mine had been proposed by various internal and external experts' groups, and in 1968 the then-governing conservative Austrian People's party (ÖVP) finally decided to shut the mine.

Political and union pressures delayed the closing until 1970, when the ÖVP was replaced by a minority Socialist government, which began to develop, slowly and painfully, a long-run phasing-out program, which supposedly will be completed by 1985.[9] In the meantime there remained the question what was to be done with the massive mountains of coal that Fohnsdorf had been and was still producing but could not sell. The next step, therefore, was to build a coal-fired power plant nearby, which polluted the air and killed the pines of the picturesque Mur Valley for miles around. The Mur, one of the most polluted rivers of Western Europe, has the unique distinction of being polluted almost solely by nationalized enterprises. Austrians ordinarily grumble about pollution but rarely challenge the polluter in court, especially if the state or the province is the culprit. In this case, however, E. Janik, the administrator of the Lichtensteinian estates in Styria and one of Austria's foremost environmentalists, took the offending power plant to court and won. This did not end the pollution, however; it merely meant that the Lichtensteins are paid annually for their losses. The coal production continues, and so does the excruciatingly slow structural adoption process.

Works-Council Behavior

The ability of the Austrian works councils to call strikes and renegotiate wages and salaries within the overall industry-wide guidelines illustrates two peculiarly Austrian conditions. Intellectually Austro-Marxism, the most radical interpretation of Marx among Social Democratic parties in the interwar period, is still quite fashionable among the relatively small but influential left wing of the Socialist party; hence the works councils are not only institutions to further social cooperation but may also be considered as instruments of worker-management confrontation.

Second, and more importantly, the operational success of supraindustry codetermination (*überbetriebliche Mitbestimmung*), through a clubby forum where employee and employer federation and chamber presidents meet with Socialist ministers, has sharply reduced the importance of industrial unions. The leaders of the national unions in turn have responded by discussing topics in their industry-wide bargaining sessions that previously were left to the works councils. The works councils have reacted to their decreasing sphere of influence by becoming quite often obstreperous and by emphasizing very short-run and parochial interests against the combined efforts of union federations, management, and government. Two cases illustrate this point.

VEW Case: In the 1975 reorganization of the nationalized steel industry, the VEW (*Vereinigte Edelstahl-werke*, a merger of two special steel manufacturers) became a subsidiary of the Voest-Alpine, the consolidated Austrian steel corporation. The Voest-Alpine in turn is owned by the nationalized industry holding corporation, ÖIAG.

The VEW, like the entire Austrian steel industry, has owned obsolete, high-cost plants, but unlike the Voest-Alpine, it has been unable to close down unneeded capacity since there were no alternative employment opportunities available in the narrow mountain valleys in which its most uneconomical factories have been located. The VEW Vorstand, strongly supported, if not pressured, by its works council, had embarked on a policy of accepting any order as long as it covered the marginal variable cost of producing it. As a consequence, the VEW has been operating at full capacity during the entire steel crisis but has incurred substantial losses over the same period. In 1977 alone VEW's total costs exceeded revenues by AS 400 million (about $27 million).

The Voest-Alpine and ÖIAG management boards persuaded the VEW Vorstand in February 1978 to introduce a long-run economy program to reduce its annual losses by about $20 million. In return ÖIAG and Voest-Alpine would help finance a $260 million long-run investment program to restructure the VEW enterprise, if the VEW management and the works council carried out its promise to institute an immediate economy program, equivalent to a 5 percent wage cut for the entire work force. Especially important was the VEW pledge to cut overtime and cease all hiring to reduce the work force through attrition. As new productive capacity was to be introduced, old labor-intensive plants were to be closed, but in the meantime VEW was only to accept orders that covered both variable and fixed costs.

The economy drive lasted exactly four months. By June 1978, management again had accepted all orders that its sales staff could obtain at prices that rarely covered even average variable costs. Moreover, in order to meet the delivery dates promised, full overtime was reintroduced, making it more than questionable that even the marginal costs of the latest orders were covered. Once more overtime utilization of old, inefficient machinery turned out products that could be delivered only at huge losses.[10] Not surprisingly, the VEW incurred a record loss of AS 731 million (about $52 million) for 1978. For 1979 the VEW anticipated "a substantially better performance."[11] The "substantially better performance" turned out to be a 1979 loss of A.S. 230 million, during a relatively "good year for European steel."

The decision to drop the economy program was prompted by works-council pressure. Faced by approaching works-council elections in the fall of 1978, the council members concluded that its behavior in February would not be honored by the work force. It is interesting and symptomatic for decision making in the nationalized industry that the works council's change of mind was accepted immediately by the Vorstand. After eight years of Socialist party government in Austria, there were very few executives in the highly politicized Austrian nationalized industries who were willing to embark on an economy program without works-council approval.

Of equal interest has been the apparent inability of higher management at the Voest-Alpine or ÖIAG level to compel the VEW Vorstand to abide by the original agreement. The Voest-Alpine incidentally, had been able to reduce its own capacity and transfer part of the work force to modern plants, although at a loss of several thousand jobs. The availability of other employment alternatives at its main locations made this transformation relatively painless. Faced with an obstinate works council and VEW Vorstand, however, the ÖIAG simply cannot force itself to impose its will on its subsidiary. The fact that the new ÖIAG chief, Oskar Grünwald, had been the chairman of the ÖIAG works council prior to his recent promotion may have been a contributory factor to the 1978 impasse, which was not resolved until the spring of 1979 when the huge 1978 losses had to be announced. A new radical saving program was then finally introduced.

The behavior of the VEW works council is completely rational if one realizes that the current Austrian government will not permit any major company (more than two thousand employees) to close. No matter how inept the management, how inefficient the plant, there will be some form of government subsidy to keep the enterprise going, at least until after the next election, regardless of whether the firm is in the public or private sector.[12] To the extent that any efficient economic system needs to facilitate the transfer of labor and capital from old to new industries, the high tax burden borne by the private sector together with the overwhelming concern with short-run work-place preservation prevents any long-run structural transformation of the production system.

Semperit Case: The combination of a socialist government willing to use subsidies to keep inefficient enterprises afloat, with union-industry cooperation on the supranational level and strong works councils on the local level delays any adjustment process to the extent that the economy can respond only to severe crises. The VEW case illustrated the difficulty of imposing unpopular decisions on an enterprise if works council and operating management combine to oppose it. The Semperit case illustrates how even corporate management, national unions, and union federations combined may be unable to cope with an obstreperous local works council.

The Semperit company is one of Austria's biggest enterprises outside the nationalized sector. Although the state-owned Creditanstalt, Austria's largest bank, holds the majority interest in the company, Semperit is generally considered a private-sector enterprise. The manufacturer of tires and industrial equipment has been in serious economic difficulties, reflected by frequently changing corporate affiliations, reorganizations, and a rapid turnover in top management. The quality of Semperit's Vorstand and the rationality of the Creditanstalt's strategy have been criticized constantly by the enterprise's middle management and outside observers.

In the early 1970s the Creditanstalt management believed that the long-run growth prospects for Semperit demanded an association with a large foreign multinational firm, which would provide needed investment and marketing capacity and carry out the necessary rationalization measures. After lengthy negotiations with Michelin, a new Swiss holding company,

Semkler-Koordinations A.G. was founded in 1973 to coordinate the production, research, and marketing policies of Semperit and Michelin's sickly subsidiary, Kleber, France's second largest tire producer.

The Creditanstalt held 55 percent of Semkler stock, 30.9 was held by Michelin, and 14.1 by the investment bank, Credit Suisse. Semkler in turn owned 67 percent of Semperit and 51 percent of Kleber. Though Michelin and Crédit Suisse were the minority owners, they had been the dominating force in Semkler, whose chief, G.M. Repoux, had been associated previously with Michelin's Swiss subsidiary. Semperit's operational managers will, at the slightest provocation, supply a long list of decisions in which Semperit interests had been sacrificed in order to help Michelin.

The cooperation between Semperit and Kleber never seemed to get off the ground, and after three years (1976-1978) of heavy losses for both Semperit and Kleber, the holding company was dissolved in January 1979. Only a complete merger, tight supranational management, and ruthless rationalization could have turned the association of two problem companies into a success. For our purpose, however, the behavior of the Semperit works council and management during the first half of 1978 is of interest.

Semperit had losses of AS 99 million (about $6.7 million) in 1977, and similar losses, which actually turned out to be even larger, had been forecast for the year 1978. Confronted with a European excess capacity in tires and related production, the company in early 1978 embarked on an economy program, which looked toward attrition to reduce the work force. At this crucial point in Semperit's existence, a group of 477 semiskilled workers in the tire division in Traiskirchen demanded an upward evaluation of their job classification, which was immediately rejected by management. Although the corporate works council had just approved Semperit's economy program, the local works council at the Traiskirchen plant (which had forty-five hundred employees) supported the reclassification.[13] When management refused to reconsider, the 477 wrappers went on strike, with local works-council approval. With the exception of the left-wing Young Socialists (Jusos) the entire country, including the national union, I.G. Chemie, condemned the strike and urged management to stand fast. After a week had passed it became quite clear that the local works-council chairman considered the issue a test of strength through which he hoped to gain sufficient prestige with the Semperit work force to further his ambition to become chairman of the corporate works council.[14]

As the strike dragged on for several weeks, the national union as well as the Austrian union federation (ÖGB) brought increasing pressure on the Traiskirchner works council to reach a compromise, but without success. At last, the president of the ÖGB, who also is the speaker (president) of the Parliament and the second most powerful person in Austria after Chancellor Kreisky, invited Semperit management, works council, and the officers of I.G. Chemie to a mediation session in his chambers at the Parliament. Management, the I.G. Chemie leadership, and the rebellious works council met with Anton Benya, who announced shortly thereafter that the strike had been settled by a compromise, in which the striking workers obtained 95 percent of their original demand.

In both the VEW and Semperit cases, the works council responded to political pressures to prevent the implementation of unpopular measures designed to increase productivity and profitability in the long run. The success with which demagogic works councils thwarted top management policies, which had the support of union-employer-government leadership, will make it increasingly difficult for responsible works-council members to agree to painful but necessary decisions unless a crisis is imminent.

When in January 1979 the Semperit-Kleber association was finally disbanded, Semperit faced such a crisis. In order to guarantee its continued existence as a viable enterprise, a capital infusion of about $77 million (AS 1 billion) was necessary. At this point the works council finally agreed to forgo all voluntary fringe benefits (benefits obtained by the works council for the Semperit employees that were in excess of the benefits set in the industry-wide collective-bargaining agreement). In addition the employees, with works-council approval, agreed to work four shifts without pay in 1979, the Semperit corporation sold its handsome headquarters building, and the Creditanstalt promised a substantial capital infusion. None of these steps will be effective, however, if the works council does not cooperate with the necessary rationalization measures.

Politics of Austrian Codetermination

Codetermination and the presence of union leaders on the supervisory boards have been given credit for the peaceful restructuring of the German mining industry in 1950, which reduced the work force by 40 percent. Under different conditions, an equivalent codetermination in which the position of the union federation has been even further strengthened through its participation in a macroeconomic council may very well have the opposite effect on any attempt to increase productivity if reduced excess benefits may be vetoed by grass-roots works councils. The Austrian press has emphasized that German management would have reacted to the strike of the tire workers by closing down the whole plant to save the wage payments to the entire two-thousand-member work force and thereby would have put the plant works council under great pressure.[15] This is undoubtedly true for German enterprises in the private sector, although the management in state-owned enterprises may very well be less hard-nosed. In no major firm in Austria today, however, is the management not caught in a web of political, social, personal, and institutional ties that connect with the government and the union leadership.

For example, since the heavily taxed Austrian enterprises have not been able to generate enough investment funds, the Kreisky administration passed a law in 1978 to permit its finance minister to grant investment credits to deserving enterprises, thus permitting government discretion, rather then market forces, to make investment decisions. The Austrian employers quickly adapted themselves to the political realities and appeared together with their works-council chairmen at the finance ministry when applying for the investment funds. The increased influence of a works-council chairman under a socialist administration further weakens the position of the owner but may even undermine the dominance of the union federations.

Under these conditions management and employers may quickly become the junior partners in the social cooperation between capital and labor, which in turn may make it increasingly difficult for the union federation leadership to support unpopular measures, since as the senior partner it will have to accept the main responsibility for joint decisions.

Conclusion

Riding on Chancellor Kreisky's coattail, the Socialists won the March 1979 election and will remain in power for another four-year term, although they lost subsequent provincial elections in the fall. The growth of union power will continue but will also foster more and more confrontations between the works councils and the union-party-management establishment. It will become increasingly difficult to take the necessary steps to restructure industry until a major breakdown in the economy occurs. In the short run, labor is no longer a variable cost anywhere in Europe. However, in Austria and Sweden it has turned into a long-run fixed cost, which immobilizes the adjustment processes of both a market and a planned economy. So far the government has been able to postpone the day of reckoning by borrowing heavily abroad to cover its large international payments and budget deficits and by relying on trade union federation president Benya to keep wage demands near or below the low inflation level. In turn, the able finance minister Androsch has kept the schilling pegged to the mark, and has actually reduced prices in part. The Androsch-Benya cooperation has preserved Austria from the economic difficulties experienced by Denmark, The Netherlands, and Sweden. It will be interesting to see whether corporative-socialist Austria will continue to perform its peculiar kind of economic miracle.

Switzerland: Direct Democracy in a Capitalistic Society

Although the early historical development of the Swiss labor movement and the Social Democratic party was very similar to that of Germany and Austria, the Alpine confederation has no formal codetermination legislation, yet it probably has more true grass-roots industrial democracy than any other European country. Switzerland's recent history has not been divided by World War II; hence its labor organizations still resemble those of the Weimar Republic. A strong reformistic Social Democratic party, with a socialist, predominantly French-speaking left wing, has been the major representative of the working class and has been closely affiliated with the Swiss Trade Union Federation (*Schweizerischer Gewerkschaftsbund*, or SGB). The second strongest union group is the Catholic Christian Workers Association (*Christlicher Arbeiter Verband*), followed by the Independent Employees Association and the Protestant Employees Association.

Swiss Trade-Union Policy

The most important trade union in Switzerland has been the 140,000-member Swiss Metall and Watch Employees Association (SMUV), a member of the SGB, whose collective-bargaining agreement with the Swiss Metall and Watch industry (ASM) has provided the guidelines for wage negotiations throughout the country.

After World War I, and especially during the depression, Swiss trade unions adhered to a strong confrontation policy toward employers, which contained at least the rhetoric of class warfare. Faced by a radical popular front in France and National Socialism in Germany, the SMUV negotiated a peace agreement (*Friedens Abkommen*) with the ASM in 1937, which replaced strikes and lockouts with virtually continuous industry-wide collective bargaining. Although the industry-wide agreements are ordinarily negotiated for a four-year period, committees meet continuously throughout the four years to consider demands for revisions, which can be raised by either side.[16] In addition, enterprises negotiate specific wage and cost-of-living arrangements within industry-wide guidelines. Moreover, the existence and jurisdiction of works councils are also negotiated locally. Works councils exist throughout the Swiss metal industry and have played a significant role in maintaining good employee-management relations on the shop floor. An attempt by a group of trade-union officials and Social Democrats to launch a constitutional amendment enabling the federal government (actually federal parliament) to enact broad worker-participation legislation was roundly defeated by the Swiss electorate in the 1976 referendum.

The basis for Swiss union federation policy has been its concept of loyalty and trust (*Grundsatz von Treue und Glauben*), which Otto Flückiger, chief of the metal-workers' union redefined recently: "Do not keep from the employee anything that can be granted to him, don't demand from the employer anything he cannot offer, but argue about that which can be granted."[17] If no agreement can be reached on what can be granted, the issue comes before binding arbitration by experts, not only in the metal industry, but virtually throughout the entire Swiss economy. Strikes in the private sector are extremely rare, and public-sector employees do not have the right to strike.

It is probably Switzerland's moral rectitude of enforcing existing laws and having unions that are guided by a concept of loyalty and trust that drives the radical chic intellectuals in Zurich and Geneva to desperation and encourages them to attack all forms of social cooperation and authority. The demand for greater grass-roots democracy in factory and community must take on anachronistic overtones on a society in which all major issues are decided by referenda and in which each canton, the size of a typical midwestern county, has more self-government than an American state. Similarly the unusually democratic structure of Swiss unions enables each employee to participate in the formation of a union's negotiation position that truly reflects the membership's wishes.

Radicals' Attack on Social Cooperation

Technical issues arise, however, that are often decided by a central bureaucracy, even in Switzerland. The radical Left has concentrated, therefore, on exploiting the opposition of local minorities to decisions that have been made at a national level—whether they concern the building of atomic power plants or the adoption of a new four-year collective-bargaining agreement in the metal industry. The demand for complete local self-determination would require unanimous approval throughout society of both parliamentary decisions and industry-wide bargaining agreements, a utopian demand that would lead to anarchy in Switzerland. As Switzerland's president, Willi Ritschard, said, "A democracy cannot survive if all decisions must need unanimous approval, since all advantages [of policy decisions] are accompanied by disadvantages, and the interest of the state cannot satisfy individual egoism.[18]

Within the SGB and especially SMUV, a left-wing opposition group, Manifest 77, chose to exploit the local-autonomy issue and demanded greater "transparency in the decision making process within the union," while simultaneously proclaiming its opposition to social cooperation and the no-strike (*Arbeitsfrieden or labor peace*) agreement with the "class enemy.''[19] The Manifest 77 group is centered predominantly in the French-speaking cantons of southwest Switzerland, where it has the support of the Independent Socialists, a small Marxist group that split from the Social Democrats in the 1930s and has had only regional influence.

The Manifest 77 was merely the latest expression of dissatisfaction with the SGB cooperative policy among the more class-conscious labor leaders in French-speaking Switzerland (especially in the cantons of Geneva, Vaud, and Valais). In the early 1970s, their demand for greater worker participation in decision making had prompted the Social Democrats and SGB to support the codetermination initiative, which was supposed to use the political-parliamentary process to give workers a legal right to participate in the decision-making processes of private and public enterprises (for example, the state-owned Swiss Federal railroads). Much of the discussion concerning the merits of the initiative pertained to the need or advisability of enacting mandatory works-council laws, when these participation forums have been established successfully through the collective-bargaining process whenever employees and unions so desired.[20] In fact, however, the Manifest 77 group and other supporters of the codetermination initiative had much more ambitious goals than a mere works-council law. They hoped that a successful referendum vote would provide the impetus for marshaling a parliamentary majority to bring to Switzerland the full worker-union participation rights of the German Montan codetermination laws.

The decisive defeat of the referendum in 1976 pushed the left-wing opposition in the SGB even further to the left. Although they were interested above all in forcing the SGB leadership into abandoning class cooperation—at least in its rhetoric—they emphasized in their intraunion opposition the extension of union democracy. The SMUV's rather heavy-handed expulsion of internal opposition leader Jean-Claude Gründisch, secretary of the SMUV local union in Monthey, did generate a fair amount of sympathy for him. An attempt to exploit this sympathy and form a rival metal union in Monthey failed, however, and weakened the left-wing opposition in both the SMUV and the Swiss Trade Union Federation.

Industrial Democracy at Work

By any realistic yardstick, Swiss society and Swiss industry enjoy the most truly democratic decision process in Western society today. Although Switzerland's political democracy is closely tied to the small size and homogeneity of the country, the democratic decision processes of Swiss unions could be easily imitated in most other European countries if the union leaderships were truly interested in industrial democracy.

The preparation for the quadrennial negotiations in the SMUV begin eithteen months before the end of the current contracts with a state-of-the-industry report by the union leadership, which is submitted to the industry conference of four hundred works delegates, who are chosen by direct election in each plant. The resulting list of negotiable issues and demands (*Problemkatalog*) is returned for further hearings to the local and regional union assemblies. Recommended changes are submitted once more to the industry conference, which acts throughout as the directly elected negotiation council but finally selects a negotiation team consisting of union officials and works representatives to meet with the employers. Once the negotiation team is selected, however, and begins to meet with the representative of the employers, all sessions remain completely confidential to avoid political pressures (*Druck der Strasse*). There are no leaks, and no statements are made until a final agreement has been reached.

All other unions operate similarly, though since they are smaller, the process is less formalized. It is striking to compare the democratic decision process in the Swiss reformistic unions with the bureaucratic-elitist procedures in the class-conscious British or Socialist Swedish unions.

The Swiss codetermination experience provides several important lessons.

1. Codetermination and industrial democracy are firmly rooted in the social, political, and historical roots of a society. Even Central Europe, ethnically, culturally, and politically quite homogeneous, has developed three distinct forms of codetermination. If it has not been possible so far to export German codetermination to Switzerland, it seems incredible that anyone could expect it to work effectively in Great Britain.

2. Codetermination and industrial democracy do not necessarily require a body of law in order to become effective. If unions are democratically led and if they are able to encourage broad participation, free collective bargaining may provide an alternate, even superior, road to employee participation.

3. The demand for more industrial democracy is based upon the political theories of left-wing intellectuals rather than upon the actual conditions in industry. The same people who attack the Swiss trade unions because they carry out the last states of their negotiations under a cloak of secrecy would gladly permit the bureaucratic British or elitist Swedish unions to dominate the entire economy. The mere presence of union representatives on boards of directors permits professional ideologues to view such a system as an expression of industrial democracy.

Switzerland and West Germany have the two most successful labor-relation systems in Europe. They also have the two governments most strongly committed to a free market economy and stable prices. It is this economic environment that has been responsible for the operational soundness of the two quite different codetermination systems. Without a free market and without a pragmatic democratic society, neither the Swiss nor the German codetermination model would have been effective.

Notes

1. For example, in Germany the ubiquitous Eugen Loderer has (since April, 1978) demanded equal codetermination (50 percent of the supervisory board seats) on the boards that supervise German radio-television networks. The German television industry consists of regional, public, non-profit companies, which are owned by the respective Länder. The supervisory boards comprise primarily representatives of the Länder governments and their opposition parties. The management is fairly autonomous but must take political realities into consideration. During the height of the Brandt administration, most German cultural institutions, including the television networks, developed a noticeable leftist bias, which has become somewhat less pronounced in recent years as a consequence of the increasing CDU-CSU strength in the provincial parliaments. Equal codetermination in the networks would give the DGB the kind of political-cultural influence that is incompatible with the survival of a democracy. There is little chance that equal codetermination will be adopted for the German radio-television industry, but few would be willing to bet that sooner or later the national unions will not obtain some representation on the supervisory boards. Of greater interest is the global demand for equal union codetermination in all aspects of life.

In Austria, the unions have already established themselves in the management forums of the nationalized radio-television network, and union leaders hold executive positions in sports and academic research organizations. No major appointment, even in the cultural sector, will be made without union approval.

2. The Austrian Social Democratic party (renamed the Socialist party after World War II) demanded a form of codetermination for the first time in its Hausfelder party conference (December 1888-January 1889). The Christian Social party also demanded employee codetermination in its 1896 platform.

3. Deutsch-Österreichisches Betriebsrätegesetz, 15 May 1919. Austria's formal name from 1919 to 1934 was Deutsch-Österreich, or German-Austria.

4. *Mitbestimmung am Arbeitsplatz* (Vienna: Bundespressedienst 1974), p. 21 (my translation).

5. In the Metall industry (steel, iron manufacturers, and all fabricators of metal-containing products) 100 percent of the workers and about 65

percent of the salaried employees are union members. The same percentages apply throughout the manufacturing and mining industries but decrease sharply in the tertiary sector, which is characterized by a large number of family-owned enterprises. All employees, however, whether union members or not, are automatically members of the chamber of labor (*Arbeiterkammer*).

Anton Benya, president of the Austrian Trade Union Federation (ÖGB) is a Socialist party leader and speaker of the Parliament. Often referred to as the "Austrian Meany," he carries considerably more weight than Meany did and is indubitably the second most influential person in Austria.

6. The Socialist governed as a minority party from 1970 to 1974 and have enjoyed a narrow but effective parliamentary majority since then. In the 1979 election they gained two additional parliamentary seats and 51 percent of the popular vote.

7. Typically, for the Austrian version of socialized finance capitalism, among the three examples given only the Austria Hotel A.G. is a profitable enterprise by American standards.

8. The new ÖIAG chief executive (*Generaldirektor*) Oskar Grünwald made a very similar statement at a July 1978 press conference. Questioned about productivity trends in the ÖIAG, Dr. Grünwald, formerly ÖIAF works-council chairman, emphasized that "the nationalized enterprises have a greater responsibility than other enterprises to consider the interests of the employees." He confirmed that the nationalized enterprises are permitted to dismiss employees only in the rarest cases, regardless of a firm's profit position, since "it is cheaper to keep people employed than pay them unemployment insurance." *Frankfurter Allgemeine Zeitung*, 25 July 1978, p. 10. The FAZ added that the willingness of the state to cover deficits makes it difficult for management and works council to make hard decisions.

The ÖIAG (Austrian Industry Corporation) is a holding company of the various nationalized enterprises that have retained their individual management. The firms owned by the nationalized banks, however, are not included in the Austrian Nationalized Industry Holding Corporation and hence are considered privately owned. In most cases the banks hold only a controlling interest and the previous owners retain a minority interest. The ability of the ÖIAG to impose its policies on each enterprise within its holding is quite limited. In the spring of 1978 the ÖIAG's chief executive resigned because he obtained insufficient support from the Socialist chancellor, Kreisky. Typically, and interestingly, he was replaced by Dr. O. Grünwald, who had been the senior union-employee representative on the ÖIAG's supervisory board and whose managerial experience outside the personnel sector is quite limited.

Both major political parties have been traditionally represented on the supervisory boards of the ÖIAG and its subsidiaries.

9. The establishment of the Socialist minority government in 1970 illustrated the power of the Austrian unions. In the 1970 election the governing ÖVP and the opposition Freedom party (national-liberals or FPÖ) lost a few seats in Parliament to the Socialists, who still lacked a majority, however. A coalition government, ÖVP-FPÖ, was certainly a possibility, especially since the difference between those two bourgeois parties is primarily historical. Benya, the chief of the ÖGB, let it be known, however, that "the Austrian worker won't stand for a coalition of the election: 'losers,' " a statement that ended immediately all talk about an ÖVP-FPÖ coalition, and the Socialists formed their first government. In 1976 the governing Socialist-Liberal (SDP-FDP) coalition in Germany lost votes and parliamentary seats to the opposition CDU-CSU but retained a slim majority very similar to the loss of the governing party in Austria in 1970.

10. There is no doubt that the VEW exports to the United States violate U.S. dumping legislation. Although the prices charged abroad are ordinarily not lower than the domestic ones, all major Austrian newspapers acknowledge freely that VEW prices do not cover full costs, and may not even cover variable costs. See "Stahlgipfel ohne Ergebnisse," *Die Presse*, 9 June 1978, p. 8, and Heinrich Mathis, "Ohne Stahlbremse in die Krise," *Die Presse*, 10 June 1978, p. 3.

11. *Die Presse*, 15 June 1979, p. 7.

12. In June 1978 alone, Chancellor Kreisky himself participated in preparing the rescue operation for two medium-sized textile companies.

13. Actually Semperit's economy drive was Austrian rather than spartan. Although the company lost money in 1977, it still had to pay profit bonuses (*Prämien*) to its work force. Since there were no profits to draw upon, it had to borrow money to distribute what once had been profit-sharing payments.

14. The Traiskirchner works-council chairman, Gustav Maierhofer, also serves as an employee-director on Semperit's supervisory board. In the May 1978 general stockholder assembly, Maierhofer was strongly attacked by several minority stockholders. In the legally required vote to approve the performance of each director, the majority stockholder, Creditanstalt, supported him. When questioned by reporters, its spokesman announced that, after all, the year 1977 and not current events was the subject of the stockholder meeting.

15. Cf. Kurt Horwitz, "Verlorene Unschuld," *Die Presse*, 13-14 May 1978.

16. See article 18, SMUV Constitution, and Regulation for Negotiation.

17. *Die Weltwoche*, 26 April 1978, p. 5 (my translation).

18. Switzerland's 1978 president, Willi Ritschard, in a debate in the Swiss Parliament. *Neue Züricher Zeitung*, 25 April 1978; also quoted in *Die Weltwoche*, 26 April 1978.

19. Named after a manifesto a group of left-wing union officials released in 1970, in which the SMUV was attacked for arriving at its decisions in secrecy.

20. In the context of Swiss politics, the "initiative" defines the process of obtaining sufficient signatures to have the electorate vote directly, through a "referendum," to adopt a constitutional amendment or merely enact a federal law. In practice the terms *initiative* and *referendum* often are used interchangeably and refer in such popular usage to the entire process.

Index

About the Author

Alfred L. Thimm received the Ph.D. in economics from New York University. He is presently professor of economics and management at Union College and the director of its Ph.D. program in administrative and engineering systems. He has served as Visiting Professor twice at the University of Munich and at the Wirtschatsuniversität of Vienna, and was also a Fulbright Research Scholar at the Technical University of Graz.

A consultant to organizations in the private and public sectors, Professor Thimm has published four books and several monographs and articles in English and German on topics in economics, management, and decision theory.

DATE DUE